Amerind Studies in Anthropology

Series Editor **John Ware**

CHACO REVISITED

NEW RESEARCH ON THE PREHISTORY OF CHACO CANYON, NEW MEXICO

EDITED BY **CARRIE C. HEITMAN**
AND **STEPHEN PLOG**

THE UNIVERSITY OF
ARIZONA PRESS

TUCSON

The University of Arizona Press
www.uapress.arizona.edu

Printed in the United States of America
21 20 19 18 17 16   7 6 5 4 3 2

ISBN-13: 978-0-8165-3160-8 (cloth)
ISBN-13: 978-0-8165-3412-8 (paper)

Cover designed by Miriam Warren
Cover photo by Stephen Plog

Publication of this book is made possible in part by funding from the College
and Graduate School of Arts and Sciences at the University of Virginia.

Library of Congress Cataloging-in-Publication Data
Chaco revisited : new research on the prehistory of Chaco Canyon, New
Mexico / edited by Carrie C. Heitman and Stephen Plog.
     pages cm — (Amerind studies in anthropology)
  Includes bibliographical references and index.
  ISBN 978-0-8165-3160-8 (cloth : alk. paper)
  1. Chaco culture—New Mexico—Chaco Canyon. 2. Chaco Canyon
(N.M.)—Antiquities. I. Heitman, Carrie C., editor. II. Plog, Stephen, editor.
III. Series: Amerind studies in anthropology.
  E99.C37C349 2015
  978.9'8201—dc23

                                        2014039733

♾ This paper meets the requirements of ANSI/NISO Z39.48-1992
(Permanence of Paper).

We, the editors, dedicate this book to Gwinn and Gordon Vivian—
devoted scholars and unwavering stewards of Chaco Canyon.

CONTENTS

ACKNOWLEDGMENTS

The editors of this volume would like to express their deepest gratitude to the Amerind Foundation and the Dean of Arts and Sciences at the University of Virginia for their support of this seminar, and the University of Arizona Press for bringing this volume to life. In the fall of 2010, their collective support allowed us to bring together a wonderful group of researchers to engage in vigorous discussions over the course of three days in Dragoon, Arizona. We would like to thank each of the scholars who gave their time and energy to participate and then to finalize their chapters for publication.

We would also like to specifically acknowledge the support of John Ware, former director of the Amerind Foundation, as well as the encouragement and guidance of University of Arizona Press editor-in-chief Allyson Carter. Lastly, we would like to thank the two anonymous reviewers for offering detailed, thoughtful comments that helped us improve the original draft of the manuscript.

This is a vibrant time in Chacoan archaeology, as indicated by the numerous books and papers published over the last decade. Debate continues on a variety of significant issues that will only be resolved by continued discussion and evaluation of the many ideas that have been presented. We are delighted to help further that discussion and evaluation with this collection of chapters.

CHACO REVISITED

Understanding Chaco

Past, Present, and Future

Stephen Plog

Over the last 40 years, our understanding of Chaco Canyon has been fundamentally altered by a significant amount of fieldwork in combination with new analyses and insightful research. For someone like myself whose career has spanned that period and who has witnessed the change, the transformation has been remarkable. Although hard to believe in retrospect—especially after all of the fieldwork, research, and publications of the National Park Service's Chaco Project in the last quarter of the twentieth century—in the decades preceding the late 1960s, Chaco was viewed by some as simply one of a number of important areas in the northern Southwest. In fact, my guess is that a systematic review of the published literature from the 1950s, 1960s, and early 1970s might reveal more publications on west-central New Mexico and east-central Arizona, particularly the University of Arizona's work at Point of Pines and Grasshopper and The Field Museum's research in the Reserve region and the Hay Hollow Valley, than on Chaco Canyon or the San Juan Basin.

Although excavations were uncommon in Chaco Canyon in the 1950s and 1960s, research in the canyon has a longer and perhaps more complex history than any other region, having gone through several markedly different stages. The most recent stage includes a diverse array of research that for the most part has not been based on new fieldwork, but rather has reexamined the remarkable, though previously rarely studied, museum collections of artifacts, faunal and floral remains, and human skeleton material from fieldwork conducted in the late nineteenth century or the first half of the twentieth century or, alternatively, has taken advantage of a wide range of web-accessible, digitized information from that early fieldwork. The diverse contributions that constitute this volume exemplify this latter stage of research and convincingly demonstrate the important new insights that can be gained from such studies. Collectively they address significant, pivotal questions such as the agricultural potential of Chaco Canyon, the extent to which small and great house inhabitants shared a common cosmology and ritual practices, the nature of kinship and sociopolitical organization at canyon great houses, and the production and distribution of the many types of artifacts—bone tools, basketry, and textiles—that occur in frequency orders of magnitude greater than in most other regions of the Southwest. Two chapters also provide tantalizing discussions of the potential insights to be gained from the analysis of the much-discussed but poorly understood great house burials.

To understand the importance of these contributions and place them in proper context, I believe it is necessary to briefly review the history of Chacoan research. The first stage in the study of the remarkable settlements in Chaco Canyon included the short, but surprisingly accurate, discussions and descriptions of the canyon by Simpson in 1849 (McNitt 1957; Simpson 1874), Jackson (1878), and the Mindeleffs' fieldwork in 1887–1888 that was never published, but left us the first set of photographs of the Chacoan great houses and landscape. The widely disseminated Hayden (1878) and Wheeler (1879) survey reports published by the U.S. government included frequent references to the canyon. Hayden's reports included William Henry Jackson's (1878) important descriptions and maps of the large Chaco great houses. Volume VII of the Wheeler report was edited by prominent American archaeologist Frederic Ward Putnam (1879) and focused on ethnography and archaeology of the Southwest, with several chapters mentioning Chaco. These reports consistently expressed admiration for the skill of Chaco architects and astonishment at the large size of many of the structures.

In part as a result of these studies, Chaco became a focus of some of the leading anthropologists of this era. Lewis Henry Morgan, one of the foremost anthropologists of the nineteenth century, included a chapter on Chaco Canyon in his seminal *Houses and House-Life of American Aborigines* (1881:153–174). In both that chapter and an earlier publication (Morgan 1869:461–474), Morgan suggests that Chaco great houses were the Seven Cities of Cibola sought by Francisco Coronado (a conclusion quickly disputed by the astute Simpson [1874:199–200]). Despite the rejection of Chaco as the Seven Cities, Morgan's discussions highlighted the significance of Chaco in publications that were widely read by scholars of that generation.

The remarkable nature of Chaco also was highlighted by the construction of a three-dimensional model of Pueblo Bonito by Jackson and W. H. Holmes that was reproduced by Ward's Scientific Establishment and sold to several museums in the United States (Fowler 2000:89) and by exhibits at the Columbian Exposition in Chicago in 1893. Not only American archaeologists but also many members of the public had become very aware of the remarkable scale and density of the canyon great houses during the last half of the nineteenth century. Examples of the widespread knowledge of Chaco include a discussion of the "wonderful ruins in the Chaco canyon of New Mexico" in an article that appeared in *The Louisiana Democrat* published in Alexandria, Louisiana (reprinted from the *Denver Republican*) on March 9, 1887, as well as articles on the Columbian Exposition that were reprinted in the *Globe Republican* of Dodge City, Kansas (September 22, 1893) and the *Colfax Chronicle* of Colfax, Louisiana (November 4, 1893). The 1893 article included considerable detail on Pueblo Bonito: "One of the most remarkable of the pueblos is that of Bonito in the canyon of Chaco in New Mexico. This home of the Indian was built in the shape of a half circle and faced out on a yawning chasm. The high walls of the houses facing to the rear served the double purpose of a fortification against enemies and protection against the elements. The buildings were all of stone and the masonry of the tribe, judged by the ruins of the towns that are left, was really marvelous. Their tools were much better than those of the other tribes of the time and the people more peaceful and industrious."

The American Museum of Natural History's Hyde Exploring Expedition to Chaco initiated the next stage in our understanding of the canyon by making Chaco the focus of one of the first major, long-term professional excavations in the Southwest. The Hyde Expedition, directed by Frederic Ward Putnam and George Pepper, conducted excavations between 1896 and 1901, almost exclusively at Pueblo Bonito. That work was supplemented by a much briefer period of fieldwork by Moorehead (1906) in 1897. Whereas the earlier studies had revealed the exceptional architectural skills of Pueblo inhabitants of the canyon and the unusual, indeed unique, density of the large Chaco great houses, the Hyde Expedition uncovered the remarkable artifact assemblages that were buried within the ruins of Pueblo Bonito: ceramic cylinder vessels, previously unknown in the Pueblo region and apparently restricted to Chaco Canyon; hundreds of wooden staffs of different shapes and remarkable craftsmanship; flutes, some with painted or carved decorations; and astonishing amounts of turquoise and jet ornaments. The richness of the artifact assemblages demonstrated that it was not only the architecture of Chaco that set it apart from other regions of the Southwest but also the extraordinary ornaments, vessels, and objects manufactured by highly skilled artisans.

Although Pepper (1905, 1906, 1909, 1920) described most of the Hyde Expedition excavations and some of the most exceptional artifacts and deposits in detail and provided (in combination with detailed field notes) important contextual information that would later prove to be invaluable (e.g., Ashmore 2007; Plog and Heitman 2010), the focus of the Hyde Expedition, following the pattern common at the time, emphasized the collection of museum-quality materials for exhibit more than an enhanced understanding of the canyon dwellings and their inhabitants. Pepper's publications and his many public lectures in the New York City region nevertheless did highlight the exceptional accomplishments of the Chaco people at a time when most Indians were dismissed as "primitive" if not "savages," and his work thus played an important role in beginning to change public perceptions of Native Americans.

After the end of the Hyde Expedition, subsequent limited field studies of the canyon (Nelson 1920) offered no significant new insights until the joint National Geographic Society and Smithsonian explorations from 1920 to 1928. Led by Neil Judd of the Smithsonian's National Museum of Natural History, the project completed excavation of the remainder of Pueblo Bonito, conducted more limited excavations at the nearby great house of Pueblo del Arroyo, examined the stratigraphy of several trash mounds at other Chaco great houses, and explored a handful of other settlements (e.g., Judd 1920, 1924, 1927, 1954, 1959, 1964, 1967; Roberts 1927, 1929). With an increased focus on stratigraphic excavations and profiles, studies of change in ceramics over time, and the use of the newly developed technique of tree-ring dating, the National Geographic Expedition greatly improved our understanding of the chronology of the canyon. Judd's work clearly demonstrated the complex pattern in the growth of Pueblo Bonito over a period of several centuries and established that not all great houses had been constructed at the same time. In addition, Judd found evidence of frequent remodeling and of planned constructions, such as the northeast foundation complex at Pueblo Bonito, that were initiated but never completed. Frank Robert's (1929) contemporaneous excavations of the much earlier pithouse village of Shabik'eshchee, along with Judd's (1924) exploration of isolated pithouses deeply buried under the modern canyon floor but exposed in the walls of Chaco wash, further enhanced our appreciation for the long and complex history of occupation in the canyon.

In addition, the discovery by Shepard (1939; see also Judd 1954:181–183) that tens of thousands of corrugated utility vessels had been brought into the canyon from a distant area, although underemphasized at the time because of Judd's (1954:235) skepticism, provided an important new insight into the broad regional connections of Chaco with the surrounding Four Corners region. Nevertheless, despite Shepard's discovery, Judd's own tantalizing references to prehistoric roads, his recognition that sites with Chacoan-style architecture existed outside the canyon, and excavations at small house sites outside the canyon by Amsden (1925) that Judd requested, Judd's focus remained firmly on the prehistory of Chaco Canyon and almost exclusively on the great houses.

The next period of exploration, primarily in the 1930s and the early 1940s, was led by Edgar Hewett and sponsored either jointly by the School of American Research (SAR) and the University of New Mexico (UNM), or solely by the university. Excavations uncovered portions on the great house of Chetro Ketl but also explored numerous small house sites on the south side of the canyon near Casa Rinconada. With the significant exceptions of Florence Hawley's efforts (e.g., 1934, 1938) to refine the chronology of Chaco generally and Chetro Ketl specifically, her pioneering definition of formal ceramic types following the conventions that were developing in the Southwest at the time (Hawley 1936), and Paul Reiter's master's thesis and dissertation (1933, 1946), the Chetro Ketl excavations largely failed to produce new and significant insights.

Hewett never published a monograph summarizing the excavations in any significant detail. Although Pepper has frequently been criticized for his report on Pueblo Bonito—a report that remains useful—few have highlighted Hewett's failure to write a Chetro Ketl report even remotely comparable to Pepper's Bonito monograph. In addition,

archival research by Joan Mathien and Joyce Raab, and by the staff of
the Chaco Research Archive, has failed to locate field notes for many of
the excavated rooms and kivas in Chetro Ketl, and—unlike the Hyde
Expedition—no complete inventory of the artifacts and ecofacts recovered has been found. Small collections of artifacts from Chetro Ketl are
held by several museums, but the sum of those assemblages is minimal
enough to suggest that a significant amount of material recovered is
now missing. We thus lack adequate information to understand the
second-largest great house in the canyon or to compare Chetro Ketl
with Pueblo Bonito or Pueblo del Arroyo. Hewett harshly criticized the
Hyde Expedition and, in particular, Richard Wetherill's continued presence in the canyon, but in retrospect Hewett's Chetro Ketl excavations
fell well below the standards of either the Hyde Exploring Expedition
or the National Geographic Project.

Fortunately, the records from the SAR and UNM excavations
of many of the small house sites are more adequate than those from
Chetro Ketl, although monographs were published on only two of the
sites excavated (Brand et al. 1937; Kluckhohn and Reiter 1939). As with
the great house excavations, the work at the small houses uncovered
the complexity of construction sequences and the chronological depth
of small house construction. Although the artifact assemblages from
the small house sites failed to match the richness of the great houses,
the excavations did uncover some turquoise, shell, and painted wood,
revealing similarities to the great houses. Most importantly, the excavation demonstrated the contemporaneity of great and small house habitations, a discovery that initiated discussions of the possible relationship
between the two types of settlements, first exemplified by Kluckhohn's
(1939) discussion and his conclusion that the residents of the two types
of settlements likely represented different groups or cultures.

For the next quarter century after the completion of the SAR and
UNM excavations in the early 1940s, much more limited fieldwork was
conducted in Chaco, largely by the National Park Service or by the Arizona State Museum under the leadership of R. Gordon and R. Gwinn
Vivian. The Park Service excavations included work at Casa Rinconada,
Kin Kletso, and Chetro Ketl by Gordon Vivian (Vivian and Mathews
1965; Vivian and Reiter 1965). Perhaps the most important discovery
during this period, however, was the Vivians' recovery of a large cache

of wooden ritual objects during repair work at Chetro Ketl (Vivian et al. 1978), the first cache of wooden objects found since the Hyde Expedition excavations in 1896 and the largest assemblage ever found in a single context in a pueblo. In addition, Gordon Vivian's initial mapping of canals and agricultural fields, aided by what at the time was an innovative use of aerial photography, subsequently was supplemented by Gwinn Vivian's excavations sponsored by the National Science Foundation (Vivian 1984, 1991, 1992; Vivian et al. 2006). The latter studies remain the most intensive and thorough efforts to understand the water control systems devised by the Chacoan people to enhance the productivity of their agricultural fields.

In the early 1970s the National Park Service initiated a new major program of study exceeding in scale the work of the Hyde Exploring Expedition, the National Geographic Society, or the UNM and SAR field schools. The Park Service's Chaco Project, in conjunction with Cynthia Irwin-Williams's contemporaneous research at Salmon Ruins (Irwin-Williams 1972; Irwin-Williams and Shelley 1980; Reed 2006) and key cultural resource management studies throughout the San Juan Basin, including the nearby great house of Bis sa'ani (Breternitz et al. 1982), fundamentally altered our understanding of the Chaco Canyon and the era between A.D. 800 and 1130 by demonstrating the broad geographical significance of the Chaco in the northern Southwest. The participating scholars recognized what A. V. Kidder, Neil Judd, Gordon Vivian, and others had observed in part, but not explored, decades earlier: the existence of large Chaco-like sites—now typically referred to as outlying great houses—scattered over a sizeable region and the presence of roads leading out of the canyon (and from some of the outliers) that connected it to the hinterland. At the same time, the Chaco Project undertook a complete survey of the park, the major exploration of a portion of Pueblo Alto and its massive trash mound, and the excavation of a large sample of small house settlements. Subsequent intensive sampling of preserved beams (Windes and Ford 1996) also has greatly improved our understanding of the nuances of construction sequences.

Over the next two decades, the Chaco Project's publication series (*National Park Service Publications in Archaeology, Chaco Canyon Studies,* and *National Park Service, Reports of the Chaco Center*) that documented those excavations—to a large extent the result of the sustained

dedication of Frances Joan Mathien and Thomas Windes—has produced a large corpus of publications. In addition, numerous analyses
of excavation data by Chaco Project personnel, particularly Lekson's
(1984) detailed examination of construction sequences at canyon great
houses and the magnitude of the effort such building episodes required,
Toll's (1985) analysis of ceramic deposition in the Alto trash mound, and
other studies such as Mathien's (e.g., 1981, 1984, 1997) investigation of
turquoise production and Akins's (1984, 1985, 1986, 2001, 2003) analyses
of fauna and human remains, have been particularly influential. These
works were recently complemented by a final series of synthetic volumes summarizing the work of the Chaco Project and offering perspectives on a wide range of topics (Lekson 2006a, 2007; Mathien 2005).

As a result of more than three decades of fieldwork, analysis, and
publication, the research of the Chaco Project has generated a richer and
more complete knowledge of Chaco and the networks that connected
the canyon to a large surrounding region. It is now established that ties
with Chaco extended throughout the northern Southwest and across
remarkable distances into Mesoamerica. In combination with continued
fieldwork throughout the Southwest, it has become increasingly clear
that many aspects of Chaco—the broad relationships, the scale of public
buildings, the density of large pueblos, the richness of material assemblages, and much more—were unprecedented in Pueblo history.

We should not be surprised, however, that given the uniqueness
and complexity of Chaco, many basic questions about Chaco remain
unresolved. In one of the books synthesizing the efforts of the Chaco
Project, Lynne Sebastian (2006:404) observed, "When it comes to
explaining how and why all of this came about, how Chacoan society
was organized and functioned, sometimes we seem no farther along
now than when the Chaco Project started more than thirty years ago."
Even basic terms such as "Chacoan" remain unclear. Toll (2006:118) has
noted, "'Chaco' has become a nebulous concept that includes different
extents and characteristics for different people." "System," "phenomenon," "big idea," "region," "world," "rituality," "interaction sphere," and
"metaphor" are just some of the concepts that people have used to characterize Chaco and the areas that seem to have some relation to Chaco.

As the above summary of fieldwork at Chaco has illustrated, the
persistence of key questions regarding Chaco is certainly not a result

of a lack of data. Indeed, Lekson (2006b:22) has argued the converse: "Southwestern archaeology is choking on its own overabundant data (compared with other regions of the world)." And nowhere in the Southwest are those data more abundant than in Chaco.

Although copious amounts of data can present analytical challenges, I nevertheless believe there are more important reasons why key questions about Chaco remain unanswered. One is the remarkable spatial scale of the Chaco social network. Few would now dispute that an understanding of Chaco demands integrating information from the canyon with the many outlying regions that had some type of connection with the core concentration of great houses. As many others have noted, to better understand Chaco, we need to consider multiple spatial scales—the canyon, the nearby hinterland (e.g., Bis sa'ani, Kin Bineola, and Pueblo Pintado), the broader San Juan Basin, and beyond—and explore the nature of social, political, religious, and economic relations at all of these different scales. Not surprisingly, as the scale of Chacoan relationships became clear, there has been considerable discussion of that larger area, of the roads and trails, and the scores of Chacoan-style great houses distributed throughout much of northwestern New Mexico, southwestern Colorado, and southeastern Utah. Also of significance, new studies have been undertaken at outliers such as Chimney Rock, the Bluff Site, and Aztec Ruins, complemented by a significant synthesis of work conducted at Salmon Ruins in the 1970s (Cameron 2008; Reed 2006, 2008).

These studies of the broader Chaco hinterland have been important and must be continued, but unfortunately there has been comparatively less emphasis on the complexity of the archaeological record in the canyon itself even though many fundamental questions regarding organization and change over time within the canyon continued to be debated. Relations at larger scales cannot be understood without clear conceptions of relations at smaller scales, and vice versa. They are complementary, not mutually exclusive. Yet Sebastian's (1992) *The Chaco Anasazi: Sociopolitical Evolution in the Prehistoric Southwest* presents the last comprehensive model of cultural patterns and temporal dynamics among settlements—small houses and great houses—in the canyon from the ninth through twelfth centuries. Moreover, there have been significant dimensions of the archaeological record in the canyon that have remained poorly understood and, until very recently, rarely studied.

A second factor contributing to the lack of progress in understanding Chaco is that while there are many models of social relationships at different spatial scales, there has been too little effort to intensively and rigorously evaluate those models. If Southwestern archaeology is indeed choking on data, I suggest that in part it has resulted from a deficiency of intensive, problem-oriented research that focuses on particular dimensions of those data to evaluate proposed models. As Gwinn Vivian (2008:372) has emphasized, there are too "many 'as it was' scenarios developed in an attempt to 'explain' the archaeological record" of Chaco and not enough studies that use "that record as a source of data to confirm or refute testable hypotheses," models, or propositions.

Post–Chaco Project: Taking Advantage of Existing Data and Collections

Fortunately, one of the many significant impacts of the Chaco Project has been the way that it served as a catalyst for new research, particularly during the last two decades. The continued attention is a remarkable testimony to the vision of John Corbett in the late 1960s and to those— Bob Lister, Tom Lyons, Alden Hayes, Jim Judge, Joan Mathien, Nancy Akins, Steve Lekson, Peter McKenna, John Schelberg, Lynne Sebastian, Mollie and Wolky Toll, Marcia Truell, Tom Windes, and several others—who brought that vision to fruition.

At that same time, however, the disciplinary landscape has changed radically since the time when Chaco Project excavations ended and this surge of new research began. The National Park Service has largely ceased sponsorship of large research efforts such as the Chaco Project or the somewhat earlier large-scale studies of Mesa Verde National Park. Archaeologists and government agencies also have become more sensitive to the rights of indigenous communities and the need to consult with them regarding excavations. This sensitivity has been reinforced by the passage of new legislation such as the Native American Graves Protection and Repatriation Act (NAGPRA).

Policies regarding new excavations on federal land nevertheless vary from one agency to another and sometimes even from one national

park to another. In Chaco Culture National Historical Park specifically, excavations of previously undisturbed settlements or rooms have
been discouraged, and therefore new excavations have virtually ceased.
Patricia Crown and Wirt Wills of the University of New Mexico have
reexamined some previously excavated areas, such as their important
exploration of Room 28 and the trenches through the Pueblo Bonito
mounds. In addition, new excavations have been allowed in isolated
instances when construction or erosion has threatened prehistoric
settlements. Thus, park archaeologists Dabney Ford and Roger Moore
have uncovered a small pithouse village scheduled to be disturbed by
expansion of utilities in the park, and the University of Virginia has
conducted studies in the area of Roberts Great House where erosional
forces are removing portions of multiple settlements.

Nonetheless, the current probability of initiating major new excavations of previously unexplored settlements in the canyon and employing new methods either not developed or not common during the era
of the Chaco Project is unfortunately extremely poor. New fieldwork
at early great houses other than Pueblo Bonito is badly needed, much
could be gained from excavations of early pithouse communities, and
studies of key areas such as the remarkable cluster of settlements in
South Gap that have been neglected by prior investigators might provide significant clues regarding social, political, and ritual organization.

The low probability of new field studies has, nevertheless, helped
spur alternative research. Much of the recent research fortunately has
demonstrated that we can explore key questions using published and
unpublished data and analyses of museum collections. Some of this new
research has been facilitated by the current decade-long effort of the
Chaco Research Archive to collect field notes, images, artifact invento-
ries, unpublished manuscripts, correspondence, and a variety of other
information on the many excavations from 1896 through the end of the
SAR-UNM era of fieldwork and to provide access to them (along with
sophisticated database queries) via an online database (http://www.
chacoarchive.org/cra). Scholars can access, and in most cases download,
that information—including context-specific information and photographs for a dozen Chaco settlements and site-level data on many other
pueblos—and conduct searches and database queries relevant to specific
research questions.

Some have previously expressed considerable skepticism about the value and extent of these data (e.g., Frazier 2005:94, 214). Toll (2006:141; see also 2001:64) has stated, "The jumble of structures and occupations and variable research in central Chaco Canyon is so confusing that we can hardly hope to understand it." Similarly, Sebastian (2006:420) has written in regard to excavations in the late 1800s and early 1900s: "The excavation techniques were crude, documentation was cursory, and curation—both the decisions about what to keep and the accessioning and record keeping for retained materials—was often abysmal. We cannot use most of the pre–World War II data to answer many of these twenty-first century questions" (although Sebastian [2006:421] also encourages researchers to "redouble our efforts to coax every bit of possible data" from the records of early excavations and the materials they recovered).

There is little question that the documentation for these early excavations is highly variable, as noted above with the excavations Hewett supervised. However, in many cases the records from prior investigations are very good, the notes are detailed, the catalog records are thorough, and the artifactual materials are available for study. Recent research that has been conducted using data from the early excavations (e.g., Ashmore 2007; Crown and Hurst 2009; Crown and Wills 2003; Cordell et al. 2008; Heitman 2011; Mills and Ferguson 2008; Neitzel 2003a, 2003b; Plog and Heitman 2010; Watson 2012), as well as some of the studies presented in this volume, demonstrate the remarkable potential of working with the early records and artifacts.

Such research is important not only because of the low probability of initiating new excavations in the canyon but also because so much of the discussion of Chaco focuses solely on great house architecture instead of examining the cultural contexts that architecture created. As Varien (2001:56) has argued, "Many discussions of Chacoan society begin and end with an analysis of public architecture." Although that architecture is the most visible and perhaps significant characteristic that distinguishes the Chacoan era, key questions about the nature of those buildings remain unresolved, as Minnis (this volume) reveals in some detail. How many people lived in Pueblo Bonito or in Chaco Canyon? Were the great houses inhabited by small numbers of individuals as some have argued (Bernardini 1999; Windes 1984, 2003), used primarily for public rituals, or simply larger versions of the typical pueblos of the northern Southwest as Pepper, Judd, and many others have proposed? How can we explain not only the extraordinary quantities of turquoise and shell at Pueblo Bonito but also the often-ignored abundance of ground stone and bone tools? Was the canyon a productive agricultural locale or an area whose inhabitants were forced to rely on corn and meat imported from other regions? What was the relation among the inhabitants of the numerous small house settlements and the great houses? I suggest that if we fail to understand the nature and dynamics of Pueblo society in the canyon itself, we have little chance of understanding the broader Chacoan world.

The Chapters

The studies presented in this volume are a result of a seminar hosted by the Amerind Foundation. Our goal in organizing the Amerind seminar, "Current Issues in the Archaeology of Chaco Canyon, A.D. 850–1150" held in October 2010, was not to emphasize a single issue, but to bring together scholars who are actively addressing a range of theoretical models, cultural historical questions, and empirical data.

The twelve chapters fall into four somewhat overlapping groups: agriculture; social organization, ritual, and cosmology; craft production; and skeletal analyses and mortuary patterns. The contributions by Geib and Heitman and by Vivian and Watson address the question of agricultural production in the canyon using very different approaches. Geib and Heitman examine the frequency of corn pollen at Chacoan sites and place those data within a broader regional context of pollen abundance at sites outside of Chaco. Of particular importance, they carefully consider the ways that corn pollen might have entered the archaeological record, a topic often not addressed in studies of pollen from archaeological sites. In doing so, they consider the biology of corn production, experimental studies of pollen distribution, and ethnographic evidence on maize processing. They demonstrate that maize pollen is comparatively abundant at the small number of Chaco sites, including both small and great houses, from which samples are available. These data suggest on-site husking of corn, a behavior that is unlikely unless corn was grown in nearby fields. The study by Geib and Heitman thus supports the conclusion that significant amounts of maize were grown in Chaco Canyon. In addition, they propose that processing of ceremonial meal that included corn pollen may have been important at some Chacoan settlements.

The chapter by Vivian and Watson nicely complements the study of Geib and Heitman by examining agricultural production from a different perspective. They first address the range of agricultural strategies that would have been possible in Chaco Canyon and surrounding areas. Local soil and geomorphology, archaeological evidence of water control features, hydrology, and historic Navajo farming methods are among the factors that they consider in relation to the potential farming methods. Next, they use some of these same data in conjunction with historic information on hydrology, vegetation cover, and Navajo fields to model the potential productivity of floodwater or *akchin* fields in the canyon. Vivian and Watson conclude that several previous studies may have underestimated the agricultural production of the Chaco Canyon region and that by using multiple agricultural strategies, the fields collectively could have produced enough food to support the population of the area they refer to as the Chaco Core, particularly if Chacoans employed cooperative food production and sharing among a group larger than a household.

A second group of studies explores issues regarding demography and mortuary behavior. Snow and LeBlanc review the many possible questions that we could ask about these topics for both the canyon alone and the broader Chacoan world, the possible methods of answering those questions, and the strengths and weaknesses of those methods. They also provide a valuable evaluation of prior studies regarding these issues. Their discussion emphasizes that while demographic and skeletal studies could be extremely valuable in addressing several key questions, the existing data and analyses are limited. At best, we might conclude that the occupants of Chaco were not members of the Uto-Aztecan language group and thus were more closely affiliated with other linguistic groups in the Southwest.

Snow and LeBlanc present important DNA data for skeletal populations from two Chacoan or post–Chacoan era settlements along the San Juan River near Farmington. The two settlements are not contemporary, though there may have been some overlap in their occupations.

They are, however, located within a few kilometers of each other. These DNA data are among the very best available for any Southwestern settlements, and thus, the remarkable differences between the two settlements in the relative frequencies of haplogroups is striking, with one more similar to populations in northern Mexico and the other to Eastern Pueblo groups. The two skeletal populations were recovered from different contexts within each pueblo, however, and this complicates interpretation of the data, as there are potential sampling biases.

Marden's chapter on the Pueblo Bonito skeletal remains is more narrowly focused, examining two case studies that illustrate the complexity of understanding mortuary patterns in two rooms of Pueblo Bonito. These examples explore the deposition of a partial human skeleton in Room 32 of Pueblo Bonito and the skeletal remains of multiple individuals in Room 33. Based on her rigorous and exhaustive taphonomic analysis, Marden concludes that George Pepper, the original excavator, found parts of one individual in both rooms. Examining some of the contextual details and spatial patterns, Marden argues that the individual was first buried in Room 33 and then parts of the skeleton were later dragged into Room 32 by carnivores, an interpretation consistent with her observation that carnivores had chewed on some of the skeletal elements in Room 32 as well as the scattered deposition of elements of the skeleton. Marden therefore questions whether the Room 32 skeletal remains were part of a ritual cache of materials in the structure. Similarly, Marden's taphonomic analysis of the skeletal material from Room 33 also revealed some unexpected distributions of skeletal elements of some of the 14 individuals buried in the room. For some individuals, different elements of the skeleton were found at different depths in the room, suggesting the wooden floor above two of the materials may have been removed at times to make offerings.

Marden's case studies provide new information that is significant to an understanding of both Room 33, a much-discussed structure because of the richness of the remains, and Room 32, a contiguous structure that has received much less attention despite its location in an important section of Pueblo Bonito. Room 32 has several other intriguing characteristics in addition to the skeletal remains discussed by Marden. Close to one portion of the partial body (pelvis and vertebrae) that she discusses, for example, lay a formalized cache of arrows and wooden staffs in the northwest room corner. In addition, a patterned set of graves goods were associated with the vertebrae and pelvis near the doorway between Rooms 32 and 33, including a wooden staff parallel to the vertebrae and a set of eight small wooden sticks burned at one end and found perpendicular to the vertebrae (Pepper 1896, 1920:138). Pepper (1920:138) suggested the sticks "may have been deposited with the body at the time of burial, and the ends burned for some special purpose." Pepper also observed that alternating levels of sand and black or charcoal-filled soil characterized the stratigraphy of the room (discussed in a later chapter by Heitman).

A full understanding of the Room 32 and 33 human remains and artifacts will require integration of the taphonomic evidence with information on associated grave goods, the vertical and spatial distributions of materials—both skeletal and artifactual—in the rooms, AMS radiocarbon dates, Pepper's stratigraphic observations and, in particular, Pepper's excavation and catalog methods. Marden's analysis, however, provides critical new information that will significantly enhance our efforts to reach a more complete understanding of these two important rooms.

A third group of chapters addresses dimensions of social and ritual life in the canyon. Both Heitman and Mills apply aspects of the house society model to help us understand Chaco. Mills begins by highlighting a particularly significant and fundamental principle of that model: we cannot separate behavior into discrete dimensions such as "economic," "ritual," or "political" because these are aspects of almost all behavior in Pueblo societies. She then explores some of the often-discussed burial data from Pueblo Bonito to suggest that many aspects of the materials in the room, including the temporal depth of their deposition and the absence of association between many objects and specific burials, suggests these two burial clusters may represent different "houses" and that one may have been more important than the other. Mills also compares and contrasts the evidence for houses with the spatial distribution and degree of variation of court kivas (minimal variation) and great kivas (much greater variation), proposing possible ties between great kivas and houses. Her study also hypothesizes a possible hierarchical distinction between the two Pueblo Bonito houses and a dichotomy between great and small houses suggested by the absence of court kivas at the small house sites. Mills's study provides a superb example of the value of early excavation data and the insights to be gained by integrating analyses of both architecture and objects.

Also basing her study on the house society model and Pueblo ethnography, Heitman addresses the extremely important question of similarities and differences among great and small houses by examining both the frequency of objects and architectural features. Although the Chacoans constructed hundreds of small house sites and at least 30 to 40 have been partially excavated since 1896, small house sites remain understudied, as Gwinn Vivian (e.g., 2008:373–374) has emphasized on many occasions. A few comparative studies have been published (e.g., Bustard 1996; McKenna and Truell 1986), but the small house sites nevertheless tend to disappear in synthetic interpretations (e.g., Lekson 2006a, 2007; Noble 2004; Van Dyke 2007). Given the abundance of small house sites, the complexity of their occupation histories, the variation among them in size and architecture, and their possible role in key activities such as craft production (Windes 1992; Mathien 2001), it is imperative that we gain a better understanding of their histories and the relations both among small houses and between small houses and great houses. Heitman takes an important step in that direction. She demonstrates houses in both types of settlements were layered with meanings by employing similar ritual practices, suggesting shared cosmologies that particularly emphasized narratives of origin. At the same time, important variation between small and great houses highlights the importance of Pueblo Bonito as the potential home of apical ancestors.

In addition to showing shared cosmology and ritual practices among small and great house inhabitants, Heitman also explores the Pueblo Bonito burial clusters. Her discussion of ancestors and heirlooms, and animation and performance complements and reinforces Mills's study.

Whiteley's examination of Chaco social organization takes a different tack by examining a potential relationship between kinship systems (defined not simply by descent, as archaeologists commonly interpret it, but rather by "four intersecting axes: terminology, descent, marriage, and residence") and architectural forms in Chaco. Kinship is important, Whiteley argues, because it is central to the dynamics of economic and political behavior and to social reproduction. Turning to the archaeological data, Whiteley notes the marked contrast between the architectural form of Pueblo Bonito (and other "D-shaped" great houses with a multiplicity of kivas, great and small) and Wijiji ("E-shaped" with two primary kivas) and explores that variation through the lens of kinship, particularly Crow and Iroquois kinship systems. Drawing on both cross-cultural comparisons and his remarkable knowledge of Pueblo societies, Whiteley notes the contrast between pluralism, as exemplified by Bonito, and dualism, as at Wijiji, in Chacoan architecture. He further suggests that Iroquois kinship "aligns well with dualistic types," while Crow-Omaha are more characteristically plural. Crow-Omaha also are strongly associated with higher population densities, sedentism, and hierarchy. However, while Omaha systems are more expansionist and outward focused, Whiteley suggests Crow systems are more "centripetal," drawing people and resources inward.

Whiteley also argues, however, that Crow-Omaha and Iroquois are not as different as some have suggested and that Pueblo societies over the last several centuries may have had a tendency to oscillate toward one form or another depending upon adaptive conditions and strategies. A tendency toward Crow forms may have been more common in situations in which alliances became more complex, social relations more hierarchical, and house society models more applicable, such as at Pueblo Bonito. When new villages or colonies were established, however, they may have tended to be more dualistic, as with Wijiji. Whiteley therefore brings a significant social and temporal dynamic to discussions of Pueblo social organization, a dynamic that has important implications for our understanding of Chaco.

Chapters by Jolie and Webster and by Watson examine long-neglected and unusually abundant materials—basketry, painted wood, and bone tools—from Chaco, although from somewhat different perspectives and purposes. Jolie and Webster begin their study by citing the common proposal that Chaco was a multiethnic community. They note the problems with the archaeological use of the concept of "ethnicity" and instead choose to focus on social identities, which have multiple axes— gender, age, and kinship, among others. They then explore identity through analyses of such perishable materials as basketry, sandals, mats, and painted wood. They propose that the high degree of technological and structural diversity in such materials at Pueblo Bonito suggests "multiple origins for the makers of Pueblo Bonito's woven items," suggesting the presence of two or three stylistically distinct groups among

the inhabitants of the great houses. At the same time, the recovery of perishable artifacts such as similar types of painted wood from both small
and great houses implies that their inhabitants participated in the same
major systems of social identity that characterized the great house communities, reinforcing Heitman's conclusions. Jolie and Webster propose
a shared social identity may have been promoted within the canyon and
across the Chacoan network by crafting portable artifacts such as bifurcated baskets or wooden staffs used in ritual contexts, which evoked a
shared Basketmaker ancestry. They further note the presence of artifacts
suggesting shared ideological ties with Mesoamerican cultures.

Jolie and Webster also identify a possible east–west division at Bonito
based on evidence such as significant differences in some of materials
occurring in the two discrete burial clusters discussed by Heitman and
Mills. They also find that the finest woven materials occur with these
clusters, further highlighting the likelihood of social differentiation
within the canyon.

Watson analyzes another understudied material, bone tools, to
explore the organization and intensity of bone tool production over
time and across space. He also examines the relationship between these
dimensions of bone tool production and political evolution in Chaco.
As with Heitman, his study is informed by ethnographic studies of the
Pueblo and by cross-cultural comparisons. Watson discovers a shift
through time in the material used for bone tools, with the skeletal elements of artiodactyls and carnivores increasingly emphasized in the last
several decades of the eleventh century, birds (e.g., hawks, eagles, sandhill cranes) becoming important in the last decades of the century, and
turkeys added by the early twelfth century. He also uncovers evidence
of inter-site variation, suggesting possible local exchange relations and
a possible variation over time in the loci of bone tool production, with
the earliest evidence of production occurring at small house settlements,
a pattern also noted for other materials such as turquoise. The general
trends suggest increasing standardization and intensification of the bone
tool industry through the end of the eleventh century and a correlation
between those changes and the intensification of great house construction and agricultural control features as well as the expansion of outliers.

Concluding the volume are two excellent chapters by discussants at
the Amerind seminar that consider a range of issues. Minnis addresses

Chaco from the perspective of his long-term research in the Paquimé region of northern Mexico and particularly emphasizes questions of relative agricultural production in the two very different regions. His additional focus on key questions about the nature of Chaco Canyon and the large surrounding hinterland also highlights the significant disagreement on these important issues noted earlier in this chapter.

Hays-Gilpin and Ware take a different tack, discussing the chapters from a broad temporal perspective that includes the pre-Chaco era but stresses the continuities and lack of continuities between Chaco and the historic Pueblos, both Eastern and Western, as well as the importance of including Pueblo people in such discussions. Their chapter in particular elaborates and comments on many of the very significant issues raised in the chapters by Heitman, Mills, and Whiteley. Hays-Gilpin and Ware, in combination with the discussions of Heitman, Mills, and Whiteley, provide multiple promising avenues for exploring cultural change over the dynamic 300-year era when the intertwined social, political, and religious dimensions of Chaco Canyon became so distinct from contemporaneous regions and so central to much of the northern Pueblo world. Collectively the four papers provide a refreshing and exceedingly promising new approach to understanding both the Chacoan era and historical change and continuity over the centuries that separated the depopulation of Chaco from the historic pueblos documented by ethnographers beginning in the late nineteenth century.

Summary

None of the chapters in the volume decisively answer any of the major questions about Chaco, but collectively the chapters take important steps toward a better understanding of social, economic, biological, and ritual dimensions of life in the canyon. After the long history of research in Chaco, the continued discovery of unanticipated dimensions of prehispanic life in the canyon, and the persistent debate about such basic questions such as the number of great house inhabitants, we should realize that an understanding of Chaco ultimately will be a collective product of many research projects over a period of years. No individual empirical study, theoretical framework, or overarching model is going to produce an eye-opening revelation that provides us at last with a clear understanding of Chaco. I am confident we will increasingly reach that understanding, however, through theoretically and ethnographically informed, methodologically rigorous, and empirically grounded studies that focus on resolving specific issues that are key to the broader questions. I believe the studies in this volume significantly contribute to that goal.

References Cited

Akins, Nancy J. 1984. Temporal Variation in Faunal Assemblages from Chaco Canyon. In *Recent Research on Chaco Prehistory*, edited by W. James Judge and John D. Schelberg, pp. 225–240. Reports of the Chaco Center No. 8. Division of Cultural Research, National Park Service, Albuquerque.

———. 1985. Prehistoric Faunal Utilization in Chaco Canyon Basketmaker III through Pueblo III. In *Environment and Subsistence of Chaco Canyon, New Mexico*, edited by Frances Joan Mathien, pp. 305–445. Publications in Archeology 18E, Chaco Canyon Studies. National Park Service, U.S. Department of the Interior, Santa Fe.

———. 1986. *A Biocultural Approach to Human Burials from Chaco Canyon, New Mexico*. Reports of the Chaco Center No. 9. Division of Cultural Research, National Park Service, Albuquerque.

———. 2001. Chaco Canyon Mortuary Practices: Archaeological Correlates of Complexity. In *Ancient Burial Practices in the American Southwest*, edited by Douglas R. Mitchell and Judy L. Brunson-Hadley, pp. 167–190. University of New Mexico Press, Albuquerque.

———. 2003. The Burials of Pueblo Bonito. In *Pueblo Bonito: Center of the Chaco World*, edited by Jill E. Neitzel, pp. 94–126. Smithsonian Books, Washington, D.C.

Amsden, Monroe. 1925. Small Sites of the Chaco. National Anthropological Archives, Smithsonian Institution, Washington, D.C.

Ashmore, Wendy. 2007. Building Social History at Pueblo Bonito: Footnotes to a Biography of Place. In *The Architecture of Chaco Canyon, New Mexico*, edited by Stephen H. Lekson, pp. 179–198. University of Utah Press, Salt Lake City.

Bernardini, Wesley. 1999. Reassessing the Scale of Social Action at Pueblo Bonito, Chaco Canyon, New Mexico. *Kiva* 64:447–470.

Brand, Donald D., Florence M. Hawley, Frank C. Hibben, et al. 1937. *Tseh So, A Small House Ruin, Chaco Canyon, New Mexico (Preliminary Report)*. The University of New Mexico Bulletin No. 308, Anthropological Series 2, No. 2. University of New Mexico, Albuquerque.

Breternitz, Cory D., David E. Doyel, and Michael P. Marshall (editors). 1982. *Bis sa'ani: A Late Bonito Phase Community on Escavada Wash, Northwest New*

Mexico. Navajo Nation Papers in Anthropology No. 14. Navajo Nation Cultural Resource Management Program, Window Rock, Arizona.

Bustard, Wendy J. 1996. Space as Place: Small and Great House Spatial Organization in Chaco Canyon, New Mexico, A.D. 1000–1150. Ph.D. dissertation, Department of Anthropology, University of New Mexico, Albuquerque.

Cameron, Catherine M. 2008. *Chaco and After in the Northern San Juan: Excavations at the Bluff Great House*. University of Arizona Press, Tucson.

Colfax Chronicle [Colfax, Louisiana] November 4, 1893. Interesting Exhibits: The Pueblos of the Aztecs in Miniature at the World's Fair.

Cordell, Linda S., H. Wolcott Toll, Mollie S. Toll, and Thomas C. Windes. 2008. Archaeological Corn from Pueblo Bonito, Chaco Canyon, New Mexico: Dates, Contexts, Sources. *American Antiquity* 73:491–511.

Crown, Patricia L., and W. Jeffrey Hurst. 2009. Evidence of Cacao Use in the Prehispanic American Southwest. *Proceedings of the National Academy of Sciences* 106:2110–2113.

Crown, Patricia L., and W. H. Wills. 2003. Modifying Pottery and Kivas at Chaco: Pentimento, Restoration, or Renewal? *American Antiquity* 68:511–532.

Fowler, Don D. 2000. *A Laboratory for Anthropology: Science and Romanticism in the American Southwest, 1846–1930*. University of New Mexico Press, Albuquerque.

Frazier, Kendrick. 2005. *People of Chaco: A Canyon and Its Culture*. W. W. Norton and Co., New York.

Globe Republican [Dodge City, Kansas] September 22, 1893. Interesting Exhibits: The Pueblos of the Aztecs in Miniature at the World's Fair.

Hawley, Florence M. 1934. *The Significance of the Dated Prehistory of Chetro Ketl*. University of New Mexico Bulletin 246. Albuquerque: University of New Mexico Press.

———. 1936. *Field Manual of Prehistoric Southwest Pottery Types*. University of New Mexico Bulletin No. 291, Anthropological Series I, No. 4. University of New Mexico Press, Albuquerque.

———. 1938. The Family Tree of Chaco Canyon Masonry. *American Anthropologist* 3:245–255.

Hayden, F. V. 1878. *Tenth Annual Report of the United States Geological and Geographical Survey of the Territories Embracing Colorado and Parts of Adjacent Territories, Report of Progress of the Exploration for the Year 1876*. U.S. Government Printing Office, Washington, D.C.

Heitman, Carrie C. 2011. Architectures of Inequality: Evaluating Kinship and Cosmology in Chaco Canyon, New Mexico, A.D. 850–1180. Ph.D. dissertation, Department of Anthropology, University of Virginia.

Irwin-Williams, Cynthia (editor). 1972. *The Structure of Chacoan Society in the Northern Southwest: Investigations at the Salmon Site—1972*. Eastern New Mexico University Contributions in Anthropology 4(3). Eastern New Mexico Printing Services, Portales.

Irwin-Williams, Cynthia, and Phillip H. Shelley (editors). 1980. *Investigations at Salmon Ruin: The Structure of Chacoan Society in the Northern Southwest, Vols. I–IV.* Eastern New Mexico University Printing Services, Portales.

Jackson, William H. 1878. Ruins of the Chaco Cañon, Examined in 1877. In *Tenth Annual Report of the United States Geological and Geographical Survey of the Territories Embracing Colorado and Parts of Adjacent Territories, Being a Report of Progress of the Exploration for the Year 1876*, edited by F. V. Hayden, pp. 431–450. U.S. Government Printing Office, Washington, D.C.

Judd, Neil H. 1920. Report on an Archaeologic Reconnaissance of Chaco Canyon, New Mexico. United States National Museum, Washington, D.C.

———. 1924. Two Chaco Canyon Pithouses. In *Annual Report for 1922, Smithsonian Institution*, pp. 399–413. Smithsonian Institution, Washington, D.C.

———. 1927. The Architectural Evolution of Pueblo Bonito. *Proceedings of the National Academy of Science* 13:561–563.

———. 1954. *The Material Culture of Pueblo Bonito.* Smithsonian Miscellaneous Collections Vol. 124. Smithsonian Institution, Washington, D.C.

———. 1959. *Pueblo del Arroyo, Chaco Canyon, New Mexico.* Smithsonian Miscellaneous Collections Vol. 138, No. 1. Smithsonian Institution, Washington, D.C.

———. 1964. *The Architecture of Pueblo Bonito.* Smithsonian Miscellaneous Collections Vol. 147, No. 1. Smithsonian Institution, Washington, D.C.

———. 1967. The Passing of a Small PIII Ruin. *Plateau* 39:131–133.

Kluckhohn, Clyde. 1939. Discussion. In *Preliminary Report on the 1937 Excavations, BC 50–51 Chaco Canyon, New Mexico*, edited by Clyde Kluckhohn and Paul Reiter, pp.151–162. University of New Mexico Bulletin 345, Anthropological Series 3, No. 2. University of New Mexico Press, Albuquerque.

Kluckhohn, Clyde, and Paul Reiter (editors). 1939. *Preliminary Report on the 1937 Excavations, BC 50–51, Chaco Canyon, New Mexico.* University of New Mexico Bulletin 345, Anthropology Series Vol. 3, No. 2. University of New Mexico Press, Albuquerque.

Lekson, Stephen H. 1984. *Great Pueblo Architecture of Chaco Canyon.* Publications in Archaeology 18B, Chaco Canyon Series. National Park Service, U.S. Department of the Interior, Santa Fe.

———. 2006b. Chaco Matters: An Introduction. In *The Archaeology of Chaco Canyon: An Eleventh-Century Regional Center*, edited by Stephen H. Lekson, pp. 3–44. School of American Research Press, Santa Fe.

———. 2009. *A History of the Ancient Southwest.* School for Advanced Research Press, Santa Fe.

Lekson, Stephen H. (editor). 2006a. *The Archaeology of Chaco Canyon: An Eleventh-Century Regional Center.* School of American Research Press, Santa Fe.

———. (editor). 2007. *The Architecture of Chaco Canyon, New Mexico.* University of Utah Press, Salt Lake City.

The Louisiana Democrat [Alexandria, Louisiana] March 1887. Nature in Ruins: An Unexplored Region in the Wonderland of the Far West.

Mathien, Frances Joan. 1981. Neutron Activation of Turquoise Artifacts from Chaco Canyon, New Mexico. *Current Anthropology* 22:293–294.

———. 1984. Jewelry Items of the Chaco Anasazi. In *Recent Research on the Chaco Prehistory*, edited by W. James Judge and John D. Schelberg, pp. 173–186. Reports of the Chaco Center No. 8. Division of Cultural Research, National Park Service, Albuquerque.

———. 1997. Ornaments of the Chaco Anasazi. In *Ceramics, Lithics and Ornaments of Chaco Canyon*. National Park Service, Santa Fe.

———. 2001. The Organization of Turquoise Production and Consumption by the Prehistoric Chacoans. *American Antiquity* 66:103–118.

———. 2005. *Culture and Ecology of Chaco Canyon and the San Juan Basin*. Publications in Archeology 18H, Chaco Canyon Series. National Park Service, U.S. Department of the Interior, Santa Fe.

McNitt, Frank. 1957. *Richard Wetherill: Anasazi*. University of New Mexico Press, Albuquerque.

McKenna, Peter J., and Marcia L. Truell. 1986. *Small Site Architecture of Chaco Canyon, New Mexico*. Publication in Archeology 18D, Chaco Canyon Series. National Park Service, Santa Fe.

Mills, Barbara J., and T. J. Ferguson. 2008. Animate Objects: Shell Trumpets and Ritual Networks in the Greater Southwest. *Journal of Archaeological Method and Theory* 15:338–361.

Moorehead, W. K. 1906. Explorations in New Mexico. *Bulletin of the Phillips Academy Department of Archaeology* 3(3):33–53.

Morgan, Lewis Henry. 1869. The "Seven Cities of Cibola." *The North American Review* 108(223):457–498.

———. 1881. *Houses and House-Life of the American Aborigines*. U.S. Government Printing Office, Washington, D.C.

Neitzel, Jill E. 2003a. Artifact Distributions at Pueblo Bonito. In *Pueblo Bonito: Center of the Pueblo World*, edited by Jill E. Neitzel, pp. 107–126. Smithsonian Press, Washington, D.C.

———. 2003b. The Organization, Function, and Population of Pueblo Bonito. In *Pueblo Bonito: Center of the Pueblo World*, edited by Jill E. Neitzel, pp. 143–149. Smithsonian Press, Washington, D.C.

Nelson, N. C. 1920. Notes on Pueblo Bonito. In *Pueblo Bonito* by George H. Pepper, pp. 381–390. Anthropological Papers of the American Museum of Natural History Vol. 27. Trustees of the American Museum of Natural History, New York.

Noble, David Grant (editor). 2004. *In Search of Chaco: New Approaches to an Archaeological Enigma*. School of American Research Press, Santa Fe.

Pepper, George H. 1896. Rooms #32 and 33, Also Measurements of Rooms. 1896–47 Accession file, Division of Anthropology, American Museum of Natural

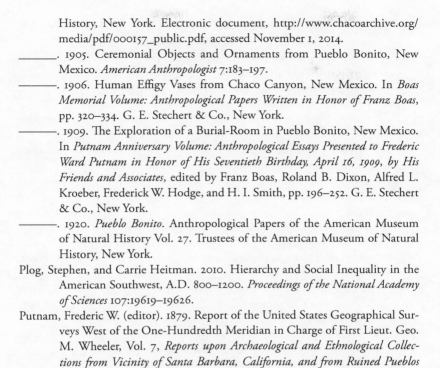

History, New York. Electronic document, http://www.chacoarchive.org/media/pdf/000157_public.pdf, accessed November 1, 2014.

———. 1905. Ceremonial Objects and Ornaments from Pueblo Bonito, New Mexico. *American Anthropologist* 7:183–197.

———. 1906. Human Effigy Vases from Chaco Canyon, New Mexico. In *Boas Memorial Volume: Anthropological Papers Written in Honor of Franz Boas*, pp. 320–334. G. E. Stechert & Co., New York.

———. 1909. The Exploration of a Burial-Room in Pueblo Bonito, New Mexico. In *Putnam Anniversary Volume: Anthropological Essays Presented to Frederic Ward Putnam in Honor of His Seventieth Birthday, April 16, 1909, by His Friends and Associates*, edited by Franz Boas, Roland B. Dixon, Alfred L. Kroeber, Frederick W. Hodge, and H. I. Smith, pp. 196–252. G. E. Stechert & Co., New York.

———. 1920. *Pueblo Bonito*. Anthropological Papers of the American Museum of Natural History Vol. 27. Trustees of the American Museum of Natural History, New York.

Plog, Stephen, and Carrie Heitman. 2010. Hierarchy and Social Inequality in the American Southwest, A.D. 800–1200. *Proceedings of the National Academy of Sciences* 107:19619–19626.

Putnam, Frederic W. (editor). 1879. Report of the United States Geographical Surveys West of the One-Hundredth Meridian in Charge of First Lieut. Geo. M. Wheeler, Vol. 7, *Reports upon Archaeological and Ethnological Collections from Vicinity of Santa Barbara, California, and from Ruined Pueblos of Arizona and New Mexico, and Certain Interior Tribes*. U.S. Government Printing Office, Washington, D.C.

Reed, Paul F. (editor). 2006. *Thirty-Five Years of Archaeological Research at Salmon Ruins, New Mexico*. 3 vols. Center for Desert Archaeology, Tucson; Salmon Ruins Museum, Bloomfield, New Mexico.

——— (editor). 2008. *Chaco's Northern Prodigies: Salmon, Aztec, and the Ascendancy of the Middle San Juan Region after AD 1100*. University of Utah Press, Salt Lake City.

Reiter, Paul D. 1933. *The Ancient Pueblo of Chetro Ketl*. Master's thesis, Department of Anthropology, Harvard University, Cambridge, Massachusetts.

———. 1946. *Form and Function in Some Prehistoric Ceremonial Structures in the Southwest*. Ph.D. dissertation, Department of Anthropology, Harvard University, Cambridge, Massachusetts.

Roberts, Frank H. H. 1927. *The Ceramic Sequence in the Chaco Canyon, New Mexico and Its Relation to the Cultures of the San Juan Basin*. Ph.D. dissertation, Department of Anthropology, Harvard University, Cambridge, Massachusetts.

———. 1929. *Shabik'eshchee Village, a Late Basket Maker Site in Chaco Canyon, New Mexico, Bureau of American Ethnology Bulletin 92*. Smithsonian Institution, Washington, D.C.

Sebastian, Lynne. 1992. *The Chaco Anasazi: Sociopolitical Evolution in the Prehistoric Southwest*. Cambridge University Press, Cambridge.

————. 2006. The Chaco Synthesis. In *The Archaeology of Chaco Canyon: An Eleventh-Century Regional Center*, edited by Stephen H. Lekson, pp. 393–422. School of American Research Press, Santa Fe.

Shepard, Anna O. 1939. Technology of La Plata Pottery. In *Archaeological Studies in the La Plata District*, edited by Earl H. Morris, pp. 249–287. Carnegie Institute of Washington, Washington, D.C.

Simpson, James H. 1874. The Ruins to Be Found in New Mexico, and the Explorations of Francisco Vasquez de Coronado in Search of the Seven Cities of Cibola. *Journal of the American Geographical Society of New York* 5:194–216.

Toll, H. Walcott. 1985. *Pottery, Production, Public Architecture, and the Chaco Anasazi System*. Ph.D. dissertation, Department of Anthropology, University of Colorado, Boulder.

————. 2001. Making and Breaking Pots in the Chaco World. *American Antiquity* 66:56–78.

————. 2006. Organization of Production. In *The Archaeology of Chaco Canyon: An Eleventh-Century Regional Center*, edited by Stephen H. Lekson, pp. 117–151. School for Advanced Research Press, Santa Fe.

Van Dyke, Ruth M. 2007. *The Chaco Experience: Landscape and Ideology at the Center Place*. School of American Research, Santa Fe.

Varien, Mark D. 2001. We Have Learned a Lot, But We Still Have More to Learn. In *Chaco Society and Polity: Papers from the 1999 Conference*, edited by Linda S. Cordell, W. James Judge, and June-el Piper, pp. 47–61. New Mexico Archaeological Council Special Publication 4. New Mexico Archaeological Council, Albuquerque.

Vivian, Gordon, and Tom W. Mathews. 1965. *Kin Kletso: A Pueblo III Community in Chaco Canyon, New Mexico*. Southwestern Monuments Association Technical Series Vol. 6. Southwestern Monuments Association, Tucson.

Vivian, Gordon, and Paul Reiter. 1965. *The Great Kivas of Chaco Canyon*. School of American Research Monograph No. 22. School of American Research, Santa Fe.

Vivian, R. Gwinn. 1984. Agricultural and Social Adjustments to Changing Environment in the Chaco Basin. In *Prehistoric Agricultural Strategies in the Southwest*, edited by Suzanne K. Fish and Paul R. Fish, pp. 242–257. Arizona State University, Tempe.

————. 1991. Chacoan Subsistence. In *Chaco & Hohokam*, edited by Patricia L. Crown and W. James Judge, pp. 57–75. School of American Research, Santa Fe.

————. 1992. Chacoan Water Use and Managerial Decision Making. In *Anasazi Regional Organization and the Chaco System*, edited by David E. Doyel, pp. 45–57. Maxwell Museum of Anthropology, Anthropological Papers

No. 5. Maxwell Museum of Anthropology, University of New Mexico, Albuquerque.

———. 2008. The Middle San Juan and Chaco Canyon. In *Chaco's Northern Prodigies*, edited by Paul F. Reed, pp. 366–375. University of Utah Press, Salt Lake City.

Vivian, R. Gwinn, Dulce N. Dodgen, and Gayle H. Hartmann. 1978. *Wooden Ritual Artifacts from Chaco Canyon, New Mexico: The Chetro Ketl Collection*. Anthropological Papers of the University of Arizona No. 32. University of Arizona Press, Tucson.

Vivian, R. Gwinn, Carla R. Van West, Jeffrey S. Dean, Nancy J. Akins, Mollie S. Toll, and Thomas C. Windes. 2006. Ecology and Economy. In *The Archaeology of Chaco Canyon*, edited by Stephen H. Lekson, pp. 45–65. School of American Research Press, Santa Fe.

Watson, Adam Stewart. 2012. *Craft, Subsistence, and Political Change: An Archaeological Investigation of Power and Economy in Prehistoric Chaco Canyon, 850 to 1200 CE*. Ph.D. dissertation, Department of Anthropology, University of Virginia, Charlottesville.

Wheeler, George M. (editor). 1879. *Report upon United States Geographical Surveys West of the One-Hundredth Meridian*. Vol. VII: Archaeology. U.S. Government Printing Office, Washington, D.C.

Windes, Thomas C. 1984. A New Look at Population in Chaco Canyon. In *Recent Research on Chaco Prehistory*, edited by W. James Judge and John D. Schelberg, pp. 75–87. Reports of the Chaco Center No. 8. Division of Cultural Research, National Park Service, Albuquerque.

———. 1992. Blue Notes: The Chacoan Turquoise Industry in the San Juan Basin. In *Anasazi Regional Organization and the Chaco System*, edited by David E. Doyel, pp. 159–168. Maxwell Museum of Anthropology, Anthropology Series No. 5. Maxwell Museum of Anthropology, University of New Mexico, Albuquerque.

———. 2003. This Old House: Construction and Abandonment at Pueblo Bonito. In *Pueblo Bonito: Center of the Pueblo World*, edited by Jill E. Neitzel, pp. 14–32. Smithsonian Institution Press, Washington, D.C.

Windes, Thomas C., and Dabney Ford. 1996. The Chaco Wood Project: The Chronometric Reappraisal of Pueblo Bonito. *American Antiquity* 61:295–310.

Reevaluating and Modeling Agricultural Potential in the Chaco Core

R. Gwinn Vivian and Adam S. Watson

While on a military expedition to the Navajo country in 1849, Lieutenant J. H. Simpson (1850:86) recorded, "The soil in the *Cañon de Chaco*, though now very arid, seems to possess the elements of fertility." In the more than a century and a half since Simpson's observation, the canyon's agricultural potential has been evaluated and debated without general consensus (e.g., Benson et al. 2006; Brand et al. 1937; Bryan 1954; Earle 2001; Force et al. 2002; Holsinger 1901; Judd 1954, 1964; Loose and Lyons 1976; Sebastian 1992; Toll et al. 1985; Vivian 1974, 1984, 1990, 1991, 1992; Vivian and Mathews 1965). Recent investigations (Benson 2011a, 2011b; Dorshow 2012; Wills and Dorshow 2012) have tended to widen the consensual gap. Of four archaeological regions evaluated by Benson (San Juan Basin, Mesa Verde, Zuni, and Los Alamos/Bandelier/Pajarito Plateau) with respect to optimal precipitation and heat, soil salinity levels, and pH values, "the San Juan Basin, including Chaco Canyon, is the least promising part of the study area in terms of dryland farming" (Benson 2011b:1). Benson and colleagues had earlier noted the incongruity of a surge in great house construction in Chaco Canyon between approximately A.D. 1030 and 1130 in a very unproductive area for maize cultivation and postulated that "increases in Chaco's population during pilgrim fairs and major construction intervals would have necessitated the importation of maize . . . from outlier sites . . . used for storage of surplus foodstuffs" (Benson et al. 2006:301). However, Dorshow, while not arguing that previous estimates were incorrect, proposed that his geospatial analysis of geomorphology and surficial hydrology suggested "that previous models of Chacoan agricultural productivity have underestimated local production capacity" (Dorshow 2012:2098).

Problems Characterizing Analyses of Chacoan Agriculture

We believe that several factors may account, at least in part, for conflicting research results regarding Chacoan agricultural potential. These include (1) association of farming primarily with Chacoan great houses, (2) a need for consensus on a Chacoan production zone, (3) minimal evaluation of soil hydrology in recorded or postulated field locations, and (4) limited investigation of Chacoan agricultural strategies. The first three problems are reviewed briefly and then current information on six known or predicted farming strategies is summarized. Ethnographic data and hydrologic modeling are then employed to more thoroughly evaluate the productive potential for a seventh strategy—*akchin* farming.

Association of Farming Primarily with Great Houses

Inasmuch as Chacoan archaeology has been focused long-term primarily on great houses, it is not surprising that references to farming in the Chaco area usually have been linked with these structures. Sebastian (1992:122) solidified this trend in her emergent leadership model in which she assumed that great houses were located adjacent to the "most productive farmland," leading to a perpetual patron-client relationship with "their neighbors." However, by approaching Chaco as a monolithic area of agricultural productivity, the immense variability of farming opportunities in the Chaco region was ignored. Such diversity—involving endless permutations of conditions including soil, vegetation, slope, elevation, runoff, antecedent moisture, sunlight, and cold air drainage—combines to set Chaco apart and would lend sustainability and resiliency to farming in Chaco. This underscores the critical need to consider agricultural production by small house communities in addition to great houses, given the number of those communities, their settlement pattern, and the multiple available strategies for farming in and outside the canyon.

A Need for Consensus on a Chacoan Production Zone

We believe this problem is a direct result of the close association of farming with great houses and the resultant failure to acknowledge multiple

Chacoan farming strategies. Inasmuch as the majority of Chacoan great houses in the inner San Juan Basin are located in the lower half of Chaco Canyon, that area, including the canyon and bordering mesas, often is identified as the Chacoan production zone (e.g., Dorshow 2012; Sebastian 1992; Wills and Dorshow 2012). Yet, there is no consensus that this zone could produce crops sufficient for the local population, thereby requiring imports from Chacoan "outliers."

Two concepts have been proposed that would expand the Chacoan production zone beyond the lower canyon but that do not extend that area to distant outliers in locales such as the Chuska Valley and the northern slopes of the Dutton Plateau east and west of Crownpoint, New Mexico. The "Chaco Halo" (Doyel et al. 1984), an oval zone encompassing approximately 312 km^2, includes most of Chaco Canyon and extends from the Kin Klizhin–Chaco Wash confluence on the west to within 10 km of Pueblo Pintado on the east—a distance of roughly 24 km. The distance from north to south is about 13 km and includes a portion of the Chacra Mesa on the south and the lower drainage of the Escavada Wash on the north. The Kin Bineola, Kin Klizhin, Pueblo Pintado, and Bis sa'ani communities do not fall within the Halo. Doyel and his co-authors introduced the "Halo" concept as a means for including a number of diverse Chacoan sites lying outside the canyon that served multiple purposes such as "adjacent agricultural production centers and perhaps seasonal occupational sites for the inhabitants of the central canyon" (Doyel et al. 1984:49).

The "Chaco Core" (Vivian 1990; Vivian et al. 2006) is a longer (42 km) but similarly narrow (18 km) oval that territorially expands the "Halo" to include the Kin Bineola, Kin Klizhin, East Community, Pueblo Pintado, and Bis sa'ani communities for a total area of approximately 672 km^2 (see Figure 2.1). The Chaco Wash runs the full length of the Core, primarily through Chaco Canyon, and the lower drainages of three primary tributaries—the Escavada, Kin Klizhin, and Kin Bineola—join the Chaco within the Core. Though Core landscapes vary, a number of zones have similar physiographic, hydrologic, and edaphic characteristics highly suitable for runoff farming, particularly akchin. This is especially true of several Core landforms (e.g., mesa slopes and side canyons) that produce increased runoff following summer storms. Similarly, summer storms and winter snow on numerous sand dunes in

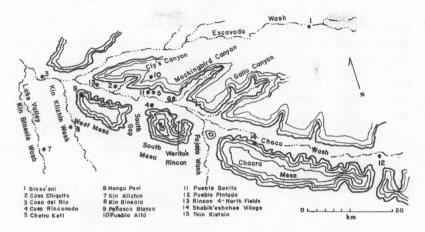

Figure 2.1. Map of sites and physiographic features in the Chaco Core.

the Core increase subsurface moisture for dune farming. We propose that over time, zones within the Core with these physiographic, hydrologic, and edaphic characteristics became the loci for interdependent agricultural Chacoan communities both within Chaco Canyon, such as the East Community, and outside Chaco Canyon, such as Pueblo Pintado and Kin Bineola.

Though both the Halo and Core concepts provide a means for defining production zones larger than lower Chaco Canyon, their usefulness can be minimized when the terms are applied to other spatial zones. For example, Benson et al. (2006:293) referenced both "Chaco Core" and "Chaco Canyon Core" but limited this zone to the lower 18 km of Chaco Canyon. Subsequently, Benson (2011b:62, Figure 1) described a 6,345 km^2 "Chaco Halo" that extended from Raton Wells on the east to the base of the Chuska Mountains on the west. And Dorshow (2012:2099, Figure 1) defines a "Chaco Core Study Area" that "encompasses the lower third of Chaco Canyon where most of the Bonito phase great houses are located (Fig. 1)," although he also identifies this same area as the "Downtown Chaco Study Area" in Figures 4 through 15.

Minimal Evaluation of Field Soil Hydrology

Past evaluations of the agricultural potential of soils in the Chaco Core (e.g., Cully and Toll 2014; Cully et al. 1982; Judd 1954, 1964; Powers et

al. 1983; Windes 1987a, 1993) were based primarily on USDA Soil Conservation Service soil taxonomic unit descriptions, soil maps, and land
class maps that emphasize pedologic profiles. Less attention has been
paid to water requirements of maize, though Benson (2011a, 2011b) has
examined this need in detail. However, it is generally acknowledged
that with the exception of dune farming, sole dependence on direct
precipitation—dry farming—is virtually impossible in the Chaco Core,
thereby making supplementary water vital for crop production. This is
a common premise guiding investigations of native crop production in
much of the Southwest, including the work of Dominguez and Kolm
(2005) in the Hopi Mesas region. However, they subsequently determined that Hopi field locales were selected "primarily on soil profile
attributes that increase moisture input and storage (as indicated by key
plant taxa) and secondarily on the availability of supplementary water"
(Dominguez and Kolm 2005:738). Planting in these locales was most
effective when combined with field clearing, planting, and maintenance
procedures advantageous to stored moisture in the soil.

Soil hydrologic profiles provide a framework for tracing and evaluating the movement of water into, within, and out of a soil profile.
Multiple variables are involved in water movement, but soil texture
is the most critical, and "textures at the extreme ends of the soil triangle, sand, silt, and clay, behave in distinctively different manners"
(Dominguez and Kolm 2005:744). Dominguez and Kolm point out
that archaeologists could use generalized soil hydrology principles to
clarify climate/soil/technology interactions as a means to better identify
and evaluate potential farming locations utilizing varied farming technologies. Dorshow (2012) has taken an important first step in applying
these principles to a segment of the Chaco Core—the lower portion of
Chaco Canyon and bordering mesas. He included soil texture as one
of six "key natural factors" integrated in a "predictive geospatial analysis of Bonito phase agricultural potential" (Dorshow 2012:2101). Soils
data were collected from aerial photos, field observations of the U.S.
Department of Agriculture, Natural Resource Conservation Service,
and the U.S. Geological Survey Geologic Map of the Pueblo Bonito
Quadrangle (Scott et al. 1984). While acknowledging that the spatial
resolution of his data was "relatively coarse," he was confident that basic
trends related to agricultural potential could be obtained from his data.

Generally, this would be true of mesas and other lands bordering the canyon on the north and south. However, given the complex depositional history of the canyon floor (Hall 2010; Love 1977), greater refinement of potentially diverse deposits in this zone could be advantageous given Dorshow's (2012:2108) conclusion that there is "significantly more high potential and less low potential land in the northern catchments, relative to the grouped southern catchments."

Limited Investigation of Chacoan Agricultural Strategies

Until quite recently, Chacoan literature has tended to deemphasize both the importance and potential of local agriculture. Lekson (2009:292n122), for example, commented that "Chaco is a famously poor place to farm, and Chacoans knew it. Perhaps Chaco was not using its precious water to raise crops better farmed elsewhere." And although Benson's (2011a, 2011b) recent study focused on "dryland (rain-on-field) agriculture," he and others (Benson et al. 2006:298) acknowledged that such farming was highly unlikely in Chaco Canyon and that maize could not have been grown there "without recourse to effective water-control systems." Wills and his students recently have challenged these conclusions in several well-documented papers (Dorshow 2012; Wills and Dorshow 2012; Wills et al. 2012). Overall, there is increasing evidence for more extensive and intensive farming in the Chaco Core (see Geib and Heitman, this volume). This is particularly true with respect to strategies designed to take maximum advantage of several diverse geomorphic settings utilizing groundwater or runoff (floodwater). These include use of groundwater in dune fields and archaeological and/or ethnographic evidence for use of runoff in terracing, check dams, floodplain, rincon canal irrigation, drainage basin canal irrigation, slope wash, and akchin (alluvial fan). The first six strategies are summarized below; akchin is evaluated in the following section.

Groundwater

Dune Fields. Upper Holocene to Upper Pleistocene eolian sand (*Qes*) in and surrounding Chaco Canyon (Scott et al. 1984) is present in both active and stabilized dunes that collect and hold water from rain and snow. Currently, stabilized dunes occur as climbing dunes in Werito's Rincon and as sand sheets on South Mesa surrounding the Tsin Kletsin great house and in several areas near South Gap to the south of West and South Mesas. Their greatest extent is as longitudinal dunes north of Chaco Canyon along the Escavada Wash in the vicinity of the Pueblo Alto great house community. They also occur on the north side of the Chaco River below the Chaco-Escavada confluence near the Peñasco Blanco great house community.

Hopi agricultural use of groundwater stored in dune sand is well-documented (Beaglehole 1937; Bradfield 1971; Hack 1942). In the latter half of the 1930s, somewhat less than 27 percent of Hopi fields were planted in stabilized sand dunes, although over 60 percent of the fields at Hotevilla were in dunes (Hack 1942:33–34). The most common locations were in longitudinal dunes on mesa tops and near the base of climbing dunes on mesa slopes. Lines of stone held brush to protect young plants from wind-blown sand marked old field areas. Similar lines of stone have not been found in the Chaco Core, though eolian action may have obliterated this evidence. However, Chaco Project experimental farming plots in dunes in Chaco Canyon, particularly Werito's Rincon, were the most successful of several field locations tested (Toll et al. 1985). Worman and Mattson (2010:474) also postulate dune farming in the Pueblo Pintado community at the eastern end of Chaco Canyon. Although roughly 1,000 ha of stabilized dunes are currently present in and near Chaco Canyon, estimating potential hectares of cropland is difficult inasmuch as the Hopi farmed only portions of dunes, particularly climbing dunes. Moreover, some dunes that were active along the Chaco and Escavada Washes a half century ago are now stabilizing or stabilized, indicating significant changes in dunes over short periods of time. Nonetheless, dune fields should be included when evaluating the agricultural potential of the Chaco Core.

Runoff

Unlike groundwater, the use of runoff or floodwater is conditioned by the quantity and velocity of flow (affected in turn by the intensity and duration of the storm producing it) as well as the size, physiography, slope, and permeability of the drainage area. Quantity and velocity were serious concerns for Chacoan farmers as was the soil hydrology of the intended fields, and use strategies varied according to local conditions and intended use.

Seven types of planting locales or fields utilizing runoff have been identified in the Chaco Core. Four archaeologically documented types include terracing, check dams, rincon canal irrigation, and drainage basin canal irrigation. Three additional types—floodplain, slope wash, and akchin—were utilized by Chaco-area Navajo; floodplain and akchin almost certainly were also Chacoan strategies. Summary data on six types follow. Modeling is then employed to evaluate akchin potential.

Terracing/Check Dams. Data on terracing and check dams are consolidated, as evidence for their use is restricted to a small zone of cliff top on the north side of Chaco Canyon in the vicinity of the Pueblo Alto great house. This area is characterized by large expanses of bedrock with minimal vegetation and soil cover. Runoff flows on the surface over cliff edges into branching side canyons for use in terraced plots or in shallow mesa-top channels where it is collected behind check dams.

Two small areas of lateral or contour terracing east of and below the Pueblo Alto great house accounted for just .3 ha of cultivatable land (Wills and Dorshow 2012; Windes 1987b). Several tiers of masonry walls 1 to 3 m in height were constructed below the side canyon cliff edges to enhance natural terracing holding sandy soil derived from cliff top deposits via wind and water action. Combined water catchment from cliff top runoff for both zones was approximately 3 ha. Hack (1942:36) reported small Hopi "gardens" high on mesa sides watered from seepage reservoirs that were reserved for special crops, including tobacco.

Several check dams—low (ca. 40–50 cm) masonry walls built in shallow, narrow bedrock drainages—were located on the cliff top above the terracing. Soil consisted of sand and minimal organic matter resting on bedrock. Windes (1978:105) described and illustrated two check dam "garden plots" in this area, but noted that pollen samples did not suggest use as a garden. Reported canyon bottom check dams are likely of Navajo origin.

Rincon Canal Irrigation. Rincon canal irrigation as presently known in the Chaco Core is restricted to the lower 8.8 km (5.5 mi) of Chaco Canyon. It has been documented primarily in side canyon ("rincon") drainages on the north side of Chaco Canyon from Mockingbird Canyon to the western terminus of the canyon near the Peñasco Blanco great house

(Vivian 1974, 1992; Vivian et al. 2006). The physiography of the lower north side of Chaco Canyon is marked by "a sheer cliff surmounted by a bench and a more gentle cliff above" (Bryan 1954:11). Sixteen south-draining rincons and one larger drainage, Cly's Canyon, are cut into the lower sheer cliff. Most rincons have one primary watercourse draining both sides of sloping bedrock catchments of the side canyon. The southern exposure curtails dense and varied vegetation and the development of soils, thereby contributing to runoff with greater velocity and in most instances a greater load of sand and silt. Today, runoff in the primary drainage when entering the main canyon tends to cut a deep channel to the Chaco Wash, impairing the development of alluvial fans.

After examining these rincons, Benson et al. (2006:311) concluded, "It is much easier to access side-canyon runoff by constructing check dams and contour terraces on the up-canyon surface of an alluvial fan, than it is to harvest runoff at the distal end of a fan after infiltration losses have been maximized." Test excavations in the lower canyon, however, produced evidence of a highly standardized pattern of collection and diversion of water from rincons to gridded fields. As described and illustrated by Vivian (1990), earthen or masonry dams at the mouths of rincons diverted water into U-shaped canals, often lined with stone or bordered by masonry, that delivered water to well constructed headgates that channeled the flow into tracts of multiple, well-defined, large (ca. 22.5 m x 13.5 m) grids (Loose and Lyons 1976). Although architectural features in these systems were designed to handle large volumes of rushing floodwater, headgates in two systems were destroyed, and in one instance, gates were repaired at least two times. Total rincon catchment was approximately 556 ha. The larger Cly's Canyon drainage (563 ha) was also tapped for floodwater, but there is currently no evidence for collecting water from the even larger Mockingbird Canyon drainage (ca. 890 ha). Estimated canal irrigated farmland from Mockingbird Canyon to the western end of Chaco Canyon is 145 ha.

The physiography and hydrology of the south side of Chaco Canyon differs from that on the north. Multiple gradated elevational benches, more varied and dense vegetation, and a more dendritic drainage pattern resulted in reduced velocity of runoff and accumulation of alluvial fans at the mouths of rincons rather than channel cutting to the Chaco Wash. However, two rincon canal irrigation systems are known on the

south side in the lower 8.8 km of the canyon, one below the Peñasco
Blanco great house and another near the Casa Rinconada great kiva
opposite the Pueblo Bonito great house (Vivian et al. 2006). Features
duplicate those on the north side of the canyon. Estimated catchment
for each system was 240 ha, and potential farming area in each case was
approximately 20 ha.

Tests by Loose and Lyons (1976:139) in the gridded fields near the
Chetro Ketl great house revealed a tan "sandy soil about 40 centimeters
thick" that overlay laminated gray clay "ranging from 5 to 20 centimeters thick" that in turn covered a "massive gray compact clay ranging
from 60 centimeters to 1 meter thick." They identified the upper laminated clay level as an "Old Field Surface" deposited by the Chaco Wash,
while the tan sandy soil was derived from side canyons, suggesting "the
field was watered from both the side canyons and the central wash"
(Loose and Lyons 1976:142). Hall's (2010) alluvial chronology of Chaco
Canyon includes frequent deposits of a massive homogenous clay as
overbank alluvium in his "Chaco unit" (2100–1000 years BP), and the
massive clay level below the grids may represent this alluvium. However, the upper levels within the grids may reflect intentional deposition
partially through canal irrigation of contrasting soil textures. Dominguez and Kolm (2005:744) determined that the layering of soil textures
"at the extreme ends of the soil triangle, sand, silt, and clay" was vital for
efficient water conductivity for agriculture. Soils in Hopi fields included
an upper zone of sand that quickly absorbed water and then acted as
mulch, a "midsoil" of silt and loam that permitted more rapid root
extraction of water, and a basal zone of clay that slowed infiltration.
Deep canal deposits in the Casa Rinconada area farming zone included
accumulations of relatively thin clay layers, thick levels of sand, and
occasional thin silt deposits. Rincon canal irrigation seemingly was
designed not only to collect and distribute water but also to move and
deposit sand, silt, clay, and organic matter on agricultural fields.

Drainage Basin Canal Irrigation. Several drainage basins of varying size
lie partially or wholly within the Chaco Core. Although they have generally similar physiography and hydrology, they vary with respect to local
geology, slope, drainage patterns, the sediment load and entrenchment
of primary watercourses, and the composition of alluvium in floodplains

bordering the watercourse. Major watercourses also change character during periods of aggradation and cycles of arroyo entrenchment.

There is limited but convincing evidence that Chacoan farmers tapped floodwater from the major watercourse ("washes") in three drainage basins for canal irrigation: the Kin Bineola, Kin Klizhin, and Gallo. On the Kin Bineola (Holsinger 1901; Judd 1954; Lyons et al. 1976; Marshall et al. 1979; Van Dyke and Powers 2014; Vivian and Palmer 2003), there were at least two and possibly three diversion dam-canal segments in the lower portion of the drainage in a catchment of approximately 1,650 km^2 (637 mi^2). Combined segments could have watered 250–300 ha. Floodwater in the Kin Klizhin (drainage area ca. 1,233 km^2 [47.5 mi^2]) was collected behind a large masonry and earthen diversion dam and diverted by canal to a field area of 130 to 150 ha (Van Dyke and Powers 2014). The Gallo, with a basin of 95 km^2 (36.3 mi^2), carried water into Chaco Canyon via Gallo Canyon to bottomland between Gallo and Mockingbird Canyons, an area of approximately 130 ha. There is no evidence that the Chaco Wash either within Chaco Canyon or below the confluence of the Chaco and Escavada Washes was used for canal irrigation. Known features of drainage basin systems include large masonry and/or earthen diversion dams (Kin Bineola, Kin Klizhin), large canals up to 16 m in width and currently averaging 1 m in depth (Kin Bineola, Gallo), smaller "distribution" canals (Kin Klizhin, Gallo), "turn-outs" on canals that presumably channeled water to fields possibly via smaller canals (Kin Bineola), and one field gate (Kin Bineola). Gridded fields are presumed to have been utilized in the Gallo system but have not been recorded.

Floodplain. Hack (1942:29–30) identified floodplain fields as areas bordering the course of a shallow arroyo that would be naturally inundated by widespread floodwater but that also might receive water diverted by earthen spreaders. It is often assumed (e.g., Benson et al. 2006; Judd 1954, 1964) that floodplain agriculture was practiced along the Chaco Wash in Chaco Canyon despite evidence that the "relatively high salinities of many Chaco Canyon soils would have negatively affected maize production during the Pre-Hispanic period" (Benson et al. 2006:298). Judd (1964:230) sought "soils formerly available for cultivation" but backfilled a number of test pits that had only "sand and silt" before locating a soil "within the banks of Bryan's post-Bonito Channel" that represented alluvium typical of the "main valley fill" (Judd 1964:231). Judd's "main valley fill" was most likely Hall's (2010:238) "overbank alluvium" deposits of massive silty clay on the canyon floor that characterized Hall's "Chaco unit" of alluvial sequences in Chaco Canyon. Love (1977:295) indicates that these sediments were derived from headwaters of the Chaco Wash and in some areas could have spread across the entire canyon floor to inter-finger "with locally derived deposits along the canyon margins." These deposits generally contained more sand, and Judd's backfilled test pits were likely in this zone. While farming on the canyon margins was feasible, the agricultural potential of the massive silty clay in the "main valley fill" would have been negligible given the largely impermeable nature and potentially high salinity of the deposit.

However, massive clay deposits did not characterize all floodplains in the Chaco Core. Judging by recorded Navajo floodplain farming at the confluence of the Chaco and Escavada Washes, in Lake Valley on the lower reaches of the Kin Bineola Wash, and along the Escavada Wash north of Chaco Canyon, these areas and others, particularly along the Chaco River below Chaco Canyon, almost certainly were utilized by Chacoan farmers (Windes 2007). The well-documented (Brugge 1980; Judd 1954) Chischilly-begay fields on the Kin Bineola drainage attest to the productivity of these fields. In 1930, he "planted 4 acres of beans to harvest 400 bushels, and 18 acres of corn which yielded 70 wagonloads" (Brugge 1980:375). Potential floodplain cropland in the Chaco Core has not been determined, but it probably equals areas of dune deposits that were estimated at about 1,000 ha. There are no soil profiles for known fields in the Kin Bineola drainage, but Dykeman (1982:82) reports that the Escavada Wash floodplain is "covered with a layer of coarse sand ranging from 30 centimeters to more than 2 meters in thickness" that blankets an "impermeable clay alluvium." Moreover, he (1982:96) notes that the most extensive soils covering the Escavada floodplain are the Stumble-Notal complex that "may have agricultural potential."

Slope Wash. The majority of 31 Navajo fields recorded on the Escavada and Alemita drainages north of Chaco Canyon were slope wash (Cully et al. 1982). There is no record of Navajo slope wash fields elsewhere in the Chaco Core, presumably because geomorphic conditions differ significantly. Cully examined three slope wash fields ranging in size from .7 to 1.5 ha, but catchment size was not reported. No facilities were employed to divert, channel, or further spread runoff. Cully et al. (1982:149) noted that fields were "placed to take advantage of moisture that has penetrated the sandier soils above . . . [a] less permeable layer." Chacoans may have utilized some form of slope wash in areas with suitable topography such as the Bis sa'ani community on the Escavada Wash, but use of slope wash was likely limited.

Modeling Agricultural Potential of Akchin in the Chaco Core

We now turn to the problem of predicting viable akchin in Chaco. In light of the difficulty of identifying potential Chacoan field systems in the absence of architectural evidence, our study begins with those areas known historically to have been under cultivation by Chaco Navajos and from which we might then extrapolate to the Chaco Core more broadly. The analysis addresses two questions: (1) What can the proven effective farming practices of historic-period Chaco Navajos tell us about the potential viability of Ancestral Puebloan farming? and (2) What are the strongest predictors of Navajo field locations?

Methods

In addressing these questions our approach is two-fold, drawing first on the ethnographic record as well as spatial and environmental data. Ethnographic evidence provides us with the location of several Navajo fields and, when coupled with spatial data, affords a means of examining the relationship between fields and their respective catchments. These relationships can be further compared with the Hopi analogues employed by other scholars (Herhahn and Hill 1998; Hill 1998; Watson 2009). The second step entails the integration of catchment runoff characteristics related to successful fields from which we can begin to construct predictive models of the potential placement of prehistoric Chacoan fields.

Ethnographic Evidence. The relative success with which the Chaco Navajos cultivated maize, melon, pumpkin, and squash is well-documented (Breternitz et al. 1982:145–154; Brugge 1980; Bryan 1954; Judd 1954:53–59;

Pepper 1896:158). Judd mapped two series of akchin fields—one maintained by Rafael in a rincon on the south side of Chaco Canyon opposite Casa Chiquita and a second set of fields managed by Dan Cly at the head of Cly's Canyon, then known as Rincon del Camino (Brugge 1980:354; Judd 1954:53–59). Several additional fields along the Escavada Wash and in South Gap were identified using aerial photographs taken by Fairchild Aerial Surveys, Inc., for the Soil Erosion Service in 1934 (see Figure 2.2). The fields in South Gap were attributed to Tomacito on the basis that the drainage was also his home site (Brugge 1980:486). The size and location of "Niggalita's fields" under cultivation at the time of the Hyde Expedition's excavations at Pueblo Bonito were estimated by visiting the approximate location, correlating nearby landscape features with those visible in photographs taken by Pepper in 1898 (see Geib and Heitman, this volume), and finally, by mapping the estimated field boundaries using handheld GPS.

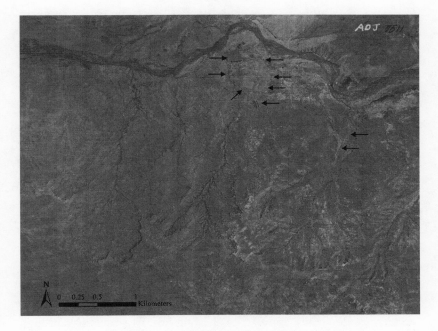

Figure 2.2. Slopes draining into Escavada Wash approximately 3 km north of Mockingbird Canyon, with Navajo agricultural fields marked by black arrows. (Courtesy Fairchild Aerial Surveys, Inc., 1934)

Hopi and Zuni floodwater farming practices have remained a subject of study since the late nineteenth century (Beaglehole 1937; Bradfield 1971; Bryan 1929; Hack 1942; Muenchrath et al. 2002; Rhode 1995; Stephen 1969). Hack's (1942) pioneering study of agriculture at Hopi, as part of the Harvard Awatovi Expedition, provides one of the most thorough accounts of Pueblo farming practices. Hack recorded a range of data from physiographic, demographic, and climatic factors to the economic implications of environmental degradation and changing farming practices. Of particular relevance to this study are Hack's observations on the relationship of cultivated areas to their respective catchments because, as he states, "all floodwater fields depend on the concentration of the runoff to a much larger area than the field itself" (Hack 1942:31). Hack found that Hopi fields generally ranged from 3 to 6 percent of the drainage and that this limited variation was a function of the catchment's soil and physiographic characteristics.

Hydrologic Modeling in Chaco. Benson et al.'s (2006:298) study of Chacoan agricultural productivity yielded several significant insights, including the authors' conclusion that high soil salinity in Chaco would have amplified crop loss—an important consideration when modeling carrying capacity. However, irrigable zones were predicted on the basis of a "runoff-rainfall ratio" or "runoff coefficient" of .03, which in turn was derived from an experimental watershed in Walnut Gulch, Arizona. Runoff is heavily dependent on numerous variables, including evapotranspiration and infiltration, which are in turn factors of soil type, mean annual temperature, and precipitation. This calls into question the reliability of runoff coefficients extrapolated from the Walnut Gulch area of southeastern Arizona to the climatically, physiographically, and ecologically dissimilar southern Colorado Plateau. Further, the use of a single runoff coefficient to account for the physiographic and floral diversity of Chaco Canyon seems to be an oversimplification, particularly given the prevalence of impervious surfaces such as the rock outcrops and slickrock that so dramatically dominate the Chacoan landscape. This study approaches the question of variability through the generation of a runoff coefficient map that incorporates multiple parameters, including ground slope, vegetative cover, soil type, and antecedent moisture.

As noted above, the recent work of Dominguez and Kolm (2005) as well as that of Sandor and colleagues (2007) at Hopi and Zuni, respectively, underscores the fundamental role of soil moisture and nutrient conditions as considerations in the selection of agricultural fields. Although such detailed information is not yet available for potential farming areas within the Chaco and Escavada watersheds, our analysis takes an important step toward achieving such a fine-grained understanding by integrating vegetative cover and soil maps with slope angle, through a GIS. The accuracy of USGS and USDA–NRCS maps often varies by quadrangle, and data can become outdated since conditions (particularly vegetative cover) have been known to change relatively rapidly (Potter and Kelley 1980).

The internal and external heterogeneity of runoff characteristics of the Chaco and Escavada watersheds makes selection of a single runoff coefficient impractical. As Pilgrim and Cordery (1993:17) observed, "estimating the value of the runoff coefficient is the greatest difficulty and the major source of uncertainty" because it represents all of the factors that affect the relation of peak flow to average rainfall intensity other than areas and response time. Overland runoff can result from long-duration, low-intensity rainfall; short-duration, high-intensity rainfall; and/or snowmelt, and it is impacted by a variety of factors including soil saturation, soil permeability, slope, vegetative cover, and climate (Pilgrim and Cordery 1993:9.1; Prakash et al. 1996:332–333). Traditionally, runoff coefficients are inferred from standard engineering tables and graphs or by the sum of scores that account for various factors (Pilgrim and Cordery 1993:9.17). The latter approach is taken here to model the diverse catchments of the Chaco Canyon and Escavada watersheds following a method initially outlined by Kennessey (1930) that has seen widespread use (Barazzuoli et al. 1989; Farina and Gaspari 1990; Spadoni et al. 2010).

The Kennessey method yields an estimated runoff coefficient by adding separate coefficients that represent soil permeability, slope angle, and vegetative cover (see Table 2.1). A weighted average is then derived for each drainage. Although there are three series of coefficient components, Kennessey provided no guidance for selecting a particular range. Barazzuoli et al. (1989:616) proposed the use of an Index of Aridity to account for climatological ranges, more specifically variability in prior antecedent soil moisture, infiltration, and evapotranspiration.

Table 2.1. Composite Runoff Coefficient Table
(Kennessey 1930).

Composite Runoff (C_d) Variables		Coefficients		
Permeability	C_p			
	1st - Very Slight	0.21	0.26	0.3
	2nd - Moderate	0.12	0.16	0.2
	3rd - Good	0.06	0.08	0.1
	4th - High	0.03	0.04	0.05
Slope angle	C_s			
	> 35%	0.22	0.26	0.3
	10% – 35%	0.12	0.16	0.2
	3.5% – 10%	0.01	0.03	0.05
	< 3.5%	0	0.01	0.03
Vegetative cover	C_v			
	1st - Bare Rock	0.26	0.28	0.3
	2nd - Pastures	0.17	0.21	0.25
	3rd - Cultivated Land with Coppices	0.07	0.11	0.15
	4th - Forest Trees	0.03	0.04	0.05
Index of aridity (I_a)		< 25	25–40	> 40

For the GIS analysis, slope angle was derived from a 10 m digital elevation model, and vegetation was mapped using the USGS National Landcover data set. Soil maps from the USDA–NRCS were used to identify soil map units for San Juan, Sandoval, and McKinley Counties. Soil units were assigned to one of Kennessey's permeability classes using a soil unit's respective saturated hydraulic conductivity, or K_{sat} (μm/sec), in accordance with guidelines established in the *USDA Soil Survey Manual* (USDA 1993). Index of aridity is then calculated using Thornthwaite's (1948) equation (see equation 2.1) with the most arid month determined using a method outlined by de Martonne (1926).

Annual precipitation patterns in Chaco (summarized in Table 2.2), as in the broader San Juan Basin, are highly variable, and the majority of annual moisture derives from short-duration, high-intensity convective storms that occur predominantly between July and September

$$I_a = \frac{\dfrac{P}{(T + 10)} + \dfrac{(12 \times p)}{t}}{2}$$

where:

P = average annual precipitation
T = average annual temperature
p = average precipitation during most arid month
t = average temperature during most arid month

Equation 2.1. Index of aridity (Thornthwaite 1948)

Table 2.2. Recorded Precipitation and Temperature for Chaco Canyon (1922–2005). (Courtesy Western Regional Climate Center; http://www.wrcc.dri.edu/cgi-bin/cliMAIN.pl?nm1647)

Month	Avg. Monthly Precip. (cm)	Avg. Monthly Max. Temp (C)	Avg. Monthly Min. Temp (C)	Avg. Monthly Temp (C)	I_a
January	1.17	6.39	−10.56	−2.08	1.48
February	1.40	9.39	−7.67	0.86	1.29
March	1.42	13.83	−5.11	4.36	0.99
April	1.19	19.22	−1.44	8.89	0.63
May	1.52	24.50	3.06	13.78	0.64
Jun	1.04	30.28	8.11	19.19	0.36
July	2.90	32.44	12.67	22.56	0.89
August	3.40	30.83	11.72	21.28	1.09
September	2.90	27.11	6.89	17.00	1.07
October	2.39	20.72	−0.06	10.33	1.17
November	1.55	12.44	−6.06	3.19	1.17
December	1.55	6.61	−10.67	−2.03	1.94
Average Annual	22.43	19.48	0.07	9.78	1.06

(Vivian 1990:20–21). The use of Thornthwaite's (1948) equation results in an Aridity Index value of 19.72 for Chaco Canyon, dictating that the first column of the Kennessey table best approximates runoff tendencies of the study area.

Derived coefficients representing slope angle, soil permeability, and vegetative cover, summarized elsewhere (Watson 2009), were summed to arrive at a runoff coefficient map (Figure 2.3). Composite runoff coefficients for each catchment were then calculated as an area-weighted average following Olyphant et al. (2002).

Assessment of the viability of field systems relative to catchments was accomplished by calculating the minimum "Cultivated Area Ratios" (Critchley and Siegert 1991) required to support maize agriculture. The method relies on the variables outlined above as well as the minimum rainfall necessary to *reliably* support maize agriculture—for our purposes minimum thresholds from the Hopi area were utilized (22.86 cm/yr; see equation 2.2). Critchley and Siegert's (1991) method also calls for

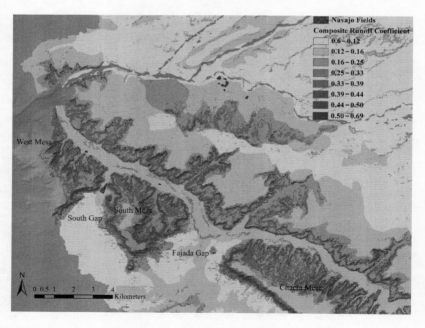

Figure 2.3. Composite runoff coefficient map of Chaco and Escavada drainages—darker areas denote higher runoff coefficients and thus greater potential for surface runoff to reach canyon bottom.

$$\frac{\text{Crop Water Requirement} - \text{Design Rainfall}}{\text{Design Rainfall} \times \text{Runoff Coefficient} \times \text{Efficiency Factor}} = \frac{\text{Catchment Area}}{\text{Cultivated Area}}$$

Equation 2.2. Cultivated area ratio calculation (Critchley and Siegert 1991)

the use of efficiency factors. An efficiency coefficient of .75 for steep, short slopes was used for the north side of Chaco Canyon, while .5 for long, gradual slopes was selected for the south side of Chaco Canyon and the slopes draining northward into the Escavada.

Yearly totals were deemed adequate to account for drought conditions. To assure a conservative assessment of field viability, extremely low average rainfall levels were obtained by selecting the 98 percent precipitation exceedance probabilities from a ranked probability plot of the prehistoric yearly rainfall retrodictions generated by Rose and colleagues (Rose 1979; Rose et al. 1982). Finally, the ranked probability plot was constructed using the method outlined by equation 2.3.

$$P_e = \frac{m}{n + 1} \times 100$$

where:

P_e = percentage of time that observation (m) will be exceeded
m = the rank of the observation
n = total number of observations used

Equation 2.3. Probability of exceedence equation (Chow et al. 1988)

Results

Beginning with field-catchment ratios, we found that Navajo fields were generally smaller relative to catchment than those found in the Hopi region (Table 2.3). However, the series of Navajo akchin fields along the Escavada Wash correspond precisely with the range of Hopi ratios and Rafael's fields approach in relative size those of Hopi. Upon further examination of the aerial photography (not pictured) where Rafael's largest field lies on the west side of the akchin at the mouth of Rafael's Rincon, a similar quadrilaterally shaped area, almost a mirror image of the main field, abuts the east side of the akchin and may represent an

Table 2.3. Navajo Field Locations, Sizes, and Relationships to Their Respective Catchments.

Field Number	Location	Field Size (ha)	Catchment Size (ha)	Field/ Catchment Ratio	Area- Weighted Runoff Coefficient	Maximum Allowable Field/ Catchment Ratio during Poor Rainfall Year (11.5 cm)	Source
Escavada #1	Southern slopes of Escavada Wash approximately 3 km north of Mockingbird Canyon	0.67	199.73	0.003	0.24		Fairchild Aerial Surveys, Inc. (1927)
Escavada #2	"	0.62	199.73	0.003	0.24		"
Escavada #3	"	1.38	199.73	0.007	0.24		"
Escavada #4	"	4.05	199.73	0.020	0.24		"
Escavada #5	"	2.57	199.73	0.013	0.24		"
Escavada #6	"	0.8	199.73	0.004	0.24		"
Total		10.09	199.73	0.051		0.12	
Escavada #7	Southern slopes of Escavada Wash approximately 3 km north–northeast of Mockingbird Canyon	1.4	274.84	0.005	0.22	0.11	Fairchild Aerial Surveys, Inc. (1927)

							Pepper Photographs, 1898 (CHCU Negative 77649, CHCU 52388)
Niggalita's Fields	Mouth of Werito's Rincon	0.64	451.61	0.001	0.34	0.17	
Tomacito's Field #1 (South Gap)	South Gap	5.23	1606.67	0.003	0.19		Fairchild Aerial Surveys, Inc. (1927); Brugge (1980:353–354)
Tomacito's Field #2 (South Gap)	"	2.75	1606.67	0.002	0.19		"
Total		7.98	1606.67	0.005		0.10	
Dan Cly's Field #1	Head of Cly's Canyon/ Rincon del Camino	0.23	83.12	0.003	0.19	0.10	Judd (1954:54)
Dan Cly's Field #2	"	0.42	336.17	0.001	0.14	0.07	"
Total		0.65	419.29	0.002			
Rafael's Field #1	Rafael's Rincon, South side of canyon, opposite Cly's Canyon	1.09	99.34	0.011	0.25		Judd (1954:53)
Rafael's Field #2	"	0.03	12.86	0.002	0.35		"
Rafael's Field #3	"	0.12	76.42	0.002	0.33		"
Total		1.12	99.34	0.011		0.17	
Sum Total		22.00	5746.08	0.004			

earlier, possibly abandoned field. This suggests that the area under cultivation as recorded by Judd may in fact have been nearly twice as large at
some earlier stage. Similar traces of abandoned fields are visible in aerial
photographs of the Escavada area (Figure 2.3), indicating that this area,
too, may have witnessed more intensive cultivation in the past.

With respect to our first question—that of the viability of farmland
in the Chaco Core—the field-catchment ratio provides indisputable
evidence that with adequate knowledge and experience, side drainages
along the Chaco and Escavada Washes were capable of supporting maize
agriculture. That the majority of Navajo fields are markedly undersized
relative to their respective catchments could be an indication that several fields exhibited low productivity. Conversely, the smaller plots
could reflect an acceptable tradeoff for Navajo farmers who may have
chosen instead to optimize the amount of water available to crops and
thus mitigate the risk of drought in any given year.

The results of analysis using Critchley and Siegert's (1991) Cultivated Area Ratio point to the latter explanation as the more plausible.
As depicted in Table 2.3, the Cultivated Area Ratios illustrate that all
of the field systems in question should be able to produce at much
larger capacities even during years of unusually low rainfall. Of note,
the results indicate that Werito's Rincon could have supported as much
as 70 ha of viable farmland.

So what then are the strongest predictors of field location? As seen
in Figure 2.4, Navajo farmers appear to have selected fields that exhibit
both large catchment size and high runoff coefficients. Where runoff
coefficients are lower, larger catchment areas tend to be favored. All fields
draw on at least 10 ha of catchment, and all of the related catchments
exhibit an area-weighted runoff coefficient greater than or equal to about
.15. Figure 2.4 also demonstrates that catchments within the Chaco
watershed tend to exhibit higher runoff coefficients than the majority
of those found along the Escavada, with more than 50 percent of Chaco
catchment runoff coefficients falling at or above .25—an indication that
the potential for viable akchin is more widespread in Chaco. The runoff coefficient map depicted in Figure 2.3 lends further support to this
conclusion. With the exception of the uplands from which the known
Navajo fields along the Escavada drew their water, the Chaco side drainages tend to display higher runoff coefficients than those of the Escavada.

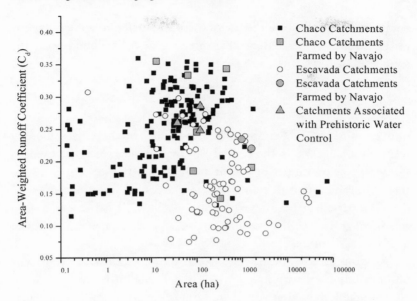

Figure 2.4. Graph of catchment area vs. area-weighted runoff coefficient. Catchments known to have been under cultivation historically or prehistorically are shown in gray; triangles represent catchments for which prehistoric water control features have been previously identified (Vivian 1990).

To expand the sample size and test the applicability of these results, three catchments for which prehistoric field systems have been previously identified (Chetro Ketl, Rinconada, and Rincon-4 North) were added to the Figure 2.4 plot. The three catchments all lie well within the threshold preferred by Navajo farmers, further demonstrating the usefulness of these factors as predictors of field location. As illustrated in Figure 2.4, numerous other potential field locations are fed by large catchments with similarly high runoff coefficients.

While evidence of Navajo farming success alone is an insufficient basis upon which to infer sizable and consistent Chacoan agricultural yields, it does provide incontrovertible proof that akchin farming is and was a viable farming strategy in a variety of geomorphic settings within the Chaco Core. By identifying those hydrologic conditions that were conducive to Navajo akchin farming, we can begin to predict where we might find evidence for Chacoan fields. Future studies aimed at modeling Chacoan agricultural potential or investigating potential prehistoric fields would benefit from the use of these parameters as a means of targeting for analysis those areas that carry a greater likelihood of having supported field systems.

Conclusion

Our examination of the agricultural potential of the Chaco Core, a relatively small zone in the central San Juan Basin centered on Chaco Canyon, was prompted by recent studies (e.g., Benson 2011a, 2011b) that determined that this area was agriculturally "very unproductive" during a period of heightened cultural activity. To better understand this incongruity, we have evaluated several aspects of past analyses of Chacoan agriculture.

We propose that the Chaco Core is the most efficient geographic unit of study for the area in question. In defining the Chaco Core as an agricultural "production zone," we do not intend to imply that maize and other crops were regularly moved between communities within this zone. Rather, we argue that this relatively confined area (less than 1,000 km^2) is characterized by a combination of physiographic and associated hydrologic settings not found in surrounding landscapes that were conducive to development of a suite of agricultural strategies, some of which (e.g., rincon canal irrigation) have not been found elsewhere in the San Juan Basin. We suggest that the use of diverse agricultural strategies within the Chaco Core by multiple communities may have buffered periodic shortages in certain locales within the Core. The akchin hydrologic modeling study reported here reinforces the postulated value of these strategies and underscores the need for additional similar analyses. Hydrologic modeling could be particularly relevant for rincon canal irrigation systems, given our preliminary results (Figure 2.4) compared with earlier investigations by Lagasse et al. (1984). We believe that the lack of attention paid to soil hydrologic profiles in recent (Benson 2011a, 2011b) evaluations of Chacoan agricultural potential may have skewed production estimates. This is especially true in Chaco Canyon where past and recent investigations have presumed that fields were primarily on the massive clay alluvium of the Chaco Wash floodplain rather than on deposits of sand, silt, and clay at the canyon margins. But, even with enhanced agricultural strategies, could Chacoans have produced sufficient foodstuffs to support a century of heightened construction activity within the Chaco Core? Benson et al. (2006:301) rejected this possibility and argued, "Increases in Chaco's population during pilgrim fairs and major construction intervals (e.g., between A.D. 1030 and 1130) would have necessitated the importation of maize even if only a few hundred individuals resided in the canyon." Their conclusions that pilgrimage fairs were held in Chaco Canyon and that labor for great house construction came from outside the canyon are a priori assumptions, neither of which has been validly confirmed. We argue that tailoring agricultural strategies to variable physiographic and hydrologic settings has temporal depth in the Chaco Core and that this practice favored a shift from generally extensive forms of agriculture to more intensive forms in the early eleventh century. This transition appears to correlate with regional shifts in precipitation levels as well as changes in spatial and temporal climatic variability. Moreover, this transition occurs at a time characterized by the establishment of new great houses and an apparent decline in the number of small house communities in Chaco Canyon.

Stone (1993:74) has observed that "without intensification, cultivation almost always degrades agricultural resources,[1] and abandonment is a basic—but not ubiquitous—reaction." However, Stone's (1993:79) note 1 is important, as he indicates that "the principal exception is the cultivation of land surfaces that are regularly renewed by natural processes, such as mud-flat horticulture in the American Midwest or akchin farming in the desert Southwest." The productive value of akchin and, for the same reason, floodplain agriculture was recognized in the Chaco Core by at least the sixth century and probably much earlier. Wills et al. (2012) point out that upper Chaco Canyon near Shabik'eshchee Village during the Basketmaker III and Pueblo I periods "might have been an exceptionally good location for farming because of combined effects of large localized watersheds and shallow bedrock forcing groundwater closer to the surface, together with organic nutrient input provided by runoff from pinyon-woodlands on adjacent mesas." These conditions existed throughout the canyon, particularly on the south side.

Windes (2007:82) reports that a number of late 800s/900s great house settlements along the Chaco River west of Chaco Canyon "typically formed where multiple drainages come together," a choice reflecting "a striking reliance on a combination of floodwater and ground-water farming, the most viable horticultural strategy in the dry, interior basin." The Chaco River in this area has a shallow (<69 cm) water table and is bordered in places by sand dunes so that farming "may have led to abnormally high crop yields that resulted in surpluses even during droughts" (Windes 2007:70). Middens at these early great houses are marked by large numbers of manos and metates, and Windes (2007:70), in discussing the Casa del Rio great house, comments that "if there was ever a site that screamed 'surplus' from extensive food processing this is it."

Similarly, Geib and Heitman (this volume) revealed that proportions of maize pollen recovered from deposits at Chacoan great houses and small sites were exceptionally high relative to other sites throughout the San Juan Basin. Given the low likelihood that such high concentrations of pollen would have been possible if maize were imported over long distances, the data contradict Benson et al.'s (2006) assertion and instead indicate substantial local production.

The archaeological record suggests that both akchin within Chaco Canyon and floodplains outside the canyon on the Chaco and Escavada Washes were sufficiently productive from the sixth through the tenth centuries to support the population of the Chaco Core, despite considerable variability in precipitation regimes. Benson and Berry (2009:98) have reported that a megadrought in the Southwest between A.D. 1130 and A.D. 1177 was preceded by a wet period occurring between A.D. 1040 and 1129. Dean and Funkhouser (2002) have more precisely documented the wet period, noting that increased precipitation in the Chaco region occurred between A.D. 990 and 1030, 1035 and 1060, and 1070 and 1115. Regionally, the period between A.D. 1025 and 1090 experienced low temporal variability but "increasing spatial variability, when conditions varied considerably from place to place across the region" (Dean and Funkhouser 2002:40). This contrasted with the preceding period from approximately A.D. 900 to 1025 when the region was marked by high temporal variability but low spatial variability.

We posit that less variation in the timing of precipitation but greater fluctuation in the location of rainfall events from A.D. 1025 to 1090 may have favored agriculture in the hydrologically and physiographically diverse Chaco Core. Moreover, under these conditions, periods of increased precipitation may have stimulated a shift from more extensive to more intensive agriculture involving the use of canal irrigation to intensify both akchin (rincon) and floodplain (drainage basin) farming. The strategy in both cases involved not only greater control over water collection and distribution but also equal distribution of critical deposits of sand, silt, and at times clay in defined fields.

Proceeding from the assumption that "nearly all agricultural production among the northern Anasazi was at the household level," Kohler and Van West (1996:170) identified periods of "cooperative behaviors" in the Mesa Verde region marked by pooling/sharing of food interrupted by periods of "defection" from any ongoing system of sharing. In both periods behavior was "based entirely on the self-interest of the participants—a rational choice model" (Kohler and Van West 1996:190). Archaeologically defined "measures" of cooperative behavior that "ought to be involved with food sharing" (Kohler and Van West 1996:181) include great kivas, great houses, roads, and growth/aggregation at the community level. Kohler and Van West (1996:190) observe that shifts between periods of pooling and defection may have ended around A.D. 1300 when "many new techniques for water harvesting used in the northern Rio Grande" may have stimulated new production conditions that "always favored cooperation under a rational choice model."

Force et al. (2002:35, Table 4) summarize the "Channel Filling" period, pre–AD 1025–1090, in Chaco Canyon as a time characterized by the resumption of great house construction (Lekson 1984), fewer small house sites (Windes 1987b, 1993, 2001, 2007), and the appearance of roads and water control features. It is noteworthy that whereas massive construction projects in great houses were initiated between A.D. 1030 and 1040, Windes (2007) has observed that smaller units at new great houses were initiated in the late 900s and early 1000s at Chetro Ketl, Pueblo Alto, and Hungo Pavi.

Given the present archaeological evidence, we propose that Chacoan rincon and drainage basin canal irrigation systems may represent cooperative behavior involving food production (leading to sharing) by a unit larger than the household. If true, what was that unit and were social mechanisms ("measures of cooperative behavior") necessary for integration of all farming systems at a community level? The predominance of Chacoan great houses on the north side of Chaco Canyon and their presence in the Kin Bineola and Kin Klizhin watersheds suggest operational links with rincon and drainage basin canal irrigation systems. Furthermore, the architectural standardization of facilities in these systems, particularly gates, may reflect intra-great house cooperative construction and possibly maintenance akin to that postulated for great house construction (e.g., Wills 2000; Windes 1987a). If great houses or great house agricultural "clustered confederacies" (Spielmann 1994) operated canal irrigation systems, was there a need to share production from more extensive farming systems including dune and akchin that may have continued to be operated by small house communities? Given the marginal conditions for agriculture in the Chaco Core, we presume that there was a need. Moreover, the range of available strategies dependent upon variable locales and labor requirements suggests that farming in Chaco was never necessarily a client-patron arrangement between residents of great houses who controlled the best lands and "their neighbors"—residents of small house sites—who contributed labor in exchange for food. We believe that this relationship may have been more complex than previously proposed.

References Cited

Barazzuoli, Piero, Senatro Izzo, Paolo Menicori, Massimiliano Micheluccini, and Massimo Salleolini. 1989. A New Practical Aid to Regional Hydrologic Planning: The Runoff Coefficient Map. *Environmental Management* 13(5):613–622.

Beaglehole, Ernest. 1937. Notes on Hopi Economic Life. *Yale University Publications in Anthropology* 15:60–88. Yale University Press, New Haven.

Benson, Larry V. 2011a. Factors Controlling Precolumbian and Early Historic Maize Productivity in the American Southwest, Part 1: The Southern Colorado Plateau and Rio Grande Regions. *Journal of Archaeological Method and Theory* 18(1):1–60.

———. 2011b. Factors Controlling Pre-Columbian and Early Historic Maize Productivity in the American Southwest, Part 2: The Chaco Halo, Mesa Verde, Pajarito Plateau/Bandelier, and Zuni Archaeological Regions. *Journal of Archaeological Method and Theory* 18(1):61–109.

Benson, Larry, John Stein, Howard Taylor, Richard Friedman, and Thomas C. Windes. 2006. The Agricultural Productivity of Chaco Canyon and the Source(s) of Pre-Hispanic Maize Found in Pueblo Bonito. In *Histories of Maize: Multidisciplinary Approaches to the Prehistory, Linguistics,*

Biogeography, Domestication, and Evolution of Maize, edited by Robert H. Tykot, John E. Staller, and Bruce F. Benz, 289–314. Academic Press, San Diego.

Benson, Larry V., and Michael S. Berry. 2009. Climate Change and Cultural Responses in the Prehistoric American Southwest. *Kiva* 75(1):87–117.

Bradfield, Maitland. 1971. *The Changing Pattern of Hopi Agriculture*. Occasional Paper No. 30. Royal Anthropological Institute of Great Britain and Ireland, London.

Brand, Donald D., Florence M. Hawley, Frank C. Hibben, et al. 1937. *Tseh So, A Small House Ruin, Chaco Canyon, New Mexico (Preliminary Report)*. University of New Mexico Bulletin No. 308, Anthropological Series 2, No. 2. University of New Mexico, Albuquerque.

Breternitz, Cory D., David E. Doyel, and Michael P. Marshall. 1982. *Bis sa'ani: A Late Bonito Phase Community on Escavada Wash, Northwest New Mexico*. Navajo Nation Papers in Anthropology No. 14. Navajo Nation Cultural Resource Management Program, Window Rock, Arizona.

Brugge, David M. 1980. *A History of the Chaco Navajos*. Reports of the Chaco Center No. 4. Division of Cultural Research, National Park Service, Albuquerque.

Bryan, Kirk. 1929. Flood-Water Farming. *Geographical Review* 19(3):444–456.

———. 1954. *The Geology of Chaco Canyon, New Mexico in Relation to the Life and Remains of the Prehistoric Peoples of Pueblo Bonito*. Smithsonian Miscellaneous Collections No. 7. Smithsonian Institution Press, Washington, D.C.

Chow, Ven T., David R. Maidment, and Larry R. Mays. 1988. *Applied Hydrology*. McGraw-Hill, Inc., New York.

Critchley, Will, and Klaus Siegert. 1991. Water Harvesting: A Manual for the Design and Construction of Water Harvesting Schemes for Plant Production. Electronic document, http://www.fao.org/docrep/U3160E/u3160e05 .htm, accessed May 5, 2008.

Cully, Anne C., Marcia L. Donaldson, Mollie S. Toll, and Klara B. Kelley. 1982. Agriculture in the Bis sa'ani Community. In *Bis sa'ani: A Late Bonito Phase Community on Escavada Wash, Northwest New Mexico*, edited by Cory D. Breternitz, David E. Doyel, and Michael P. Marshall, pp. 115–166. Navajo Nation Papers in Anthropology No. 14. Navajo Nation Cultural Resource Management Program, Window Rock, Arizona.

Cully, Anne C., and Mollie S. Toll. 2014. Evaluation of Agricultural Potential on Four Additions to Chaco Culture National Historical Park. In *An Archaeological Survey of the Additions to Chaco Culture National Historical Park*, edited by Ruth M. Van Dyke and Robert P. Powers, chapter 3, Reports of the Chaco Center No. 13. Division of Cultural Research, National Park Service, Albuquerque. Electronic document, http://www.chacoarchive .org/ChacoAdditionsSurvey/chapter_3, accessed October 29, 2014.

60 *R. Gwinn Vivian and Adam S. Watson*

Dean, Jeffrey S., and Gary Funkhouser. 2002. Appendix A. Dendroclimatology and Fluvial Chronology in Chaco Canyon. In *Relation of "Bonito" Paleo-channels and Base-Level Variations to Anasazi Occupation, Chaco Canyon, New Mexico*, by Eric R. Force, R. Gwinn Vivian, Thomas C. Windes, and Jeffrey S. Dean, pp. 39–41. Arizona State Museum Archaeological Series 194. Arizona State Museum, University of Arizona, Tucson.

de Martonne, E. M. 1926. Une nouvelle fonction climatologique: L'indice d'aridité. *La Météorologie*, Paris 2:449–458.

Dominguez, Steven, and Kenneth E. Kolm. 2005. Beyond Water Harvesting: A Soil Hydrology Perspective on Traditional Southwestern Agricultural Technology. *American Antiquity* 70(4):732–765.

Dorshow, Wetherbee Bryan. 2012. Modeling Agricultural Potential in Chaco Canyon during the Bonito Phase: A Predictive Geospatial Approach. *Journal of Archaeological Science* 39 (2012):2098–2115.

Doyel, David E., Cory D. Breternitz, and Michael P. Marshall. 1984. Chacoan Community Structure, Bis sa'ani Pueblo and the Chaco Halo. In *Recent Research on Chaco Prehistory*, edited by W. James Judge and John D. Schelberg, pp. 37–54. Reports of the Chaco Center No. 8. Division of Cultural Research, National Park Service, Albuquerque.

Dykeman, Douglas D. 1982. The Physical Setting of the Bis sa'ani Community. In *Bis sa'ani: A Lake Bonito Phase Community on Escavada Wash, Northwest New Mexico*, edited by Cory D. Breternitz, David E. Doyel, and Michael P. Marshall, pp. 73–115. Navajo Nation Papers in Anthropology No. 14. Navajo Nation Cultural Resource Management Program, Window Rock, Arizona.

Earle, Timothy. 2001. Economic Support of Chaco Canyon Society. *American Antiquity* 66(1):26–35.

Farina, D., and A. Gaspari. 1990. Application of the Kennessey Method for the Determination of the Runoff Coefficient and Aquifer Recharge in Mountain Regions. In *Hydrology in Mountainous Regions I: Hydrological Measurements, the Water Cycle*, Vol. 193. International Association of Hydrological Sciences Press, Wallingford, Oxfordshire, UK.

Force, Eric R., R. Gwinn Vivian, Thomas C. Windes, and Jeffrey S. Dean. 2002. *Relation of "Bonito" Paleo-channels and Base-Level Variations to Anasazi Occupation, Chaco Canyon, New Mexico*. Arizona State Museum Archaeological Series No. 194. Arizona State Museum, University of Arizona, Tucson.

Hack, John Tilton. 1942. The Changing Physical Environment of the Hopi Indians of Arizona. Reports of the Awatovi Expedition, Peabody Museum, Harvard University, Report No. 1. Papers of the Peabody Museum of American Archaeology and Ethnology Vol. 35, No. 1. Harvard University, Cambridge.

Hall, Stephen A. 2010. New Interpretations of Alluvial and Paleo-vegetation Records from Chaco Canyon, New Mexico. In *Geology of the Four Corners Country*, New Mexico Geological Society Fall Field Conference Guidebook, 61, edited by James E. Fassett, Kate E. Zeigler, and Virgil Lueth, pp. 231–246. New Mexico Geological Society, Socorro.

Herhahn, Cynthia, and J. Hill. 1998. Modeling Agricultural Production Strategies in the Northern Rio Grande Valley, New Mexico. *Human Ecology* 26(3):469–487.

Hill, J. Brett. 1998. Ecological Variability and Agricultural Specialization among the Protohistoric Pueblos of Central New Mexico. *Journal of Field Archaeology* 25(3):275–294.

Holsinger, S. J. 1901. *Report on Prehistoric Ruins of Chaco Canyon, New Mexico.* Ordered by General Land Office Letter "P," December 18, 1900. General Land Office, Mississippi. On file, National Anthropological Archive, Washington, D.C.

Judd, Neil M. 1954. *The Material Culture of Pueblo Bonito.* Smithsonian Miscellaneous Collections Vol. 124. Smithsonian Institution, Washington, D.C.

———. 1964. *The Architecture of Pueblo Bonito.* Smithsonian Miscellaneous Collections Vol. 147, No. 1. Smithsonian Institution, Washington, D.C.

Kennessey, B. 1930. *Lefikyasi téniezok és retenciok.* Vizugy, Koziemények.

Kohler, Timothy A., and Carla R. Van West. 1996. The Calculus of Self-Interest in the Development of Cooperation: Sociopolitical Development and Risk among the Northern Anasazi. In *Evolving Complexity and Environmental Risk in the Prehistoric Southwest*, edited by Joseph A. Tainter and Bonnie Bagley Tainter, pp. 169–196. Proceedings, Santa Fe Institute, Studies in the Sciences of Complexity Vol. 24. Addison-Wesley, New York.

Lagasse, Peter F., William B. Gillespie, and Kenneth G. Eggert. 1984. Hydraulic Engineering Analysis of Prehistoric Water-Controlled Systems at Chaco Canyon. In *Recent Research on Chaco Prehistory*, edited by W. James Judge and John D. Schelberg, pp. 187–211. Reports of the Chaco Center No. 8. Division of Cultural Research, National Park Service, Albuquerque.

Lekson, Stephen H. 1984. *Great Pueblo Architecture of Chaco Canyon.* Publications in Archeology 18B, Chaco Canyon Studies. National Park Service, U.S. Department of the Interior, Santa Fe.

———. 2009. *A History of the Ancient Southwest.* School for Advanced Research Press, Santa Fe.

Loose, Richard W., and Thomas R. Lyons. 1976. The Chetro Ketl Field: A Planned Water Control System in Chaco Canyon. In *Remote Sensing Experiments in Cultural Resource Studies: Nondestructive Methods of Archeological Exploration, Survey, and Analysis.* Assembled by Thomas R. Lyons, pp. 133–156. Reports of the Chaco Center No. 1. Division of Cultural Research, National Park Service, Albuquerque.

Love, David W. 1977. Dynamics of Sedimentation and Geomorphic History of Chaco Canyon National Monument, New Mexico. Guidebook of the San Juan Basin III, Northwestern New Mexico, edited by J. E. Fassett, pp. 291–300. New Mexico GeologicSociety Guidebook, 28th Field Conference.

Lyons, Thomas R., Robert K. Hitchcock, and Basil G. Pouls. 1976. The Kin Bine-
    ola Irrigation Study: An Experiment in the Use of Aerial Remote Sens-
    ing Techniques in Archeology. In *Remote Sensing Experiments in Cultural
    Resource Studies: Non-destructive Methods of Archeological Exploration, Sur-
    vey and Analysis*, assembled by Thomas R. Lyons, pp. 115–131. Reports of
    the Chaco Center No. 1. Division of Cultural Research, National Park
    Service, Albuquerque.

Marshall, Michael P., John R. Stein, Richard W. Loose, and Judith E. Novotny.
    1979. *Anasazi Communities of the San Juan Basin*. Public Service Company
    of New Mexico, Albuquerque, and New Mexico Historic Preservation
    Bureau, Santa Fe.

Muenchrath, Deborah A., Maya Kuratomi, Jonathan A. Sandor, and Jeffrey
    A. Homblurg. 2002. Observational Study of Maize Production Sys-
    tems of Zuni Farmers in Semiarid New Mexico. *Journal of Ethnobiology*
    22(1):1–33.

Olyphant, Greg, Ginger Korienek, Sally Letsinger, Kevin Spindler, and Denver
    Harper. 2002. GIS-Based Hydrologic Modeling of Watersheds that Drain
    into Lake Michigan: Examples from the Watersheds of Trail Creek and
    the East Little Calumet River. Indiana Geological Survey, Bloomington.
    Electronic document, http://igs.indiana.edu/survey/projects/hydrotools/
    html_files/index.cfm, accessed January 19, 2009.

Pepper, George H. 1896. Diary of G. H. Pepper from August 1st 1896 to Septem-
    ber 28, 1896. Manuscript on file with the Archives of the Hyde Exploring
    Expedition, Department of Anthropology, American Museum of Natural
    History, New York. Chaco Research Archive Accession 000157.

Pilgrim, David H., and Ian Cordery. 1993. Flood Runoff. In *Handbook of Hydrol-
    ogy*, edited by David R. Maidment, pp. 9.1–9.42. McGraw-Hill, New York.

Potter, L. D., and N. E. Kelley. 1980. Aerial Photointerpretation of Vegetation of
    Chaco Canyon National Monument. In *Cultural Resources Remote Sens-
    ing*, edited by Thomas R. Lyons and Frances Joan Mathien, pp. 87–104.
    Cultural Resources Management Division, National Park Service, Wash-
    ington, D.C.

Powers, Robert P., William B. Gillespie, and Stephen H. Lekson. 1983. *The Outlier
    Survey: A Regional View of Settlement in the San Juan Basin*. Reports of the
    Chaco Center No. 3. Division of Cultural Research, National Park Service,
    Albuquerque.

Prakash, Anand, Richard J. Heggen, Victor M. Ponce, John A. Repogle, and Henry
    C. Riggs. 1996. Runoff, Streamflow, Reservoir Yield, and Water Quality.
    In *Hydrology Handbook*, edited by Richard J. Heggen, pp. 331–435 2nd ed.
    American Society of Civil Engineers, New York.

Rhode, David. 1995. Estimating Agricultural Carrying Capacity in the Zuni
    Region, west-central New Mexico. In *Soil, Water, Biology and Belief in Pre-
    historic and Traditional Southwestern Agriculture*, edited by W. H. Toll, pp.

85–100. Archaeological Special Publication 2. New Mexico Archaeological Council, Albuquerque.

Rose, Martin. 1979. *Preliminary Annual and Seasonal Dendroclimatic Reconstructions for Four Climatic Regions Including and Surrounding Chaco Canyon.* Manuscript on file, Chaco Culture National Historical Park Museum Archive, University of New Mexico, Albuquerque.

Rose, Martin, William J. Robinson, and Jeffrey S. Dean. 1982. *Dendroclimatic Reconstruction for the Southeastern Colorado Plateau.* Manuscript on file with the Report Submitted in Fulfillment of Contract PX 7486–7–0121, Laboratory of Tree-Ring Research, University of Arizona, Tucson.

Sandor, Jonathan A., Jay B. Norton, Jeffrey Homburg, Deborah A. Muenchrath, Carleton S. White, Stephen E. Williams, Celeste I. Havener, and Peter D. Stahl. 2007. Biogeochemical Studies of a Native American Runoff Agroecosystem. *Geoarchaeology* 22(3):359–386.

Scott, Glenn R., Robert B. O'Sullivan, and David L. Weide. 1984. Geologic Map of the Chaco Culture National Historical Park, Northwestern New Mexico. Miscellaneous Investigations Series, Map I-1571. Department of the Interior, U.S. Geological Survey, Washington, D.C.

Sebastian, Lynne. 1992. *The Chaco Anasazi: Sociopolitical Evolution in the Prehistoric Southwest.* Cambridge University Press, Cambridge.

Simpson, James Harvey. 1850. Journal of a Military Reconnaissance from Santa Fe, New Mexico to the Navajo Country. In *Report of the Secretary of War to the 31st Congress, 1st Session, Senate Executive Document No. 65*, pp. 55–168. Union Office, Washington, D.C.

Spadoni, M. M. Brilli, F. Giustini, and M. Petitta. 2010. Using GIS for Modeling the Impact of Current Climate Trend on the Recharge Area of the S. Susanna Spring (Central Apennines, Italy). *Hydrological Processes* 24:50–64.

Spielmann, Katherine A. 1994. Clustered Confederacies: Sociopolitical Organization in the Protohistoric Rio Grande. In *The Ancient Southwestern Community: Models and Methods for the Study of Prehistoric Social Organization*, edited by W. H. Wills and Robert D. Leonard, pp. 45–54. University of New Mexico Press, Albuquerque.

Stephen, Alexander M. 1969 [1936]. *Hopi Journal of Alexander M. Stephen*, edited by Elsie Clews Parsons. Columbia University Press, New York.

Stone, Glenn Davis. 1993. Agricultural Abandonment: A Comparative Study in Historical Ecology. In *Abandonment of Settlements and Regions: Ethnoarchaeological and Archaeological Approaches*, edited by Catherine M. Cameron and Steve A. Tomka, pp. 74–81. New Directions in Archaeology. Cambridge University Press, Cambridge.

Thornthwaite, C. Warren. 1948. An Approach toward a Rational Classification of Climate. *Geographical Review* 38(1):55–94.

Toll, H. Wolcott III, Mollie S. Toll, Marcia L. Newren, and William B. Gillespie. 1985. Experimental Corn Plots in Chaco Canyon: The Life and Hard

Times of *Zea Mays* L. In *Environment and Subsistence of Chaco Canyon, New Mexico*, edited by Frances Joan Mathien, pp. 79–133. Publications in Archeology 18E, Chaco Canyon Studies. National Park Service, U.S. Department of the Interior, Santa Fe.

USDA. 1993. *Soil Survey Manual*. U.S. Dept. of Agriculture Handbook 18. U.S. Government Printing Office, Washington, D.C.

Van Dyke, Ruth M., and Robert P. Powers. 2014. Summary and Conclusions. In *An Archaeological Survey of the Additions to Chaco Culture National Historical Park*, edited by Ruth M. Van Dyke and Robert P. Powers, chap. 9. Reports of the Chaco Center No. 13. Division of Cultural Research, National Park Service, Albuquerque. Electronic document, http://chacoarchive.org/cra/, accessed November 1, 2014.

Vivian, R. Gordon, and Tom W. Mathews. 1965. *Kin Kletso: A Pueblo III Community in Chaco Canyon, New Mexico*. Technical Series 6(1):1–115. Southwest Parks and Monuments Association, Globe, Arizona.

Vivian, R. Gwinn. 1974. Conservation and Diversion, Water Control Systems in the Anasazi Southwest. In *Irrigation's Impact on Society*, edited by Theodore E. Downing and McGuire Gibson, pp. 95–112. Anthropological Papers of the University of Arizona No. 25. University of Arizona, Tucson.

————. 1984. Agricultural and Social Adjustments to Changing Environments in the Chaco Basin. In *Prehistoric Agricultural Strategies in the Southwest*, edited by Suzanne K. Fish and Paul R. Fish, pp. 243–257. Arizona State University Anthropological Research Papers No. 33. Arizona State University, Tempe.

————. 1990. *The Chacoan Prehistory of the San Juan Basin*. Academic Press, San Diego.

————. 1991. Chacoan Subsistence. In *Chaco and Hohokam: Prehistoric Regional Systems in the American Southwest*, edited by Patricia L. Crown and W. James Judge, pp. 57–75. School of American Research Advanced Seminar Series. School of American Research Press, Santa Fe.

————. 1992. Chacoan Water Use and Managerial Decision Making. In *Anasazi Regional Organization and the Chaco System*, edited by David E. Doyel, pp. 45–58. Maxwell Museum of Anthropology, Anthropological Papers No. 5. Maxwell Museum of Anthropology, University of New Mexico, Albuquerque.

Vivian, R. Gwinn, and Douglas Palmer. 2003. A Reevaluation of the Kin Bineola Water Control Systems. Manuscript on file, Museum Collection of the Chaco Culture National Historical Park, University of New Mexico, Albuquerque.

Vivian, R. Gwinn, Carla Van West, Jeffrey S. Dean, Nancy Akins, Mollie Toll, Tom Windes. 2006. Chacoan Ecology and Economy, Appendix B. In *The Archaeology of Chaco Canyon: An Eleventh-Century Pueblo Regional Center*, edited by Stephen H. Lekson, pp. 429–457. School of American Research Press, Santa Fe.

Watson, Adam S. 2009. Watersheds and "Big Men": Reassessing the Role of Hydrology and Differential Agricultural Success in Chacoan Political Evolution. Paper presented at the 74th Annual Meeting of the Society of American Archaeology, Atlanta, Georgia.

Wills, W. H. 2000. Political Leadership and the Construction of Chacoan Great Houses, AD 1020–1140. In *Alternative Leadership Strategies in the Prehispanic Southwest*, edited by Barbara J. Mills, pp. 19–44. University of Arizona Press, Tucson.

Wills, W. H., F. Scott Worman, Wetherbee Dorshow, and Heather Richards. 2012. Shabik'eshchee Village in Chaco Canyon: Time to Move Beyond the Archetype. *American Antiquity* 77(2):326–350.

Wills, W. H., and Wetherbee Bryan Dorshow. 2012. Agriculture and community in Chaco Canyon: Revisiting Pueblo Alto. *Journal of Anthropological Archaeology* 31(2012):138–155.

Windes, Thomas C. 1978. *Stone Circles of Chaco Canyon, Northwestern New Mexico.* Reports of the Chaco Center No. 5. Division of Chaco Research, National Park Service, Albuquerque.

———. 1987a. *Investigations at the Pueblo Alto Complex, Chaco Canyon,* Vol. I. Publications in Archeology 18F, Chaco Canyon Studies. National Park Service, U.S. Department of the Interior, Santa Fe.

———. 1987b. *Investigations at the Pueblo Alto Complex, Chaco Canyon,* Vol. II, Part 2. Publications in Archeology 18F, Chaco Canyon Studies. National Park Service, U.S. Department of the Interior, Santa Fe.

———. 2001. House Location Patterns in the Chaco Canyon Area: A Short Description. In *Chaco Society and Polity: Papers from the 1999 Conference,* edited by Linda S. Cordell, W. James Judge, and June-el Piper, pp. 31–45. New Mexico Archaeological Council Special Publication 4. Albuquerque, New Mexico.

———. 2007. Gearing Up and Piling On: Early Great Houses in the Interior San Juan Basin. In *The Architecture of Chaco Canyon, New Mexico,* edited by Stephen H. Lekson, pp. 45–92. University of Utah Press, Salt Lake City.

Windes, Thomas C. (editor). 1993. *The Spadefoot Toad Site: Investigations at 29SJ 629, Chaco Canyon, New Mexico,* Vol. I. Reports of the Chaco Center No. 12. Division of Cultural Research, National Park Service, Albuquerque.

Worman, F. Scott, and Hannah V. Mattson. 2010. Arroyos and Agriculture: Geoarchaeological Investigations at Pueblo Pintado. *Kiva* 75(4):447–482.

3

The Relevance of Maize Pollen for Assessing the Extent of Maize Production in Chaco Canyon

Phil R. Geib and Carrie C. Heitman

Opinion is hardly unanimous, but many authors endorse the idea that Chaco Canyon is and was a marginal place for growing corn (*Zea mays*), a chief source of food energy for Puebloan groups in the Southwest. Poor soils with "toxic" levels of salts, inadequate and unpredictable precipitation, and a short growing season have all been identified as contributing to the agricultural marginality of the place (Benson 2011a; Bryan 1954; Force et al. 2002; Judd 1954:59–61). Benson has been the most vocal proponent of this view of late, and his research has culminated in the conclusion that "the San Juan Basin, including Chaco Canyon, appears to be the least promising area for dryland farming; that is, it is too dry and its soils are N-poor, saline and too basic (high pH values) for the production of maize" (Benson 2011a:49–50; Benson 2011b). The Chaco Project's experimental maize fields in the late 1970s seem to bear out this statement: "Chaco, under modern conditions, is indeed marginal as a corn growing environment" (Toll et al. 1985:124). If Chaco Canyon is as marginal for farming as many claim, then the cultural achievements of the Puebloans that lived there are all the more remarkable, and this marginality has figured prominently in many interpretations about how and why Chaco Canyon developed as it did (Judge 1979, 1989; Schelberg 1981, 1982; Sebastian 1983, 1991, 1992; Vivian 1984, 1990). Chacoans had to import not only beams for building, pottery for cooking and storage, and stone for flaked tools but also even the staff of life—corn. And when you add in such exotics as turquoise, parrots, copper bells, and cacao, the potential "trade" deficit looms large. If Chaco Canyon did not provide even enough food for basic sustenance, what was it that made the place so special in the first place? More importantly, what literally fueled the obvious cultural fluorescence of Chaco Canyon and its massive labor-intensive construction projects? Wills and Dorshow (2012:138) observe that "the popular perspective that Chaco was mysterious or enigmatic is largely a response to this view of the canyon as agriculturally marginal."

Yet, how do we know what the agricultural potential of the canyon was during the Bonito phase (ca. A.D. 850–1140) or that Chacoans could not provide for themselves? Perhaps the pendulum has swung too far toward a pessimistic assessment of the maize farming in and around the canyon. Certainly, Navajo farmers with considerable traditional knowledge and a real stake in the outcome successfully grew corn within Chaco Canyon (Judd 1954:52–59), and in 1898, George Pepper photographed Navajo fields on the floodplain of Chaco Canyon proper that produced a bountiful corn harvest (Figure 3.1a). Since photo documentation is not anecdotal, it seems a sufficient counter to assertions that farming of the Chaco floodplain was impossible because of high salinity. Judd's records of Navajo maize harvests evidently come from a time of more favorable precipitation and growing-season length, but this, too, could have characterized much of the Bonito phase. Figure 3.1b shows another Navajo field on the main floodplain at harvest time. Navajo farmers clearly experienced agricultural risk (Huntington 1914:81), but evidently the canyon proved a sufficient attraction to entice early settlement by them (Brugge 1986), perhaps precisely because of its productive potential. Farming potential was likely the prime motivation for initial Basketmaker settlement, a time when supplemental extra-local sources of maize were improbable. Since everything is relative, Chaco Canyon may have seemed like a small Eden in the context of the vast "dreary wastes" (Huntington 1914:81) of the San Juan Basin at large.

To his credit, Benson, like others before, has collected soil samples and processed meteorological and proxy climate data to demonstrate the marginality of Chaco for farming. He has also worked to chemically fingerprint the geographic sources of maize found at Chaco and elsewhere in the San Juan Basin (Benson 2011c; Benson et al. 2003, 2006, 2008, 2009). This research grew out of previous speculations that corn and other staples may have been imported into Chaco Canyon (Altschul 1978; Cordell 1979; Cordell and Plog 1979; Judge 1979; Lyons and Hitchcock 1977) and an exploratory study using concentrations of elements in corn and soils for isolating potential source areas (Cordell

Figure 3.1. Navajo cornfields in Chaco Canyon: (a) field on the margin of
the main floodplain at harvest time in 1898 (note the pile of husks in the
foreground, with corn ears in a heap next to the standing individual) (Courtesy
Maxwell Museum of Anthropology, University of New Mexico, Neg. No.
88.41.16); (b) Roy Newton in his cornfield on the floodplain of Chaco Wash
at the intersection with Escavada Wash. (Courtesy Chaco Culture National
Historical Park Museum Collection, chacoarchive.org, Neg. No. 78146)

et al. 2001, 2008). Corn sourcing is certainly an interesting approach, but one with many complexities and confounding issues yet to be resolved (Cordell et al. 2008). Troubling, too, is that Athabaskan-age cobs from Chaco (Gallo Cliff Dwelling) are also identified as coming from non-local sources: the Totah, Lobo Mesa, and Dinetah regions (Benson et al. 2009:403). Given the documentation of Navajo farming in Chaco Canyon, a local origin for most historic cobs from the canyon is expected. If locally grown Navajo corn is potentially misidentified as non-local, then what about the prehistoric specimens?

In the face of findings and claims as to the marginality of Chaco for farming purposes, it is certainly worth considering other evidence that bears upon the extent to which maize and other crops were grown there. Our main objective is to consider how corn pollen at Chacoan sites might inform about agricultural practices. This involves placing the pollen data generated by the Chaco Project (Cully 1985, 1988) within a regional context and incorporating the findings of experimental research with pollen washes from various portions of maize ears (Geib and Smith 2008). The latter have important implications for under-standing how corn pollen might enter the archaeological record and the probabilities behind various behavioral interpretations of pollen counts. Equally significant is the Puebloan ethnographic record concerning the harvesting and processing of corn and the ceremonial use of corn pollen and plants. We discuss four different aspects, including (1) the pollen ecology of maize, (2) a brief review of experimental maize pollen washes and the implications for behavioral interpretations, (3) a review of the Puebloan ethnographic record pertaining to the use of maize and how this may relate to the patterns seen in pollen spectra, and (4) a summary of the available maize data for Chaco Canyon and how it compares on a regional scale.

Pollen Ecology of Maize and Experimental Washes

A useful starting point is to consider how corn pollen might enter the archaeological record, which requires a brief review of maize pollina-tion. *Zea mays* is monoecious, having separate male and female flower-ing parts on a single plant; the tassels are the male or pollinating flowers, with the female flowering structures in the ears tightly enclosed by husks.

Flowering generally occurs in two stages with close synchrony: pollen shed then silking. Male function preceding female function (protandry) helps limit self-pollination. Pollen dispersal usually begins two to three days prior to silk emergence and continues for five to eight days (Aldrich et al. 1986). As a wind-pollinated plant (anemophilous), corn, like all grasses, produces abundant pollen, with each tassel containing two to five million pollen grains borne in anthers, and an average-sized plant is estimated to produce between fifteen and fifty million grains (Miller 1982). As anthers open, the pollen grains pour out, to be carried away by breezes and to settle by gravity. Compared to other wind-pollinated species, maize pollen is relatively large and heavy, with the spherical grains falling rapidly (settling speed of 17–31 cm/second depending on degree of dehydration [Aylor 2002]), which generally limits dispersal. Although capable of being carried moderate distances by strong winds, especially with updrafts like dust devils, most corn pollen settles within 15 m of the plant, as estimated by cross-breeding studies or counts on surfaces (e.g., Bannert and Stamp 2007; Bannert et al. 2008; Pleasants et al. 2001). Much of the pollen falls directly on the broad hairy surfaces of the corn plant and adheres to the fine sticky hairs (trichomes) of the silks, which serve to catch and anchor the pollen grains. Silks are the functional stigmas of the female flowers, and each must be pollinated in order for an ovule to be fertilized and develop into a kernel. The tight outer wrapping of the ears protects the developing kernels and precludes the deposition of any corn pollen upon them.

The nature of maize pollination holds at least two important implications for inferences drawn from corn pollen recovered from archaeological sites. First, maize pollen is unlikely to end up at a site through natural processes like other wind-pollinated plants such as pine or other grasses unless that site is located within or quite close to a cornfield, especially on the downwind side. Even then, corn pollen deposition is likely to be minimal relative to other environmental pollen rain, so proportionally swamped. Although each corn plant produces millions of pollen grains, many other plants produce far more, at least in aggregate, including other grasses and even some entomophilous plants, with counts for some pines at more than 1,000 million grains per plant (Khanduri and Sharma 2002). In modern maize fields, Martin and Byers (1965) report that the amount of corn pollen present is often no greater than around 1 percent, and Dean (1995:Table 22.2) reports values between 0 percent and 11 percent with a mean of 4 percent for modern plowed and irrigated cornfields. The overall low proportion reflects the proportional swamping of corn pollen by that from other taxa.

The second implication is that storing or processing shucked corn ears or kernels is unlikely to deposit corn pollen in any significant quantities within the archaeological record. This claim was verified by experimental pollen washes of 26 maize samples, including kernels, silks, and husks (Geib and Smith 2008). Pollen of any type was rare in all of the maize washes: 23 (88 percent) produced counts of 11 or less total pollen grains, and the material on the slides was extremely clean. The pollen washes of separate portions of 3 corn ears revealed a dramatic reduction in corn pollen after removal of the outer husks (Figure 3.2). Indeed, except for the outer husks, nearly no corn pollen was recovered from the other portions of the maize ears, and none came from the husked ears. Although husking removed all of the maize pollen in a controlled experiment, prehistoric people probably husked corn less carefully, and

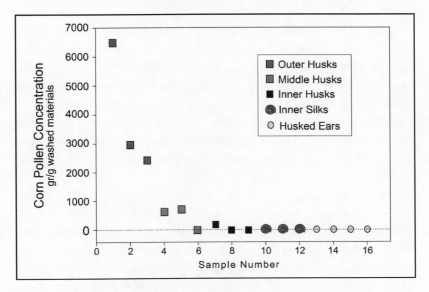

Figure 3.2. Concentration of corn pollen (grains/gram washed materials) from husked ears, inner silks, and husks removed sequentially from outside to inside (n=16) (Geib and Smith 2008:Figure 6). Maize pollen aggregates were totally absent from these samples, even the outer husks.

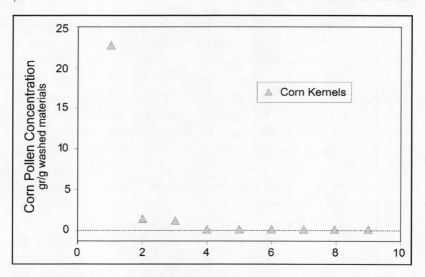

Figure 3.3. Concentration of corn pollen (grains/gram washed materials) from corn kernels removed from cobs in traditional manner (n=9).

handling could transfer pollen from the outer husks to kernels. To test this possibility, Geib and Smith (2008) also made pollen washes of 9 samples of kernels from corn ears husked and shelled following traditional practices. These washes also revealed a largely similar absence of maize pollen (Figure 3.3), with just 3 of the 9 samples containing any maize grains. The maximum was just 7 grains in one sample for a concentration value of 23 grains per gram; another sample had 3 grains and the third a single grain for concentration values of less than 2 grains per gram.

The basic finding of the experimental washes is that maize pollen is generally absent or exceedingly rare on kernels or shucked ears, the items that archaeologists are most interested in making inferences about. With little or no maize pollen actually present on kernels or shucked ears, it seems unlikely that storing or processing this resource would produce a directly related pollen signature, or one detectable relative to other pollen taxa in a standard archaeological sample. Maize ears or kernels not grown locally but imported from some distant agricultural fields are even less likely to produce anything but trace amounts of pollen in a standard archaeological sample.

   Corn pollen will be most abundant where outer corn husks or other plant portions, especially male flowers and leaves, are deposited. As such, harvesting practices become critical. Was husking done in the field or adjacent field house with shucked ears transported back to the residential site? Alternatively, were whole ears brought back to the settlement for husking there? Ethnographies demonstrate that Puebloans did both in the recent past, with field husking common among the Hopi (e.g., Stephen 1969 [1936]:940–941, 953) and Zuni (Cushing 1920:211), but with unhusked ears brought back to such villages as Cochiti, San Ildefonso, and Santa Clara (Goldfrank 1927; Robbins et al. 1916) where the husking was done communally in plaza spaces. Since wagons and draft animals were used at the Rio Grande pueblos (and at Zuni), it is difficult to know the time depth for settlement husking. Figure 3.1a demonstrates a probable common practice for Navajos in Chaco, that of removing husks in the field. Since this eliminates extraneous weight, it might have been the preferred method in prehistory unless maize fields were very close to a residence. Field husking and drying would further reduce weight, and field drying is a documented practice, with the ears left in the field for many weeks (Hough 1918). Field husking would also leave organic debris to rot in the field, thereby returning much-needed nutrients to the soil. Corn husks and even whole plants could enter sites for ceremonial and other purposes; thus, it is to this aspect that we now turn.

Puebloan Use of Maize Pollen

Puebloan ethnographies document many other ways for corn pollen to enter the archaeological record at settlements, primarily because offerings of corn pollen (or a corn meal/pollen mix) is an ever-present component of Pueblo ritual practice (Table 3.1). Contexts for such offerings range from the habitual daily routine of an individual offering corn pollen to the rising sun, to more restricted ceremonial contexts involving ritual specialists. According to Parsons, "It seems probable that anciently every Pueblo sprinkled corn meal or pollen at sunrise and said a prayer. Elders and ceremonialists still do so" (Parsons 1939:179). This practice is repeatedly described in myth (e.g., Acoma: Stirling 1942:3, 5, 7, 13) and songs (Santo Domingo: White 1935:97–99). In the origin myth of

Table 3.1. Summary of Contexts and Occasions when Puebloans Sprinkle Corn Meal/Pollen.

Use Category	Specific Context	Page References from Parsons (1939)
On people	Initiates	672
	Newborns	46
	The deceased	70, 73, 293
	Racers	311, 816
	Dancers	563, 634, 685, 816, 831, 836
	Kachinas	174, 318, 381, 461, 468, 472, 567, 569, 570, 579, 735, 742, 748, 749, 753, 755, 757n., 761, 772, 773, 778, 785, 787, 801, 1099
	Warriors	648
On ritual paraphernalia/ features	Fetishes	654, 701–792
	Masks	294, 755, 850
	Scalps	645
	Prayer sticks & feathers	283, 284, 292, 315, 558, 567, 581, 775, 816, 955
	Kiva *sipapu*	383
	Kiva foot drum	512, 631, 667
	Medicine bowl	360–361, 375, 689, 704
	Staffs	327, 491n., 577, 606, 703
As part of a ceremony	To mark a ritual position	294, 366, 373, 512–513, 674n., 687, 700, 704,711, 755, 759, 839, 867n.
	Sprinkled down a kiva hatch	293, 295n., 362, 568, 574, 607, 617
	Offered to the sacred directions	260, 558, 827
	To create a meal road	18, 362, 693, 697, 706, 834
	In front of a line of dancers	616, 620
	To create a ground painting	294

(continued)

Table 3.1. Summary of Contexts and Occasions when Puebloans Sprinkle Corn Meal/Pollen (*continued*)

Use Category	Specific Context	Page References from Parsons (1939)
On plants and animals	Snakes	244, 293, 512
	Deer or rabbit	293, 304, 540, 760, 847
	Ants	293, 714
	Crops	547
	Plants and trees	277, 293, 785
	Eagles	296–297
To the heavens	Sun	36, 139, 179–180, 212, 218, 292, 311, 468, 517, 544, 557, 562, 583, 584, 593, 606, 672, 695, 703, 747, 775, 816, 904, 1079n.
	Moon or stars	583
At sacred places	Springs or rivers	375, 558, 584, 587, 788
	On altar or shrine	358, 361, 603, 633, 634, 635, 667, 677, 680, 690, 704, 714, 741, 769, 818, 819

Note: From a survey of Parsons's *Pueblo Indian Religion* (1939).

Acoma, Stirling (1942:5) describes how the two sisters first taught the people how to gather corn pollen and, with corn meal, offer it to the rising sun each morning.

Admittedly there is a great deal of overlap or conflation in the use of both corn pollen and corn meal as "prayer meal" across the Pueblo Southwest. Working at Isleta, Parsons notes that her informant used these terms indiscriminately and warns the reader to bear this lack of distinction in mind when reading ceremonial accounts (1932:275; see also 1939:296). Goldfrank (1927:68) notes the same lack of native differentiation at Cochiti but that shamans specifically keep corn pollen in a small clay bowl called a "pollen basket." Corn pollen may be used alone or mixed with ground shell and turquoise, or with micaceous hematite, or combined with pollen from other plants (Parsons 1939:296). Similarly, corn meal may also be used alone or added to such mixtures. Space limitations preclude an exhaustive listing of

the host of contexts and occasions in which corn pollen/meal is sprinkled; suffice it to say that they are numerous and varied and many
occur daily.

Corn pollen can also enter the record in other ceremonial ways that
involve the use of corn plants, especially the upper portions of stalks
that include the male tassels after pollination. Examples include ceremonies at Walpi where corn plants are set up in clay pedestals to create
a mock cornfield, with plants subsequently being knocked over and
distributed to women and children (Fewkes 1900:608–609, 617) or the
common practice at Nima'n ceremonies of handing out gifts tied to a
corn stalk to young children. Also at Nima'n, the Hemis Katsinas enter
the plaza carrying armloads of freshly cut green corn, ears still on the
stalks (also for the Lalakon dance [Stephen 1969 [1936]:936–937]). Ceremonies like this could introduce quantities of maize pollen to a settlement, and although these specific ones may lack sufficient time depth,
similar practices might date back to the Basketmaker period. Ritual can
even introduce corn pollen to granaries: at Cochiti four unhusked ears
of corn, referred to as "the mothers," are saved and placed in the four
corners of a corn storage room and the husked ears are piled on top of
them, whereas at Laguna, an entire corn stalk is placed in each corner of
a granary (Goldfrank 1927:92).

There are many examples of corn husks being used for various purposes such as wrappers around ceremonial items, for rolling
tobacco or other ceremonial or medicinal plants, in food preparation,
or even for artifacts. Nonetheless, the husks selected for this are likely
to be fresh ones from the interior of cobs rather than the weathered
ones on the exterior, and examination of ethnographic and prehistoric
items in museums that include maize husks supports this claim. As
the maize ear pollen wash study demonstrated, corn pollen occurs
in abundance on the outer husks but with little to none on interior
leaves. As such, use of corn husks at sites is unlikely to be a major con-
tributor of maize pollen to the archaeological record. This is also true
if husks were saved for fuel, something that might have occurred in
wood-deprived Chaco during the Bonito phase, since hot fire destroys
pollen (Ruhl 1986), and husks would have burned quickly and been
reduced to ash.

The Chaco Canyon Pollen Record

With the forgoing as context, we turn to the pollen data for Chaco Canyon proper, which is limited compared to the large amount of excavation that has occurred. Cully (1985, 1988) reports pollen counts from 4 sites: 2 small sites (29SJ627 and 29SJ629, hereinafter 627 and 629) and select rooms of Pueblo Alto and Kin Nahasbas. The last site has just 5 samples, which might be poorly representative of the site as a whole. Clary (1987) provides pollen counts for 4 additional samples from Pueblo Alto, 3 from mealing bins of Room 110 and 1 from wall niche 9, also in this room. The total number of samples reported from this effort is 93, and more than half (62.8 percent) of these produced adequate counts, which means a minimum of 200 grains following Barkley (1934; see Rull 1987). A 200 grain count provides about a 75–85 percent accurate representation for common pollen types (Dimbleby 1985; Martin and Byers 1963). Twenty-nine of the samples (31.2 percent) have pollen proportions calculated on counts of less than 200 grains, with 91 grains the lowest. Fifteen samples were essentially "sterile," with no count given, but evidently listed to record the observation of corn pollen (and cactus in one instance); one of these sterile samples is for mealing bin 6 at Pueblo Alto, which produced a count of just 17 grains.

Cully analyzed her samples in the late 1970s for the Chaco Project, a time when palynological research in archaeology was still in its formative stages (at least in the New World). Sampling strategies, processing technique, and counting methods have continued to evolve, and even during the Chaco Project, the procedures for sampling rooms changed, such that the approach for 627 (the first site analyzed) differed from 629 and Pueblo Alto. Most analysts these days include tracer or marker grains (e.g., *Lycopodium* spores) as a "spike" to a sample prior to processing, which allows calculation of pollen concentration (PC) and pollen accumulation rate (Maher 1981; Stockmarr 1971). Marker grains also allow calculation of confidence intervals for estimates (Rull 1987) and the specification of how many grains need to be counted in order to discover rare pollen types (Dean 1995). Absolute pollen frequencies allow an estimate of the deposition of a pollen type (such as corn) that is independent of any other pollen type. Although this approach is now standard practice in the Southwest, most comparisons are still done with proportions, such that the grains of a given taxon are presented relative to the total grains counted in a sample. Since only four of the Chaco samples from the 1970s were spiked (the four samples analyzed by Clary), we mainly restrict our comparisons to proportions. Dean (2006) demonstrates that PC values can be calculated after the fact if the pollen residue from the original samples still exists, but this requires doing new counts after spiking the samples.

Not surprisingly, corn pollen is present in the Chaco samples (Table 3.2); indeed, Cully observed it in nearly all of them (<80 percent occurrence for the three sites with adequate sample size), even in some that did not produce adequate counts. Aside from mere presence, corn pollen is quite abundant in several of the samples, accounting for 10 percent or more of the pollen counted in more than 35 percent of the samples from each site (Figure 3.4). This is significant since it greatly exceeds the amount of corn pollen commonly present on modern maize fields, which is often around 1 percent (Martin and Byers 1965; cf. Dean 1995:Table 22.2). Of course fields are open settings where environmental

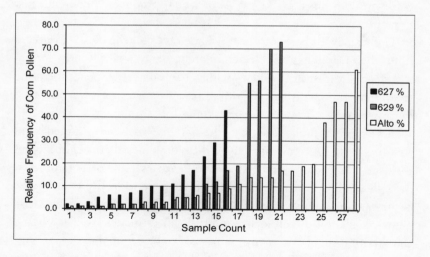

Figure 3.4. Relative frequency of corn pollen in samples with "adequate" counts from 29SJ627, 29SJ629, and Pueblo Alto, Chaco Canyon, New Mexico. (Data from Cully 1985)

Table 3.2. Summary of Corn Pollen Data from Chaco Canyon Sites.

Attribute	627	629	Alto	Nahasbas
n of samples reported	24	28	36	5
n of samples with reported counts	19	23	31	5
% of samples with reported counts	79.2	82.1	86.1	100.0
n of 200+ grain counts	9	14	21	5
% 200+ grain counts	47.4	60.9	67.7	100.0
n of counted samples with corn	16	21	29	2
% of counted samples with corn	84.2	91.3	93.5	40.0
n of total samples with corn	21	26	33	2
% of total samples with corn	87.5	92.9	91.7	40.0
n of samples with 10%+ corn	8	8	13	2
% of samples with 10%+ corn	42.1	34.8	41.9	40.0
Average corn proportion	10.4	14.9	14.9	16.2
Standard deviation	11.2	23.6	19.6	23.2
Lower quartile	2.5	1.5	2	—
Median	7.0	2	7	—
Upper quartile	13.0	14.5	17	—
Maximum	43.0	73.0	68	50.0
Total pollen grains counted	3,198	4,668	6,010	1,090
Total corn pollen grains counted	343	640	1,038	190
% corn pollen grains counted	10.7	13.7	17.3	17.4

Note: Data from Clary 1987; Cully 1985, 1988.

pollen rain from prolific producers can swamp the maize signal, whereas most archaeological samples come from closed environments where the pollen record is accumulated by humans to some unknown degree.

One way of trying to evaluate the pollen record from the Chaco Canyon sites is to compare it against the results obtained for other sites in the greater San Juan Basin and beyond (e.g., Dean 1999; Gish 1994a, 1994b; Smith 1999; Smith et al. 1999). This can be done in many different ways, but we take a broad-brushed approach, focusing on variability in maize pollen occurrence. Rather than finely parsing the data, we examine site departures in corn pollen representation in two ways:

(1) the average relative frequency of corn pollen in the samples for a given site, and (2) the average count of corn pollen relative to the total pollen sum for each site. We specifically exclude modern samples and post-occupation fill at sites and also exclude fecal specimens, such as those from Bis sa'ani (Cully 1982). Fecal pollen counts are a significant source of information about diet and other aspects of plant use (e.g., Bryant and Dean 2006; Dean 2006), but few Chacoan sites in addition to Bis sa'ani have preserved specimens, most notably Salmon Ruins (Reinhard et al. 2006a, 2006b) and Pueblo Bonito (Karl Reinhard, personal communication 2013). The contexts that we included are diverse but mostly intramural, especially structure and pit surfaces. After calculating two regional means of corn pollen representation, we computed departures therefrom (anomalies) for each site, which were then transformed to Z-scores. We recognize that this approach is insensitive to potentially important variability introduced by context, site age, sampling, processing, counting, and other details, but with sufficiently large sample sizes, both within sites and across the region as a whole, any patterns disclosed are likely to be robust, and they should have comparative heuristic value at a broad scale. Use of absolute corn frequencies could be more informative but cannot at present be done with Cully's Chaco data. As discussed below, pollen counts for Pueblo Alto and Pueblo Bonito obtained more recently by Susan Smith for the University of New Mexico allow comparison using maize pollen concentration in a summary fashion.

Our current database has over 1,200 pollen samples from 50 sites and a total pollen sum of more than 235,000 grains. Given this scale, the patterns should be telling us something about differential corn pollen accumulation at sites across the region. The plots of Z-scores (Figure 3.5) by the two different methods closely mirror each other; indeed, the r^2 for the correlation between the data sets is 0.98. The zero line marks the mean in these figures, which we assume represents the baseline frequency of corn pollen at habitations resulting from prehistoric Puebloan use of this domesticate. Both means are somewhat positively skewed by the few sites with high levels of corn pollen, which includes the Chaco Canyon sites. For example, the average proportion of corn pollen per sample is 3.6 compared to a median 1.5. The median value is similar to the proportion of corn pollen in modern fields where deposition

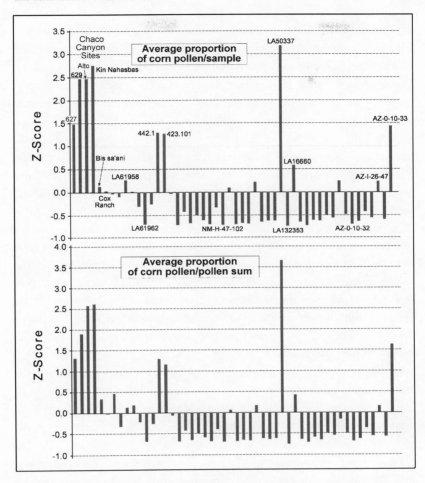

Figure 3.5. Plots of the anomalies from the mean of corn pollen representation calculated by two different methods; Chaco Canyon sites are shown in sequence to the far left.

is largely mediated by natural processes. Positive departures denote those sites with greater than average corn representation and vice versa for negative departures; bar height signifies the extent of departure in standard deviations. The small number of sites with positive departures include all four Chaco Canyon sites grouped on the far left: 629, Alto, and Kin Nahasbas are more than two standard deviations above the mean with 627 just less than 1.5 standard deviations above the mean.

Even though the Chaco Canyon sites are a significant part of the reason for the mean being pulled higher than the median, these sites are
still quite divergent; they would appear even more divergent based on
the median value of corn pollen representation. Higher than average
amounts of corn pollen is not true for Chacoan outliers, since Bis sa'ani
and Cox Ranch have near-average values.

The only site in our database with more abundant maize pollen than
the Chaco Canyon sites is LA50337 (Clary 1993), located along the La
Plata River in northwestern New Mexico. Many of the samples from
this site with abundant corn pollen came from plaza contexts where
ears may have been husked and ceremonies performed. Situated as it is
in a prime agricultural setting, one that Benson et al. (2007:301) identify as "an excellent area for maize production and exportation," a high
incidence of maize pollen at LA50337 is perhaps unsurprising. Yet the
Chaco Canyon sites are little different and contain far more maize pollen than other sites located in seemingly less marginal settings. If we
were to plot the maize pollen departures as isopleths, there would be
a peak at Chaco Canyon and another along the La Plata River, with
plenty of negative space.

Further support for concluding that Chacoan sites have extraordinarily high amounts of corn pollen comes from the trash mounds of
Pueblo Alto and Pueblo Bonito. Susan Smith and Susan Fish have both
analyzed additional samples from Pueblo Alto, specifically the trash
mound, and Smith has also analyzed samples from the Pueblo Bonito
trash mound. This work was done for Wirt Wills and Patricia Crown,
and the data are not yet available. Some summary results presented by
Susan Smith at a recent SAR symposium, however, provide a useful
glimpse of the findings. These more recent pollen counts fully support
the overall trend in maize pollen occurrence in Cully's samples, and
Smith does this with a more robust quantification measure, that of
maize PC (Fish's data is based on proportions). Susan Smith (personal
communication 2010) found that maize pollen concentration (grains/
gr of sample) for both the Alto and Bonito mounds was far above
other sites in the region for which she had comparative data. Whereas
non-Chacoan sites had maximum values of less than 400 grains/gr
and in most cases less than 200 grains/gr, samples from both Chacoan
great house trash mounds had upwards of 500 maize grains per gram

and most samples had more than 1,000 grains per gram. Susan Fish also found high proportions of corn pollen in most of the samples that she analyzed from the Pueblo Alto trash mound, most between 30–60 percent (Susan Smith, personal communication 2010). Wills and Dorshow (2012:147) conclude from these recent pollen counts that "Pueblo Alto shows one of the strongest signals for on-site processing of maize plants."

Given that the mean of corn pollen representation in Figure 3.5 represents the basic frequency of deposition deriving from prehistoric Puebloan use of this domesticate, it is worth considering how and why corn pollen entered the Chaco Canyon sites at frequencies well above the norm for the region. Maize pollen may have simply blown into archaeological contexts as part of the background pollen rain, but only if the sampled habitations were very close to agricultural fields. Even then, deposition within the relatively closed setting of structure interiors by wind or other natural processes should have been minimal. To the extent that natural processes were involved, this would suggest that agricultural fields were proximate to all sampled sites, including Pueblo Alto. Nonetheless, it seems reasonable to assume that most corn pollen at settlements results from human activity of one sort or another, with natural processes playing a minimal role. But what sort of activities? Is it the storage and processing of corn ears and kernels, as often inferred? Given the experimental results reported previously, we have to say no. Storage of ears or kernels and the processing of kernels into flour or by parching or popping are unlikely to deposit corn pollen in the archaeological record at frequencies higher than the overall mean or even at the mean. If true for locally grown maize, the produce imported from afar would be even less likely to generate such a pollen signature. The activities that are most likely to result in corn pollen deposition have little to do with corn kernels or corn ears per se regardless of where they originate.

Activities that could deposit corn pollen in the proportions seen at Chaco Canyon sites include the onsite husking of corn ears and various ceremonial activities that involve corn pollen or corn stalks. High corn pollen frequencies might be expected in plazas or open areas next to structures, where husking would be performed. Yet plazas are also important places for ceremonies, such that maize pollen could accumulate in them from these activities alone. What remains unknown is whether ceremonial deposition would produce as robust a maize pollen signature as seen in many of the Chaco samples, especially considering that few if any came from places of probable ritual activity. The small sites of 627 and 629 are well positioned to have been locations of on-site maize ear husking, located as they are along the south side of the Chaco floodplain. Given Alto's elevated position away from the potential farmland of the canyon bottom, the site might seem an unlikely location for corn husking. Yet, Wills and Dorshow (2012:142) have recently argued that "agricultural production was integral to the Pueblo Alto community" and further that "the mesa top around Pueblo Alto is so suitable for maize and bean cultivation today that even inexperienced archaeologists can get plants to grow [there]" (2012:146). If this claim has merit, then ear husking might well have occurred at Alto as well, and this could account for the high frequency of maize pollen that all analysts have documented at the site. Nonetheless, except for the recently analyzed mound samples, the Chaco Canyon pollen record comes from structure interiors, doubtful places for husking. For sites situated in close proximity to fields, there could have been ample opportunity for maize pollen to be introduced to structure interiors on the bodies and clothing of field workers, children, or dogs. Yet by such incidental processes, the frequency of corn pollen seems more likely to be low and certainly not at the levels documented for the Chaco sites.

The mealing bin pollen data from Pueblo Alto provides an intriguing hint at a ritual activity that could partially account for some of the high maize frequencies: the preparation of ceremonial meal. Cully analyzed three samples from mealing bins one through three from Room 110, and Karen Clary analyzed the other three plus one from a wall niche in the same room. Clary spiked her samples so that these are the only reported samples from Chaco that allow calculation of pollen concentration; for maize this ranged from a low of 105 grains per gram to a high of 11,844. It is worth mentioning that the "low" value is actually quite high compared with most samples from the Southwest. The lowest relative frequency of corn pollen in the seven samples is 20 percent, with most samples containing more than 40 percent maize pollen (Figure 3.6). Given the experimental maize washes, the grinding of kernels alone is a highly improbable means to produce these frequencies of

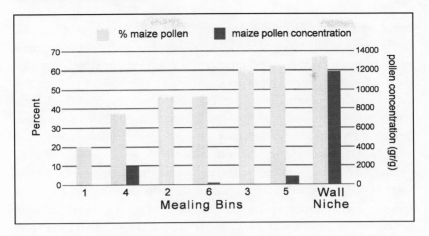

Figure 3.6. Bar graph of the proportion of maize pollen and maize pollen concentration for six mealing bins and a wall niche of Room 110 from Pueblo Alto (data from Clary 1987); note that mealing bin 6 only had a total pollen count of 17 grains.

maize pollen. Not only would maize pollen rarely occur on kernels but also any that did would be proportionally swamped by the numerous other types of environmental pollen that would have settled on ears as they dried in the sun after husking. The activity that could account for the incidence of maize pollen in the mealing bin samples is the preparation of "prayer meal" as described in various ethnographies, where corn pollen or male flowers are added to kernels and ground together. The preparation of ceremonial meal, whether for public gatherings or simply as an exchange commodity (prayer meal from a sacred place) might help account for the massed (four or more) mealing bins seen at Pueblo Bonito (Rooms 90 and 291), Pueblo del Arroyo (Room 55), Pueblo Alto (Room 110), small house site Bc 51 (Room 47), and likely other Chacoan great houses.

The consumption of ceremonial meal consisting of a pollen flour mix would also account for the high incidence of maize pollen in some of the human feces from Chaco Canyon (Clary 1984), Salmon Ruins (Reinhard et al. 2006a, 2006b) and Pueblo Bonito (Karl Reinhard, personal communication 2013). Williams-Dean (1986:198–199; also Williams-Dean and Bryant 1975) attributed the high incidence of corn pollen in Antelope House feces as possibly resulting from the consumption of corn silks, meaning the dried ones exterior to the husks that actually received pollen rain. Whether such items were commonly consumed is an open question, though Pepper (1920) reported corn silk quids from Pueblo Bonito. However, Williams-Dean also found that some of the maize pollen in the feces appeared crushed, which was thought to represent the grinding of pollen-covered maize kernels with manos and metates (Williams-Dean 1986:199). Reinhard et al. (2006b:Tables 1 and 3) also obtained high maize counts and concentration values in the feces from Salmon Ruins along with a considerably higher incidence of crushed maize pollen than at Antelope House. They interpreted this evidence as indicating the consumption of "pollen-bearing, maize-based foods such as stews" (Reinhard et al. 2006a:103). Given the experimental wash data summarized earlier, this seem unlikely unless maize pollen was being purposefully added to the kernels during the processing, which is exactly what occurs in the preparation of ceremonial meal. This might occur not just with collected pollen but also with entire tassels. Pollen is nutritionally beneficial, and Simms (1985) has shown that cattail pollen, which was commonly consumed in the Great Basin, is the highest-ranked plant food, above even oak and pinyon nuts.

Conclusion

As with most aspects of archaeology, single data sets alone seldom provide clear answers. It is only by integrating and fully accounting for disparate lines of evidence that a more comprehensive understanding is achieved. The frequency of corn pollen in the Chaco Canyon samples appears high, well above the incidence of corn pollen in modern fields where, despite dense planting, corn pollen proportions are below many of the Chaco samples, sometimes well below. By creating a regional pollen database to look at the incidence of corn pollen at prehistoric habitations scattered across the San Juan Basin and somewhat beyond, we obtained an even better datum point for evaluating the frequency of corn pollen in the Chaco Canyon samples. The regional pollen database demonstrates quite markedly that the four Chaco Canyon sites with analyzed samples have frequencies of maize pollen well above the regional average. This finding is fully corroborated by more recently analyzed samples from the trash mounds of Pueblo Alto and Pueblo Bonito (Susan Smith, personal communication 2010).

Any interpretation of what the anomalously high maize pollen proportions might mean should factor in what we currently know from experimental pollen washes coupled with knowledge about how maize pollen could enter the archaeological record based on Puebloan ethnography. Even armed with such information, there are still inferential gaps between pollen counts and past behavior. It is obvious that pollen analysis will never be able to answer how much corn was grown in the canyon. Nonetheless, the transport of maize ears or kernels into Chaco Canyon from growing areas of the Chaco Halo or beyond cannot account for the high incidence of maize pollen at Chaco settlements unless such transport involved the highly improbable movement of corn ears in the husk or tasseled corn plants. While it is possible that some corn plants were brought to the canyon from surrounding communities for special ceremonies—a practice that could account for some of the maize pollen deposited in some samples, perhaps especially at great houses—it cannot account for the overall abundance of maize pollen across the board, especially at small sites.

The high proportions of maize pollen at Chacoan sites imply significant local production of this domesticate similar to the high proportions at the La Plata site of LA50337. The occurrence of maize husks, stalks, and silks in samples from structure interiors at small and large Chacoan sites also strongly supports significant local production and harvesting. Perhaps the best indication of this, on account of preservation, comes from Pueblo Bonito, which yielded samples of husks, stalks, corn silk quids, and tassels. The Chaco Research Archive database (http://www.chacoarchive.org/cra) lists 22 incidences of husks, 5 of stalks, 2 of silk quids, and 1 of a corn tassel from Bonito; doubtless this is just a minor fraction of what was actually present (see Pepper 1920:37, 70, 96–97, 105, 107). The alternative that we find highly unlikely is one where legions of Puebloans weighed down by maize ears in the husk trudged across the clay flats of the San Juan Basin bringing in the staple to be distributed to small and great houses alike for the requisite husking and consequent scattering of maize pollen.

Although Chaco Canyon may have been marginal for growing corn, the pollen record implies that there was significant local production of maize, as much by the Alto data as by that from the small sites of 627 and 629. Vivan and Watson (this volume) argue that diverse agricultural strategies were employed by prehistoric occupants to take full advantage of the hydrological and physiographical diversity of the Chaco Core. The pollen record similarly indicates that we should not underestimate the productive potential of the canyon. This includes the central flood-plain as well as seldom considered areas such as argued by Wills and Dorshow (2012) and Vivian and Watson (this volume). In this regard, careful pollen sampling could reveal which portions of the canyon were actually farmed, perhaps coupled with the sampling of packrat (*Neotoma* sp.) middens both for pollen and macroremains (e.g., Hall 2010). The occurrence of maize remains in such contexts well away from habitations is hard to square with the maize importation model, but easily accounted for by local maize production in every suitable setting.

The abundance of maize pollen in mealing bins at Pueblo Alto strongly suggests the purposeful addition of pollen or anthers while grinding kernels to flour. This is further supported by the high incidence of maize pollen, especially broken grains, in human feces from both Salmon Ruins and Pueblo Bonito. Based on ethnographic homology this would have occurred in the preparation of ceremonial meal to be used for prayer making. Prayer meal from such a special place as Chaco Canyon and one of its illustrious great houses may have been in high demand within the region characterized by Chacoan outliers, providing one local commodity to help balance the economic and social debts of canyon residents. The practice of purposefully mixing in maize pollen or tassels during the preparation of meal can account for the high proportions of maize pollen at Chacoan sites, a behavior that was ritually salient while also being nutritionally beneficial.

Acknowledgments

We greatly appreciate the sharing of pollen data by Susan Smith, Glenna Dean, and Jan Gish. The careful pollen analyses of these individuals (including calculation of pollen concentration) and publication of data tables giving full counts ensures that results can be used to the greatest extent in making regional comparisons. Others kindly sharing data include Karen Adams and Andrew Duff. We greatly appreciate the helpful comments on drafts of this chapter by Susan Smith, Karl Reinhard, and two anonymous reviewers. Thanks also to Steve Plog for the invitation to participate in the Amerind Seminar.

References Cited

Aldrich, Samuel R., Walter O. Scott, and Robert G. Hoeft. 1986. *Modern Corn Production*. 3rd ed. A&L Publications, Champaign, Illinois.

Altschul, Jeffrey H. 1978. The Development of the Chacoan Interaction Sphere. *Journal of Anthropological Research* 34(1):109–146.

Aylor, Donald E. 2002. Settling Speed of Corn (*Zea mays*) Pollen. *Journal of Aerosol Science* 33:1601–1607.

Bannert, Michael, and Peter Stamp. 2007. Cross-Pollination of Maize at Long Distance. *European Journal of Agronomy* 27:44–51.

Bannert, Michael, André Vogler, and Peter Stamp. 2008. Short-Distance Cross-Pollination of Maize in a Small-Field Landscape as Monitored by Grain Color Markers. *European Journal of Agronomy* 29:29–32.

Barkley, Fred A. 1934. The Statistical Theory of Pollen Analysis. *Ecology* 15:283–289.

Benson, Larry. 2011a. Factors Controlling Pre-Columbian and Early Historic Maize Productivity in the American Southwest, Part 2: The Chaco Halo, Mesa Verde, Pajarito Plateau/Bandelier, and Zuni Archaeological Regions. *Journal of Archaeological Method and Theory* 18(1):61–109.

———. 2011b. Factors Controlling Pre-Columbian and Early Historic Maize Productivity in the American Southwest, Part 1: The Southern Colorado Plateau and Rio Grande Regions. *Journal of Archaeological Method and Theory* 18(1):1–60.

———. 2011c. Who Provided Maize to Chaco Canyon after the Mid-12th-Century Drought? *Journal of Archaeological Science* 37:621–629.

Benson, Larry, Michael S. Berry, Edward A. Jolie, et al. 2007. Possible Impacts of Early-11th, Middle-12th, and Late-13th-century Droughts on Western Native American and the Mississippian Cahokians. *Quaternary Science Reviews* 26(3–4):336–350.

Benson, Larry, L. Cordell, K. Vincent, H. Taylor, J. Stein, G. L. Farmer, and K. Futa. 2003. Ancient Maize from Chacoan Great Houses: Where Was It Grown? *Proceedings of the National Academy of Sciences* 100:13111–13115.

Benson, L. V., H. E. Taylor, K. A. Peterson, B. D. Shattuck, C. A. Ramotnik, and J. R. Stein. 2008. Development and Evaluation of Geochemical Methods for the Sourcing of Archaeological Maize. *Journal of Archaeological Science* 35:912–921.

Benson, L. V., J. R. Stein, and H. E. Taylor. 2009. Possible Sources of Archaeological Maize found in Chaco Canyon and Aztec Ruin, New Mexico. *Journal of Archaeological Science* 36:387–407.

Benson, Larry, John Stein, Howard Taylor, Richard Friedman, and Thomas C. Windes. 2006. The Agricultural Productivity of Chaco Canyon and the Source(s) of Pre-Hispanic Maize Found in Pueblo Bonito. In *Histories of Maize*, edited by John E. Staller, Robert H. Tykot, and Bruce F. Benz, pp. 289–314. Elsevier, New York.

Brugge, David M. 1986. *Tsegai: An Archeological Ethnohistory of the Chaco Region*. National Park Service, Washington, D.C.

Bryan, Kirk. 1954. The Geology of Chaco Canyon, New Mexico, in Relation to the Life and Remains of the Prehistoric People of Pueblo Bonito. Smithsonian Miscellaneous Collections Vol. 122. Smithsonian Institution Publication 4140. Smithsonian Institution, Washington, D.C.

Bryant, Vaughn M., and Glenna W. Dean. 2006. Archaeological Coprolite Science: The Legacy of Eric O. Callen (1912–1970). *Palaeogeography, Palaeoclimatology, Palaeoecology* 237(2006):51–66.

Clary, Karen H. 1984. Anasazi Diet and Subsistence as Revealed by Coprolites from Chaco Canyon. In *Recent Research on Chaco Prehistory*, edited by W. James Judge and John D. Schelberg, pp. 265–279. Reports of the Chaco Center No. 8. Division of Cultural Research, National Park Service, Albuquerque.

———. 1987. An Analysis of Pollen from Anasazi Period Mealing Bins from Room 110, Pueblo Alto (29SJ389), Chaco Canyon, New Mexico. Castetter Laboratory for Ethnobotanical Studies Technical Series Report No. 201. Contract PX7029–7–0391. Manuscript. on file, NPS Chaco Culture NHP Museum Archive, University of New Mexico, Albuquerque.

———. 1993. Pollen Analysis of LA 50337, The La Plata River, Northeastern New Mexico. In *The Excavation of a Multicomponent Anasazi Site (LA 50337) in the La Plata River Valley, Northeastern New Mexico*, edited by Bradley J. Vierra, pp. 281–321. Archaeological Notes 19. Museum of New Mexico Office of Archaeological Studies, Santa Fe.

Cordell, Linda S. 1979. Prehistory: Eastern Anasazi. In *Southwest*, edited by Alfonso Ortiz, pp. 131–151. Handbook of North American Indians, Vol. 9, William C. Sturtevant, general editor. Smithsonian Institution, Washington, D.C.

Cordell, Linda S., Stephen R. Durand, Ronald C. Antweiler, and Howard E. Taylor. 2001. Toward Linking Maize Chemistry to Archaeological Agricultural Sites in the North American Southwest. *Journal of Archaeological Science* 28:501–513.

Cordell, Linda S., and Fred Plog. 1979. Escaping the Confines of Normative Thought: A Reevaluation of Puebloan Prehistory. *American Antiquity* 44:405–429.

Cordell, Linda S., H. Wolcott Toll, Mollie S. Toll, Thomas C. Windes. 2008. Archaeological Corn from Pueblo Bonito, Chaco Canyon, New Mexico: Dates, Contexts, Sources. *American Antiquity* 73:491–511.

Cully, Anne C. 1982. Pollen Analysis from Sites on Block VIII–IX, Navajo Indian Irrigation Project, San Juan County, New Mexico. Castetter Laboratory for Ethnobotanical Studies Technical Series No. 61. Department of Biology, University of New Mexico, Albuquerque.

———. 1984. The Distribution of Corn Pollen at Three Sites in Chaco Canyon. In *Recent Research on Chaco Prehistory*, edited by W. James Judge and John D. Schelberg, pp. 251–264. Reports of the Chaco Center No. 8. Division of Cultural Research, National Park Service, Albuquerque.

———. 1985. Pollen Evidence of Past Subsistence and Environment at Chaco Canyon, New Mexico. In *Environment and Subsistence of Chaco Canyon, New Mexico*, edited by Frances J. Mathien, pp. 135–245. Publications in Archaeology 18E, Chaco Canyon Studies. National Park Service, U.S. Department of the Interior, Santa Fe.

———. 1988. Appendix I. Five Pollen Samples from Kin Nahasbas. In *Kin Nahasbas Ruin, Chaco Culture National Park, New Mexico*, edited by Francis J. Mathien and Thomas C. Windes, pp. 289–293. National Park Service, Branch of Cultural Research, Santa Fe.

Cushing, Frank Hamilton. 1920. *Zuni Breadstuff.* Indian Notes and Monographs Vol. VIII. Museum of the American Indian, Heye Foundation, New York.

Dean, Glenna. 1995. In Search of the Rare: Pollen Evidence of Prehistoric Agriculture. In *Soil, Water, Biology, and Belief in Prehistoric and Traditional Southwestern Agriculture*, edited by H. Wolcott Toll, pp. 353–359. New Mexico Archaeological Council Special Publication 2. New Mexico Archaeological Council, Albuquerque.

———. 1999. Pollen Evidence of Human Activities in the Southern Chuska Mountains. In *Chuska Chronologies, Houses, and Hogans: Archaeological and Ethnographic Inquiry along the N30–N31 between Mexican Springs and Navajo, McKinley County, New Mexico*, by Jonathan E. Damp, pp. 493–601. Zuni Cultural Resources Enterprise Research Series No. 10. Pueblo of Zuni, Zuni, NM.

———. 2006. The Science of Coprolite Analysis: The View from Hinds Cave. *Palaeogeography, Palaeoclimatology, Palaeoecology* 237:67–79.

Dimbleby, Geoffrey W. 1985. *The Palynology of Archaeological Sites*. Academic Press, Orlando.

Fewkes, Jesse W. 1900. Property-Right in Eagles among the Hopi. *American Anthropologist* 2:690–707.

Force, Eric, R. Gwinn Vivian, Thomas C. Windes, and Jeffrey S. Dean. 2002. *Relation of "Bonito" Paleo-channels and Base-Level Variations to Anasazi Occupation, Chaco Canyon, New Mexico*. Arizona State Museum Archaeological Series No. 194. Arizona State Museum, University of Arizona, Tucson.

Geib, Phil R., and Susan J. Smith. 2008. Palynology and Archaeological Inference: Bridging the Gap between Pollen Washes and Past Behavior. *Journal of Archaeological Science* 35:2085–2101.

Gish, Jannifer W. 1994a. Appendix H. Palynology. In *Across the Colorado Plateau: Anthropological Studies for the Transwestern Pipeline Extension Project*.

Volume IX—Appendices, edited by Ronna J. Bradley and Richard B. Sullivan, pp. H-1–H-31. Office of Contract Archaeology and Maxwell Museum of Anthropology, Albuquerque.

———. 1994b. Appendix D. Pollen Methodology. In *Across the Colorado Plateau: Anthropological Studies for the Transwestern Pipeline Extension Project. Volume X—Appendices*, edited by Richard B. Sullivan, pp. D-1–D-39. Office of Contract Archaeology and Maxwell Museum of Anthropology, Albuquerque.

Goldfrank, Esther S. 1927. *The Social and Ceremonial Organization of Cochiti.* Memoirs of the American Anthropological Association No. 22. American Anthropological Association, Menasha, Wisconsin.

Hall, Stephen H. 2010. Early Maize Pollen from Chaco Canyon, New Mexico, USA. *Palynology* 34:125–137.

Hough, Walter. 1918. The Hopi Indian Collection in the United States National Museum. *Proceedings of the United States National Museum* 54(2235):235–296.

Huntington, Ellsworth J. 1914. *The Climatic Factor as Illustrated in Arid America.* Carnegie Institute of Washington Publication No. 192, pp. 75–82. Carnegie Institute, Washington, D.C.

Jarosz, Nathalie, Benjamin Loubet, Brigitte Durand, Xavier Foueillassar, and Laurent Huber. 2005. Variations in Maize Pollen Emission and Deposition in Relation to Microclimate. *Environmental Science & Technology* 39:4377–4384.

Judd, Neil M. 1954. *The Material Culture of Pueblo Bonito.* Smithsonian Miscellaneous Collections Vol. 124. Smithsonian Institution, Washington, D.C.

Judge, W. James. 1979. The Development of a Complex Cultural Ecosystem in the Chaco Basin, New Mexico. In *Proceedings of the First Conference on Scientific Research in the National Parks*, Vol. II, edited by Robert M. Linn, pp. 901–906. National Park Service Transactions and Proceedings Series No. 5. U.S. Government Printing Office, Washington, D.C.

———. 1989. Chaco Canyon–San Juan Basin. In *Dynamics of Southwest Prehistory*, edited by Linda S. Cordell and George J. Gumerman, pp. 209–261. Smithsonian Institution, Washington, D.C.

Khanduri, Vinod P., and Chandra M. Sharma. 2002. Pollen Productivity Variations. Pollen-Ovule Ratio and Sexual Selection in *Pinus roxburghii. Grana* 41:29–38.

Lyons, Thomas R., and Robert K. Hitchcock. 1977. Remote Sensing Interpretation of an Anasazi Land Route System. In *Aerial Remote Sensing Techniques in Archaeology*, edited by Thomas R. Lyons and Robert K. Hitchcock, pp. 111–134. Reports of the Chaco Center No. 2. University of New Mexico and National Park Service, Albuquerque.

Maher, Louis J. 1981. Statistics for Microfossil Concentration Measurements Employing Samples Spiked with Marker Grains. *Review of Palaeobotany and Palynology* 32:153–191.

Martin, Paul S., and William Byers. 1965. Pollen and Archaeology at Wetherill Mesa. In *Contributions of the Wetherill Mesa Archaeological Project*, assembled by H. Douglas Osborne, pp. 122–135. Memoirs of the Society of American Archaeology No. 19. Society of American Archaeology, Salt Lake City.

Miller, Paul D. 1982. Maize Pollen: Collection and Enzymology. In *Maize for Biological Research*, edited by William F. Sheridan, pp. 279–282. A Special Publication of the Plant Molecular Biology Association. Charlottesville, VA.

Parsons, Elsie Clews. 1932. Isleta, New Mexico. Bureau of American Ethnology, 47th Annual Report. Smithsonian Institution, Washington, D.C.

———. 1939. *Pueblo Indian Religion*. 2 vols. University of Chicago Press, Chicago.

Pepper, George H. 1920. *Pueblo Bonito*. Anthropological Papers of the American Museum of Natural History Vol. 27. American Museum Press, New York.

Pleasants, John M., Richard L. Hellmich, Galen P. Dively, Mark K. Sears, Diane E. Stanley-Horn, Heather R. Mattila, John E. Foster, Peter Clark, and Gretchen D. Jones. 2001. Corn Pollen Deposition on Milkweeds in and near Cornfields. *Proceedings of the National Academy of Sciences* 98:11919–11924.

Poehlman, John Milton, and David Allen Sleper. 1995. *Breeding Field Crops*, Vol. XV. Iowa State University Press, Ames.

Reed, Paul F. (editor). 2006. Thirty-Five Years of Archaeological Research at Salmon Ruins, New Mexico, Vol. 3, *Archaeobotanical Research and Other Analytical Studies*. Center for Desert Archaeology, Tucson; Salmon Ruins Museum, Bloomfield, New Mexico.

Reinhard, Karl J., Sherrian K. Edwards, Teyona Daymon, and Debra K. Meier. 2006a. Pollen Concentration Analysis of Salmon Ruin and Antelope House: Documenting Anasazi Dietary Variation. *Journal of Palaeogeography, Palaeoclimatology, and Palaeoecology* 237:92–109.

Reinhard, Karl J., Sara LeRoy-Toren, and Dennis R. Danielson. 2006b. Salmon Ruin Coprolites: San Juan Diet. In *Thirty-Five Years of Archaeological Research at Salmon Ruins*, Vol. 3, edited by Paul F. Reed, pp. 875–888. Center for Desert Archaeology, Tucson; Salmon Ruins Museum, Bloomfield, New Mexico.

Robbins, Wilfred W., John P. Harrington, and Barbara Freire-Marreco. 1916. *Ethnobotany of the Tewa Indians*. Bureau of American Ethnology Bulletin 34. Smithsonian Institution, Washington, D.C.

Ruhl, Donna L. 1986. Extraction and Thermal Alteration of Pollen Embedded in Clay. Ceramic Notes No. 3, edited by Prudence M. Rice, pp. 118–124. Ceramic Technology Laboratory, Florida State Museum, Gainesville.

Rull, Valentí. 1987. A Note on Pollen Counting in Palaeoecology. *Pollen et Spores* 29:471–480.

Schelberg, John D. 1981. *Analogy, Social Complexity, and Regionally Based Perspectives*. Paper presented at the 46th Annual Meeting of the Society for American Archaeology, San Diego.

————. 1982. Economic and Social Development as an Adaptation to a Marginal Environment in Chaco Canyon, New Mexico. Ph.D. dissertation, Department of Anthropology, Northwestern University, Evanston, Illinois.

Sebastian, Lynne. 1983. Regional Interaction: The Puebloan Adaptation. In *Economy and Interaction along the Lower Chaco River: The Navajo Mine Archaeology Program*, edited by Patrick F. Hogan and Joseph C. Winter, pp. 445–452. Office of Contract Archeology and Maxwell Museum of Anthropology, University of New Mexico, Albuquerque.

————. 1991. Sociopolitical Complexity and the Chaco System. In *Chaco and Hohokam. Prehistoric Regional Systems in the American Southwest*, edited by Patricia L. Crown and W. James Judge, pp. 109–134. School of American Research Press, Santa Fe.

————. 1992. The Chaco Anasazi. *Sociopolitical Evolution in the Prehistoric Southwest*. Cambridge University Press, Cambridge.

Simms, Steven R. 1985. Acquisition Cost and Nutritional Data on Great Basin Resources. *Journal of California and Great Basin Anthropology* 7:117–126.

Smith, Susan J. 1999. Pollen Analysis. In *Anasazi Community Development in the Cave-Redrock Valley Archaeological Excavations along the N33 Road in Apache County, Arizona*, edited by Paul E. Reed and Kathy Niles Hensler, pp. 851–869. Navajo Nation Papers in Anthropology No. 33. Navajo Nation Archaeology Department, Window Rock, Arizona.

Smith, Susan J., Meredith H. Matthews, Kathy Niles Hensler, and LeeAnna Schniebs. 1999. Analysis of Subsistence: Pollen, Macrobotanical, and Faunal Remains. In *A Pueblo I Household on the Chuska Slope: Data Recovery at NM-H-47-102, along Navajo Route 5010(1) near Toadlena, New Mexico*, edited by Kathy N. Hensler, Paul F. Reed, Scott Wilcox, Joell Goff, and John A. Torres, pp. 39–49. Navajo Nation Papers in Anthropology No. 35. Navajo Nation Archaeology Department, Window Rock, Arizona.

Stephen, Alexander. 1969 [1936]. *Hopi Journal of Alexander M. Stephen*, edited by Elsie Clews Parsons. 2 vols. Columbia University Press, New York.

Stirling, Matthew. 1942. *Origin Myth of Acoma and Other Records*. Bulletin No. 135, Bureau of American Ethnology. Smithsonian Institution, Washington, D.C.

Stockmarr, J. 1971. Tablets with Spores Used in Absolute Pollen Analysis. *Pollen et Spores* 13:615–621.

Toll, H. Wolcott III, Mollie S. Toll, Marcia L. Newren, and William B. Gillespie. 1985. Experimental Corn Plots in Chaco Canyon. The Life and Hard Times of *Zea Mays* L. In *Environment and Subsistence of Chaco Canyon, New Mexico*, edited by Frances Joan Mathien, pp. 79–133. Publications in Archeology 18E, Chaco Canyon Studies. National Park Service, U.S. Department of the Interior, Santa Fe.

Vivian, R. Gwinn. 1984. Agricultural and Social Adjustments to Changing Environment in the Chaco Basin. In *Prehistoric Agricultural Strategies in the*

Southwest, edited by Suzanne K. Fish and Paul R. Fish, pp. 242–257. Anthropological Research Papers No. 33. Arizona State University, Tempe.

———. 1990. *The Chacoan Prehistory of the San Juan Basin*. Academic Press, San Diego.

White, Leslie. 1935. *The Pueblo of Santo Domingo*. Memoirs of the American Anthropological Association No. 43. American Anthropological Association, Menasha, Wisconsin.

Williams-Dean, G. 1986. Pollen analysis of human coprolites. In *Archeological Investigations at Antelope House*, edited by Don P. Morris, pp. 189–205. National Park Service Publications in Archaeology, vol. 19. National Printing Office, Washington, D.C.

Williams-Dean, Glenna, and Vaughn M. Bryant Jr. 1975. Pollen Analysis of Human Coprolites from Antelope House. *Kiva* 41:97–111.

Wills, W. H., and Wetherbee B. Dorshow. 2012. Agriculture and Community in Chaco Canyon: Revisiting Pueblo Alto. *Journal of Anthropological Archaeology* 31(2):138–155.

4

A Perishable Perspective on Chacoan Social Identities

Edward A. Jolie and Laurie D. Webster

Although Chaco Canyon is frequently described by archaeologists today as a multiethnic or culturally diverse community (e.g., Cordell and Judge 2001; Lekson 2006), few studies have attempted to characterize the identities or affinities of the people who resided in Chaco Canyon or participated in its social and ritual life. Previous research has yielded evidence suggesting the existence of multiple socially, culturally, or biologically distinct groups, both at Pueblo Bonito and within the canyon (Akins 1986; Judd 1954; Kluckhohn 1939; Schillaci 2003; Vivian 1990; Wills 2009), and these data provide an important starting point for investigating questions about social identity, sociocultural diversity, and the roles that these phenomena may have played in the developments for which Bonito phase Chaco Canyon is famous. Yet, in contrast to the voluminous literature on durable products such as architecture, ceramics, and lithics, perishables have been largely ignored in past research on Chacoan society because of preservation bias. Until we began our studies of the Chaco perishables in 2006, virtually no research had been conducted on these collections, despite their potential to contribute new data for evaluating different models about Chacoan society and the Chaco regional system.

In this chapter, we use the technological and design style of perishable artifacts to explore questions related to Chaco Canyon as a multiethnic community, Chacoan social identity, and Chaco's relationships with outlying areas. Because perishable data are unevenly distributed across the archaeological landscape, some of these questions are more amenable to study than others. Diverse assemblages of perishable artifacts were recovered from the massive, multistoried great houses of Pueblo Bonito, Pueblo del Arroyo, and Chetro Ketl, especially the first site, but only meager, poorly preserved collections survived at other

canyon sites. Small house specimens, for example, are mostly carbonized and very friable (e.g., Bc 51, Bc 59; see also Tschopik 1939), whereas
the Chetro Ketl collections are small and poorly documented, limiting
their value for analysis. Most perishables appear to date to the Bonito
phase, with small quantities of McElmo and Mesa Verde phase material deriving from Kin Kletso, Bc 288 (Gallo Cliff Dwelling), and a few
other sites.

Exploring Chacoan Social Identities

Individuals embody multiple identities informed by sociocultural and
biological realities that include, but are not limited to, age, gender, kin
group, settlement history, ancestry, language, class, religion, race, and ethnicity. That such identity markers can and often do crosscut and inform
wider social and cultural identities underscores just how fluid larger group
identities are, as well as the degree to which identities shift or change in
response to different circumstances (e.g., Jenkins 2008; Jones 1997). Conceptually, "social identity" refers to the ways in which people define and
organize themselves as individuals and as members of social groups. This
term overlaps considerably in popular usage and meaning with "cultural
identity," but cultural identity is usually invoked in reference to identity
formations associated with social groups above the community level and
is often treated by archaeologists as synonymous with ethnic or "tribal"
identity (Bernardini 2005; Cameron 2005). By comparison, social identity tends to emphasize identity formations operating at smaller social and
spatial scales that imply a narrower set of social categories and identity
groups. One advantage to investigating social identity as conceived in
this way is that it appreciates the actions of multiple independent smaller
social groups in creating and maintaining regional patterns of social interaction and identities, while requiring attentiveness to spatial as well as
temporal scales. This perspective also incorporates recent research that
reminds us of the dynamic, multidirectional nature of mobility in the
Southwest and the observation that prehispanic groups were constantly
or regularly in movement and had few boundary constraints (e.g., Bernardini 2005; Lekson 1995; Ortman and Cameron 2011).

From this position, we prefer to focus our attention on "social identity" as opposed to "ethnicity" because, in broader anthropological

usage, the latter denotes real or perceived group membership within the context of contemporary nation-states. In our view, ethnicity is an inappropriate term to use in reference to any form of social identity in the prehispanic Southwest, and the notion of Chaco as a multiethnic community is misleading. It is more profitable to think of Chaco as a potentially socioculturally diverse or heterogeneous community resulting from the aggregation of multiple groups of people of different ethno-linguistic, culture-historical, or enculturative backgrounds, a consequence of which may be multiple social identities operating at different scales (Jolie 2015).

Because sociocultural diversity is not an easily quantified variable, it must be examined archaeologically at multiple scales from the perspective of indirect evidence. One way to infer and characterize social diversity is to look for evidence of behaviors and institutions that contribute to it, such as migration, social interaction, and small-scale sociopolitical formations, including the descent groups (households, clans, moieties) and sodalities that prevail among historic Southwestern societies. In this way, we may begin to understand social diversity not simply as a demographic state, which tells us little about interaction and identities, but also as a social condition that invites examination of attendant social processes, including cooperation, conflict, assimilation, hybridity, and so on, that result from the convergence of multiple social groups and identities.

If social diversity existed within Chaco Canyon, recent literature on craft learning and transmission indicates that it should be reflected at some scale in multiple learning networks that are the product of social interaction and enculturation reflected in the technological choices made by individuals during artifact production (Crown 2007; Lave and Wenger 1991; Lyons and Clark 2008; Minar and Crown 2001; Stark et al. 2008; Whiting and Edwards 1988). Although there is no reason to presume that identifiable patterns in perishable artifact style correlate with discrete social identity groups, such propositions can be evaluated with reference to independent lines of evidence, such as ceramics and architecture, and reference to ethnographic analogy.

To explore this and related questions, in the first part of this chapter we draw on the analyses of technological stylistic patterning in more than 1,200 coiled baskets, plaited mats, and fine plaited sandals from

Pueblo Bonito, other sites in Chaco Canyon, and beyond (Jolie 2015) to examine whether clusters of technological features can be identified that might reflect weavers related through the processes of learning and teaching these crafts and to provide insight into geographic affinities and social identities. Coiled baskets, plaited matting, and fine twill plaited sandals are three classes of woven artifacts found in and beyond Chaco that are well suited to exploring social identity in this way because even very tiny fragments embody multiple production decisions that inform on stylistic variation. They are also intersecting technologies (Hagstrum 2001) that require similar technological knowledge, resources, and labor, although the production of each is organized differently. For example, in contrast to coiled baskets, which ethnographies and cross-cultural data suggest are more likely to be traded within and between villages or given as gifts (e.g., Ford 1972; Tanner 1983; Teiwes 1996), mats and footwear are typically produced at the scale of individual households (Driver and Massey 1957; Ortiz 1979). Generally, if mats or sandals "travel" at all, they are likely to only move as far from home as their maker or wearer does.

At Chaco, we know that, minimally, coiled baskets and plaited sandals were locally produced because we have unfinished examples (Jolie 2015; see also Watson, this volume). Examining stylistic variability across these three woven artifact classes helps mitigate the effects that imported items may have on our ability to identify patterns that reflect social diversity at the scale of individual sites, particularly when non-ritual products, which are considered especially informative for inferring demographic connections and social ties (Lyons and Clark 2008), are included.

In the second part of this chapter, we consider two groups of perishable artifacts that we propose communicate symbolic or emblematic style and that may have been used to reproduce and reinforce group identity within Chaco Canyon and across the regional system (Connerton 1989; Mills 2004, 2008, this volume; Mills and Walker 2008; Van Dyke and Alcock 2003). They are (1) artifacts that convey a shared Basketmaker ancestry, and (2) artifacts that embody southern technologies and suggest connections with Mesoamerican worldviews. Insights derived from these data complement the finer-scale stylistic analyses of baskets, mats, and sandals, and contribute to an understanding of Chacoan social identities in a regional context.

Basket, Mat, and Sandal Evidence for Social Diversity within Chaco Canyon

Oral traditions and historic and ethnographic accounts imply that the ancestors of today's diverse Pueblo communities were, like many societies, neither linguistically, biologically, nor culturally homogeneous (e.g., Bernardini 2005; Dozier 1954, 1966; Ortiz 1979; Parsons 1925, 1928, 1932). Within Chaco Canyon and across the regional system, social diversity has been suggested based on studies of architectural variability (Meyer 1999; Van Dyke 1999, 2003), while differences in settlement patterning as well as the dichotomy between great houses and small houses have been argued to reflect canyon-level diversity (Bustard 1996, 2003; Judge and Cordell 2006; Lekson et al. 2006; Whiteley, this volume). Building on earlier proposals by Kluckhohn (1939) and Vivian and Mathews (1965), Vivian (1970, 1990) argues that the site-size dichotomy within the canyon resulted from two distinctive social organizational structures, corresponding to two cultural groups that developed along unique culture-historical trajectories on opposite sides of Chaco Canyon. Most recently, Wills (2009) has argued convincingly that architecture, ceramic styles, and refuse disposal patterns, among other evidence, support cultural discontinuity within the canyon between about A.D. 1100 and 1150 that can be linked to the development of McElmo-style architecture and ceramics.

Bioarchaeological and mortuary data complement these studies, suggesting the presence of multiple biologically distinct groups within the canyon and raising the possibility that at least two biologically distinct groups occupied Pueblo Bonito simultaneously, represented by the north and west burial clusters (Akins 1986, 2003; Heitman and Plog 2005; Schillaci 2003; Schillaci and Stojanowski 2003; see also Snow and LeBlanc, this volume). Such studies further suggest that each burial cluster exhibits sufficient internal cohesiveness to imply genetic relatedness among the individuals from a given burial group, possibly reflecting "family burial facilities" (Akins 2003).

While poor preservation, contextual information, and chronological control make it difficult to evaluate the specific findings of prior studies, the results of technological stylistic analyses of coiled baskets, plaited mats, and fine plaited sandals suggest patterns that complement previous research. Some of the salient findings of these analyses are summarized below, but the interested reader is referred to Jolie (2015) for more details and discussion.

Pueblo Bonito

The largest assemblage of coiled baskets, plaited mats, and fine twill plaited sandals from Chaco Canyon derives from Pueblo Bonito (n=207) and is more than four times larger than the next biggest collection of the same from Chetro Ketl (n=48). Ceramic and dendrochronological cross-dating allow many individual artifacts to be ascribed to either the Early to Classic (A.D. 850–1110), or the Classic to Late (A.D. 1040–1140) Bonito periods, but the uneven distribution of the sample between rooms and, to a degree, across the site, makes spatial analysis more complicated. To explore spatial patterning in stylistic features, Jolie (2015) arbitrarily quartered Pueblo Bonito's architectural plan using the north-south trending central plaza room block as one dividing line and an invisible line extending from the northern wall of Room 148 in the central plaza as an east-west dividing line. Conveniently, if admittedly coarse grained, these divisions correspond reasonably well to the architectural growth of the pueblo during the Bonito phase reconstructed by Windes (2003; see also Lekson 1986) and facilitate linking stylistic patterns in space to chronological trends in the site's use and expansion. Initial construction of the northwestern and northeastern rooms generally dates between about A.D. 860 and the early 1000s, whereas the rooms in the southeast and southwest were primarily added after A.D. 1040. Evidence for the renovation and re-use of rooms was taken into account when assigning likely date ranges to individual specimens.

In general terms, the primary structural attributes of Pueblo Bonito coiled basketry (e.g., foundation type and arrangement, stitch type, starting and finishing methods) are consistent with observed trends in prehispanic Pueblo production standards throughout the northern Southwest (e.g., Morris and Burgh 1941). As at most prehispanic Pueblo sites, two rod and bundle coiling sewn with non-interlocking stitches is the dominant structural type, followed by one rod foundation coiling with interlocking stitches as a distant second. However, of the seven total structural techniques documented at Pueblo Bonito, four are known from western burial cluster rooms 320A and 326. That the two most abundant of the unique vessel forms (cylinder baskets and

elliptical trays) in the western burial cluster were made by three different coiling techniques suggests that weavers from overlapping but distinctive craft learning networks contributed these items to the rooms,
either as mortuary furniture, periodic offerings to commemorate venerated ancestors, or some combination thereof.

Variation in coiled basket wall fineness or texture, a product of stitch
and coil width and density, is also apparent within Pueblo Bonito. On
average, baskets from mortuary contexts are finer than non-mortuary
specimens, but insufficient data exist to evaluate differences between
Pueblo Bonito's burial clusters. To varying degrees, textural differences
correspond to the arbitrary spatial subdivisions that map generally onto
the site's architectural growth over time (Figure 4.1). More specifically,
stitch and coil data suggest basket wall textural differences between vessels
from rooms in the northwest and northeast. They also indicate that baskets deriving from the southeastern portion of the pueblo sort differently
from northern specimens, which are more similar to each other. Among
northern rooms, the apparent east vs. west difference hinges on wall texture, with northeastern wares coarser on average than northwestern wares.

Demonstrable contrast between Classic through Late Bonito subphase (A.D. 1040–1140) coiling from the southeastern rooms at Pueblo
Bonito, and coiling from Early to Classic Bonito subphase (A.D. 850–
1110) contexts from northern rooms, is of a different kind. Coiled baskets from the northern rooms, which include the earliest rooms built
during the mid- to late ninth century A.D., show a positive relationship
between stitch and coil density, whereas specimens from southeastern
rooms indicate a trend toward greater stitch density at the expense of
fatter coils, and thus lower coil density. Chronology is clearly a factor
here, but it is initially unclear whether the difference is attributable to a
progressive shift over time in basketweavers' preferences for wall texture
appearance or a later influx of coiled wares produced by weavers belonging to a different learning network, one that prioritized consistency in
stitch density over coil density.

Given the small sample (n=12) of coiled baskets more securely assign-
able to Classic to Late Bonito subphase contexts, and what is known
about the conservative nature of coiled basketry production and findings
from studies that consider basketry technological change over time (e.g.,
Adovasio 1986; Adovasio and Gunn 1986; Adovasio and Pedler 1994;
Polanich 1994; Thulman 2013), it is highly unlikely that this observed

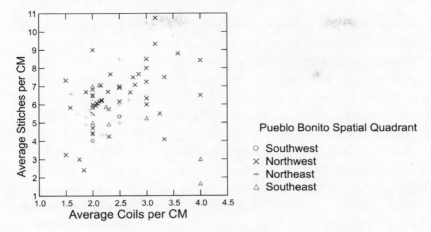

Figure 4.1a. Scatter plot of Pueblo Bonito coiled basketry stitches and coils per centimeter by arbitrary spatial quadrant.

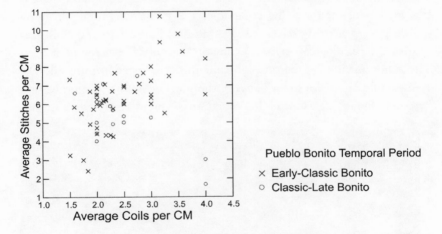

Figure 4.1b. Scatter plot of Pueblo Bonito coiled basketry stitches and coils per centimeter by temporal period.

shift in the relationship between stitch and coil density occurred randomly within a span of roughly 100 years, when the preceding two or more centuries demonstrate relative consistency in the same attributes. The most parsimonious explanation is the introduction of coiled wares woven by individuals who belonged to an overlapping but historically distinct learning network that conveyed different ideas about "appropriate" stitch and coil density as they relate to wall texture.

The A.D. 1040s to 1070s construction dates for the majority of the rooms in Pueblo Bonito's southeast quadrant (Lekson 1986; Windes 2003) provide a terminus *post quem* for this potential demographic development, and they are consistent with arguments for an influx of non-local people(s) around or after about A.D. 1100 (Wills 2009). Furthermore, such a demographic development perceived from the perspective of coiled basketry is also potentially correlated with the post–A.D. 1085 construction of the north-south–oriented wall that bisects Pueblo Bonito to create two plazas and separates two great kivas (Judd 1964:198, 207; Lekson 1986:141–42). This and other synchronous architectural changes have been cited as evidence of an emergent dualism linked to the development of moieties at Pueblo Bonito (Fritz 1978; Heitman, this volume; Heitman and Plog 2005; Vivian 1970, 1990; see also Whiteley, this volume).

Analyses of Pueblo Bonito's twill plaited mats and sandals generally complement the foregoing observations. Data on structurally intricate twill plaited matting selvages (edge finishes) indicate the possibility of greater technological stylistic variation in southeastern rooms relative to other portions of the pueblo, while intricate selvage widths and element folding angles differ between the northwestern and southeastern rooms (Figure 4.2). Chronological control is poor, but the data suggest

Figure 4.2. Fragment of a 2/2 twill plaited mat with intricate selvage from Room 3a at Pueblo Bonito, catalog number H/8932. (Courtesy of the Division of Anthropology, American Museum of Natural History)

that intricate selvages became wider and structurally more complex during Classic and Late Bonito times. Given the unlikelihood that these modifications enhanced mat structural integrity appreciably, this may indicate that wider and more complex mat edge finishes reflected and signaled greater time investment and increased symbolic significance. Variation in mat strip width and fabric density reveals no clear spatio-temporal patterns, but this may be a product of natural constraints on the dimensions of the rush (*Schoenoplectus* sp.) culms used in matting.

Other Sites in Chaco Canyon

Unsurprisingly, given the adjacency of these sites, Pueblo Bonito and Chetro Ketl's coiled baskets appear most similar to each other in terms of weave texture (Figure 4.3). The possibility exists for greater affinity between Chetro Ketl's coiled wares and those from Pueblo Bonito's northern rooms, which date principally to Early and Classic Bonito subphase times. If this stylistic similarity reflects overlapping learning networks, as seems plausible, then it may indicate that some fraction of the individuals responsible for Chetro Ketl's coiled basketry shared stronger ties to, and interacted more directly with, the occupants of Pueblo Bonito responsible for the wares from the northern rooms during the tenth through mid-eleventh century A.D. If this was the case, then Chetro Ketl's coiled baskets, assumed to date between about A.D. 1040 and 1140 (Lekson 1986), bear little similarity to Pueblo Bonito's stylistically distinctive wares from the southeastern rooms, which may be linked to newcomers arriving sometime after A.D. 1040/1070, based on construction dates assigned to those room blocks.

Whereas coiled basketry reveals little about small house and great house sociocultural and temporal differences, comparative data on twill plaited matting and sandals afford some preliminary insights. In Chaco Canyon, as across the northern Southwest, 2/2 interval (over two, under two) plaited matting is overwhelmingly preferred. However, the samples of small house matting from Bonito phase Bc 51 and Mesa Verde phase Bc 288 are primarily 3/3 interval, indicating the possibility of differences between the other two small houses that produced primarily 2/2 twill plaited matting and the Pueblo Bonito and Chetro Ketl great houses.

Intricate selvages on mats from Bc 288 appear to be wider on average than examples from other canyon sites, and they also evidence two

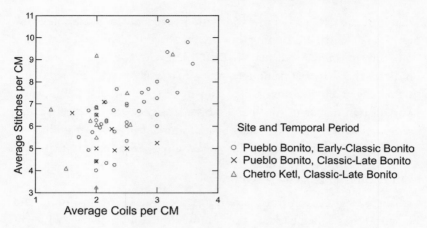

Figure 4.3. Scatter plot of stitch and coil-density data for two rod and bundle bunched foundation, non-interlocking-stitch coiled baskets from Pueblo Bonito and Chetro Ketl by temporal period.

unique intricate selvage variants. Combined with an atypical 1/1 plaited mat with a unique selvage variant of Late Bonito or McElmo age from Tsin Kletsin, and the unusual 3/3 twill construction of one sandal from Bc 288, available twelfth-century A.D. data, though limited, suggest a stylistic departure from earlier Bonito phase products consistent with more marked craft learning network differences. These data may be taken as additional support for proposals of an A.D. 1100s demographic discontinuity (Wills 2009).

Beyond Chaco

Significant and broadly contemporaneous comparative samples of perishable artifacts from the northern Southwest are limited to the well-preserved data from Aztec West Ruin (Morris 1919, 1924, 1928), a Chacoan outlier located some 80 km north of Chaco, Antelope House in Canyon del Muerto, Arizona (Adovasio and Gunn 1986), and thirteenth-century sites in the Mesa Verde region of southwest Colorado (Osborne 2004). Although Salmon Ruins yielded a small assemblage, this material is largely carbonized and very poorly preserved (Webster 2006).

Similarities across the northern Southwest in the primary structural techniques employed in coiled basketry, plaited matting, and fine twill plaited sandals indicate a deep shared history for these technologies.

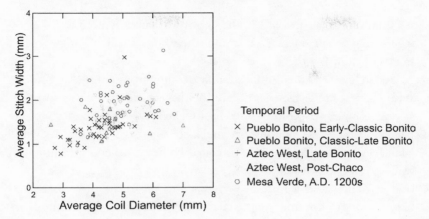

Figure 4.4. Scatter plot of coiled basket stitch and coil dimensions from Pueblo Bonito, Aztec Ruin West, and sites in the Mesa Verde region. Only two rod and bundle bunched foundation, non-interlocking stitch, and three rod bunched foundation, non-interlocking stitch specimens are plotted.

Putting aside the suite of unique coiled vessel forms associated specifically with Chaco Canyon that are discussed below, Chaco Canyon coiled baskets are on average finer than those from the other regions sampled (Figure 4.4). Middle San Juan vessels from Aztec and Salmon Ruins overlap with the range of variation observed in Chaco Canyon material, but they tend to be intermediate between Chaco and Mesa Verde in terms of wall texture or fineness. Although Chaco Canyon sandals are finer relative to other sites, plaited mats and fine twill plaited sandals are generally quite similar, and this may reflect both the constraints imposed on the product by the plaiting technique and the raw materials used.

Comparison of stylistic data from Pueblo Bonito, Aztec West, and Antelope House, and the Mesa Verde region makes clear the distinctiveness of thirteenth-century Mesa Verde products relative to the other regions sampled. Products from the Mesa Verde region dating to the A.D. 1200s differ principally from the other assemblages in the following ways: (1) coiled baskets exhibit coarser wall textures and a different decorative style; (2) plaited matting was only a minor product woven in significantly smaller quantities relative to other regions; and (3) Mesa Verde sandals show a strong preference for broadleaf yucca as a raw

material source, as opposed to the narrowleaf yucca typically used elsewhere, and they evidence a distinctive method of splicing in new elements by knotting them on the soles of the sandals.

Securely dated Late Bonito subphase coiling from Aztec (A.D. 1100–
1130) bears some stylistic similarity to Chaco Canyon coiling, but the
sample is small. By comparison, post-Chaco (A.D. 1130–1290) woven
perishables at Aztec demonstrate much stronger stylistic affinities with
Mesa Verde products in terms of coiled basketry structural technique,
wall texture, and decorative style, as well as matting selvage construction attributes and a shift in preference to broadleaf yucca as a raw
material source for sandals. The character of these post-Chaco similarities between Aztec and Mesa Verde is not of a magnitude to substantiate
the movement of people south to Aztec from Mesa Verde, but rather a
shift toward greater intensity of interaction between Aztec's occupants
and populations to the north.

Perishable Objects That Expressed a Shared Basketmaker Identity

If Chacoan society was composed of different social and/or biological
groups, as accumulating evidence suggests, what mechanisms were used
to integrate these groups and promote cooperation? One way of integrating diverse groups and consolidating social identities is through a
shared ideology that uses "social memories of an imagined, shared past to
construct common identities among peoples of different backgrounds"
(Van Dyke 2007:128). In our view, the shared or imagined ancestral tradition most often evoked at Chaco was a Basketmaker tradition, made
manifest in the perpetuation and ritualization of Basketmaker forms
(see also Webster et al. 2014). Many aspects of the Chacoan worldview
were already in place by Basketmaker III, and memories of this past figured prominently in the construction of Chacoan ideology (Van Dyke
2007:63, 70; see also Mills, this volume; Vivian and Mathews 1965:29).

Several classes of perishable ritual artifacts from Chaco Canyon
appear to signal ancestral ties with Basketmaker groups and may have
been used to construct a shared Chacoan social identity. We argue that
connections were made through the use of portable ritual artifacts conceptually linked to Basketmaker prototypes. Analogs for many of these

artifacts have been recovered from Basketmaker sites in the Lukachukai-Chuska Mountains area, including those in the Prayer Rock District and Canyon del Muerto. Selected utilitarian forms of Basketmaker material culture appear to have acquired a ceremonial use by mid- to late Basketmaker III, becoming core components of Pueblo I and Pueblo II ritual systems. The use of this Basketmaker symbolism reached a fluorescence at Chaco during the eleventh and early twelfth centuries. Most of these artifacts were recovered from great houses, but a few were found at small house sites.

Burden Baskets, Bifurcated Baskets, and Ceramic Basket Effigies

The idea that certain ceremonial objects found at Chaco signaled ancestral connections to Basketmaker groups is not new, but it was proposed more than half a century ago by Morris and Burgh (1941:54–59) and Judd (1954:306–320) in reference to the bifurcated burden baskets and ceramic bifurcated burden basket effigies found at Chaco and a few other sites in the northern Southwest (Figure 4.5). In their view, the prototype for the Chacoan bifurcated burden basket was the large, decorated, conical Basketmaker carrying basket of the San Juan region. During Late Basketmaker II times, as the economic focus shifted from the gathering of wild foods to more intensive agriculture, carrying baskets evolved into elaborately decorated forms (Morris and Burgh 1941:54, Figure 15). Miniature clay versions, usually unfired, were produced that served no utilitarian purpose. Morris and Burgh (1941:54) speculated that carrying baskets began to shift from the utilitarian to the ceremonial realm by mid-Basketmaker III.

Clay effigies of bifurcated burden baskets recovered from Pueblo Bonito, Pueblo del Arroyo, and Kin Kletso recall Basketmaker miniature clay burden baskets that imply recognition of the burden basket's import in sustaining individual and community life, if not also a developmental connection (Jolie 2015; Judd 1954:316, Plate 88, 1959:23, 163, 317, Figure 100, Plate 35). Basketmaker II–III clay effigies of carrying baskets have been recovered from the Kayenta area (Guernsey 1931:Figures 26a and b), Canyon del Muerto (Morris 1927:Figures 6f and 10–12), the Prayer Rock District (Morris 1980:Figures 92g–i), west of the Colorado River in Utah (Morss 1931:50), and Shabik'eschee Village in Chaco

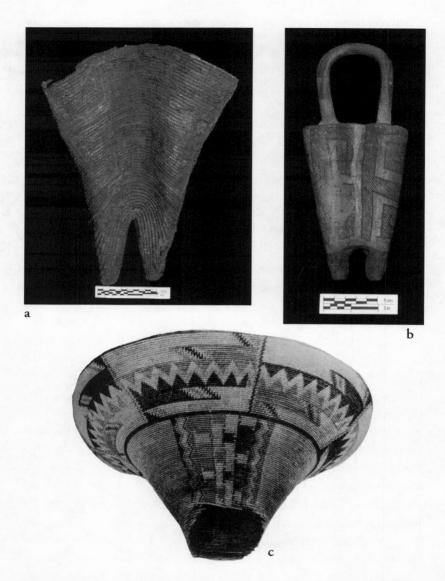

a

b

c

Figure 4.5. Burden baskets and basket effigy: (a) complete bifurcated burden basket with painted design from Room 320, Pueblo Bonito, catalog number NMNH A335293; (b) a ceramic bifurcated burden basket effigy from Room 27, Pueblo del Arroyo, catalog number NMNH A334637; (c) Basketmaker II/III burden basket from Pictograph Cave, Canyon del Muerto, Arizona, adapted from Morris and Burgh (1941:frontispiece). Scale in 4.5a is 10 cm. (Photographs 4.5a and 4.5b by Edward Jolie, courtesy of the Smithsonian Institution National Museum of Natural History)

Canyon (Roberts 1929:125). The presence of a burden basket effigy at this last site suggests the presence of these baskets in Chaco Canyon during Basketmaker III times, although no perishable artifacts from this period have survived.

The earliest known bifurcated baskets and related ceramic effigies appear to date to the A.D. 1000s in Chaco Canyon. At least five bifurcated burden baskets, some with woven and painted decoration, were recovered from Pueblo Bonito, all from rooms 320A and 326 in the western cluster of burial rooms (Jolie 2015; Judd 1954:307–320). Another possible example was recovered from an unknown context at Kin Kletso (Jolie 2015). Several probable additional large burden baskets, not evidencing bifurcation, were recovered from Rooms 13, 53 or 56/63, and 62 in the northern arc of rooms (Judd 1954:171, 234–235; Pepper 1920:68–69, 234–235, Figure 100). Pepper (1920:68) identified the Room 13 basket as an "altar painting," but our analysis identified it as a very large clay-coated and painted burden basket.

Morris and Burgh (1941:54) proposed a connection between Basketmaker III carrying baskets, clay carrying basket effigies, and clay female effigies and suggested that they constituted the ritual paraphernalia of a cult related to human fertility and bountiful harvests. Judd (1954:307, 320; see also Morris and Burgh 1941:56) suggested that the Chaco bifurcated baskets were used to store and transport the ritual paraphernalia of a cult, probably a women's society, descended from Basketmaker times. Recent research by Jolie (2015) on the bifurcated basket complex agrees with much of Morris and Burgh's (1941) and Judd's (1954) interpretations, but differs in seeing earlier Basketmaker basket effigies as more likely children's toys and models and placing more emphasis on the increasing symbolic importance of burden baskets to ideas about water, fertility, and maize agricultural productivity. That the bifurcated vessel form and associated ritual practices survived the decline of the Chaco regional system, at least into the late A.D. 1200s or early 1300s, is supported by nearly two dozen examples of bifurcated burden baskets and ceramic burden basket effigies from sites across northeastern and east-central Arizona (Jolie 2015). Although they are clearly bifurcated burden baskets, the form of the thirteenth-century basketry examples is distinct from earlier Chaco specimens and appears much more standardized in terms of vessel shape and decorative embellishment. The geographical restriction of these later vessels and effigies to points west of Chaco suggests strong social and ceremonial ties with Chaco, if not also destinations for migrants leaving the canyon.

Carved Ceremonial Wooden Staffs

Several other forms of perishable ceremonial artifacts from Chaco also suggest an ancestral connection with Basketmaker material culture. Certain ceremonial staffs from Rooms 32 and 33 at Pueblo Bonito appear to represent continuations or adaptations of Basketmaker implements. For example, the long ceremonial sticks with a spatulate blade at one end (Pepper's Types 3 and 4) are nearly identical to some forms of digging sticks from Basketmaker caves in the Prayer Rock District (cf. Pepper 1920:Figures 58 and 60 with Morris 1980:Figures 90d–g), except that the Chaco examples are equipped with attachments for feathers. One of Pepper's Type 2 sticks and several of his curved sticks also closely resemble Prayer Rock examples (cf. Pepper 1920:Figures 57a and 61 with Morris 1980:Figures 84f and a, respectively; additional Basketmaker examples of these curved sticks are in the unpublished Canyon del Muerto collections). The simple curved crook of Basketmaker times is not reported from Chaco, but the staff with a clawlike end (Pepper 1920:145–146, Figure 55) could be a Chaco variation.

Twined Sandals

Another item of Basketmaker material culture perpetuated at Chaco is the finely woven twined cordage sandal. This style of yucca footwear developed during Basketmaker II and reached its greatest complexity during mid- to late Basketmaker III (Hays-Gilpin et al. 1998). Like burden baskets, some twined sandals may have acquired a ceremonial use by this time (Webster 2008:183).

Compared to other forms of Basketmaker-style perishables at Pueblo Bonito, twined sandals are more evenly distributed throughout the pueblo. Several were recovered from the northern arc of rooms, including at least one confidently dated to the Early Bonito phase (Figure 4.6), based on stylistic criteria and its close association with a fine twill plaited sandal that produced an AMS date with a median

Figure 4.6. Twined sandal from Room III, Pueblo Bonito, catalog number H/9183. Sandal probably dates to the Early Bonito subphase. (Photograph by Laurie Webster, courtesy of the Division of Anthropology, American Museum of Natural History)

calibrated calendar age of A.D. 829 (Jolie 2015). Twined sandals were also recovered from trash deposits in the north, east, and west wings of the pueblo. No examples were identified in the northern burial cluster, but western burial Room 326 yielded a pair of twined sandals in an elliptical basket (Judd 1954:76).

Twined sandals were also recovered from the great houses of Pueblo del Arroyo (Judd 1959:9, 124), Chetro Ketl (Reiter 1933:23, 41, Plates VII, XI(1); Vivian 1931:23–27, Figures 8 and 9), and Kin Kletso (Jolie, unpublished data). Although they are not identified as twined sandals in the published reports, we have also identified fragments of these sandals in Pueblo II and III collections from sites such as Tsin Kletsin, 29SJ1360, and Bc 58 within the canyon, and at Bis sa'ani just outside the canyon. Farther north, examples are known from Salmon and Aztec Ruins (Webster 2006, 2008). Thus, twined sandals are one Basketmaker-style perishable artifact known to occur at both great house and small house sites.

Perishable Objects Suggesting Southern Ideologies

Mesoamerican influences in Chacoan society have been a focal point for scholarly debate for decades. In Chaco Canyon, long-distance exchange and interaction are well evidenced by the presence of macaws, copper bells, pseudo-cloisonné, and most notably, cacao (chocolate) residue on pitchers and unique cylinder vessels analogous to Mesoamerican forms used for consuming a cacao-based beverage (Crown and Hurst 2009; Nelson 2006). These articles, as well as several types of perishable artifacts that we discuss below, suggest the existence of real or imagined ideological ties to Mesoamerica and northern Mexico among at least some Chaco residents. Some scholars have suggested that Mesoamerican-style prestige items and symbols were adopted by Chacoan religious or political leaders to enhance their positions of leadership and legitimize their status (Mathien 2005:271), whereas others have attributed their source to Toltec high-status elites or *pochteca* traders (e.g., Frisbie 1988; Reyman 1978). More recently, Mathiowetz (2011) has suggested that a suite of Mesoamerican ideas entered the Southwest via the Aztatlán tradition of West Mexico. Regardless of the mechanisms by which Mesoamerican concepts and art forms spread into Chaco, several perishable and durable artifact classes at Chaco, especially Pueblo Bonito, appear to reflect ideas from that region.

Cylinder Baskets

Cylinder baskets first appear in Chaco and are nearly exclusive to Pueblo Bonito (Judd 1954:166–171, 306, Plate 45; Pepper 1909:227–228, 1920:164–173, Figure 71), where they presumably functioned in a fashion analogous to the ceramic cylinder vessels and were also influenced by Mesoamerican forms (Crown and Hurst 2009). This basket form has no precedent in Basketmaker contexts, but the association of two examples, one large and one small and both encrusted with turquoise mosaic, with an elaborate Room 33 burial directly radiocarbon dated to the late ninth century A.D. (Plog and Heitman 2010), suggests that cylinder baskets pre-date the ceramic versions. Recent reanalysis indicates at least 13 and perhaps as many as 21 cylinder baskets are represented in the existing Pueblo Bonito collections (Jolie 2015). If the latter number is accurate, then 13 of these specimens derive from the western burial cluster rooms, and the rest were spread throughout the pueblo. Associated chronological information suggests that cylinder baskets were most common at Chaco during the A.D. 1000s, but they may have persisted into the 1100s. These cylinder baskets, at least five of which bear woven or painted designs, exhibit sufficient variability in overall dimensions, structural type, and stitch splicing mechanics to suggest that they were produced by multiple weavers belonging to overlapping but distinct craft learning networks (Jolie 2015). The singular cylinder basket example not from Pueblo Bonito derives from the so-called Magician's Burial from Ridge Ruin near Flagstaff, Arizona (McGregor 1943). That specimen, encrusted with turquoise mosaic, was associated with the extraordinarily rich burial of an adult male who was interred with a host of ritual paraphernalia, including an elliptical tray, multiple clay-coated and painted baskets, and several carved wooden staffs, among many other perishable items (Jolie, unpublished data; McGregor 1943). The burial, thought to reflect a ritual leader and war chief of high standing, is dated to the last half of the twelfth century.

Hourglass-Shaped or Elliptical Trays

Another probable form of ceremonial coiled basketry lacking a direct analog in Basketmaker and Pueblo I assemblages is the shallow, elliptical or hourglass-shaped tray (Judd 1954:165–166, 306–307, Plate 44). Most known examples come from Pueblo Bonito, but at least seven other examples are known: one from the Magician's Burial at Ridge Ruin, one from Antelope House in Canyon del Muerto, one from Burial 9 in Room 33 at Aztec West Ruin, one from Grand Gulch, two looted examples from Horse Rock Ruin, and one from a tributary of Allen Canyon, the latter four from southeastern Utah (Adovasio and Andrews 1990; Adovasio and Gunn 1986; Jolie 2015; Osborne 2004:345; Plog 1979:Figure 11, lower). Of the six known Bonito examples, four are from Room 326 in the western burial cluster and fragmentary specimens derive from Rooms 2 and 54. The trays from Room 326 at Pueblo Bonito and Room 33 at Aztec were both associated with an adult female burial and contained a type of artifact that Judd and others have routinely described as a bone flesher or scraper, but what was more likely a woman's yucca processing tool (cf. Osborne 2004:426–430). The non-funerary basket from Allen Canyon also contained several of these tools. In contrast, the contents of the Antelope House and Ridge Ruin specimens strongly suggest ritual accoutrements.

Judd (1954:307) noted a similarity between the hourglass shape of these trays and the bases of bifurcated baskets, which led him to suggest a possible relationship between the elliptical baskets and Basketmaker wedge-shaped burden baskets. Another more intriguing possibility is that the Chaco elliptical baskets were modeled after the oblong "medicine baskets" or "shaman's baskets" used in Mesoamerica and Peru (e.g., Powell and Grady 2010:Figure 2.14; Zingg 1940). Although the elliptical baskets from the San Juan region vary in their construction styles, they seem to be conceptually linked by their association with ritual paraphernalia and women's work (Jolie 2015).

Clay-Coated Painted Baskets

Clay-coated painted baskets are another ceremonial form that, in Chaco Canyon, is presently known only from Pueblo Bonito. Six examples were also recovered from Chacoan deposits at Aztec West Ruin (Jolie 2015). These coiled baskets were coated with red or pink clay on both faces, then painted with geometric designs. Four were recovered at Pueblo Bonito from Rooms 13, 37, 83, and 300A, all of which are located in the northern arc of the pueblo. Strikingly, none are known from burials. The example from Room 13, which Pepper (1920:68–69) identified as an "altar painting," is probably the remains of a burden basket. A fragment from adjacent Room 300 has a black zigzag design (Judd 1954:Figure 101). The fragmentary remains of a large basket from nearby Room 83, not discussed by Pepper, are decorated with a polychrome two-dimensional zigzag design (Figure 4.7). The specimen from Room 37 is too small to permit observation about its painted design.

Clay-coated painted baskets are associated with high-status and ritual contexts (Odegaard and Hays-Gilpin 2002). Although painted baskets are widely distributed in the Southwest, not all were clay coated or made in the same way. All early examples of clay-coated painted baskets are covered with a red clay coating and painted with polychrome designs. The Pueblo Bonito baskets are believed to be the earliest examples of this vessel style in the Southwest and, together with the Late Bonito subphase Aztec specimens, share a very similar production

Figure 4.7. Clay-coated painted basket fragments from Room 83, Pueblo Bonito, catalog numbers H/7040 and H/7041. (Photograph by Laurie Webster, courtesy of the Division of Anthropology, American Museum of Natural History)

sequence (Jolie 2015). Later examples are known primarily from northeastern and east-central Arizona, date between about A.D. 1150 and the 1300s, and differ from and are more varied than Chacoan examples with respect to raw materials, color palette, and decorative style (Jolie 2015; Odegaard and Hays-Gilpin 2002).

Clay-coated and painted basketry technology is truly unique in the context of North American basketweaving traditions, but prehispanic Mesoamerica was host to a number of intersecting technologies that arguably identify it as the ultimate source for the technology used to produce the Chacoan specimens (Jolie 2015). The best and most direct Mesoamerican analog for clay-coated and painted baskets is a Middle Preclassic (ca. 1400 to 800 B.C.) partially preserved bowl recovered from an adult female burial at Tlatilco in the Basin of Mexico (García Moll 1973; García Moll et al. 1991:80, 259). Here, both faces of a coiled basket were coated with at least four layers of mineral pigment, though the design could not be reconstructed. On the exterior, an initial red pigment coat was covered with white, then red again, then yellow pigment. On the interior, a red coat was followed by green, then red, green again, and yellow. Farther south, two much younger examples of pigment-coated basketry derive from mortuary contexts at Copán, Honduras, and Altun Ha, Belize, suggesting the persistence of this technology in the Maya region until at least the A.D. 600s (Bell et al. 2000, 2004; Pendergast 1982:54–68). Other similar technologies that spread through ancient Mesoamerica and northern and western Mexico and suggest links to Southwestern clay-coated and painted baskets include lacquer, pseudo-cloisonné, stuccoed ceramics, and textile-clay laminates (Beaubien 2003; Ekholm 1940, 1942; Holien 1977; Jolie 2015).

Tabular Carved and Painted Wood

Several collections of painted and carved wood were recovered from sites in Chaco Canyon, including the great house villages of Chetro Ketl (Vivian et al. 1978), Pueblo Bonito (Judd 1954:275–276, Figures 42, 75, and 76, Plate 78; Pepper 1920:101, 159, Figure 139, Plate 8a), Pueblo del Arroyo (Judd 1959:131, Figure 29), and Kin Kletso (Vivian and Mathews 1965:101), and the small house community of Bc 50 (Tseh So) (Brand et al. 1937:96). Most are decorated with blue-green, red, white, yellow, or black paint, and are cross-dated to the late eleventh or early twelfth century. The Chetro Ketl assemblage contains more than 200 pieces, including parts of birds, scalloped objects resembling turkey tail fans, decorated slats and discs, a plume circle, crescents or horns, lightning lattices, and several other forms. Pueblo Bonito did not produce a unified assemblage, only isolated pieces, including a well-preserved pair of large wand-like objects from Room 168 (Webster 2011:Figure 2a). Except for the painted board from Room 32, all painted wood at Pueblo Bonito was recovered from the eastern half of the pueblo (Judd 1954:276). Pueblo del Arroyo produced only a few pieces, including a painted wooden sandal form from the northern block of rooms, and Kin Kletso yielded only one example. Interestingly, one of the most complete assemblages of painted wood from Chaco Canyon was recovered from the floor of Room 1 at the small house of Bc 50 (Tseh So). The style of painting on these artifacts shows close parallels with the Chetro Ketl assemblage (Vivian et al. 1978:22–23).

These painted wood assemblages have no known precedent at Basketmaker sites on the Colorado Plateau, but numerous examples of carved and painted wood have been recovered from dry caves in the Mogollon culture area, especially the Gila River and its tributaries, where carved and painted wooden objects played a major role in ceremonial practice (Cosgrove 1947; Hough 1914; Lambert and Ambler 1961; Martin et al. 1952; see also Webster 2007). Most Mogollon examples are thought to postdate A.D. 1000, but a radiocarbon-dated basket from Bear Creek Cave suggests that at least some of these items are contemporaneous with the Bonito phase at Chaco (Jolie 2015). Although this painting technology appears to have southern antecedents (Vivian et al. 1978:27–31), the strong thematic emphasis on birds exhibited by the Chaco assemblages suggests stylistic continuity with traditions on the Colorado Plateau.

Tie-Dye Cotton Textile

The only woven textile from Chaco that exhibits clear southern influence is a previously unpublished tie-dye cotton textile alluded to by Pepper (1920:138) in his description of a burial in Room 32 at Pueblo Bonito. This textile has recently been located (Figure 4.8). Tie-dye is a resist-dye technique that involves tying sections of a fabric before immersing it in dye to produce a negative design where the cloth is tied and the dye is unable to penetrate. A similar style of shirt or cloak is depicted on a human effigy from Room 316 at Bonito (Judd 1954:Figure 60). The Pueblo Bonito tie-dye textile is the easternmost and the earliest known example of tie-dye in the Southwest. Other examples are reported from the Kayenta region, the Verde Valley, and southern Arizona (Webster et al. 2006:Table 1). The roots of this tradition appear to lie in Mesoamerica and Peru, where the technique was used to decorate clothing of the nobility and ruling elites, including that of the Toltec royalty (Anawalt 1990:298). The dot-in-a-square motif commonly produced by this technique was conceptually linked to maize agriculture, serpents, and fertility (Webster et al. 2006).

Figure 4.8. Tie-dye textile fragments from Room 32, Pueblo Bonito, catalog number H/15752, originally part of H/4605. (Photograph by Laurie Webster, courtesy of the Division of Anthropology, American Museum of Natural History)

Conclusion

In this chapter, we have used perishable artifacts to explore Chacoan social identity, sociocultural diversity, and integrative symbols in Chaco Canyon. Variation in the technological style of coiled baskets, plaited mats, and fine plaited sandals suggests the existence of at least two, and perhaps three, distinct but overlapping craft learning networks that arguably correspond to different social groups at Pueblo Bonito. These findings complement prior studies that see evidence for multiple socially and biologically diverse groups at the site. A chronological dimension to the observed spatial patterning, when considered with the meager data from other Chaco Canyon sites, lends additional support to arguments that the canyon witnessed a cultural discontinuity around A.D. 1100.

We have also proposed two sources of symbolic and ritual influence at Chaco Canyon: one that expressed a relationship to Basketmaker ancestors and another that evoked connections with broader

Mesoamerican worldviews. The available data imply the importance of Pueblo Bonito, more so than any other site, in perpetuating and likely reformulating perishable artifact types that were symbolic of a shared Basketmaker identity, as well as "introducing" new technologies and vessel forms with connections to Mesoamerican technologies and worldviews. After the decline of the Chaco regional system, technologies, including bifurcated baskets, clay-coated and painted baskets, and perhaps cylinder baskets, ceased to be produced within the canyon, but persisted in modified form among communities occupying northeastern and east-central Arizona throughout the thirteenth century A.D., hinting at the persistence of long-term social ties between Chaco Canyon and these regions since Basketmaker times.

If oral traditions and ethnographic and historic accounts of sociocultural diversity in the Pueblo Southwest are any indication, the accumulating evidence for such diversity in Chaco Canyon and across the regional system is not surprising. Yet, what remain to be considered are the plausible impacts of such diversity on the development of Chacoan society and identities. Here, the perishable artifacts suggest additional avenues of investigation.

Symbols, ritual practices, and religions are widely recognized for their ability to bring disparate peoples together to pursue a common goal or set of goals. That so many distinctive types of perishable artifacts at Chaco have strong symbolic or ritual connotations is revealing of the role of ritual in the development of Pueblo Bonito and Chacoan society more broadly. While this observation itself is not new, the perishable artifact data contribute a new avenue of inquiry into the spatiotemporal dimensions of ritual at Pueblo Bonito and beyond. Some of the most ritually significant perishable artifacts, such as bifurcated baskets and clay-coated and painted baskets, have restricted spatial distributions at Pueblo Bonito that indicate distinctive uses. Spatial separation in the portions of the pueblo where both of the aforementioned artifact types are found strongly suggests that they reflect paraphernalia associated with ritual practices administered by different social units. By extension, other perishable artifacts of symbolic or ritual import with wider distributions, such as elliptical trays, twined sandals, and tie-dye textiles, likely indicate social interaction, integration, and participation with Chaco at larger spatial scales.

While these observations do not bear directly on questions of cultural and social diversity, they do enhance our understanding of the role that *diversity in ritual practice* may have played in integrating the inhabitants of Pueblo Bonito and perhaps other social groups within and beyond Chaco Canyon. We believe that some of the classes of ritual perishable artifacts we have discussed reflect distinctive sets of beliefs, or ritual associations such as sodalities, and that their particular histories are tied to the diverse peoples who brought them to Chaco Canyon at different times, principally during the Early and Classic Bonito subphases (Jolie 2015). Further, although we have no data that bear directly on the question of linguistic diversity, the possibility that multiple languages were spoken in Chaco Canyon is becoming increasingly likely. One important implication of sociocultural and linguistic diversity for ceremonialism is multilingualism, which, based on ethnographic insights, would have provided opportunities for greater partitioning or secluding of important ritual and other knowledge, particularly across different generations that experienced different levels and degrees or forms of multilingualism (cf. Dozier 1954; Kroskrity 2009).

To address the complicated social phenomena that we have taken as our focus in this chapter, we recognize that much more work remains to be done, both with additional classes of perishable artifacts and by integrating the perishables data with those of other media, such as architecture, ceramics, lithics, and rock art. Articulating a single "Chacoan identity," let alone multiple "Chacoan identities," is a herculean task, given the extent to which social identity is a moving target. Acknowledging the complexity of such endeavors, we plan to focus our future attention on improving our chronological control of perishable data sets that can be used to target the correlates of specific social identity markers and evaluate existing hypotheses for sociocultural diversity. Critical to this process will be a bottom-up approach that emphasizes the actions and motivations of smaller social units in creating and maintaining the regional patterns that archaeologists have observed.

Acknowledgments

We are indebted to the staff at the many museums too numerous to list here who kindly facilitated collections access during our research.

We especially thank David Hurst Thomas and Anibal Rodriguez of the American Museum of Natural History, Deborah Hull-Walski and David Rosenthal of the Smithsonian's National Museum of Natural History, and Wendy Bustard of the National Park Service's Chaco Museum for accommodating our often-lengthy research visits. Chip Wills, Patty Crown, and Ruth Jolie also provided critical support and input, for which we are extremely grateful. Generous financial support for this research has been supplied by Sigma Xi, the Department of Anthropology at the University of New Mexico, the Mellon Foundation, and an NSF Doctoral Dissertation Improvement grant to Jolie (award no. 0853134).

References Cited

Adovasio, J. M. 1986. Artifacts and Ethnicity: Basketry as an Indicator of Territoriality and Population Movements in the Prehistoric Great Basin. In *Anthropology of the Desert West: Essays in Honor of Jesse D. Jennings*, edited by Carol J. Condie and Don D. Fowler, pp. 43–89. University of Utah Anthropological Papers No. 110. University of Utah Press, Salt Lake City.

Adovasio, J. M., and R. L. Andrews. 1990. The Horse Rock Ruin (42SA10550) Basketry Cache: An Unparalleled View of Regional Pueblo Perishable Technology. Paper presented at the 55th Annual Meeting of the Society for American Archaeology, Las Vegas, Nevada.

Adovasio, J. M., and Joel D. Gunn. 1986. The Antelope House Basketry Industry. In *Archaeological Investigations at Antelope House*, by Don P. Morris, pp. 306–397. National Park Service, Washington, D.C.

Adovasio, J. M., and D. R. Pedler. 1994. A Tisket, a Tasket: Looking at Numic Speakers through the "Lens" of a Basket. In *Across the West*, edited by David B. Madsen and David H. Rhode, pp. 114–123. University of Utah Press, Salt Lake City.

Akins, Nancy J. 1986. *A Biocultural Approach to Human Burials from Chaco Canyon, New Mexico*. Reports of the Chaco Center No. 9. Division of Cultural Research, National Park Service, Albuquerque.

———. 2003. The Burials of Pueblo Bonito. In *Pueblo Bonito: Center of the Chacoan World*, edited by Jill E. Neitzel, pp. 94–106. Smithsonian Institution Press, Washington, D.C.

Anawalt, Patricia Rieff. 1990. The Emperor's Cloak: Aztec Pomp, Toltec Circumstances. *American Antiquity* 55:291–307.

Beaubien, Harriet F. 2003. Textile-Clay Laminates: A Special-Use Material in Ancient Mesoamerica. Electronic document, http://www.famsi.org/reports/01010/, accessed June 16, 2014.

Bell, Ellen E., Robert J. Sharer, David W. Sedat, Marcello A. Canuto, and Lynn A. Grant. 2000. The Margarita Tomb at Copán, Honduras: A Research Update. *Expedition* 42(3):21–25.

Bell, Ellen E., Robert J. Sharer, Loa P. Traxler, David W. Sedat, Christine W. Carrelli, and Lynn A. Grant. 2004. Tombs and Burials in the Early Classic Acropolis at Copan. In *Understanding Early Classic Copan*, edited by Ellen E. Bell, Marcello A. Canuto, and Robert J. Sharer, pp. 131–157. University of Pennsylvania Museum of Archaeology and Anthropology, Philadelphia.

Bernardini, Wesley. 2005. Reconsidering Spatial and Temporal Aspects of Prehistoric Cultural Identity: A Case Study from the American Southwest. *American Antiquity* 70:31–54.

Brand, Donald D., Florence M. Hawley, Frank C. Hibben, et al. 1937. *Tseh So, A Small House Ruin, Chaco Canyon, New Mexico (Preliminary Report)*. University of New Mexico Bulletin No. 308, Anthropological Series 2, No. 2. University of New Mexico, Albuquerque.

Bustard, Wendy. 1996. Space as Place: Small and Great House Spatial Organization in Chaco Canyon, New Mexico, AD 1000–1150. Ph.D. dissertation, Department of Anthropology, University of New Mexico, Albuquerque.

————. 2003. When a House Is Not a Home. In *Pueblo Bonito: Center of the Chacoan World*, edited by Jill E. Neitzel, pp. 80–93. Smithsonian Books, Washington, D.C.

Cameron, Catherine M. 2005. Exploring Archaeological Cultures in the Northern Southwest: What were Chaco and Mesa Verde? *Kiva* 70:227–254.

Connerton, Paul. 1989. *How Societies Remember*. Cambridge University Press, Cambridge.

Cordell, Linda S., and W. James Judge. 2001. Perspectives on Chaco Society and Polity. In *Chaco Society and Polity: Papers from the 1999 Conference*, edited by Linda S. Cordell, W. James Judge, and June-el Piper, pp. 1–12. New Mexico Archaeological Council Special Publication No. 4. New Mexico Archaeological Council, Albuquerque.

Cosgrove, C. Burton. 1947. *Caves of the Upper Gila and Hueco Areas in New Mexico and Texas*. Papers of the Peabody Museum of American Archaeology and Ethnology Vol. 24, No. 2. Harvard University, Cambridge.

Crown, Patricia L. 2007. Learning about Learning. In *Archaeological Anthropology: Perspectives on Method and Theory*, edited by James Skibo, Michael W. Graves, and Miriam Stark, pp. 198–217. University of Arizona Press, Tucson.

Crown, Patricia L., and W. Jeffrey Hurst. 2009. Evidence of Cacao Use in the Prehispanic American Southwest. *Proceedings of the National Academy of Sciences* 106:2110–2113.

Dozier, Edward P. 1954. *The Hopi-Tewa of Arizona*. University of California Publications in American Archaeology and Ethnology Vol. 44, No. 3. University of California Press, Berkeley.

————. 1966. *Hano: A Tewa Indian Community in Arizona.* Holt, Rinehart & Winston, New York.

Driver, Harold E., and William C. Massey. 1957. *Comparative Studies of North American Indians.* Transactions of the American Philosophical Society Vol. 47, Pt. 2.

Ekholm, Gordon F. 1940. Prehistoric "Laquer" from Sinaloa. *Revista Mexicana de Estudios Antropológicos,* 4(1–2):10–15.

————. 1942. *Excavations at Guasave, Sinaloa, Mexico.* Anthropological Papers of the American Museum of Natural History Vol. 38, Pt. II. American Museum of Natural History, New York.

Ford, Richard I. 1972. Barter, Gift, or Violence: An Analysis of Tewa Intertribal Exchange. In *Social Exchange and Interaction,* edited by Edwin N. Wilmsen, pp. 21–45. Anthropological Papers, Museum of Anthropology, University of Michigan No. 46. Museum of Anthropology, University of Michigan, Ann Arbor.

Frisbie, Theodore R. 1988. New Light on the Pochteca Concept and the Chaco Phenomenon. In *Diné Bíkéyak: Papers in Honor of David M. Brugge,* edited by Mehila S. Duran and David T. Kirkpatrick, pp. 87–97. Papers of the Archaeological Society of New Mexico No. 24. Archaeological Society of New Mexico, Albuquerque.

Fritz, John M. 1978. Paleopsychology Today: Ideational Systems and Human Adaptation in Prehistory. In *Social Archaeology: Beyond Subsistence and Dating,* edited by Charles L. Redman, Mary Jane Berman, Edward V. Curtain, William T. Langhorne Jr., Nina M. Versaggi, and Jeffrey C. Wanser, pp. 37–59. Academic Press, New York.

García Moll, Roberto. 1973. Rara muestra de cestería del preclasico medio. *Boletín de Instituto Nacional de Antropología e Historia* 2:23–26.

García Moll, Roberto, Daniel Juárez Cossío, Carmen Pijoan Aguade, Ma. Elena Salas Cuesta, and Marcela Salas Cuesta. 1991. *Catálogo de entierros de San Luis Tlatilco, México: Temporada IV.* Instituto Nacional de Antropología e Historia, Mexico City.

Guernsey, Samuel. 1931. *Explorations in Northeastern Arizona.* Papers of the Peabody Museum of American Archaeology and Ethnology Vol. 7, No. 1. Harvard University, Cambridge.

Hagstrum, Melissa. 2001. Household Production in Chacoan Canyon Society. *American Antiquity* 66(1):47–55.

Hays-Gilpin, Kelly Ann, Ann Cordy Deegan, and Elizabeth Ann Morris. 1998. *Prehistoric Sandals from Northeastern Arizona: The Earl H. Morris and Ann Axtell Morris Research.* Anthropological Papers of the University of Arizona No. 62. University of Arizona Press, Tucson.

Heitman, Carolyn C., and Stephen Plog. 2005. Kinship and the Dynamics of the House: Rediscovering Dualism in the Pueblo Past. In *A Catalyst for Ideas: Anthropological Archaeology and the Legacy of Douglas W. Schwartz,* edited by Vernon L. Scarborough, pp. 69–100. School of American Research Press, Santa Fe.

Holien, Thomas E. 1977. Mesoamerican Pseudo-cloisonné and Other Decorative Investments. Ph.D. dissertation, Department of Anthropology, University of Southern Illinois, Carbondale.

Hough, Walter. 1914. *Culture of the Ancient Pueblos of the Upper Gila River Region, New Mexico and Arizona.* United States National Museum Bulletin No. 87. Government Printing Office, Washington, D.C.

Jenkins, Richard. 2008. *Social Identity.* 3rd ed. Routledge, London.

Jolie, Edward A. 2015. Cultural and Social Diversity in the Prehispanic Southwest: Learning, Weaving and Identity in the Chaco Regional System, AD 850–1140. Ph.D. dissertation, Department of Anthropology, University of New Mexico, Albuquerque.

Jones, Siân. 1997. *The Archaeology of Ethnicity: Constructing Identities in the Past and Present.* Routledge, London.

Judd, Neil M. 1954. *Material Culture of Pueblo Bonito.* Smithsonian Miscellaneous Collections Vol. 124. Smithsonian Institution, Washington, D.C.

———. 1959. *Pueblo del Arroyo, Chaco Canyon, New Mexico.* Smithsonian Miscellaneous Collections Vol. 138, No. 1. Smithsonian Institution, Washington, D.C.

———. 1964. *The Architecture of Pueblo Bonito.* Smithsonian Miscellaneous Collections Vol. 147, No. 1. Smithsonian Institution, Washington, D.C.

Judge, W. James, and Linda S. Cordell. 2006. Society and Polity. In *The Archaeology of Chaco Canyon: An Eleventh-Century Pueblo Regional Center*, edited by Stephen H. Lekson, pp. 189–210. School of American Research Press, Santa Fe.

Kluckhohn, Clyde. 1939. Discussion. In *Preliminary Report on the 1937 Excavations, Bc 50–51, Chaco Canyon, New Mexico*, edited by Clyde Kluckhohn and Paul Reiter, pp. 151–162. University of New Mexico Bulletin 345, Anthropological Series 3, No. 2. University of New Mexico Press, Albuquerque.

Kroskrity, Paul V. 2009. Narrative Reproductions: Ideologies of Storytelling, Authoritative Words, and Generic Regimentation in the Village of Tewa. *Journal of Linguistic Anthropology* 19:40–56.

Lambert, Marjorie F., and J. Richard Ambler. 1961. *A Survey and Excavation of Caves in Hidalgo County, New Mexico.* School of American Research Monograph 25. School of American Research Press, Santa Fe.

Lave, Jane, and Etienne Wenger. 1991. *Situated Learning: Legitimate Peripheral Participation.* Cambridge University Press, Cambridge.

Lekson, Stephen H. 1986. *Great Pueblo Architecture of Chaco Canyon, New Mexico.* University of New Mexico Press, Albuquerque.

Lekson, Stephen H. (editor). 1995. Migration and the Movement of Southwestern Peoples. *Journal of Anthropological Archaeology* 14:99–250.

————. 2006. *The Archaeology of Chaco Canyon: An Eleventh-Century Pueblo Regional Center.* School of American Research Press, Santa Fe.

Lekson, Stephen H., Thomas C. Windes, and Peter J. McKenna. 2006. Architecture. In *The Archaeology of Chaco Canyon: An Eleventh-Century Pueblo Regional Center,* edited by Stephen H. Lekson, pp. 67–116. School of American Research Press, Santa Fe.

Lyons, Patrick D., and Jeffrey J. Clark. 2008. Interaction, Enculturation, Social Distance, and Ancient Ethnic Identities. In *Archaeology Without Borders: Contact, Commerce, and Change in the U.S. Southwest and Northwestern Mexico,* edited by Laurie D. Webster and Maxine E. McBrinn, pp. 185–207. University Press of Colorado, Boulder.

Martin, Paul S., John B. Rinaldo, Elaine A. Bluhn, Hugh C. Cutler, and Roger Grange Jr. 1952. *Mogollon Cultural Continuity and Change: The Stratigraphic Analysis of Tularosa and Cordova Caves.* Fieldiana: Anthropology Vol. 40. Field Museum of Natural History, Chicago.

Mathien, Frances Joan. 2005. *Culture and Ecology of Chaco Canyon and the San Juan Basin.* Publications in Archaeology 18H, Chaco Canyon Studies. National Park Service, U.S. Department of the Interior, Santa Fe.

Mathiowetz, Michael. 2011. *The Diurnal Path of the Sun: Ideology and Interregional Interaction in Ancient Northwest Mesoamerica and the American Southwest.* Ph.D. dissertation, Department of Anthropology, University of California, Riverside. ProQuest, Inc., Ann Arbor.

McGregor, John C. 1943. *Burial of an Early American Magician.* Proceedings of the American Philosophical Society 86(2):270–298.

Meyer, Daniel A. 1999. Masonry and Social Variability in the Chaco System. Ph.D. dissertation, Department of Anthropology, University of Calgary, Alberta.

Mills, Barbara J. 2004. The Establishment and Defeat of Hierarchy: Inalienable Possessions and the History of Collective Prestige Structures in the Pueblo Southwest. *American Anthropologist* 106:238–251.

————. 2008. Remembering While Forgetting: Depositional Practices and Social Memory at Chaco. In *Memory Work: Archaeologies of Material Practices,* edited by Barbara J. Mills and William H. Walker, pp. 81–108. School for Advanced Research Press, Santa Fe.

Mills, Barbara J., and William H. Walker (editors). 2008. *Memory Work: Archaeologies of Material Practices.* School for Advanced Research Press, Santa Fe.

Minar, C. Jill, and Patricia L. Crown (editors). 2001. Learning and Craft Production. *Journal of Anthropological Research* 54:369–493.

Morris, Earl H. 1919. *The Aztec Ruin.* Anthropological Papers Vol. 26, Pt. 1. American Museum of Natural History, New York.

————. 1924. *Burials in the Aztec Ruin.* Anthropological Papers Vol. 26, Pt. 3. American Museum of Natural History, New York.

———. 1927. *The Beginnings of Pottery Making in the San Juan Area: Unfired Prototypes and the Wares of the Earliest Ceramic Period.* Anthropological Papers Vol. 28, Pt. 2. American Museum of Natural History, New York.

———. 1928. *Notes on Excavations in the Aztec Ruin.* Anthropological Papers Vol. 26, Pt. 5. American Museum of Natural History, New York.

Morris, Earl H., and Robert F. Burgh. 1941. *Anasazi Basketry: Basket Maker II through Pueblo III: A Study Based on Specimens from the San Juan River Country.* Carnegie Institution Publication No. 533. Carnegie Institution, Washington, D.C.

Morris, Elizabeth Ann. 1980. *Basketmaker Caves in the Prayer Rock District, Northeastern Arizona.* Anthropological Papers of the University of Arizona No. 35. University of Arizona Press, Tucson.

Morss, Noel. 1931. *The Ancient Culture of the Fremont River in Utah. Report on the Explorations under the Claflin-Emerson Fund, 1928–29.* Papers of the Peabody Museum of American Archaeology and Ethnology Vol. 12, No. 3. Harvard University, Cambridge.

Nelson, Ben A. 2006. Mesoamerican Objects and Symbols in Chaco Canyon Contexts. In *The Archaeology of Chaco Canyon: An Eleventh-Century Pueblo Regional Center*, edited by Stephen H. Lekson, pp. 339–371. School of American Research Press, Santa Fe.

Odegaard, Nancy, and Kelley Hays-Gilpin. 2002. Technology of the Sacred: Painted Basketry in the Southwest. In *Traditions, Transitions, and Technologies: Themes in Southwestern Archaeology*, edited by Sarah H. Schlanger, pp. 307–331. University Press of Colorado, Boulder.

Ortiz, Alfonso (editor). 1979. *Southwest.* Handbook of North American Indians, Vol. 9, William C. Sturtevant, general editor. Smithsonian Institution, Washington, D.C.

Ortman, Scott G., and Catherine M. Cameron. 2011. A Framework for Controlled Comparisons of Ancient Southwestern Movement. In *Movement, Connectivity, and Landscape Change in the Ancient Southwest*, edited by Margaret C. Nelson and Colleen Strawhacker, pp. 233–252. University Press of Colorado, Boulder.

Osborne, Carolyn M. 2004. *The Wetherill Collections and Perishable Items from Mesa Verde.* Self-published on www.lulu.com.

Parsons, Elsie Clews. 1925. *The Pueblo of Jemez.* Papers of the Southwestern Expedition No. 3. Yale University Press, New Haven, Connecticut.

———. 1928. The Laguna Migration to Isleta. *American Anthropologist* 30:602–613.

———. 1932. Isleta, New Mexico. In *Forty-Seventh Annual Report of the Bureau of American Ethnology, 1929–1930*, pp. 193–466. U.S. Government Printing Office, Washington, D.C.

Pendergast, David M. 1982. *Excavations at Altun Ha, Belize, 1964–1970*, Vol. 2. Royal Ontario Museum, Toronto.

Pepper, George H. 1909. The Exploration of a Burial Room in Pueblo Bonito, New Mexico. In *Putnam Anniversary Volume Anthropological Essays: Presented to Frederic Ward Putnam in Honor of His Seventieth Birthday, April 16, 1909*, edited by Franz Boas, Roland B. Dixon, Alfred L. Kroeber, Frederick W. Hodge, and H. I. Smith, pp. 196–252. G. E. Stechert & Co., New York.

———. 1920. *Pueblo Bonito*. Anthropological Papers of the American Museum of Natural History Vol. 27. Trustees of the American Museum of Natural History, New York.

Plog, Fred. 1979. Prehistory: Western Anasazi. In *Southwest*, edited by Alfonso Ortiz, pp. 108–130. Handbook of North American Indians, Vol. 9, William C. Sturtevant, general editor. Smithsonian Institution, Washington, D.C.

Plog, Stephen, and Carrie Heitman. 2010. Hierarchy and Social Inequality in the American Southwest, AD 800–1200. *Proceedings of the National Academy of Sciences* 107(46):19619–19626.

Polanich, Judith Kessler. 1994. Mono Basketry: Migration and Change. Ph.D. dissertation, Department of Anthropology, University of California, Davis.

Powell, Melissa, and C. Jill Grady. 2010. *Huichol Art and Culture: Balancing the World*. Museum of New Mexico Press, Santa Fe.

Reiter, Winifred Stamm. 1933. Personal Adornment of the Ancient Pueblo Indians. Master's thesis, Department of Archaeology and Anthropology, University of New Mexico, Albuquerque.

Reyman, Jonathan E. 1978. Pochteca Burials at Anasazi Sites? In *Across the Chichimec Sea: Papers in Honor of J. Charles Kelley*, edited by Carroll L. Riley and Basic C. Hedrick, pp. 242–259. Southern Illinois University Press, Carbondale.

Roberts, Frank H. H., Jr. 1929. *Shabik'eschee Village: A Late Basket Maker Site in the Chaco Canyon, New Mexico*. Bureau of American Ethnology Bulletin 92. U.S. Government Printing Office, Washington, D.C.

Schillaci, Michael A. 2003. The Development of Population Diversity at Chaco Canyon. *Kiva* 68:221–245.

Schillaci, Michael A., and Christopher M. Stojanowski. 2003. Postmarital Residence and Biological Variation at Pueblo Bonito. *American Journal of Physical Anthropology* 120:1–15.

Stark, Miriam T., Brenda J. Bowser, and Lee Horne (editors). 2008. *Cultural Transmission and Material Culture: Breaking Down Boundaries*. University of Arizona Press, Tucson.

Tanner, Clara Lee. 1983. *Indian Baskets of the Southwest*. University of Arizona Press, Tucson.

Teiwes, Helga. 1996. *Hopi Basket Weaving: Artistry in Natural Fibers*. University of Arizona Press, Tucson.

Thulman, David K. 2013. The Role of Nondeclarative Memory Systems in the Inference of Long-Term Population Continuity. *Journal of Archaeological Method and Theory*, doi: 10.1007/s10816-013-9175-6.

Tschopik, Harry, Jr. 1939. Artifacts of Perishable Materials. In *Preliminary Report on the 1937 Excavations, Bc 50–51, Chaco Canyon, New Mexico*, edited by Clyde Kluckhohn and Paul Reiter, pp. 94–130. University of New Mexico Bulletin 345, Anthropological Series 3, No. 2. University of New Mexico Press, Albuquerque.

Van Dyke, Ruth M. 1999. The Chaco Connection: Evaluating Bonito Style Architecture in Outlier Communities. *Journal of Anthropological Archaeology* 18:471–506.

———. 2003. Bounding Chaco: Great House Architectural Variability across Time and Space. *Kiva* 69:117–139.

———. 2007. *The Chaco Experience: Landscape and Ideology at the Center Place*. School for Advanced Research Press, Santa Fe.

Van Dyke, Ruth M., and Susan E. Alcock (editors). 2003. *Archaeologies of Memory*. Blackwell Publishers, Oxford, England.

Vivian, R. Gordon. 1931. Basketry of Chetro Ketl. Manuscript on file, Archive 2107, The Museum Collections of Chaco Culture National Historical Park Service, Albuquerque.

Vivian, R. Gordon, and Tom W. Mathews. 1965. *Kin Kletso: A Pueblo III Community in Chaco Canyon, New Mexico*. Southwestern Monuments Association Technical Series Vol. 6, Pt. 1. Southwestern Monuments Association, Globe, Arizona.

Vivian, R. Gwinn. 1970. An Inquiry into Prehistoric Social Organization in Chaco Canyon, New Mexico. In *Reconstructing Prehistoric Pueblo Societies*, edited by William A. Longacre, pp. 59–83. School of American Research Press, Santa Fe.

———. 1990. *The Chacoan Prehistory of the San Juan Basin*. Academic Press, San Diego.

Vivian, R. Gwinn, Dulce N. Dodgen, and Gayle H. Hartmann. 1978. *Wooden Ritual Artifacts from Chaco Canyon, New Mexico: The Chetro Ketl Collection*. Anthropological Papers of the University of Arizona No. 32. University of Arizona Press, Tucson.

Webster, Laurie D. 2006. Worked Fiber Artifacts from Salmon Pueblo. In *Thirty-Five Years of Archaeological Research at Salmon Ruins, New Mexico*, Vol. 3, *Archaeobotanical Research and Other Analytical Studies*, edited by Paul F. Reed, pp. 893–1012. Center for Desert Archaeology, Tucson; Salmon Ruins Museum, Bloomfield, New Mexico.

———. 2007. Mogollon and Zuni Perishable Traditions and the Question of Zuni Origins. In *Zuni Origins: Toward a New Synthesis of Southwestern Archaeology*, edited by David A. Gregory and David R. Wilcox, pp. 270–317. University of Arizona Press, Tucson.

————. 2008. An Initial Assessment of Perishable Artifact Relationships among Salmon, Aztec, and Chaco Canyon. In *Chaco's Northern Prodigies: Salmon, Aztec, and the Ascendancy of the Middle San Juan Region after AD 1100*, edited by Paul F. Reed, pp. 167–189. University of Utah Press, Salt Lake City.

————. 2011. Perishable Ritual Artifacts at the West Ruin of Aztec, New Mexico: Evidence for a Chacoan Migration. *Kiva* 77(2):139–172.

Webster, Laurie D., Kelley A. Hays-Gilpin, and Polly Schaafsma. 2006. A New Look at Tie-Dye and the Dot-in-a-Square Motif in the Prehispanic Southwest. *Kiva* 71(3):317–348.

Webster, Laurie D., Linda S. Cordell, Kelley Hays-Gilpin, and Edward A. Jolie. 2014. In Praise of Collections Research: Basketmaker Roots of Chacoan Ritual Practices. In *Archaeology in the Great Basin and Southwest: Papers in Honor of Don. D. Fowler*, edited by Nancy J. Parezo and Joel C. Janetski, pp. 322–335. University of Utah Press, Salt Lake City.

Whiting, Beatrice Blyth, and Carolyn Pope Edwards. 1988. *Children of Different Worlds: The Formation of Social Behavior*. Harvard University Press, Cambridge, Massachusetts.

Wills, W. H. 2009. Cultural Identity and the Archaeological Construction of Historical Narratives: An Example from Chaco Canyon. *Journal of Archaeological Method and Theory* 16:283–319.

Windes, Thomas C. 2003. This Old House: Construction and Abandonment at Pueblo Bonito. In *Pueblo Bonito: Center of the Chacoan World*, edited by Jill E. Neitzel, pp. 14–32. Smithsonian Books, Washington, D.C.

Zingg, Robert M. 1940. *Report on Archaeology of Southern Chihuahua*. University of Denver Contributions 3. Center of Latin American Studies I. University of Denver, Denver.

5

Bones as Raw Material

Temporal Trends and Spatial Variability in the Chacoan
Bone Tool Industry

Adam S. Watson

Although debate persists over the precise timing and nature of the transformation, there is widespread agreement among Chaco scholars that
the canyon witnessed unprecedented and far-reaching sociopolitical
changes during the ninth, tenth, and eleventh centuries A.D. However,
the extent to which these developments entailed corresponding shifts in
economic organization remains unclear. Through an analysis of Chaco's
bone industry, this research assesses the scale, intensity, and organization of Chacoan craft production through time, addressing two fundamental questions: To what degree does access to and selection of raw
materials vary across time and space? Do potential shifts in production
correlate with the increasing political centralization of the Early, Classic, and Late Bonito phases (850–1140 A.D.)?

Since the Hyde Exploring Expedition commenced excavations at
Pueblo Bonito nearly 120 years ago, excavations in and around Chaco
Canyon have yielded more than 3,500 bone and antler artifacts. Ubiquitous throughout sites from Basketmaker III through Pueblo III periods, these decorative and utilitarian objects were manufactured from
the remains of at least 17 different mammal and bird species and range
in form from decorative beads, pendants, and tubes to awls, punches,
flakers, and scrapers, among others. Despite the apparent time depth
and at times great intensity of the Chacoan bone tool industry and its
important implications for other dimensions of the Chacoan economy,
these artifacts have received comparatively little attention in studies of
the organization of craft production.

Previous research into Chacoan economy has focused principally
upon turquoise and shell ornament production and ceramic and chipped
stone industries (Cameron 1984; Cameron and Toll 2001; Mathien 1997,

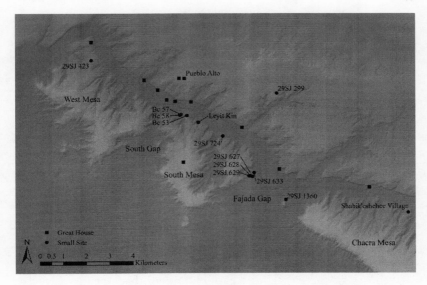

Figure 5.1. Map of Chaco Canyon and sites examined in this study.

2001; Toll 1984, 1985, 1991, 2001, 2006; Toll and McKenna 1997), and past studies of Chacoan bone artifacts have been limited to site-specific analyses of assemblages recovered during the course of the Chaco Project excavations (1972–1979) (McKenna 1984; Miles 1987, 1992, 1993). The purpose of this study is to examine variability in bone artifacts at the inter-site level spanning the sixth through twelfth centuries A.D., focusing on one great house (Pueblo Alto), eight small house sites (Leyit Kin, Bc 53, Bc 57, 29SJ627, 29SJ628, 29SJ629, 29SJ633, and 29SJ1360), and three Basketmaker III sites (Shabik'eshchee Village, 29SJ423, and 29SJ519), as shown in Figure 5.1.

Background

Variability in raw material is evaluated through study of the relationship between patterns of species procurement and the frequency with which particular species and skeletal elements served as raw materials. Through an examination of trends in the availability of raw material, this analysis can thereby assess the degree to which raw material choice may have covaried with supply or was driven by other impetuses such as durability and expediency.

Framing the Study of Craft Production

In simple terms, craft production is the transformation of raw materials into usable objects, and specialization can be defined as the heightened repetition and regularity of such an activity in exchange for some other service or commodity (Costin 1991:3). For Earle (1987:64), this is the "economic essence of complex society" in that specialization involves the development of economic interdependence, differentiation, and control and thereby supports a non-subsistence sector that in turn increases the potential for population growth. Cautioning scholars to avoid a preoccupation with the level of complexity implied by specialization, Brumfiel (1995:129) reminds us that part-time or non-specialized production commonly complicates the daily lives of individual craftspeople far more than those participating in more *complex* economies.

Schortman and Urban (2004:207) point out that "the pervasive distinction between elite industries used to fashion hierarchy and mundane crafts instrumental in the proliferation of heterarchical social distinctions probably simplifies complex ancient realities." In fact, both processes may have operated simultaneously, promoting the development of a complex "multi-centered political economy" in which power was dispersed and different craft industries supported diverse political, corporate, and ritual endeavors (Schortman and Urban 2004:208–209). Along similar lines, Wattenmaker (1998) found that in many instances elite oversight of relatively simple manufacturing of readily available raw materials was limited or non-existent. It is thus important, she argues, to bear in mind that apparently mundane objects may well delineate social boundaries unrelated to social inequality (Wattenmaker 1998:202–203).

The "ritual mode of production," a concept introduced by Spielmann (2002), is particularly relevant to the Pueblo Southwest. Drawing on ethnographic sources from Melanesia and New Guinea (Damon 1989; Firth 1950; Malinowski 1922; Rappaport 1984; Wagner 1989), Spielmann observed that in small-scale societies "the scale of economic production necessary for ritual performance is critical to understanding economic intensification" (Spielmann 2002:196). With communal ritual as the driving force, craft production and feasting are supported by the wider population rather than elite sponsors, and as a result, the goal is not "profits" but "superlative performance and participation" (Spielmann 2002:197).

Costin (1991:7–18) offered a useful framework for describing and understanding the organization of production. Varying along four axes, the continua include *context*, or the affiliation of producers with the sociopolitical structure, that is, "attached" or "independent" specialists; *concentration*, or the geographic organization of production; *scale*, or the size and principles of labor recruitment for production units; and *intensity*, or the amount of time dedicated by producers to their craft.

A fundamental distinction exists between attached and independent specialization. While the former is characterized by specialists who are bound to and provide solely for elite patrons, the latter consists of specialists who produce goods or services for a broader demand or market. A third type introduced by Ames (1995), that of *embedded* specialists, includes those systems in which production to meet the needs of elites occurs under non-coercive conditions and forms an essential part of the local economy. "Attached specialization" in Costin's (1991) terms is not widely regarded as an appropriate characterization of productive strategies in the prehistoric Southwest. However, high levels of production and exchange, both in terms of scale and intensity, are evident archaeologically and in modern ethnographic accounts (Bayman 1999:252).

Similarly, while the density of finished goods in Chaco indicates large-scale production, there is little evidence of attached specialization, prompting several scholars (Hagstrum 2001; Mathien 1997; Saitta 1999; Toll and McKenna 1997; Windes 1992) to suggest the existence of either independent or embedded specialists. Toll and McKenna (1997:207–208), for instance, contend that ceramics produced in Chaco were destined for unspecified local and regional trade networks—a pattern more typical of independent specialization. The presence of part-time specialists in ornament production is implied by the presence of at least one ornament workshop at a Chacoan small site (29SJ629). While finished ornaments of turquoise, shell, and other materials are rare at this and nearly all other small sites, they appear in remarkable quantities in great house contexts (Mathien 1997:110; Plog and Heitman 2010:19622; Windes 1992:162). Great house demands for labor in the ornament industry thus are well-defined and its apparent connection with ritual and possibly elite behavior is consistent with embedded specialization. The high concentrations of rare ceramic forms at Pueblo Bonito also attest to the potential for embedded, if infrequent, specialized ceramic production. The distinction between independent and embedded specialist, while of heuristic utility, was in practice probably fluid and contextually dependent, with elevation of production levels varying in response to demands such as ritual or periodic exchange.

The production of basketry and textiles and the working of animal hides using bone implements are well-documented historically among the Pueblos and likely comprised a major craft production sector in the canyon (Cushing 1979:183; Hagstrum 2001:52; Hill 1982:51–52, 91, 103–108). Certainly, the diversity of perishable artifacts discussed by Jolie and Webster (this volume) is a testament to the breadth and intensity of Chacoan craft industries.

Ethnographic Evidence for Specialization and Material Correlates. Ford (1972) observed that Tewa villages varied in size, relative "wealth," and level of participation in exchange systems and that certain pueblos specialized in particular craft products such as blankets, baskets, and pottery while others specialized in particular services such as midwifery or ceremonials (Ford 1972:40). Exchange networks within and between Pueblos tended to follow kinship relations or established friendships. The most common contexts for trade were those of informal individual exchanges, craft fairs, and goods bartered in exchange for ceremonial services (Ford 1972:36, 44). Still other ethnohistoric sources illustrate the diversity of craft goods, including basketry, textiles, and hides that were commonly traded among Rio Grande Pueblos (Hammond and Rey 1953:624–626, 645; Hill 1982:91, 94, 99).

It should be noted that all of the above activities were regularly undertaken at the household scale, and intensification of production would be reflected archaeologically by the presence of raw and finished goods exceeding the needs of the immediate household.

Economic intensification at Hopi, including the mobilization of labor for spinning and weaving of wool (and likely cotton to a larger extent during prehistoric times), the manufacture of baskets, communal hunting of rabbits and coyotes (and apparently deer and antelope in earlier periods), and the production of corn meal, primarily occurs in three contexts—marriage-based and general kin-related exchange and dance-related feasts (Eggan 1950:50–51, 55–56, 60; Titiev 1944:37–38, 228–229, 237). Eggan (1950:60) described these production and exchange relations:

> On all important ritual occasions the father's sisters, whether own or ceremonial, play an important role in relation to ego and his lineage, and their efforts are repaid by the latter. The exchanges consequent upon initiations of various kinds furnish a goodly portion of the economic exchange of goods in Hopi society, and from each lineage and household there is a constant inflow and outgo of food, clothing, and other wealth.

The first and second scenarios—those of marriage-based and general kin-related exchange relationships—were probably common in prehistoric Pueblo society and represent the base-level of production and exchange. Such instances would have entailed levels of production only slightly above immediate domestic needs, and presumably this pattern would be difficult to detect archaeologically.

In contrast, a surge in craft production associated with a dance-related feast may yield material correlates visible in the archaeological record. One expectation is that demands exceeding "normal" household needs would necessitate increases in the number of bone tools required for the working of basketry and hides and in weaving and in the frequency of lapidary stones and drills required for the production of ornaments. As craft production intensifies and tool manufacture becomes more standardized, diversity in raw material selection might be expected to decline. Of course, with finite raw material sources, the opposite may be true. That is, with resource scarcity the intensification of production could require the utilization of every bit of raw material, regardless of material type, which in turn would result in greater diversity. It is a complex question and one to which we will return.

Ethnographic data demonstrate that intensification of production is a logical outcome of expanding exchange networks and increases in the scale of social participation in communal ritual. In the case of Chaco, the expansion of social, political, and economic networks are reflected in great house construction; communal ritual centered on great kivas (Watson 2012); potential pilgrimage fairs and road networks; the import of ceramics, lithics, and exotics; and overall population growth.

Methods

Based on the expectations outlined above, this study assesses overall trends in the Chacoan bone tool industry and investigates whether discernible shifts in patterns of production correlate with the increasing political centralization of the Early, Classic, and Late Bonito phases. Bone tools were likely employed in a variety of tasks, including hide working, basketry production, pottery manufacture, and corn shucking, all of which apply stress to and degrade bone to varying degrees. It follows that durability should be a principal concern in raw material choice (Margaris 2009). Thus, the intensification in production and use of bone tools would be expected to result in a trend away from less durable and expedient types of bone tools toward durable raw materials and more standardized forms.

To address these questions, the data under consideration include the worked-bone assemblages recovered and analyzed during the course of the Chaco Project as well as three additional assemblages examined by the author (see Table 5.1). Broad temporal trends in raw material selection are assessed by comparing site-specific faunal procurement strategies with species selected as raw material for bone tools using correspondence analysis (CA). Where CA is unable to adequately clarify spatial and temporal variability in species choice, more fine-grained approaches are utilized. To examine richness and diversity, Simpson's Measure of Evenness ($E_{1/D}$) and Simpson's Diversity Index (D) are applied to examine changes in skeletal element choice through time (Magurran 2004:114–116) (see equations 5.1 and 5.2).

As noted, a scarcity of preferred raw materials, mass production of tools, or a lack of labor available for the time-intensive production of

$$D = \sum p_i^2$$

where:

D = Simpson's Diversity Index
$p_i p_i$ = the proportion of individuals in the ith species

Equation 5.1. Simpson's Diversity Index (D)

$$E_{1/D} = \frac{(^1/_D)}{S}$$

where:

D = Simpson's Diversity Index
S = number of species in sample

Equation 5.2. Simpson's Measure of Evenness ($E_{1/D}$)

bone tools also have the potential to produce declines in standardization. Scarcity of raw material and the possibility of mass production are assessed through a comparison of overall faunal exploitation and temporal trends in the frequencies of tools, while the effect of labor shortages must be considered as an alternative explanation for possible decreases in standardization.

Analysis of the Bc 53 (29SJ396), Bc 57 (29SJ397), and Leyit Kin (29SJ750) assemblages was completed in the Archaeobiology Laboratory of the Smithsonian Institution's National Museum of Natural History. A variety of observations and metrics were recorded, and every effort was made to ensure consistency with the criteria and terminology utilized by Chaco Project analysts. Bone artifacts were identified to element and lowest taxonomic levels using the Smithsonian's vertebrate zoology comparative osteological collections.

Where possible, date ranges for bone tool assemblages from Chaco Project sites were obtained directly from reports (McKenna and Truell 1986; Miles 1987, 1992, 1993). The chronology of Bc 57 is based on radiocarbon dates and mean ceramic dates obtained by the author, while temporal assignment of the Leyit Kin collection was made on the basis of Dutton's excavation report (1938:82–94).* The majority of worked bone could be assigned to one of five broad time periods (Basketmaker III, Early Pueblo I, and the Early, Classic, and Late Bonito subphases). Temporal trends in faunal procurement were based on the synthesis by Akins (1985).

---

*Unfortunately, the Leyit Kin sample that was able to be relocated represents approximately half of the overall bone artifact assemblage, representing 13 of the original 32 contexts excavated.

Table 5.1. Worked Bone Artifacts from Chacoan Sites Examined in This Study.

								Tool Type
Site	Awl	Needle	Pin	Antler Flaker	End Scraper	Tool Blank	Weaving Tool	Tinkler
29SJ299	6		1		1	2		2
Pueblo Alto (29SJ389)	96	2	4	2	13			
Bc 53 (29SJ396)	33	2		2	3			
Bc 57 (29SJ397)	34	1			14			
29SJ423	3							
29SJ519	1							
29SJ627	94	6	1		6	2		1
29SJ628	78	3			3	1	1	1
Spadefoot Toad site (29SJ629)	14	2			3		1	1
Eleventh Hour site (29SJ633)	5		1					1
29SJ724	13	1				9	3	2
Leyit Kin (29SJ750)	20	1			2	1		
29SJ1360	39	5	3	2	3	7		2
Shabik'eshchee (29SJ1659)	10				3		1	
TOTAL	446	23	10	6	51	22	6	10

Results

Spatial Variation

Before proceeding with the analysis of bone tool manufacture patterns, a brief discussion of spatial and temporal variability in production loci is warranted (Table 5.2). In fact, relatively few bone artifacts were found

Tool Type											
Gaming Piece	Ornament	Punch	Spatulate	Rubbing Tool	Sounding Rasp/Whistle	Waste Product	Drill	Multi-use Tool	Fragment	Unknown	TOTAL
1	19								1	12	45
2	13	3		3	2			1		102	243
	0									8	48
	14								2	5	70
	5									7	15
	14							1		8	
7	23	4	3	1	2				4	94	248
1	5	3	1		2					41	140
1	4		2							26	54
	1								2	8	18
	0									5	33
	6									10	40
	0	3					1		1	17	83
1	9	1				1			3	14	43
13	113	14	6	4	6	1	1	2	13	357	**1104**

in contexts that reflect craft production; as much as 94 percent of bone artifacts were found discarded in refuse deposits. However, during the Basketmaker III period through the Early Bonito subphase, bone tool manufacture and use appears to have been centered within pithouses and kivas. The sizable assemblage found in situ within Pithouse B at site 1360 lends support to this interpretation, but it remains unclear whether

Table 5.2. Bone Artifact Provenience by Time Period.

Time Period	Square Room				Kiva/Pithouse				Extramural Area				Trash Midden	
	Fill	%	Floor	%	Fill	%	Floor	%	Fill	%	Floor	%	Fill	%
Basketmaker III/Early Pueblo I	1	0.4	0	0.0	197	71.1	66	23.8	11.0	4.0	2	0.7	0	0.0
Early Bonito	46	17.1	14	5.2	127	47.2	48	17.8	6.0	2.2	0	0.0	28	10.4
Classic Bonito	10	17.2	2	3.4	4	6.9	0	0.0	3.0	5.2	0	0.0	39	67.2
Late Bonito	71	41.0	3	1.7	88	50.9	1	0.6	8.0	4.6	2	1.2	0	0.0
TOTAL	128	16.5	19	2.4	416	53.5	115	14.8	28	3.6	4	0.5	67	8.6

Context

the apparent decline in osseous artifacts recovered from floor-associated contexts during subsequent periods reflects a change in cultural practices or the vagaries of archaeological preservation and recovery. The presence of a small amount of worked bone from floor deposits within roomblocks during the Classic and Late Bonito subphases implies that these areas were the focus of at least some craft production. The Late Bonito increase in intramural discard of bone artifacts is attributable to a broader temporal shift in canyon-wide refuse disposal patterns (Wills 2009:297–298; Windes 1987:617–618).

Species Variability in Raw Material Choice

The initial step in this analysis is an exploration of temporal variation in resource availability and identification of sites exhibiting similar or disparate bone tool production strategies. Capable of depicting multiple dimensions of variability within a data set, CA is a particularly useful approach.

As is visible in Figure 5.2a, axis one of the CA plot captures meaningful temporal patterning in overall faunal procurement strategies with earlier sites (299, 423, 628, 724, and 1360) toward the left-hand side of the distribution and the later components of sites 627, 629, 633, and Pueblo Alto toward the right-hand side of the plot. The plot delineates two, possibly three, groups of sites—the first is defined by procurement of artiodactyls, and this group may be subdivided based on a differential emphasis on pronghorn on the one hand and deer and bighorn on the other. The second clear grouping reflects a twelfth-century bias at Pueblo Alto and 29SJ 633 toward exploitation of turkey. Due to the overwhelming focus on cottontail, jackrabbit, and various species of artiodactyl (bighorn sheep, mule deer, and pronghorn antelope) throughout most periods, there is significant overlap among sites occupied from Basketmaker III through Pueblo II. Given the increase in turkey exploitation at many Chacoan sites during the late eleventh and early twelfth centuries, this distribution of sites trending toward the right of the plot is unsurprising.

Axis 1 of Figure 5.2b also appears to capture a temporal dimension in bone tool raw material choice. Extending toward the left of the plot are the Basketmaker III sites in which jackrabbit appears to have been a common raw material source. From the origin toward the right of the

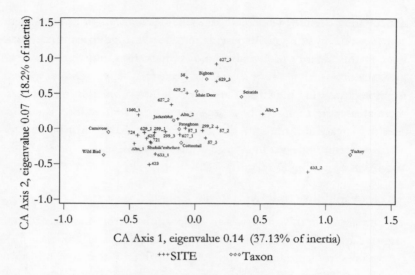

Figure 5.2a. CA plot of Basketmaker III through Pueblo III faunal procurement patterns.

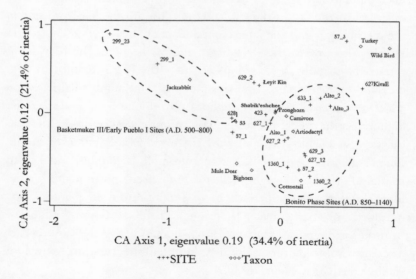

Figure 5.2b. CA plot of Basketmaker III through Pueblo III bone tool raw materials sources; the category "Wild Bird" includes worked bone identified to taxonomic class Aves.

plot lies a roughly temporally sequential distribution of Bonito phase sites dominated by artiodactyl remains and later turkey during the latest component at Bc 57. Thus, from Basketmaker III to the ensuing Pueblo periods, there is a perceptible temporal shift from the use of leporids in bone tool production toward artiodactyl, carnivores, and turkey. The tight grouping of Bonito phase sites suggests a high degree of similarity, but the possibility of additional inter-site variability warrants further investigation.

To summarize the CA, a broad temporal trend in worked-bone production is evident. Established by the Early Bonito subphase, site assemblages reflect a widespread preference for more durable artiodactyl and carnivore skeletal elements, a pattern consistent with increasing raw material standardization across all sites.

Figures 5.3, 5.4, and 5.5 depict the temporal relationship between number of identified specimens (NISP) for all faunal assemblages and the frequency with which species were selected as raw material for bone implements and ornaments. Again, artiodactyl, a category that includes pronghorn, bighorn, and mule deer, as well as specimens identified as large mammal, remains the most common raw material source across the Early, Classic, and Late Bonito subphases. Despite particularly high NISP counts throughout, exploitation of cottontail and jackrabbit as tool stock exhibits very little fluctuation through time. Carnivore elements were widely accessible during Early Bonito and were accordingly utilized with some frequency. Interestingly, as availability declined during the Classic and Late Bonito subphases, demand for carnivore skeletal elements in bone tool manufacture remained high, suggesting that cultural preferences dictated its continued importance as a raw material. Access to turkey and other bird species was relatively unchanged from the Early to Classic Bonito subphases, but demand for bird bone apparently soared during Classic Bonito. During the Late Bonito subphase, the availability of turkey increased markedly, but use of turkey bone rose only slightly compared to other species.

Thus, comparison of faunal exploitation trends and raw material choice through time reveals that raw material selection is neither strongly correlated with nor limited by the availability of resources.

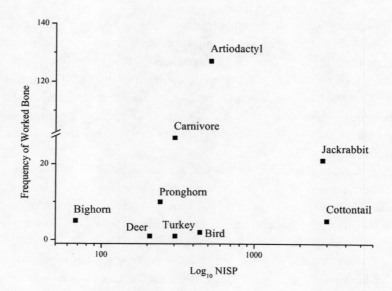

Figure 5.3. Comparison of raw material choice versus NISP for Early Bonito.

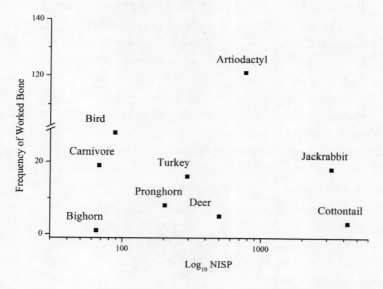

Figure 5.4. Comparison of raw material choice versus NISP for Classic Bonito.

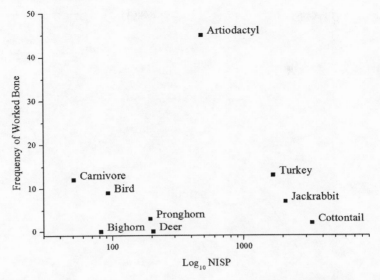

Figure 5.5. Comparison of raw material choice versus NISP for Late Bonito.

Rather, raw material selection appears to have been driven by other factors such as tool-making traditions or craft production intensity.

Ternary plots provide an opportunity to explore more subtle, site-specific trends in species procurement and bone tool production; sites were separated into groups by Early, Classic, and Late Bonito subphases, highlighting several notable trends. The obliteration of species-diagnostic anatomical features is common during the manufacturing process and use-life of bone tools. For this reason, comparisons of relative frequencies of fauna were limited to the broad categories "artiodactyl," "leporid," and "carnivore," to which even heavily worn bone artifacts can often be assigned.

Starting with the Early Bonito phase (Figure 5.6), faunal exploitation at sites 1360 and Bc 57 diverged markedly from other Early Bonito phase sites (627, 629, and Pueblo Alto), with an emphasis on artiodactyls. In addition, carnivore procurement appears relatively high at both 1360 and the earliest component at 629. Otherwise, Early Bonito phase sites all exhibit a general preference for leporid remains. While the rate of artiodactyl procurement varied widely, deer, pronghorn, and bighorn skeletal parts comprise the overwhelming majority of raw materials selected for bone tool manufacture at all sites. Among the Marcia's

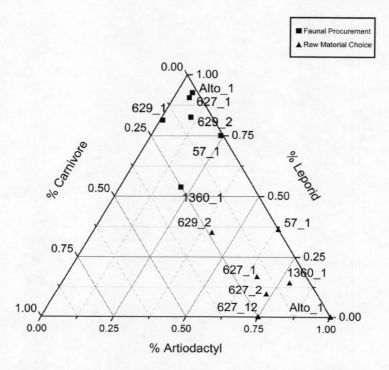

Figure 5.6. Ternary plot of Early Bonito subphase faunal procurement patterns and raw material choice.

Rincon sites (627 and 629), more durable carnivore bone was favored, while less durable, expedient tools fashioned from leporid remains were common at both 629 and Bc 57. Overall frequency of bone artifacts dating to this period is the lowest of the entire Bonito phase, and the Fajada Gap sites (627, 629, 1360) account for the majority of the worked-bone sample.

Although emphasis on artiodactyl increased slightly and leporid procurement remained relatively unchanged from the preceding period (Figure 5.7), the Classic Bonito subphase witnessed a drop in hunting of carnivores and an increase in the frequency of bird remains, a pattern most evident at Bc 57. Selection of leporids as raw material for tools declined at most sites, Leyit Kin being the exception. The trend suggests a general shift away from expedient tools toward more durable forms. Relative to other species, the rate at which bird species—including

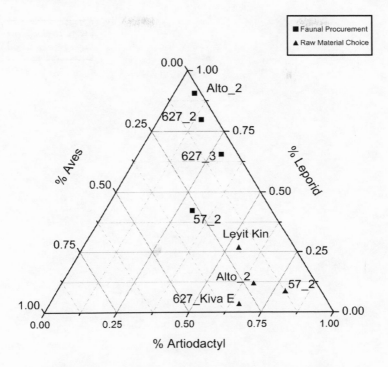

Figure 5.7. Ternary plot of Classic Bonito subphase faunal procurement patterns and raw material choice.

Cooper's hawk, Canada goose, sandhill crane, and turkey—were utilized as raw material for tools and tube beads increased by an average of 20 percent from preceding periods.

The Late Bonito subphase pattern (Figure 5.8) is similar to that of the Classic Bonito subphase, with a continued preference for artiodactyl elements in tool manufacture. Whereas the number of bone ornaments exhibited only a slight (5 percent) increase from the Early to Classic Bonito subphases, the number of bone tubes and pendants manufactured from bird bone increased by 20 percent during the Late Bonito subphase. The pattern is striking, and it reflects a significant shift in the bone tool industry. Despite low rates of carnivore procurement, the frequency of its use as raw material displayed a marked increase at Pueblo Alto and the Marcia's Rincon sites 627 and 633. The total frequency of bone tools remained high at Pueblo Alto and

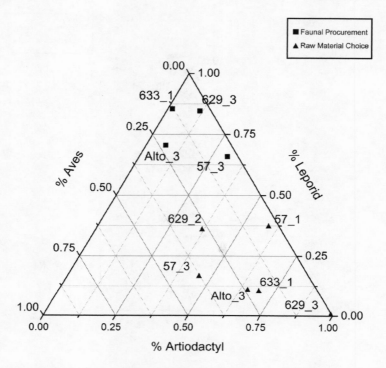

Figure 5.8. Ternary plot of Late Bonito subphase faunal procurement patterns and raw material choice.

Bc 57 but appears to have been on the decline among the Marcia's Rincon sites.

To assess the significance of these trends, a chi-square comparison was performed of species-related raw material selection and time period (Table 5.3). For the Early and Classic Bonito subphases, the chi-square test reveals that time period and species selected for manufacture of worked-bone objects are interrelated (χ^2 = 16.934, p < .01, df = 3). Examination of the adjusted residuals confirms that bird remains are indeed significantly overrepresented among Classic Bonito deposits, consistent with the trend observed above. In contrast, the results of the chi-square comparison of Classic and Late Bonito worked-bone manufacture (Table 5.4) were not significant, χ^2 = .829 (p = .842, df = 3), but the expected frequencies and adjusted residuals do highlight the continued growth in intensity of bird bone utilization.

Table 5.3. Chi-Square Table with Adjusted Residuals Comparing Species Selected as Raw Material for Bone Tools and Ornaments during the Early and Classic Subphases at Pueblo Alto, 29SJ 627, 29SJ 629, Leyit Kin, and Bc 57.

| | Time Period | | | |
| | Early Bonito | | Classic Bonito | |
Taxon	Observed (Expected)	Adjusted Residual	Observed (Expected)	Adjusted Residual
Artiodactyl	149 (143.11)	1.028	281 (286.89)	−1.028
Aves	5 (18.64)	−4.044*	51 (37.36)	4.044*
Carnivore	31 (29.96)	1.018	50 (54.04)	−1.018
Leporid	33 (29.29)	0.902	55 (58.71)	−0.902

Expected values are shown in parentheses; χ^2 = 16.934, (p < 0.001, df = 3). For adjusted residuals, * denotes p < 0.01.

Table 5.4. Chi-Square Table with Adjusted Residuals Comparing Species Selected as Raw Material for Bone Tools and Ornaments during Classic and Late Bonito Subphases at Pueblo Alto, 29SJ627, 29SJ629, 29SJ633, Leyit Kin, and Bc 57.

| | Time Period | | | |
| | Classic Bonito | | Late Bonito | |
Taxon	Observed (Expected)	Adjusted Residual	Observed (Expected)	Adjusted Residual
Artiodactyl	281 (276.6)	0.585	328 (332.4)	−0.585
Aves	51 (55.4)	−0.8601	71 (66.6)	0.8601
Carnivore	50 (50.9)	−0.1771	62 (61.1)	0.1771
Leporid	55 (54.1)	0.1854	64 (64.9)	−0.1854

Expected values are shown in parentheses; χ^2 = 0.829 (p = 0.842, df = 3).

Analysis using ternary plots reinforces the pattern visible in the CA in which artiodactyl, and to a lesser degree carnivore, elements were the raw material of choice. When combined with the disproportionately higher frequency of bone tools recovered from sites in the Marcia's Rincon and Fajada Gap areas of Chaco relative to contemporaneous occupations at Bc 57 and Pueblo Alto, the data suggest that the former areas may have been the focus of early intensification of bone tool manufacture and use (Watson 2012). Use of bird bone in tube and ornament manufacture increased in prevalence during the Classic Bonito subphase. The trend persists through the Late Bonito subphase and signals an important shift in the Chacoan bone industry in which the production of ritual or sumptuary items increased in importance relative to utilitarian objects such as awls and scrapers.

In view of the similarity in raw material choice among the Marcia's Rincon sites (627, 629, 1360) and the clear evidence for differential access to artiodactyls (Figure 5.6), it is tempting to infer exchange between these neighboring sites. While a plausible alternative interpretation is that despite limited access to artiodactyls the 627 and 629 inhabitants' supply of raw material was adequate to meet production needs, it should also be noted that the assemblage from Pithouse B at site 1360 contained an unusually high density of bone tools, including several artiodactyl lower limb bones in varying stages of reduction and modification for use as bone tools. This evidence for specialized bone tool production has prompted other researchers to conclude that such bone tool production was "in excess of need" and may have been intended for local exchange (McKenna 1984:323–345, 387). If indeed the pattern reflects local exchange, then it is perhaps not surprising that site 629, which yielded the strongest evidence for a turquoise and shell ornament workshop (Mathien 2001), exhibits less standardization in bone tool manufacture and significantly lower overall counts of bone tools compared to neighboring contemporaneous sites. Similarly, based on a canyon-wide study of abraders, Akins (1987) found that passive lapidary, believed to have been associated with ornament production, was overrepresented at each of the Marcia's Rincon sites, leading Akins to conclude that production was more commonly associated with small sites rather than great houses (Akins 1987:375–379).

Analysis of species-related raw material choice revealed a temporal trend indicative of intensification of production through time as well as a preference for more durable raw materials. However, as Emery noted, "The actual 'raw material' of the bone worker . . . is the skeletal element" (Emery 2009:8). An examination of skeletal element choice in bone tool manufacture affords an alternate means for testing the hypothesis that intensification was positively correlated with the sociopolitical changes of the Early, Classic, and Late Bonito subphases.

Skeletal Element Diversity. Fluctuations in richness, evenness, and diversity through time were assessed by focusing only on the broad tool category, "awl," the only tool type for which sample size was adequate across multiple sites (see Table 5.5). When richness was plotted against sample size, no sample-size effect was evident. The Early Bonito subphase is marked by a decrease in diversity of skeletal elements from the preceding Basketmaker III period, a pattern echoed in the diversity of species utilized (Table 5.6). Decreasing evenness in skeletal element selection appears to be the result of the increasing standardization of awl manufacture wherein large mammal metapodials constituted the preferred raw material. That both diversity and evenness of element and species selection increased slightly during Classic Bonito is unexpected but appears minor in comparison to the change that followed. The Late Bonito subphase contrasts sharply with preceding periods—a pattern not detected previously through examination of species choice. A dramatic increase in both diversity and evenness among skeletal elements reflects a growing disregard for earlier standards of awl manufacture. In fact, a review of the data revealed that the metapodials so heavily favored in antecedent periods are of minor importance during Late Bonito. Moreover, this apparent ambivalence for tool raw material

Table 5.5. Richness, Evenness, and Diversity Measures by Skeletal Elements Selected for Use in the Manufacture of Bone Awls at Sites Bc 57, 29SJ519, 29SJ628, 29SJ629, 29SJ633, and Pueblo Alto.

	Skeletal Element			
Period	Richness	Evenness (Simpson's $E_{1/D}$)	Diversity (Simpson's D)	n
Basketmaker III/Early Pueblo I	9	0.55	4.91	18
Early Bonito	8	0.41	3.26	30
Classic Bonito	12	0.43	5.16	19
Late Bonito	15	0.90	13.50	18

Table 5.6. Richness, Evenness, and Diversity Measures by Species Selected for Use in the Manufacture of Bone Awls at Sites Bc 57, 29SJ519, 29SJ628, 29SJ629, 29SJ633, and Pueblo Alto.

		Taxon		
Period	Richnesss	Evenness (Simpson's $E_{1/D}$)	Diversity (Simpson's D)	n
Basketmaker III/Early Pueblo I	7	0.82	5.76	14
Early Bonito	6	0.49	2.96	13
Classic Bonito	6	0.64	3.86	9
Late Bonito	7	0.55	3.84	13

extends across all sites in the sample (Pueblo Alto, Bc 57, 29SJ629, and 29SJ633). When juxtaposed with the steady trend toward increased standardization through the Early and Classic Bonito subphases, the Late Bonito shift in awl manufacture is all the more compelling.

Still, concerns over equifinality remain, as disparate production conditions have the potential to generate similar diversity values. As shown in Figure 5.5, the lack of correlation between resource availability and raw material choice and the overall decrease in frequency of bone tools during Late Bonito rules out the possibility that higher diversity and evenness values are attributable to either resource limitations or the effects of mass production. In light of the Late Bonito population decline (Judge and Cordell 2006:206), decreases in available labor should not be discounted as factors in the abandonment of previously held production standards.

Conclusion

This analysis revealed two dominant temporal trends in the Chacoan worked-bone industry. Species variation was characterized by a gradual increase in reliance on artiodactyls from Basketmaker III through the Early and Classic Bonito subphases, followed by a Late Bonito trend toward the use of bird, especially turkey, in the manufacture of bone tubes. While raw material preferences in awl manufacture became increasingly standardized throughout Early and Classic Bonito, the Late Bonito transition is marked by a lack of adherence to previous principles of bone tool production.

In spatial terms, there appear to have been at least two production centers that emerged and declined in overlapping succession during the Early, Classic, and Late Bonito subphases. Production arose first among the Marcia's Rincon and Fajada Gap sites during Early Bonito, followed by Pueblo Alto during the Classic Bonito subphase. By the Late Bonito subphase, bone tool use had diminished among the Marcia's Rincon sites but remained steady at Alto. While bone tools appeared regularly at sites in the Rinconada area, the magnitude does not approach that of either the Marcia's Rincon/Fajada Gap sites or Pueblo Alto.

The appearance of the earliest evidence for intensification of bone tool production and use among the smaller, more dispersed villages rather than great houses is consistent with other correlates of Chacoan craft production (Akins 1987; Mathien 2001; Windes 1992). The industry itself appears to have undergone a significant shift; bone tool manufacture and use reached an apex during the Early and Classic Bonito subphases, but they were subsequently eclipsed by a growing demand for tubes and ornaments during the Late Bonito subphase. Spanning Early Pueblo I and the Bonito phase, a limited number of bone whistles fashioned from bird and jackrabbit elements were recovered from sites 627 and 628 and Pueblo Alto. It remains unclear how many of the bone tubes manufactured might have been destined for use in whistles. If the rise in frequency in bone tubes is at all indicative of greater use of whistles, then the pattern could signal ritual elaboration and a proliferation of politico-religious specialists, as Corbett (2004) has suggested.

Greater standardization in awl forms implies intensification of hideworking and basketry production during Early and Classic Bonito, while reduced standardization during Late Bonito suggests that these perishable industries declined in importance relative to bone tube manufacture. This evidence for craft intensification coincides with other signs of social change in and around Chaco, including great house and great kiva construction, the development of Chacoan outliers (Sebastian 2006:399–401), and agricultural intensification (Vivian and Watson, this volume). The pronounced shift in tool production standards during Late Bonito may stem from a variety of factors, including declining exchange networks, labor shortages, or the arrival of migrant populations bearing different tool-making traditions. While more research is needed to better understand this period, it is clear that changes in the bone industry are tied to these broader shifts in the Chacoan political and economic landscape during the Early, Classic, and Late Bonito subphases.

In this volume, Jolie and Webster have noted the dominance in ritual contexts at Pueblo Bonito of large carrying baskets, ceremonial staffs with spatulate ends, and wooden flutes during the Early and Classic Bonito subphases that are indicative of continuity with Basketmaker III traditions. Although diversity in basketry styles during this period suggests the integration of disparate groups, the total absence of these artifact forms from subsequent Late Bonito deposits marks an apparent disruption in production traditions. Coupled with similar patterns in the related worked-bone industry, the discontinuity further underscores the pervasiveness of Late Bonito changes manifested in economic and ritual realms. Whether such a shift reflects demographic change, as some researchers have argued (Judd 1959:168–172; Vivian and Mathews 1965:109–111; Wills 2009), remains a source of debate.

The Pueblo Bonito collections alone account for nearly half of all bone artifacts recovered from Chaco Canyon, and analysis of this assemblage is underway. Substantial bone artifact assemblages were also found during the excavation of Bc 50, Bc 51, Talus Unit, and Chetro Ketl. In other words, well over half of the existing bone tools from Chaco Canyon remain to be analyzed, and as this analysis has demonstrated, exploration of temporal and spatial trends in this often-overlooked industry provides an essential perspective on Chacoan political and economic change.

Acknowledgments

I would like to thank Dr. Melinda Zeder of the Archaeobiology Program at the National Museum of Natural History in whose laboratory this research was completed. Thanks are due to Wendy Bustard of the Chaco Culture National Historical Park, Dave Phillips of the Maxwell

Museum of Anthropology, and Melissa Powell of the Museum of Indian Arts and Culture for facilitating access to these remarkable collections. I am grateful to Steve Plog and Carrie Heitman for the invitation to participate in the Amerind seminar and to two anonymous reviewers for their helpful feedback on an earlier version of this chapter.

References Cited

Akins, Nancy J. 1985. *Prehistoric Faunal Utilization in Chaco Canyon Basketmaker III through Pueblo III*. Environment and Subsistence of Chaco Canyon, New Mexico. National Park Service, Albuquerque.

———. 1987. The Abraders of Pueblo Alto. In Investigations at the Pueblo Alto Complex, Chaco Canyon, New Mexico 1975–1979, Vol. III, *Artifactual and Biological Analyses*, edited by Frances Joan Mathien and Thomas C. Windes, pp. 359–380. Publications in Archeology 18F, Chaco Canyon Studies. National Park Service, U.S. Department of the Interior, Santa Fe.

Ames, Kenneth. 1995. Chiefly Power and Household Production on the Northwest Coast. In *Foundations of Social Inequality*, edited by T. Douglas Price and Gary M. Feinman, pp. 155–187. Plenum, New York.

Bayman, James. 1999. Craft Economies in the North American Southwest. *Journal of Archaeological Research* 7(3):249–299.

Brumfiel, Elizabeth M. 1995. Heterarchy and the Analysis of Complex Societies: Comments. *Archeological Papers of the American Anthropological Association* 6(1):125–131.

Cameron, Catherine M. 1984. A Regional View of Chipped Stone Raw Material Use in Chaco Canyon. In *Recent Research on Chaco Prehistory*, edited by W. James Judge and John D. Schelberg, pp. 137–152. Reports of the Chaco Center No. 8. Division of Cultural Research, National Park Service, Albuquerque.

Cameron, Catherine M., and H. Wolcott Toll. 2001. Deciphering the Organization of Production in Chaco Canyon. *American Antiquity* 66(1):5–13.

Corbett, Raymond. 2004. The Development of Ceremonial Integration in Chumash Society. In *Foundations of Chumash Complexity*, edited by Jeanne E. Arnold, pp. 65–73. Perspectives in California Archaeology 7. Cotsen Institute of Archaeology, Los Angeles.

Costin, Cathy L. 1991. Craft Specialization: Issues in Defining, Documenting, and Explaining the Organization of Production. In *Archaeological Method and Theory*, Vol. 3, edited by Michael B. Schiffer, pp. 1–56. University of Arizona Press, Tucson.

Cushing, Frank H. 1979. *Zuni: Selected Writings of Frank Hamilton Cushing*. University of Nebraska Press, Lincoln.

Damon, Frederick. 1989. Introduction. In *Death Rituals and Life in the Societies of the Kula Ring*, edited by Frederick Damon and Roy Wagner, pp. 3–19. Northern Illinois University Press, DeKalb.

Dutton, Bertha P. 1938. *Leyit Kin, a Small House Ruin, Chaco Canyon, New Mexico*. University of New Mexico and School of American Research No. 7. University of New Mexico Bulletin No. 333, Monograph Series 1(5). University of New Mexico, Albuquerque.

Earle, Timothy. 1987. Specialization and the Production of Wealth: Hawaiian Chiefdoms and the Inka Empire. In *Specialization, Exchange, and Social Complex Societies*, edited by Elizabeth M. Brumfiel and Timothy K. Earle, pp. 64–75. Cambridge University Press, Cambridge.

Eggan, Fred. 1950. *Social Organization of the Western Pueblos*. University of Chicago Press, Chicago.

Emery, Kitty F. 2009. Perspectives on Ancient Maya Bone Crafting from a Classic Period Bone-Artifact Manufacturing Assemblage. *Journal of Anthropological Archaeology* 28(4):458–470.

Firth, Raymond (editor). 1950. *Primitive Polynesian Economy*. Humanities Press, New York.

Ford, Richard I. 1972. Barter, Gift, or Violence: An Analysis of Tewa Intertribal Exchange. In *Social Exchange and Interaction*, edited by Edwin N. Wilmsen, pp. 21–45. Anthropological Papers No. 46. Museum of Anthropology, University of Michigan, Ann Arbor.

Hagstrum, Melissa. 2001. Household Production in Chaco Canyon Society. *American Antiquity* 66(1):47–55.

Hammond, George P., and Agapito Rey. 1953. *Don Juan de Oñate: Colonizer of New Mexico*. University of New Mexico Press, Albuquerque.

Hill, W. W. 1982. *An Ethnography of Santa Clara Pueblo, New Mexico*. Edited and annotated by Charles H. Lange. University of New Mexico Press, Albuquerque.

Judd, Neil M. 1959. *Pueblo del Arroyo, Chaco Canyon, New Mexico*. Smithsonian Miscellaneous Collections Vol. 138. Smithsonian Institution, Washington, D.C.

Judge, W. James, and Linda S. Cordell. 2006. Society and Polity. In *The Archaeology of Chaco Canyon: An Eleventh-Century Pueblo Regional Center*, edited by Stephen H. Lekson, pp. 189–210. School of American Research Press, Santa Fe.

Magurran, Anne E. 2004. *Measuring Biological Diversity*. Blackwell Publishing, Malden, Massachusetts.

Malinowski, Bronislaw (editor). 1922. *Argonauts of the Western Pacific*. Routledge, London.

Margaris, Amy. 2009. The Mechanical Properties of Marine and Terrestrial Skeletal Materials. *Ethnoarchaeology* 1(2):163–184.

Mathien, Frances Joan. 1997. Ornaments of the Chaco Anasazi. In *Ceramics, Lithics and Ornaments of Chaco Canyon*, edited by Frances Joan Mathien, pp. 1119–1220. Publications in Archeology 18G, Chaco Canyon Studies. National Park Service, U.S. Department of the Interior, Santa Fe.

———. 2001. The Organization of Turquoise Production and Consumption by the Prehistoric Chacoans. *American Antiquity* 66(1):103–118.

McKenna, Peter J. 1984. *The Architecture and Material Culture of 29SJ1360, Chaco Canyon, New Mexico*. Reports of the Chaco Center No. 7. Division of Cultural Research, National Park Service, Albuquerque.

McKenna, Peter J., and Marcia L. Truell. 1986. *Small Site Architecture of Chaco Canyon, New Mexico*. Publications in Archaeology 18D. National Park Service, U.S. Department of the Interior, Santa Fe.

Miles, Judith. 1987. Bone Artifacts from Pueblo Alto. In Investigations at the Pueblo Alto Complex, Chaco Canyon, New Mexico 1975–1979, Vol. III, *Artifactual and Biological Analyses*, edited by Frances Joan Mathien and Thomas C. Windes, pp. 651–677. Publications in Archeology 18F, Chaco Canyon Studies. National Park Service, U.S. Department of the Interior, Santa Fe.

———. 1992. Analysis of Bone Artifacts from 29SJ 627. In Excavations at 29SJ 627 Chaco Canyon, New Mexico, Vol. II, *The Artifact Analyses*, edited by Frances Joan Mathien, pp. 371–402. Reports of the Chaco Center No. 11. Division of Cultural Research, National Park Service, Albuquerque.

———. 1993. Bone Artifacts from a Chacoan Small Site. In The Spadefoot Toad Site: Investigations at 29SJ629, Chaco Canyon, New Mexico, Vol. II, *Artifactual and Biological Analyses*, edited by Thomas C. Windes, pp. 317–341. Reports of the Chaco Center No. 12. Division of Cultural Research, National Park Service, Albuquerque.

Plog, Stephen, and Carrie Heitman. 2010. Hierarchy and Social Inequality in the American Southwest, AD 800–1200. *Proceedings of the National Academy of Sciences* 107:19619–19626.

Rappaport, Roy. 1984. *Pigs for the Ancestors*. 2nd ed. Yale University Press, New Haven, Connecticut.

Saitta, Dean J. 1999. Prestige, Agency, and Change in Middle Range Societies. In *Material Symbols: Culture and Economy in Prehistory*, edited by John E. Robb, pp. 135–149. Occasional Paper No. 26. Center for Archaeological Investigations, Carbondale, Illinois.

Schortman, Edward, and Patricia Urban. 2004. Modeling the Roles of Craft Production in Ancient Political Economies. *Journal of Archaeological Research* 12(2):185–226.

Sebastian, Lynne. 2006. The Chaco Synthesis. In *The Archaeology of Chaco Canyon: An Eleventh-Century Pueblo Regional Center*, edited by Stephen H. Lekson, pp. 393–422. School of American Research Press, Santa Fe.

Spielmann, Katherine A. 2002. Feasting, Craft Specialization, and the Ritual Mode of Production in Small-Scale Societies. *American Anthropologist* 104(1):195–207.

Titiev, Mischa. 1944. *Old Oraibi: A Study of the Hopi Indians of Third Mesa.* Papers of the Peabody Museum of American Archaeology and Ethnology Vol. 22, No. 1. Harvard University, Cambridge.

Toll, H. Wolcott. 1984. Trends in Ceramic Import and Distribution in Chaco Canyon. In *Recent Research on Chaco Prehistory*, edited by W. James Judge and John D. Schelberg, pp. 115–135. Reports of the Chaco Center No. 8. Division of Cultural Research, National Park Service, Albuquerque.

———. 1985. *Pottery, Production, Public Architecture, and the Chaco Anasazi System.* Ph.D. dissertation, Department of Anthropology, University of Colorado. University Microfilms, Ann Arbor.

———. 1991. Material Distributions and Exchange in the Chaco System. In *Chaco and Hohokam Prehistoric Regional Systems in the American Southwest*, edited by Patricia L. Crown and W. James Judge, pp. 77–107. School of American Research Press, Santa Fe.

———. 2001. Making and Breaking Pots in the Chaco World. *American Antiquity* 66(1):56–78.

———. 2006. Organization of Production. In *The Archaeology of Chaco Canyon: An Eleventh-Century Pueblo Regional Center*, edited by Stephen H. Lekson, pp. 117–151. School of American Research Press, Santa Fe.

Toll, H. Wolcott, and Peter J. McKenna. 1997. Chaco Ceramics. In *Ceramics, Lithics, and Ornaments of Chaco Canyon. Analyses of Artifacts from the Chaco Project, 1971–1978*, edited by Frances Joan Mathien, pp. 1119–1220. Publications in Archeology 18G, Chaco Canyon Studies. National Park Service, U.S. Department of the Interior, Santa Fe.

Vivian, Gordon, and Tom W. Mathews. 1965. *Kin Kletso: A Pueblo III Community in Chaco Canyon, New Mexico.* Southwestern Monuments Association, Technical Series, Globe, Arizona.

Wagner, Roy. 1989. Conclusion: The Exchange Context of the Kula. In *Death Rituals and Life in the Societies of the Kula Ring*, edited by Frederick Damon and Roy Wagner, pp. 254–274. Northern Illinois University Press, DeKalb.

Watson, Adam S. 2012. *Craft, Subsistence, and Political Change: An Archaeological Investigation of Power and Economy in Prehistoric Chaco Canyon, New Mexico, 850 to 1200 CE.* Ph.D. dissertation, Department of Anthropology, University of Virginia. University Microfilms, Ann Arbor.

Wattenmaker, Patricia. 1998. *Household and State in Upper Mesopotamia: Specialized Economy and the Social Uses of Goods in an Early Complex Society.* Smithsonian Institution Press, Washington, D.C.

Wills, W. H. 2009. Cultural Identity and the Archaeological Construction of Historical Narratives: An Example from Chaco Canyon. *Journal of Archaeological Method and Theory* 16(4):283–319.

Windes, Thomas C. 1987. Investigations at the Pueblo Alto Complex, Chaco Canyon, New Mexico, 1975–1979, Vol. II, *Architecture and Stratigraphy*. Publications in Archaeology 18F, Chaco Canyon Studies, National Park Service, U.S. Department of the Interior, Santa Fe.

————. 1992. Blue Notes: The Chacoan Turquoise Industry in the San Juan Basin. In *Anasazi Regional Organization and the Chaco System*, edited by David E. Doyel, pp. 159–168. Maxwell Museum of Anthropology, Anthropological Papers No. 5. Maxwell Museum of Anthropology, University of New Mexico, Albuquerque.

6

Human Burials of Chaco Canyon

New Developments in Cultural Interpretations through Skeletal Analysis

Kerriann Marden

Beginning in the ninth century, Chaco Canyon saw the construction of distinctive large-scale masonry architecture that, by the late tenth century, had taken on the massive form that has come to characterize the Chaco culture system. However, the great houses of Chaco Canyon were abandoned long before European contact, leaving behind no record of why these large structures were originally built or what function they served. Pueblo Bonito, which was among the earliest and most centrally located of the Chaco great houses, entombed dozens of individuals in two small clusters of intramural burial chambers. Many of the skeletal remains were disordered, while others were intact and buried with a remarkable array of grave goods, engendering a range of theories regarding who these persons were and why they were buried within the walls of this important structure. To address these questions, the present study uses methods derived from bioarchaeology and forensic anthropology by first reassociating the commingled human skeletal remains, then performing taphonomic analysis of these skeletons to identify postmortem changes. Reassociation permits more accurate assessment of sex and age of these individuals, as well as of the health status of these individuals in life and of their treatment at death. This chapter offers two case studies that demonstrate how reassociation of the remains from this burial assemblage can inform previous interpretations of these burials at both the population and the individual level.

Chaco Canyon, located in northwestern present-day New Mexico, is often interpreted as the origin and the epicenter of the broader Chaco culture system, a regional system characterized by "extensive exchange and ritual cohesion" (Crown and Hurst 2009:1). Central to Chacoan culture is the "great house" architectural form—massive masonry structures that began to flourish in Chaco Canyon during the late ninth and early tenth century (Windes 2003). Pueblo Bonito (29SJ387) has been called "typical, perhaps archetypical" of the Chaco great house architectural form (Lekson 2006:11). Located in the geographic center of the canyon, Pueblo Bonito is among the earliest of the great houses and, with continual remodeling and expansion, eventually became among the largest—some have argued it was the largest in the canyon (e.g., Neitzel 2007; Plog 1997; but see Vivian 1990:403).

Extensive excavations at Pueblo Bonito have revealed two clusters of burial rooms—one cluster in the northern portion of the great house and a second cluster in the western side* (Judd 1954; Moorehead 1906; Pepper 1920). These rooms contained dozens of human remains, and many of the bodies were in considerable anatomical disarray, while others were in anatomical position in association with rich deposits of exotic grave goods and ceremonial objects (Judd 1954; Neitzel 2003; Pepper 1920). In fact, the amount of turquoise found in Room 33 of the northern cluster exceeds that found with all other recorded Chaco Canyon burials combined (see Akins 1986:Table B.1). As Mills (this volume) notes, the "ritual," "economic," and "political" aspects of Ancestral Puebloans were tightly interwoven. The juxtaposition of anatomical disorder and wealth in the graves in Pueblo Bonito has led archaeologists to speculate broadly on the function of Pueblo Bonito, on the social roles of the persons buried within these rooms, and on the reason for the apparent disparity in their treatment at death.

This chapter employs two case studies from the northern burial cluster to demonstrate how a comprehensive osteological analysis of the human remains from Pueblo Bonito can enhance interpretation of the mortuary customs and ritual behavior practiced at this site. Starting with reassociation of commingled human skeletal elements, this study employs

---

*In this analysis, the rooms in which burials were found are sometimes termed "burial chambers" or "tombs," but in all cases, these terms refer to the same concept of bounded architectural rooms containing a number of human remains.

taphonomy (study of the type, degree, and distribution of postmortem changes) to reveal information about bone preservation and spatial orientation of the remains in situ. These data are then concatenated with careful investigation of the archival records regarding provenience, position, and associated grave goods for each individual in an effort to reconstruct the mortuary practices at this site and to aid in interpretation of site formation processes reflected in the human remains.

Recent scholars have exhorted researchers to reexamine the records and collections from the early years of excavation in Chaco Canyon and to find new approaches to the data that allow an examination of internal societal dynamics (Plog 2010:379; Sebastian 2006:421). As the only archaeological remnants of the corporeal body, human remains are the most intimately linked to the persons they represent and thus are a crucial element of reconstructing social identity. A wealth of information can be gleaned from examination of skeletal remains, and analysis of the manner in which an individual's body was treated at death can help to enrich the understanding of mortuary behaviors and their cultural significance (Goldstein 2001).

The Archaeological Context of the Remains

The northern burial rooms of Pueblo Bonito were excavated in more than one episode and by more than one expedition team. However, the remains that pertain to the present study were all collected during the Hyde Exploring Expedition's excavations, led by George Pepper. In 1896, these excavations unearthed 12 individuals in Room 33 in the northern part of the structure, some of whom were described as being found in anatomical disarray. Below these partially disordered remains, Pepper and his crew discovered two relatively undisturbed subfloor burials with an elaborate arrangement of exotic grave goods (Pepper 1899, 1909, 1920). In the adjoining room, Room 32, the bones of a torso, a pelvis, and a single femur were discovered. All of the remains from these two rooms are now housed at the American Museum of Natural History (AMNH). Unfortunately, although the crania were each cataloged separately, almost all of the postcranial bones of the 12 individuals above the floor of Room 33 were accessioned as a single lot of commingled bones, along with the partial remains from Room 32.

Previous Osteological Analyses of the Pueblo Bonito Human Skeletal Series

The Pueblo Bonito burial assemblage has long been debated, and yet, the social status of the individuals, the population from which they came, and the reason for their entombment within the large structure continue to be debated (Marden 2011). Although several osteological studies have been conducted on the skeletal remains from Pueblo Bonito, most of these have focused on cranial morphometrics—collection of descriptive data on the size and shape of skulls (Hoffman 1879; Hrdlička 1931; Neumann 1950; Seltzer 1944; Spuhler 1954; Stewart 1936a, 1936b, 1937) or femoral length (Akins 1986; Corruccini 1972; Malville 2008). To date, no study of the remains found in the northern burial cluster has attempted to reassociate the commingled skeletal remains found in these burial chambers to permit a comprehensive assessment of demographic, taphonomic, and pathologic information in the burial assemblage. This methodological omission has led to some persistent problems in the interpretation of these remains, at both the individual and the population level.

The Individual Level—Interpretation of Social Identity

At the individual level, failure to recognize which skeletal elements comprise a specific set of human remains inhibits accurate determination of sex, stature, pathological changes, and taphonomic changes, inhibiting interpretation of who each individual was and how each was treated at death. For example, demographic analysis of an assemblage relies on the accurate ascription of sex to each individual. However, only 2 of the 13 skulls in the AMNH collection had associated postcrania. Remains from other rooms in the northern burial cluster are held by the Field Museum of Natural History and the Peabody Museum of Archaeology and Ethnology, and of these only one of the four in the Field Museum and the single individual at the Peabody Museum had associated postcrania. With the single individual housed at the Harvard Peabody, this totals 4 individuals out of 18 to which sex could be reliably ascribed. Cranial remains are notoriously problematic in sex determination, with an accuracy rate of only 77–87 percent reported among highly experienced forensic anthropologists working with modern

skeletal populations (Klepinger 2006:31), as opposed to up to 96 percent accuracy when using the most sexually dimorphic skeletal region,
the pelvis (Mays and Cox 2000:119). Sex determination from cranial
morphology only becomes more difficult when working with ancient
human remains. "Populations vary markedly in this respect. For some
groups, cranial morphology provides a reliable basis for sex determination; for others, it does not" (Buikstra and Ubelaker 1994:19). T. Dale
Stewart noted that sex determination among the Pueblo Bonito burials
was challenging, "chiefly when the skeleton is incomplete or when those
of several individuals have been mixed" (1936a:5).

The Population Level—Interpretation of Relationships between Groups

At the population level, failure to reassociate the remains prevents
accurate demographic assessment that will affect analyses of the
nature of the assemblage and the relationship among the individuals
within it. Akins's (1986) bioarchaeological analysis of Chaco Canyon
human remains is without doubt the most often referenced research
on human remains from Chaco Canyon, and it can be considered the
seminal mortuary and bioarchaeological analysis for Chaco. A number
of Akins's other publications are founded on these same data (Akins
2001, 2003; Akins and Schelberg 1984), and several other authors have
also based their conclusions regarding the relative health and mortuary
treatment of the human remains from Chaco Canyon on the results
of this study (e.g., Ashmore 2007; Heitman and Plog 2005; Lamphere
2000; Malville 2008; Martin 1994, 2000; Mathien 2001; Neitzel 2000;
Nelson et al. 1994; Plog 1997; Schillaci and Stojanowski 2003; Schillaci et al. 2010; Sobolik 2002; Stodder 2005; Stodder and Martin 1992;
Stodder et al. 2002; Wilcox 1993; Wills 2009). Yet of the 97 burials
from Pueblo Bonito that Akins (1986) enumerates in her Appendix
B.1, only 34 were included in some of her mortuary analyses because
most of the remains were reported as having been found in disarray,
so that the in situ location of these remains and association with grave
goods could not easily be reconstructed. Akins therefore excluded
almost two-thirds of all human remains found in Pueblo Bonito and
almost all of the commingled adults from Room 33. Although this

choice was certainly supportable considering Akins's research question and methodological approach, exclusion of these individuals from the analysis skews all aspects of the mortuary record. This approach loses much of the information that is potentially the most valuable and the most interesting for understanding the treatment of human remains at Pueblo Bonito.

Reassociation of Skeletal Remains

As Hays-Gilpin and Ware note in their contribution to this volume, social distinctions in life often correlate with differences in the treatment of the body after death. However, in order to retroactively reconstruct those differences in life, one must accurately interpret differences in the treatment of the dead. Reconstruction of mortuary ritual is facilitated by reconstruction and analysis of the remains themselves. The present study began with the meticulous refitting of broken fragments (conjoining) and reassembling of isolated bones into discrete bodies (reassociation). Conjoining broken fragments into bones and reassociating individual bones into discrete individuals greatly increases their scientific potential.

Reassociation of disturbed, commingled, and partial human remains permits interpretation of the type and distribution of taphonomic features (postmortem changes to human remains). Taphonomic analysis can help us to understand and explain the condition of human remains by providing information about perimortem trauma, postmortem treatment of the body, naturally occurring processes acting on the body over time, and post-recovery damage to the bones. "The key to understanding archaeological mortuary behavior is to reconstruct the ritual context in which burial data are created. It is this intention that represents the greatest problem for the interpretation, but it is also an opportunity to infer elements of conceptual life" (Roksandic 2002:100). Taphonomy can help to illuminate some of the "big questions" of archaeological interpretation by reconstructing how people treat the bodies of the deceased in a particular cultural context, thus illuminating past cultural traditions and indicating the relationships between the dead and the living (Behrensmeyer 1975; Micozzi 1991; Saul and Saul 2002).

Careful examination of skeletal remains integrates people into the social structure, the architecture, and the physical landscape they inhabited (Brown 1995). As such, mortuary data is crucial to interpretations of social complexity and societal change (Akins and Schelberg 1984; Parker Pearson 1999).

The remainder of this chapter presents two detailed case studies that demonstrate the utility of reassociation and taphonomic analysis in interpreting mortuary behavior and social identity. In each case, direct analysis of the skeletal remains provides unique insight into the treatment of the dead and helps to inform the archaeological interpretation of the burial context.

Case Study 1: Interpretation of the Remains in Room 32

The sealed outer doorway of Room 32 was breached by Pepper during his first field season, revealing a room that had remained untouched for a considerable time span. However, the room was filled with blown sand, suggesting that the doorway had remained open for a period of time after it had fallen into disuse (Pepper 1909:197). The first human remains encountered during formal excavations of Pueblo Bonito were found in this room. This partial skeleton consisted of 13 vertebrae, a complete pelvic girdle, a femur, several ribs, a clavicle, and a scapula:

> The human backbone and pelvis which were found in the southwest corner were the next objects to receive attention. They were intact and were lying northwest by southeast, the pelvis being toward the northern point and six inches above the level of the western doorway. The vertebrae were lying in an almost horizontal position, 10 of them were intact and in position, as were also the sacrum and the pelvic bones. Three vertebrae fell in removing the surface dirt, but they had probably been in place when the body was found. . . . Wrapped around the bones and extending into the western doorway, there is a mass of burnt cloth, the greater part of which was simply woven textiles of finely spun yucca cord (Pepper 1920:138).

Pepper's field notes further clarify that a "mass of burnt cloth was found in the mouth of the western door part of it resting up against the

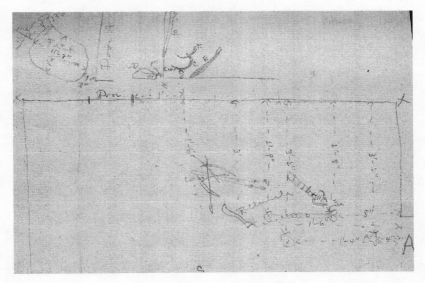

Figure 6.1. Detailed view of Pepper's plan sketch of partial human remains found in Room 32 (doorway to Room 33 is in right side of image). (Courtesy Division of Anthropology, American Museum of National History)

north side [*sic*]" (Pepper 1896).* In his field notes from Room 32, Pepper stated that "the jeweled bird #192 was found below the mass of bones and about 4" above the door level—the mass of bones ranging from 6" to 1'3'"" (Pepper 1896), presumably also measured from the door sill. Pepper's first accompanying sketch reveals the relative positions of these skeletal elements, showing the jumble of wooden implements and ribs as well as the clavicle, femur, and vertebral column (Figure 6.1).

Pepper also describes several small wooden sticks in association with the remains. Pepper's field notes contain two sketches of these remains, both depicting the vertebrae and pelvises in apparent anatomical order in situ, consistent with his published description. The first sketch Pepper generated did not depict the ossa coxarum (pelvic bones), but these bones are clearly shown in his second, more detailed sketch of these remains (Figure 6.2).

---

* It should be noted that an expert on ancient Southwestern textiles did not think that this piece of fabric showed any signs of burning, but rather decay (Laurie Webster, personal communication 2010). This cloth also bears a decorative pattern that is now dark brown in color, which may have been mistaken for heat damage in the field.

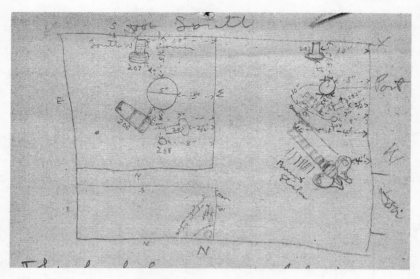

Figure 6.2. The second sketch of human remains from Room 32 clearly shows the ossa coxarum in anatomical order with the sacrum and vertebrae (doorway to Room 33 is in right side of image). (Courtesy Division of Anthropology, American Museum of National History)

Pepper's field notes (1896) also list the pelvic bones specifically in his description of the remains found in anatomical order and again reference the small sticks:

> The back bone and pelvis were intact and were lying NW by SE, the pelvis being toward the former point. The pelvis was 6″ above the level of the W doorway and the vertebrae were almost on a longitudinal plane. The sacrum and pelvic bones were intact and in position as were 10 of the vertebrae. The other vertebrae (3) fell when the man was removing the surface dirt and these too were probably in place. The vertebrae that were in place are numbered and run from 1 to 10, being numbered consecutively according to position. There were seven sticks that had been burnt off at one end, they were in a slanting position and rested against the lower part of the vertebrae. They were on the western side. Under the vertebrae and extending into the western doorway was a mass of burnt cloth.

Plog and Heitman refer to the configuration of these skeletal elements as a "highly patterned association of the vertebrae and pelvis with burial goods, the preservation of the ceremonial sticks, arrows, and cloth" (2010:19622). However, Pepper's notes and sketches seem to reflect a somewhat haphazard arrangement of the partial remains in this room, rather than a highly patterned association. Moreover, the scattered arrangement of some of the bones, the fact that only the bones of the torso, pelvis, and left leg are present in this room, and the fact that several of these bones exhibit damage consistent with carnivore gnawing suggest that these bones are part of a burial in Room 33 that were dragged into Room 32 by scavengers (Marden 2011).

The catalog file for the AMNH does not record any human remains originating in this room, and Akins reported that "the remains could not be located at the American Museum of Natural History" (1986:115). However, combined osteological analysis and archival research permitted the identification and analysis of the remains from Room 32. Examination of the large commingled skeletal lot from Room 33 (Catalog Number H/3658) revealed that the skeletal elements from Room 32 were at some point concatenated into that lot. Catalog Number H/3658 contains one set of vertebrae that—unlike any other bones—is marked in ink with the numbers 1–10 in a careful hand (Figure 6.3). This corresponds with Pepper's description of 10 of the vertebrae found in Room

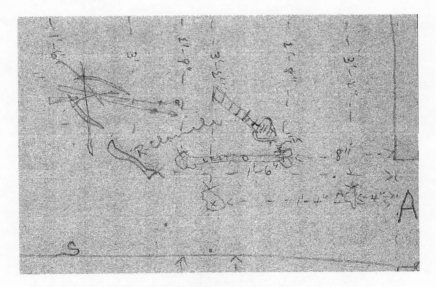

Figure 6.3. Detailed view of Pepper's sketch of remains in Room 32. Note that the femur appears to be marked "Left" and "O." (Courtesy Division of Anthropology, American Museum of National History)

32 found "intact and in position" (1920:133), which he described in his notes as "numbered and run from 1 to 10, being numbered consecutively according to position" (Pepper 1896).

These 10 numbered vertebrae were housed in a separate plastic bag in the drawer with all of the other vertebrae, along with 3 more thoracic vertebrae that reassociate precisely to the 10 numbered vertebrae to form a contiguous column. This further supports the contention that these numbered vertebrae are the 10 that Pepper found with the pelvis in Room 32, from which "other vertebrae (3) fell when the man was removing the surface dirt and these too were probably in place" (Pepper 1896).

Unfortunately, none of the pelvic bones or sacra in this skeletal assemblage seem to bear any markings to indicate that they were from Room 32, but through the process of meticulous reassociation, a sacrum and pelvis in AMNH Catalog Number H/3658 were found to reassociate to the numbered vertebrae. The lumbosacral joint is highly morphologically specific, so a precise fit between these elements can be taken as an indication that these bones represent a single individual. The sacroiliac joints are also highly specific for reassociation, and in this case, the auricular surfaces of both pelvises and of the sacrum are coated in adhesive, further confirming that these bones belong together, as no other bones in the assemblage have adhesive on the joints. These bones are also consistent in their relative lack of arthritic changes and the excellent overall cortical quality.

These pelvic bones revealed a small amount of superficial damage consistent with carnivore chewing. A pair of femora and tibiae that are consistent with the overall age, rugosity, robusticity, and cortical condition of this vertebral column and pelvis were also found among the commingled remains in AMNH Catalog Number H/3658. Like the pelvic bones, these limb bones exhibit damage consistent with having been chewed extensively by carnivores, including puncture marks, tooth furrowing, and tooth scoring (Haglund 1997; White 1992; White and Folkens 2000). No other femora of compatible age, sex, and cortical characteristics exhibited similar damage. Most notable, however, was a distinctive ovoid mark drawn in black ink on the distal anterior left femoral shaft that was only noticed after these bones were reassociated to this individual. This mark appears to be the letter *O*, consistent with the letter *O* that Pepper used to designate the left femur in Room 32 in his sketches. No other long bones in the assemblage were marked in ink in this way. This femur is an excellent morphological antimere for the right, leaving little doubt that the two bones are from the same individual. Taken together, the skeletal and archival evidence indicates that part of this individual was recovered from Room 32, while the remainder was found in Room 33.

Since partial Skeleton #10 from Room 33 and the partial remains from Room 32 represent a single individual, it is most likely that the body was first entombed in Room 33 with all of the other remains. The remains in Room 32 were found entangled in a mass of cloth, which Pepper concluded was their burial wrappings. This cloth trailed from the doorway leading to Room 33, which suggests that it had been dragged through the door with the bones.

The most parsimonious explanation for the location of part of this body in Room 32 is that this thorax and pelvis were dragged there from their original burial location in Room 33 by scavengers; the bones would have held together relatively well due to their mummified condition (the leg and foot of Skeleton #10 in Room 33 were also described as "desiccated" by Pepper). Vertebral elements can retain their anatomical association quite well due to their relatively strong ligamentous structures (Brain 1981), especially when mummified.* Furthermore, no other remains were buried above Skeleton #10 to impede scavenger access, and according to recent radiocarbon dating of these remains, the legs associated with this individual were among the most recent of the burials in this room (Plog and Heitman 2010:19623, Table 1), suggesting that they would have been most accessible to scavengers.

Pepper's notes indicate that the mandible of Skull #10, to which the vertebral column and pelvis from Room 32 has been confidently reassociated (Marden 2011), was still in place with the skull, and that the cranium was broken but is nonetheless nearly complete. Actualistic experiments have demonstrated that the temporomandibular joint is among the earliest joints in the body to disarticulate during natural

---

* The fact is exemplified by the partially intact vertebral column of Skeleton #2 from this room, which is still held together today by mummified tissue (see Marden 2011).

decomposition processes (Micozzi 1997:177). Therefore, any movement of the cranium after decomposition has begun is unlikely to include the mandible. Also, the stain pattern on the broken fragments of cranium is uniform across the fracture lines and is most pronounced on the posterior of the skull, consistent with the position in which Pepper described it, suggesting that the cranium was found in the position in which it decomposed. The taphonomic evidence indicates that the intact cranium and mandible were in their original place of deposition when found, suggesting that it must be the torso, rather than the skull, that was moved.

Whether one contends that this is a primary or secondary burial, it is more parsimonious to conclude that the intact torso, pelvis, and femur were chewed and dragged by scavengers from their original position among the burials in Room 33 into the adjacent room, rather than the alternate explanation that the body was originally placed alone in Room 32, laid out carefully with a display of burned sticks. If the entire body was originally in Room 32, then the cranium, mandible, tibiae, feet, and arms would have had to have been subsequently carried into Room 33, along with the right leg and foot (which were also still wrapped in fragments of cloth) and placed in roughly anatomical order along the far wall, leaving a space for the absent vertebral column and torso. Then the ribs, left femur, clavicle, scapula, and upper vertebrae, still entangled in burial wrapping, would have to have been strewn about Room 32 without disturbing the vertebrae from their position near the sticks. It is not possible to rule out this scenario, but it seems far less probable than the simpler explanation that the remains in Room 32 were dragged away from the rest of the body (probably by the same scavenging carnivores that left tooth scoring and chewed ends on the bones), which was found in relatively anatomical order in Room 33.

The issue of whether these remains were originally entombed in Room 32 is important to the interpretation of this burial assemblage because much has been made of the apparent ritual significance of a solitary, headless body laid out in association with burned sticks in Room 32. Pepper speculated that the sticks found upright in the sand next to the vertebral column in Room 32 "may have been deposited with the body at the time of the burial, and the ends burned for some special purpose" (1920:138). It is tempting to interpret the presence of these burned sticks as an indication that this is the primary place of entombment of this body and that this suggests elaborate ritualistic treatment. Unfortunately, the final location of this vertebral column has been invested with an archaeological significance that appears to be inconsistent with the taphonomic and skeletal evidence, and this location has taken on an interpretation of ritual significance that does not seem to be supported by the condition of the bones. Actualistic evidence gleaned from forensic contexts has demonstrated the importance of understanding the potential of scavenging to destroy or scatter body parts, to alter or destroy evidence of the original context of the body's placement, and to create diagnostic damage to the remains (Haglund 1997:367). The movement of part of Skeleton #10 from Room 33 to Room 32 seems to have produced all of these effects.

Case Study 2: Interpretation of the Subfloor Burials in Room 33

Directly beneath the 12 individuals buried in the fill of Room 33 (including Skeleton #10 described above), Pepper discovered a floor of wooden planks that covered two more burials (Skeletons #13 and #14). These burials have received a tremendous amount of attention due to the large quantity of turquoise that was associated with the bodies, which is among the primary reasons for the interpretation of Pueblo Bonito as a residence and/or sepulcher for socioeconomic, sociopolitical, or religious elites:

> On the removal of the above-mentioned specimens and the debris around them, a floor appeared. This was made of boards which averaged a foot in width and from three-quarters of an inch to an inch in thickness. These boards were laid side by side, in an east and west direction; and the floor thus formed no doubt presented a flat surface when it was new. When found, the boards were somewhat decayed, and were warped, from the effect of the water, to so great an extent that the surface was very uneven. The boards curved upward from the center, owing to the decaying bodies in the sand below them and to the pressure of the material above. From the appearance of the boards, it was evident that they had been made for the purpose indicated. In the

eastern end of one of them, a hole about four inches in diameter had
been cut, for what reason, it is impossible to say. (Pepper 1909:221–222)

It has been proposed that the plank flooring "may have physically
symbolized the boundary of the underworld and upperworld, a proposal
strengthened by Pepper's discovery that a hole four inches in diameter
had been cut near the eastern end of one of the wooden planks, perhaps
as a *sipapu* . . . [which is a] passage to the underworld through a small
hole in the earth, often represented in Pueblo ceremonial structures by
a small hole in the floor" (Plog and Heitman, 2010:19624). Pepper had
made this suggestion himself, stating that "this may have been an opening of symbolic character, similar to the *sipapu*, the entrance to the
underworld" (Pepper, 1909:249). However, Pepper described no other
sipapus, and Judd specifically remarked that he did not find any other
clear indication of a *sipapu* or similar feature anywhere in Pueblo Bonito.
"In all the [National Geographic] Society's Chaco Canyon investigations no kiva-floor hole was found that could positively be identified as
a *sipapu* except, possibly, that in Kiva Q" (Judd 1954:43, 207). It seems
incongruous that such an important cosmological ritual feature would
appear in such a prominent room so early at Pueblo Bonito, but then
disappear entirely from the site's ritual spaces.

Alternately, it seems feasible that this small aperture in the floor-
board might have served a functional purpose, rather than serving as
a symbolic ritual, allowing the board to be easily lifted. It is possible
that this roughly hand-sized hole in the plank was created to provide an
intentional means of access to the subfloor area, which may be important in understanding the enormous caches of turquoise objects buried
beneath the floor. The amount of turquoise buried beneath the floor of
Room 33 is unprecedented, exceeding anything found within the walls
of Pueblo Bonito or at any other known site in Chaco Canyon.* In
fact, at the time that these rooms were excavated, the wealth of Pepper's
Room 33 burials was so renowned that subsequent Chaco archaeologists
judged their own finds against it. Neil Judd wrote on June 14, 1921, "I

---

*It should also be noted that Peñasco Blanco has never been fully excavated, but
was described by looters in the historic period as a rich site for turquoise (NMJ/
NAA), so Pueblo Bonito may not in fact be unique in this respect.

still have hopes of finding something worthwhile in the way of specimens although our results thus far tend to indicate that Pep left little
or nothing" (Letter to B. T. B. Hyde, on file, Neil Merton Judd Papers,
National Anthropological Archives, National Museum of National History, Smithsonian Institution, Washington, D.C.).

The published description of these grave goods is extensive and rich
in detail (Pepper, 1909, 1920). Even in summary, it is evident that this
subfloor burial assemblage is remarkable. Skeleton 13 was buried with a
total of 5,890 turquoise beads and 10 turquoise pendants of varying size
that Pepper interpreted as associated with the burial. Also found with
this burial were 3 shell beads, 4 turquoise "sets" for use in inlays, a piece
of turquoise matrix, and a small piece of shell (Pepper, 1909: 222). Skeleton #14, buried over two feet below Skeleton #13, had an even greater
amount of turquoise, including 8,385 turquoise beads and 545 turquoise
pendants of various sizes and forms (Pepper 1909:223–226). Pepper also
found 7 turquoise sets, 5 jet inlays, 12 beads of shell and stone, 2 carved
pieces of turquoise, and 1 large inlay carved from red stone, as well
as several uncounted pieces of shell ornaments, turquoise matrix, and
small turquoise sets in direct association with this burial (Pepper 1909,
223–231). Along with the ornaments found in direct association with the
skeletons, there were caches of rare objects throughout the rest of the
room in this subfloor space. These include a shell trumpet, a cylindrical
basket encrusted with turquoise mosaic sets filled with thousands of
turquoise and shell beads and pendants; a basket decorated with turquoise and shell beads; caches of turquoise beads and pendants clustered around the post in the northeastern corner of the room; a cache of
turquoise beads and pendants, malachite and shell near the post in the
northwestern corner; turquoise beads and pendants, a jet inlay, and a
shell pendant in the southeastern corner; and dozens of pieces of malachite, shell bracelets, and a bone bracelet in the southwestern corner
(Pepper 1909:226–236).

It is possible that this abundance of ornaments and rare objects may
have been amassed all at one time for burial beneath the floor with these
individuals: perhaps these objects were collected from citizens as a trib-
ute to these individuals upon their deaths or perhaps this represents the
hoard of personal possessions these two individuals had accrued in life.
However, it is also possible that these objects were slowly accumulated

over time, with the hole in the plank serving as a handle to remove the flooring and to allow access to the subfloor space for repeated additions to the assemblage. This interpretation gains some support from Pepper's description of multiple caches of turquoise objects "grouped about the post at various depths" in the northeastern corner under the floor (1909:234), suggesting multiple episodes of deposition within this subfloor space over months, years, or even decades. The fact that the hole is located at the eastern end of the plank—the end closest to the doorway—further supports this possible explanation. This links both to the concepts of ritual foundation deposits and of periodic ritual renewal (Mills, this volume).

Careful reassociation of the skeletal remains from this room has revealed cases of commingling that are not evident in the archival record, which may indicate unintentional displacement of remains in the process of repeated access to the subfloor area over time. Certain skeletal elements from the large, commingled catalog number of remains found in the fill above the floor (H/3658) and the two burials found below (H/3671 and H/3672) were mixed. In the cases in which remains were mixed, the elements were labeled with the catalog number with which the bones were housed in the museum, rather than the number of the skeleton to which they belong anatomically (i.e., elements that refit the skeletal remains found above the floor are numbered with the catalog number for subfloor burials and vice versa), indicating that Pepper was not aware that the remains were commingled as they were excavated.

In some cases of commingling, anatomically adjacent bones exhibit markedly different taphonomic condition, suggesting that these burials may have been disturbed even though they were beneath the floor, which is consistent with an interpretation that the floor planks were periodically lifted. The most notable instance is the fourth cervical vertebrae of Skeleton #14, the most deeply buried individual in the room. This individual was found buried several feet beneath the floor, but the remains that were accessioned under this catalog number were incomplete, lacking the cervical vertebrae. These cervical vertebrae were found in the commingled accession lot, and they were an unquestionable morphological fit to both the cranium and thoracic vertebrae of 3672 into a complete individual, who is unique in this room for his robust size.

Moreover, the cervical vertebrae exhibit markedly different taphonomic features, with C4 exhibiting a much lighter color and weathered cortical condition inconsistent with the rest of the skeleton (see Marden 2011:717, Figure A188 for illustration). This strongly indicates that this vertebra was exposed to a significantly different microenvironment in situ than the other vertebrae belonging to this individual—and unlike that of any other skeletal elements among the subfloor burials, this bone appears bleached and weathered. This distinctive taphonomic condition supports the possibility that the floor of the room was periodically removed, which would allow the commingling (either intentional or accidental) of isolated elements among these remains.

Pepper asserted that these "bodies were placed near each other, and, from the positions in which they were found, it would seem that they had been buried at the same time" (1909:248–249). However, the relative position of the remains is not particularly consistent with a paired burial. Skeleton #14 was discovered at a level approximately 71 cm lower than that of Skeleton #13 (see Plog and Heitman 2010:19623, Figure 3). Along with the differential depth, there are marked differences in body placement between these two individuals. Skeleton #13 was oriented with the head northeast and laid on the right side, whereas Skeleton #14 was positioned with the head to the north in a supine position with the legs slightly flexed (Pepper 1909:223). Rather, it seems more likely that these burials were placed in the room at different times and that the tremendous amounts of objects placed with them were amassed over some span of time.

Interestingly, two of the individuals from the fill to whom commingled elements found beneath the floor were reassociated have been sampled for radiocarbon dates, and both were among the earlier burials placed in the room fill. Skeleton #6 (Catalog Number H/3664) was dated to A.D. 776–989, and Skeleton #12 (Catalog Number H/3670) was dated to A.D. 676–894, as compared to a date range of A.D. 690–944 and 690–940 for Skeletons 13 and 14 (Plog and Heitman, 2010:19623, Table 1). Since these were among the earliest burials placed in the room fill, if the floor planks were removed while these bodies were in the room, it is feasible that their skeletal elements could have fallen beneath the floor planks in the process. Pepper's notes do not contain adequate information about the body position of Skeleton #6, but it is noteworthy that Skeleton #12 was aligned east to west, parallel to the direction of the floorboards. This orientation would have permitted lifting of the boards even after these bodies were placed in the room.

If the tremendous cache of turquoise found beneath the floor of Room 33 was deposited over an extended period of time, this potentially alters the interpretation of the social identity of the two subfloor burials with which these grave goods were associated. Rather than serving as a single deposit of grave goods as marker of elite status, the mass of turquoise found with subfloor burials may have been deposited there for some other purpose over a span of decades or even centuries and may in fact have been associated with the subsequent burials in the fill, or with the site itself. This alternate interpretation of a long-term accumulation of grave goods associated with the burial chamber, rather than a single burial episode with massive amounts of wealth, helps to support the concept of "a shared ideology and a strong sense of shared community" in Chaco Canyon (Hays-Gilpin and Ware, this volume).

Conclusion

The mortuary behavior and social identity of the individuals interred at Pueblo Bonito will be debated by Chaco scholars for years to come. The present study highlights the crucial role of direct skeletal analysis in informing this debate—and especially the importance of reassociation of commingled remains in interpreting burial contexts. Although this is a meticulous and time-consuming process, it is an essential step in the accurate analysis of the demographic profile, taphonomic features, and pathological conditions of any burial population. The development of sound methodological approaches is central to the development of bioarchaeology (Larsen 2000; Wright and Yoder 2003), and the use of best practices can have a profound effect on the outcome of research. Analysis of the reassociated skeletal evidence from the northern burial cluster provides a fresh perspective on the mortuary treatment of these individuals that tests some of the assumptions of previous archaeological interpretations.

Osteological analysis certainly does not offer the final word in the ongoing debate over the purpose and function of Pueblo Bonito or of the social identity of the burials entombed therein. However, direct analysis of the bodies themselves adds an important element to the discussion that has heretofore been generally overlooked or misunderstood. The debates over the interpretation of commingled, disordered burials in the Southwest in general, and Pueblo Bonito in particular, will certainly persist. The case studies presented here offer an example of how skeletal reassociation and taphonomic analysis may better contextualize the treatment of human remains within the broader archaeological record.

References Cited

Akins, Nancy J. 1986. *A Biocultural Approach to Human Burials from Chaco Canyon, New Mexico*. Reports of the Chaco Center No. 9. Division of Cultural Research, National Park Service, Albuquerque.

———. 2001. Chaco Canyon Mortuary Practices. Archeological Correlates of Complexity. In *Ancient Burial Practices in the American Southwest: Archaeology, Physical Anthropology, and Native American Perspectives*, edited by Douglas R. Mitchell and Judy L. Brunson-Hadley, pp. 167–190. University of New Mexico Press, Albuquerque.

———. 2003. The Burials of Pueblo Bonito. In *Pueblo Bonito: Center of the Chacoan World*, edited by Jill E. Neitzel, pp. 94–106. Smithsonian Institution Press, Washington, D.C.

Akins, Nancy J., and John D. Schelberg. 1984. Evidence for Organizational Complexity as Seen from the Mortuary Practices at Chaco Canyon. In *Recent Research on Chaco Prehistory*, edited by William J. Judge and John D. Schelberg, pp. 103–113. Reports of the Chaco Center No. 8. Division of Cultural Research, National Park Service, Albuquerque.

Antón, Susan C. 1989. Intentional Cranial Vault Deformation and Induced Changes in the Cranial Base and Face. *American Journal of Physical Anthropology* 79:253–267.

Ashmore, Wendy. 2007. Building a Social History at Pueblo Bonito: Footnotes to a Biography of Place. In *Architecture of Chaco Canyon, New Mexico*, edited by Stephen H. Lekson, pp. 179–198. University of Utah Press, Salt Lake City.

Behrensmeyer, Anna K. 1975. The Taphonomy and Paleoecology of Plio-Pleistocene Vertebrate Assemblages East of Lake Rudolf, Kenya. *Bulletin of the Museum of Comparative Zoology* 146:473–578.

Brain, C. K. 1981. *The Hunters or the Hunted? An Introduction to African Cave Taphonomy*. University of Chicago Press, Chicago.

Brown, James A. 1995. On Mortuary Analysis—with Special Reference to the Saxe-Binford Research Program. In *Regional Approaches to Mortuary Analysis*, edited by Lane A. Beck, pp. 3–26. Plenum, New York.

Buikstra, Jane E., and Douglas H. Ubelaker. 1994. *Standards for Data Collection from Human Skeletal Remains.* Arkansas Archaeological Survey Research Series No. 44. Arkansas Archaeological Survey, Fayetteville.

Cheverud, James M., Luci A. P. Kohn, Lyle W. Konigsberg, and Steven R. Leigh. 1992. Effects of Fronto-occipital Artificial Cranial Vault Modification on the Cranial Base and Face. *American Journal of Physical Anthropology* 88(3):323–345.

Corruccini, Robert S. 1972. The Biological Relationships of Some Prehistoric and Historic Pueblo Populations. *American Journal of Physical Anthropology* 37:373–388.

Crown, Patricia L., and W. Jeffrey Hurst. 2009. Evidence of Cacao Use in the Prehispanic American Southwest. *Proceedings of the National Academy of Sciences* 106:2110–2113.

Goldstein, Lynne. 2001. Ancient Southwest Mortuary Practices: Perspectives from outside the Southwest. In *Ancient Burial Practices in the American Southwest: Archaeology, Physical Anthropology, and Native American Perspectives,* edited by Douglas R. Mitchell and Judy L. Brunson-Hadley, pp. 249–253. University of New Mexico Press. Albuquerque.

Haglund, William D. 1997. Dogs and Coyotes: Postmortem Involvement with Human Remains. In *Forensic Taphonomy: The Postmortem Fate of Human Remains,* edited by William D. Haglund and Marcella H. Sorg, pp. 367–381. CRC Press, Boca Raton.

Heitman, Carolyn, and Stephen Plog. 2005. Kinship and the Dynamics of the House: Rediscovering Dualism in the Pueblo Past. In *A Catalyst for Ideas: Anthropological Archaeology and the Legacy of Douglas W. Schwartz,* edited by Vernon L. Scarborough, pp. 69–100. School of American Research Press, Santa Fe.

Hoffman, Walter James. 1879. Report on the Chaco Cranium. In *Tenth Annual Report of the United States Geological and Geographical Survey of the Territories, Embracing Colorado and Parts of Adjacent Territories, Being a Report on the Progress of the Exploration for the Year 1876,* by F. V. Hayden. Pt. III. Archeology, pp. 451–457. U.S. Government Printing Office, Washington, D.C.

Hrdlička, Aleš. 1931. Catalogue of Human Crania in the United States National Museum Collections: Pueblos, Southern Utah Basket-makers, Navaho. *Proceedings of the United States National Museum* 78(2845):1–95.

Judd, Neil Merton. 1954. *The Material Culture of Pueblo Bonito.* Smithsonian Miscellaneous Collections Vol. 124. Smithsonian Institution, Washington, D.C.

Klepinger, Linda L. 2006. *Fundamentals of Forensic Anthropology.* John Wiley & Sons, Hoboken, New Jersey.

Lamphere, Louise. 2000. Gender Models in the Southwest: A Sociocultural Perspective. In *Women and Men in the Prehispanic Southwest: Labor, Power and Prestige*, edited by Patricia L. Crown, pp. 379–401. School of American Research Press, Santa Fe.

Larsen, Clark S. 2000. *Skeletons in Our Closet: Revealing Our Past through Bioarchaeology*. Princeton University Press, Princeton, New Jersey.

Lekson, Stephen J. 2006. Chaco Matters: An Introduction. In *The Archeology of Chaco Canyon: An Eleventh-Century Pueblo Regional Center*, edited by Stephen H. Lekson, pp. 3–44. School of American Research Press, Santa Fe.

Malville, Nancy J. 2008. Stature of Ancestral Pueblo Populations: Population Density, Social Stratification, and Dietary Protein. In *Reanalysis and Reinterpretation in Southwestern Bioarchaeology*, edited by Ann L. W. Stodder, pp. 105–129. Arizona State University Anthropological Research Papers No. 59. Arizona State University, Tempe.

Marden, Kerriann. 2011. Taphonomy, Paleopathology and Mortuary Variability in Chaco Canyon: Using Modern Methods to Understand Ancient Cultural Practices. Ph.D. dissertation, Department of Anthropology, Tulane University, New Orleans.

Martin, Debra L. 1994. Patterns of Diet and Disease: Health Profiles for the Prehistoric Southwest. In *Themes in Southwest Prehistory*, edited by George J. Gumerman, pp. 87–108. School of American Research Press, Santa Fe.

———. 2000. Bodies and Lives: Biological Indicators of Health Differentials and Division of Labor by Sex. In *Women and Men in the Prehispanic Southwest: Labor, Power and Prestige*, edited by Patricia L. Crown, pp. 267–300. School of American Research Press, Santa Fe.

Mathien, Frances Joan. 2001. The Organization of Turquoise Production and Consumption by the Prehistoric Chacoans. *American Antiquity* 66:103–218.

Mays, Simon, and Margaret Cox. 2000. Sex Determination in Skeletal Remains. In *Human Osteology in Archaeology and Forensic Science*, edited by Margaret Cox and Simon Mays, pp. 117–130. Greenwich Medical Media Ltd., London.

Micozzi, Marc S. 1991. *Postmortem Change in Human and Animal Remains: A Systematic Approach*. Charles C. Thomas, Springfield, Illinois.

———. 1997. Frozen Environments and Soft Tissue Preservation. In *Forensic Taphonomy: The Postmortem Fate of Human Remains*, edited by William D. Haglund and Marcella H. Sorg, pp. 171–180. CRC Press, Boca Raton.

Mitchell, Douglas R., and Judy L. Brunson-Hadley. 2001. Introduction. In *Ancient Burial Practices in the American Southwest: Archaeology, Physical Anthropology, and Native American Perspectives*, edited by Douglas R. Mitchell and Judy L. Brunson-Hadley, pp. 1–8. University of New Mexico Press, Albuquerque.

Moorehead, Warren K. 1906. *A Narrative of Explorations in New Mexico, Arizona, Indiana, etc.* Department of Archaeology, Bulletin No. 3. Phillips Academy, Andover, Massachusetts.

Neitzel, Jill E. 2000. Gender Hierarchies: A Comparative Analysis of Mortuary Data. In *Women and Men in the Prehispanic Southwest: Labor, Power and Prestige*, edited by Patricia L. Crown, pp. 137–168. School of American Research Press, Santa Fe.

———. 2003. Artifact Distributions at Pueblo Bonito. In *Pueblo Bonito: Center of the Chacoan World*, edited by Jill E. Neitzel, pp. 107–126. Smithsonian Institution Press, Washington, D.C.

———. 2007. Architectural Studies of Pueblo Bonito: The Past, the Present, and the Future. In *Architecture of Chaco Canyon, New Mexico*, edited by Stephen H. Lekson, pp. 127–154. University of Utah Press, Salt Lake City.

Nelson, Ben A., Debra L. Martin, Alan C. Swedlund, Paul R. Fish, and George J. Armelagos. 1994. Studies in Disruption: Demography and Health in the Prehistoric American Southwest. In *Understanding Complexity in the Prehistoric Southwest*, edited by George J. Gumerman and Murray Gell-Mann, pp. 59–112. Santa Fe Institute Studies in the Sciences of Complexity, Proceedings Volume XVI. Addison-Wesley, Reading, Massachusetts.

Neumann, Georg K. 1950. Racial Differentiation in the American Indian. Ph.D. dissertation, Department of Anthropology, University of Chicago, Chicago.

Parker Pearson, Mike. 1999. *The Archaeology of Death and Burial*. Texas A & M University Press, College Station.

Pepper, George H. 1896. Rooms #32 and 33, Also Measurements of Rooms. 1896–47 Accession file, Division of Anthropology, American Museum of Natural History, New York. Electronic document, http://www.chacoarchive.org/media/pdf/000157_public.pdf, accessed November 1, 2014.

———. 1899. Paper presented at the American Museum, March 18, 1899. On file at Archives of Latin American Library, Tulane University.

———. 1909. The Exploration of a Burial Room in Pueblo Bonito, New Mexico. In *Putnam Anniversary Volume: Anthropological Essays, Presented to Frederic Ward Putnam in Honor of His Seventieth Birthday, April 16, 1909, by His Friends and Associates*, edited by Franz Boas, Roland B. Dixon, Alfred L. Kroeber, Frederick W. Hodge, and H. I. Smith, pp. 196–252. G. E. Stechert & Co., New York.

———. 1920. *Pueblo Bonito*. Trustees of the American Museum of Natural History, New York.

Plog, Stephen. 1997. *Ancient Peoples of the American Southwest*. Thames and Hudson, London.

———. 2010. Reflections on the State of Chacoan Research: A Review Essay. *Kiva* 75(3):377–395.

Plog, Stephen and Carolyn Heitman. 2010. Hierarchy and Social Inequality in the American Southwest, AD 800–1200. *Proceedings of the National Academy of Sciences* 107:19619–19626.

Roksandic, Mirjana. 2002. Position of Skeletal Remains as a Key to Understanding Mortuary Behavior. In *Advances in Forensic Taphonomy: Method, Theory, and Archaeological Perspectives*, edited by William D. Haglund and Marcella H. Sorg, pp. 99–117. CRC Press, Boca Raton.

Saul, Julie M., and Frank P. Saul. 2002. Forensics, Archaeology, and Taphonomy: The Symbiotic Relationship. In *Advances in Forensic Taphonomy: Method, Theory, and Archaeological Perspectives*, edited by William D. Haglund and Marcella H. Sorg, pp. 71–97. CRC Press, Boca Raton.

Schillaci, Michael A., and Christopher M. Stojanowski. 2003. Postmarital Residence and Biological Variation at Pueblo Bonito. *American Journal of Physical Anthropology* 120:1–15.

Schillaci, Michael A., Dejana Nikitovic, and Lianne Tripp. 2010. Juvenile Growth in Prehistoric–Early Historic Pueblo Indians. Paper presented at the 67th Annual Meeting of the American Association of Physical Anthropologists.

Sebastian, Lynne. 2006. The Chaco Synthesis. In *The Archeology of Chaco Canyon: An Eleventh-Century Pueblo Regional Center*, edited by Stephen H. Lekson, pp. 393–422. School of American Research Press, Santa Fe.

Seltzer, Carl C. 1944. *Racial Prehistory in the Southwest and the Hawikuh Zunis*. Papers of the Peabody Museum of American Archaeology and Ethnology Vol. 23, No. 1. Harvard University, Cambridge.

Sobolik, Kristin D. 2002. Children's Health in the Prehistoric Southwest. In *Children in the Prehistoric Puebloan Southwest*, edited by Kathryn A. Kamp, pp. 125–151. University of Utah Press, Salt Lake City.

Spuhler, James N. 1954. Some Problems in the Physical Anthropology of the American Southwest. *American Anthropologist* 56:604–619.

Stewart, T. Dale. 1936a. Skeletal remains from Chaco Canyon. Draft of paper presented at the 7th annual meeting of the American Association of Physical Anthropologists, Yale University, New Haven, Connecticut, April 30–May 2, 1936. Manuscript on file, Office of the Physical Anthropology Collections Manager, National Museum of Natural History, Smithsonian Institution.

———. 1936b. Skeletal Remains from the Chaco Canyon, New Mexico. *American Journal of Physical Anthropology* 21(2):17. Supplement.

———. 1937. Different Types of Cranial Deformity in the Pueblo Area. *American Anthropologist* 39(1):169–171.

Stodder, Ann L. W. 2005. Treponemal Infection in the Prehistoric Southwest. In *The Myth of Syphilis: The Natural History of Treponematosis in Pre-Columbian North America*, edited by Mary L. Powell and Della C. Cook, pp. 227–280. University of Florida Press, Gainesville.

Stodder, Ann L. W., and Debra L. Martin. 1992. Native Health and Disease in the Prehistoric Southwest before and after Spanish Contact. In *Disease and Demography in the Americas: Changing Patterns before and after 1492*, edited by John W. Verano and Douglas H. Ubelaker, pp. 55–73. Smithsonian Institution Press, Washington, D.C.

Stodder, Ann L. W., Debra L. Martin, Alan Goodman, and Daniel R. H. Reff. 2002. Biological Stress and Cultural Longevity in the American Southwest. In *The Backbone of History: Health and Nutrition in the Western Hemisphere*, edited by Richard H. Steckel and Jerome C. Rose, pp. 481–505. Cambridge University Press, New York.

Vivian, R. Gwinn. 1990. *The Chacoan Prehistory of the San Juan Basin*. Academic Press, San Diego.

White, Tim D. 1992. *Prehistoric Cannibalism at Mancos 5MTUMR-2346*. Princeton University Press, Princeton, New Jersey.

White, Tim D., and Pieter A. Folkens. 2000. *Human Osteology*. 2nd ed. Academic Press, San Diego.

Wilcox, David R. 1993. The Evolution of the Chacoan Polity. In *Chimney Rock: The Ultimate Outlier*, edited by J. McKim Malville, pp. 163–199. Archaeological Symposium. Lexington Books, Lanham, Maryland.

Wills, Wirt H. 2009. Cultural Identity and the Archaeological Construction of Historical Narratives: An Example from Chaco Canyon. *Journal of Archaeological Method and Theory* 16:283–319.

Windes, Thomas C. 2003. This Old House: Construction and Abandonment at Pueblo Bonito. In *Pueblo Bonito: Center of the Chacoan World*, edited by Jill E. Neitzel, pp. 14–32. Smithsonian Books, Washington, D.C.

Wright, Lori E., and Cassaday J. Yoder. 2003. Recent Progress in Bioarchaeology: Approaches to the Osteological Paradox. *Journal of Archaeological Research* 11:43–70.

7

A Biological Perspective on Chacoan Identity

Meradeth Snow and Steven A. LeBlanc

Who lived in Chaco Canyon? This question is not easy to answer, and in fact, it is not easy to even define. But it should not be ignored. We need to use all the lines of evidence we can to decipher what the Chaco phenomenon was all about. This is particularly true because of the unique nature of Chaco. We cannot understand the general historical patterns by combining data from many separate but similar situations. There was only one Pueblo Bonito, only one Aztec Ruin. Because we cannot find other similar sites, or similar settlement patterns, we must squeeze the data we do have as hard as we can. We need to be reminded of this because the current biologic data from Chaco Canyon and the great house communities is rather weak and thin. But it is all we have.

The question of who the people living in Chaco Canyon were is really several different questions. Was the entire system (if it was a system) multiethnic in the sense that people would have spoken different languages and considered themselves to be ethnically different? Was the population in the canyon the result of immigration? Or conversely, was the canyon the source of people who built great houses in other areas? Or was the situation more subtle, for example with elite lineages living for many generations in the canyon, with non-elites migrating in, especially women, and still other people coming and going on a short-term basis? Can we make biological comparisons with modern people and get some idea about what language family was spoken in Chaco? What was the biologic composition of great house communities? Were these communities mainly a local phenomenon, with the inhabitants of their great houses related to the people in the surrounding local communities? Or did they have foreign elites in residence? Answers to any of these questions would help us draw a picture of what Chaco was all about.

In reality, the answers to most of these questions are beyond our ability to answer. One reason is that gene flow and culture are different. The other is that the Chaco world was not really all that big, and there was probably not that much biological variability within the entire region to begin with. Differences between groups would have been subtle. And there is the perennial problem with the quantity and quality of the data we have at our disposal.

There are several classes of potentially relevant data to address some of the above questions. First, there are indirect measures of genetic relatedness, such as discrete dental traits, discrete non-dental traits, and craniometrics. Each class of data has its own problems with how accurately they reflect actual genes that are not under significant selection in the time frames of relevance. Each of these lines of evidence also varies in how much data, including comparative data, are available. This latter problem is compounded by the comparability between studies. Not only is there the potential and demonstrably real problem of inter-recorder measurement error but also the issue that different researchers have had a tendency to use different sets of markers and measurements, further making comparisons between the few published studies difficult.

Recently, it has been possible to directly determine DNA sequences from ancient individuals. To date, such data, with rare exceptions, has been confined to mitochondria DNA (mtDNA). This mtDNA has the benefit of being passed down through matrilineal descent and is not subject to recombination. It also contains enough variability to be useful for the types of questions listed above. However, it does not provide information about patrilines, and it is not a general measure of relatedness. With mtDNA you might be able to argue that two individuals were mother and daughter but be unable to exclude whether two individuals were maternal cousins. While the potential is large for this type of inquiry, to date, we have only very limited relevant modern mtDNA and extremely limited ancient mtDNA.

Finally, there has been almost no biological relatedness work that has directly focused on the Chaco phenomenon writ large. There has been some that focused on Chaco Canyon, but only one or two studies that really look at Chaco Canyon and a set of great house communities in a comparative way. Most of the information we have pertains to how populations from a particular site relate to populations from other sites. Only for Pueblo Bonito has any attempt been made to look at intra-site variability. And when one compares a site such as Pueblo

Bonito with other sites, the other sites are often not contemporary, are multicomponent, or have small sample sizes. So, by necessity most of these comparisons become rather regional in scope. These comparisons tend to be, How does Pueblo Bonito compare with the late Mogollon of Arizona, or the Rio Grande, or the Mesa Verde area (not confined to the Chaco time frame)? We have only a couple of comparisons of the canyon sites with other Pueblo II communities and none with Pueblo I sites. So, most of the obvious comparisons of interest cannot presently be made. In spite of these limitations, we will try to summarize what is currently known.

The Interpretive Background

It is worth considering what we know about the archaeology and bio-logical reality before considering the work that has been done. The over-all demographic situation is certainly relevant. One issue we need to be mindful of is, How many people are we talking about? This question is frequently ignored in this type of discussion, but it is relevant, espe-cially if we are asking about migration or gene flow. A movement of 1 or 2 individuals into a small group of 10–15 could be detectable, but the same movement into a community of 200 would be lost in a genera-tion or two. How much could a founding population have expanded in the time frame under consideration? Revisiting population estimates for the canyon is not the issue here, but rather consideration of the conse-quences of some relative population numbers.

Clearly, many of the great house communities go back to Pueblo I times, so it surely is not the case that they were all occupied by migrants from the canyon. Some great house communities might have been founded by canyon migrants, but most must not have been. So, there are two different questions: Could some of the great house communities, such as Salmon, been founded by migrants from the canyon? Or, could elites from the canyon (if there were any) have become elites of such communities? If, for the sake of argument, the canyon began to be the loci of elite behavior at A.D. 800, or 900, or 1050 (different models could justify any of these dates, and the implications are quite different), then how many elites could have been produced? Let us assume great houses such as Pueblo Bonito held 30 elites at any one time. We would expect

they would have had considerable demographic reproductive capabil-
ity (especially with the likelihood of multiple wives for elite males). We
can assign a potential growth rate of 2 percent to these elites. While this
may seem high, elites are well fed, and given that the overall Southwestern environment was conducive to population growth at that time, it is
probably realistic (Read and LeBlanc 2003). We can also assume that the
number of elites living in the great houses remained constant (or else
the estimate of 30 elites would be quickly wrong), and so by necessity the
additional individuals would have moved out of each great house.

How many would have moved out? A growth rate of 2 percent results
in a population doubling approximately every 35 years. That is, the elites
of Pueblo Bonito would have been able to populate another great house
every 35 years. If this happened over a 200-year span, enough growth to
found another great house would have happened 6 times. If the 3 initial
canyon great houses were doing this, they could have spawned about
20 more great house elite sets. But, of course, the same would have
been true for each spawned great house, and if out-of-the-canyon great
houses had fewer elites than, say Bonito, the number of great houses
that could have been populated becomes very much greater than the
number that is known or could have existed. That is, it is biologically
possible that founding elites from the 3 earliest great houses could have
produced enough other elites to found all the other great houses, both
in the canyon and outside of it, if this process went on for a bit over
200 years.

However, if great house expansion did not really get underway until
the last century of Chacoan activity, the numbers are very different.
Three or so great houses could have spawned about two and one-half
great house community elites each, and these new ones would have had
little time to spawn additional ones. It is very hard to see how enough
elites could have been produced from a core handful of great houses
to have resulted in the 100+ great houses known in less than a century,
even if the out-of-the-canyon great houses were occupied by groups
smaller than those in the canyon-founding great houses. Incidentally,
even if only males moved and married locally, the demographics remain
the same.

This demographic argument is not worth pursuing further unless we
know when the canyon great houses were initially occupied and when

out-of-canyon great houses were built. Note that it is not dependent on the size of the elite groups. All that is needed is that the groups of elites that found great houses are no larger than the groups of elites that spawned them.

To summarize, if the Chaco phenomenon lasted 200 or more years, it is quite possible that all the elites were related in all the great houses. If the out-of-the-canyon great house phase was 100 years or less, it is not possible they were all related. An alternative scenario is that elites did not leave to found out-of-canyon great houses. (This would assume that this might have been true in a few instances, but not consistently.) In this case, there should have been an increase in the numbers of elites living in the canyon great houses. If such elites existed, where are they?

There are three reasonable possibilities that can be compared, assuming there were elites in the first place: (1) the canyon great houses did not have elites for much of their history, (2) excess elites started founding great houses right away, or (3) most offspring of elites were not elites. Only with the excess elites founding out-of-the-canyon great houses on a long-term basis would there be any likelihood of finding related elites in these communities. However, there are no proposed elites that have been identified from any such great houses, with the possible exception of Aztec Ruin. So, in order to find such potential elites biologically, we would need to have a very distinctive genetic pattern for canyon elites and a large enough sample from out-of-the-canyon great house communities to recognize it. The chances of finding such a pattern are rather remote. Also, if there were not elites for most of the Chacoan span, then trying to find relationships among the few that would have existed is also essentially hopeless.

So, using the demographic constraints and likely outcomes, only under the most perfect of circumstances would we find evidence for elite genetic relationships between the canyon and out-of-the-canyon great house communities. However, we might be able to see genetic relationships within the canyon great houses. We also might be able to find relationships between great house communities and canyon communities, but these would need to involve far more people than just elites. While the potential relationships among canyon great houses and the sites of Salmon Ruins and Aztec Ruins are particular cases, which are considered below, the most promising opportunity for finding intra-system genetic relationships is with inward gene flow. This time, the demographics work in our favor. If we had a good sample of great house community genetics we might be able to find links to the canyon. For example, it would be quite realistic to test the model of females moving into the canyon from some distances (Kohler and Turner 2006). Timothy Kohler and Kathryn Turner suggest the phenomenon was common and should be recognizable. The problem here is the traditional methods of dental traits or craniometrics are population based, not individual based, so we would need to find entire communities moving into the canyon using these lines of data. It is unlikely that this happened or that we would be lucky enough to have the right out-of-the-canyon and the right canyon samples. In theory, direct genetic data on individuals could find such patterns, but no such data currently exist.

A final thought relating to population numbers considers the numbers of burials from Pueblo Bonito. If we assume there were 100 burials interred over a span of 200 years, this implies an average momentary population of 25 individuals. Not all scholars would have the population of Pueblo Bonito as being so small, although numbers this low have been suggested. Thus, it is likely these individuals were drawn from a subset of the population or were drawn from a different pool altogether. All subsequent interpretation must keep this factor in mind.

Relevant Studies

Besides the DNA information presented here, there are several other studies that are especially relevant. These involve craniometrics and discrete dental traits. It should be noted that there is another type of data—non-dental discrete cranial traits. Such data has been recorded for the Southwest (e.g., Mackey 1980), but not for Chacoan-related populations. Some researchers feel that craniometrics, that is, measurements of the skull such as the shape of the orbits, are very sensitive genetically derived traits and are superior to dental trait data (Akins 1986; Schillaci and Stojanowski 2005). This argument is probably true when there is no cranial deformation and diet and behaviors, such as using teeth as tools, are reasonably the same among all the individuals measured. Other researchers feel that the skeleton is too plastic for such measurements to reliably reflect genetics. For these people, developmental factors can affect traits significantly, especially where inherent differences are small initially. They feel that dental data are less susceptible to developmental factors that may interfere with results obtained from craniometrics. The differences between data types are compounded in that one set of data is interval and the other ordinal or binary, so they lend themselves to different analytic techniques. Overall, the relative merits of the two approaches are probably somewhere in the middle. There are surely some genes being reflected in these data, but the above concerns combined with the small sample size means we need to treat these results with caution.

In doing this type of analysis, what one would like are studies where some population comparisons are included that have reasonably established relationships that can be used as reference. If they meet our expectations, then we can have more confidence in the rest of the results. For example, in the case of some of the dental trait studies that have been done, we find that Point of Pines and Grasshopper sites appear rather similar when compared with other sites. Or we find that Awatovi and modern Hopi appear similar. This is what we would expect, and it provides a measure of confidence that the other relationships have some validity. When such expectations are not met, one has to question the validity of any of the relationships.

There have been several craniometric analyses focusing on Chaco. Some earlier studies not considered here are well summarized by Nancy Akins (1986), but none of these focused on Chaco or had very relevant comparative populations. Akins (1986) did the most comprehensive craniometric comparison for canyon samples. She measured all the extant useable crania from Pueblo Bonito and did include some, but not all, of the possible other crania from the canyon. She did not make any comparisons with any samples from outside the canyon and did not publish the basic measurements. Michael Schillaci and colleagues (2001) did a more comprehensive study, which has several parts and in its entirety is well-constructed but was not nearly as complete for Pueblo Bonito or the canyon overall as the Akins (1986) study.

For both studies, as noted, the questions of how much cranial measurements reflect underlying genetics and how much they are impacted by environmental factors is an issue. Michael Schillaci and Christopher Stojanowski (2005) address this issue well, but it still remains an issue. On a worldwide scale the nature of the diet can have an impact on cranial development. However, for the Southwest, the diet for the time periods involved was probably quite similar over the region, and this is not likely to impact the results. However, cranial deformation was widely practiced, in varying degrees and forms. While the measurements were selected to minimize the impact of such deformation, extreme cases could have had some impact.

One part of the overall Schillaci project was a study of crania from the Rio Grande. It is not directly related to Chaco but is methodogically relevant (Schillaci and Stojanowski 2005). Because the crania were from sites that were relatively recent and at varied geographic distances from each other, we have some predictions about what the results should look like. These expectations are reasonably met. The sample sizes are not any larger than for Schillaci's other studied populations, and as the Rio Grande would be expected to be more homogenous than the Southwest as a whole, we have some confidence that the method he used is robust. Another of his compared samples was from the Southwest as a whole, with an out-population from Mesoamerica (Schillaci et al. 2001). These results are less convincing, because some of our expectations about which populations should be similar to each other do not seem to be met. For example, Schillaci's Salado sample is more closely related to Mesa Verde and Te'ewi than any of the rest of his Southwest sample, and Pueblo Bonito is more closely related to several towns in the Rio Grande than it is to Aztec Ruin. These similarities are unlikely, so we might legitimately question inferences about Chaco, the particulars of which are discussed below.

One study of theirs deals with Chaco in more detail using the same data sets (Schillaci and Stojanowski 2003), and it is discussed in more detail below. He did not use the full potential Pueblo Bonito sample, as did Akins. On the plus side, he provides some evidence that the method is robust, and there are good comparative samples from Chacoan or possibly Chacoan populations. On the negative side, several Chacoan-related populations were not included in his studies, and many of his population samples are very small. For example, his Mesa Verde sample is seven individuals, and the Te'ewi and Village of the Great Kivas samples only have six individuals each. These sample sizes are painfully small. Even one sampled individual who moved into the community or one individual with some particularly strong environmental effects could skew the results in these cases.

Discrete dental traits would appear to have a strong genetic basis, but studies based on them suffer from several difficulties. The amount of variability in a region such as the Southwest is not very great, and many of the traits are continuous in form but need to be recorded as discrete categories, thus reducing the observed variability that does exist. Also, tooth wear and tooth loss can greatly reduce the number of teeth that can be recorded for these traits. While there is an overall Southwestern discrete dental trait study by Turner (1993), the most relevant dental trait study is that by Durand et al. (2010), although it suffers from some sample size and comparative sample problems. The authors are well aware of the limitations and are planning a new study using additional data. But for the present, in the study available, the prehistoric samples are all from Pueblo Bonito or the middle San Juan. There are no Mesa Verde, Rio Grande, or other comparative samples. The only other comparisons are made with modern Western Pueblos, Athabaskans, or Yuman speakers. Sample sizes are a bit larger than for the morphometrics, but not all individuals had all teeth present. For example, the sample for Salmon Ruins was 18, but 7 of the dental traits had less than 10 scorable teeth. The 2 La Plata samples had scores for 12 and 15 individuals, respectively, not all of which had complete dentitions.

Overall, these studies are useful; however, their limitations need to be accepted. None have the sample sizes one would wish or include the relevant populations one would like to have for comparison. They are, however, what we have and are therefore valuable for the information they can provide.

Internal Chacoan Comparisons

There are several studies that compare individuals within Pueblo Bonito. The two that are relevant are Akins (1986) and Schillaci and Stojanowski (2003). Both studies are based on craniometrics. Akins (1986) provides a more complete data set and compares the north (16) and west (19) burial clusters with 9 other individuals from the canyon. Schillaci and Stojanowski (2003) compare 12 individuals from the north burial cluster with 15 from the west cluster. Unfortunately, no list of exactly which burials were compared is provided in their publication, and clearly not all potential burials were considered. Unfortunately, neither study provides the raw data, so the studies cannot be combined.

Several results were proposed for Pueblo Bonito in one or both of the above-mentioned studies. First, the two burial cluster groups were significantly different from each other. Second, there was no evidence for matrilineality or patrilineality. Finally, the north cluster had more divergence between the sexes than the west cluster had, and based on other comparisons, the north cluster was more divergent from the rest of the Chaco sample and from the rest of the Southwest than was the west cluster. Since these two studies used the same method on almost the same crania, the fact that their results generally match is not surprising.

Given the smallish sample sizes, and the lack of comparisons with other Chaco Canyon skeletons, especially from small sites, it is perhaps best to say that there is considerable variability within the single site of Pueblo Bonito and that there may be some culturally meaningful difference between the two burial clusters. Incidentally, such high intra-site variability is a pattern also found in Mimbres non-metric dental traits (LeBlanc et al. 2008), so it is perhaps less dramatic than it might appear. No other internal comparisons for the canyon are currently available. One possibility is that individuals from the two clusters were drawn from different populations, perhaps one of which was composed of individuals who were of different statuses or did not reside in the community. Both the way they were interred and their apparent genetic differences imply some significant biological and cultural differences between the two groups.

Pueblo Bonito vs. Other Communities

Comparing Pueblo Bonito with other contemporary sites is extremely difficult due to the present lack of relevant comparative samples. Based on craniometrics, Pueblo Bonito is not much like Village of the Great Kivas, which is slightly similar to Heshotauthla, according to Schillaci and Stojanowski (2003). (This is what we would predict if similarity is based on geographical distance.) They argue that the west group burials are similar to some sites in the Rio Grande, while the north cluster is more like Western Anasazi populations. However, this analysis has the west cluster of Pueblo Bonito most like Pot Creek Pueblo and very unlike Te'ewi, which would hardly fit any models we might have for archaeological relationships, because these two sites were geographically rather close, and presumably populations from both sites spoke Tanoan languages. While it is certainly possible the burials from the west cluster were related to later populations in the Rio Grande, it seems hard to accept that they were related to one Tanoan group and not another.

Pueblo Bonito has also been studied for discrete dental traits. There are two relevant studies, one by Turner (1993) and one by Durand et al. (2010). The Turner study is the best known. It was a pan-Southwestern study and did not focus on Pueblo Bonito or even the Chacoan phenomenon. There has been a reanalysis of the Turner data with a cleaner set of comparison populations, and these results are probably more robust than those given in the earlier publication, which was not so narrowly focused on the Southwest (LeBlanc and Turner 2010; LeBlanc et al. 2008). As noted, dental traits have been shown to be fairly strongly genetic, and they are very useful for broad comparisons. The discrete dental trait data shows Pueblo Bonito to fit in the northern Southwest, somewhat but not especially close to the Rio Grande. Pueblo Bonito does not align with Mesa Verde, Hopi, Zuni, or the Rio Grande in any particular way.

Overall, there seems to be no evidence for Pueblo Bonito as to its linguistic/ethnic affiliation based on dental traits, and based on craniometrics, it would appear it was a mixed population. This later statement needs to be stated in a different way. As is discussed below, there does seem to be only slight correlation between dental trait similarities among populations that can be proposed to have spoken Uto-Aztecan. Pueblo Bonito does not fit within this group. So, perhaps what can be said is that there is some slight negative evidence that the people buried in Pueblo Bonito did not speak Uto-Aztecan.

The second dental trait study by Durand et al. (2010) is much more narrowly focused than Turner's (1993), and it does much more directly address Chacoan connections, but it is best considered when looking at great house communities.

Ancient DNA and Chaco Great House Communities

Before discussing the available data, a brief background on ancient DNA seems warranted. With a few exceptions, all the indigenous

people of the Americas belong to one of five mtDNA haplogroups:
A, B, C, D, and X. In the Southwest, most non-Athapaskans are haplogroup B (Hap B), with moderate to low frequencies of haplogroup C,
and relatively rare haplogroups A and D. By comparing the frequencies
of the different haplogroups, it is possible to establish potential relationships between populations, as more closely related populations are
expected to often have similar frequencies of the different haplogroups.
There are difficulties with this approach, however, as often there is a
very small sample (particularly when samples are broken down by
time frame and individual site), which weakens the statistical power
of comparisons.

Another means of analyzing DNA from populations past and present that allows for a more robust comparison is sequencing the individual base pairs of a portion of the mtDNA molecule. Within the
mtDNA, a portion known at the hypervariable region is known for
its rapid mutation rate. Several of the haplogroups (A, B, C, and X)
have diagnostic mutations within this hypervariable region and additional mutations beyond the diagnostic set apart matrilineal haplotypes. Often the core or base version of the hypervariable region will
be common, and an individual with this haplotype is not necessarily
closely related to others that share it. But other haplotypes can be
quite rare, and individuals who share them should be expected to have
had a recent common female ancestor. However, establishing relationships through the paternal line cannot be done with mtDNA, as it
is solely passed matrilineally. So, only very specific types of relationships are recognized with this approach. A number of modern population samples do have such hyper-variable data, and it is possible to
look for such relationships and use them in comparisons. At present,
almost none of the very limited ancient mtDNA has such hypervariable region data.

As an aside, the same logic prevails with Y-chromosome data, where
short tandem repeats, in conjunction with diagnostic single nucleo-
tide polymorphisms, are used to look for Y-chromosome differences
among modern populations. Unfortunately, due to the low concentration of nuclear DNA in comparison to mtDNA in individual samples,
Y-chromosome analysis is difficult in some aDNA analyses. Nuclear
autosomal DNA provides a series of mutations that would enable the

level of genetic difference to be determined, such as cousin, sibling, etc., as well as information about rare mutations that would show lineal genetic relationships. There is currently no data, modern or ancient, of this type for the Southwest.

MtDNA can provide unique data and it is useful, but it does not necessarily address many of the questions we might wish to consider. It is, however, the only data we have, and even then it is very limited.

We currently have only two mtDNA studies that involve any populations related to Chaco. The few other studies involve earlier (Basketmaker II) or non-Chacoan populations. The first relevant study, that of Shawn Carlyle (2003), obtained mtDNA data for 21 individuals that dated from Pueblo II or later. This was a very early study, and he obtained only haplogroup data, not haplotype (sequence) data. The sample included one individual from Bonito, one from Kin Bineola, six from Aztec, and four from White House Overhang in Canyon de Chelley. The other study described here (building on data presented in Snow et al. 2007, 2010) provides mtDNA data that includes two sites near Farmington, New Mexico, that are either Chacoan or slightly later in time. The sites themselves, belonging to the Point Community, are located on the property of Mr. Bolack, an avocational archaeologist who excavated portions of the sites. His meticulous records and preservation of artifacts have allowed for placing the individual human remains at each of the sites, as well as aided in further excavation of the sites by current San Juan Community College field schools under the direction of Linda Wheelbarger. The two sites with larger samples of human remains for analysis are the Tommy site (100+ burials) and the Mine Canyon site (39 burials). Both sites are located near the San Juan River and are about a mile apart. Based on the pottery excavated from the sites, the Tommy site dates to the late Pueblo I/Pueblo II time frame and the Mine Canyon site to early Pueblo III times.

Previously, haplogroup results from 48 individuals from both the Mine Canyon site and Tommy site were published by Snow et al. (2010). Haplogroups A, B, C, and D were found in varying frequencies at the sites. The Tommy site fit in with other Southwestern sites with its high frequency of haplogroup B, and it was statistically indistinguishable from the other ancient samples in the region (from Carlyle 2003;

LeBlanc et al. 2007). In contrast, the Mine Canyon site was significantly different from all of them due to its anomalous high frequency of haplogroup A.

It has previously been proposed that the Tommy site residents had moved from their village to then occupy the Mine Canyon site. The other biological (craniometric, etc.) data supported a conclusion that these sites' occupants were very similar to one another (Greene 2007). The DNA evidence seemed to contradict this pattern of similarity between the sites. When the hypervariable region of the mtDNA was sequenced, the samples from the Mine Canyon site provided another interesting twist.

Of the eight haplogroup A samples from the Mine Canyon site, including both old and new data, it was noted that seven of these samples had two derived mutations that set them apart from the rest of the haplogroup A samples. These mutations (at np 16257 and 16263) were also noted among several Zuni samples, creating a link between these two populations. At some point in the past, it seems that the Zuni and Mine Canyon individuals shared a matriline.

Also intriguing about these samples is the fact that this similar motif (either with both mutations or with a single one of them) has also been found in the Chumash of California (Monroe et al. 2013). The possibility that trade between the two regions (as has been suggested by rare artifacts found in the Southwest that have California coastal origins) may have led to gene flow is an intriguing thought. Of course, there is also the possibility that these mutations are homologous or are much more ancient and are found in these two regions due to a common ancestor much further in the past.

Due to the questions that arose from the previous research at these two sites, a larger sample was studied to see if it would result in further clarification of the distinction between the two settlements. For additional study, 36 individuals were collected (17 from the Mine Canyon site and 19 from the Tommy site), which brought the total sample to 33 individuals from the Mine Canyon site and 75 individuals from the Tommy site. From these samples, data from 10 additional samples (6 from the Mine Canyon site and 4 from the Tommy site) brought the final sample size to 58 individuals. The combined haplogroup frequencies for Mine Canyon are Hap A = 44%, Hap B = 50%, Hap C = 6%,

Table 7.1. Mine Canyon and Tommy Sites Haplogroup Data.

	A%	B%	C%	D%	N
Mine Canyon	44	50	6	0	18
Tommy	3	68	15	15	40

and no Hap D. The Tommy site has Hap A = 3%, Hap B = 68%, Hap C = 15%, and Hap D = 15% (see Table 7.1). A Fisher's Exact Test showed that the addition of these samples did not significantly alter the original haplogroup distribution previously reported. When compared to one another, the two sites were significantly distinct. For this reason, these sites are treated separately in terms of comparing them to other populations and other statistical analyses.

The new data do result in the Mine Canyon site having more haplogroup B than previously reported—it now makes up fully half the samples from the site. There is still a higher-than-expected frequency of haplogroup A in the sample, however, which distinguishes the population from all of the other Southwestern populations used for comparison. When compared to Mesoamerican samples, it was statistically most similar to the Huichol, Cora, and Nahua-Atocpan (as per data from Kemp et al. 2010), as well as the Athapaskan Navajo.

The Tommy site, on the other hand, saw relatively little change with the additional samples (which is to be expected, as there were only four added: two Bs, one C, and one D). In comparing it with other populations in the region (using a Fisher's Exact Test), the Tommy site was statistically indistinguishable from the Fremont population to the north (which comes from an aDNA sample done by Parr et al. 1996) at the 0.05 level of probability. It was almost rather similar to Carlyle's (2003) sample of Eastern Anasazi.

The haplogroup A samples from the Mine Canyon site nearly all shared the same haplotype (or hypervariable region) motif. This allows for a more detailed analysis of these individuals, as it is possible to pinpoint the fact that they are matrilineally related to one another. Six of the seven burials that share the 16257 and 16263 motif come from Kiva B at the site, with the exception of a single individual who was buried in the midden. These unique haplogroup A samples constitute 43 percent of the samples from this part of the site and two-thirds of the haplotyped

individuals. Also accompanying the haplogroup A individuals were two
haplogroup B individuals, a single haplogroup C individual, and several
individuals who have not been haplotyped.

Kiva B presents an interesting situation: the kiva has 14 burials in and
around it, leading Mr. Bolack and others to believe there might have
been some kind of catastrophe that led to these deaths at around the
same time. This kind of event is not unheard of in the Southwest, with
instances dating back even to the Archaic period. The minimal amount
of grave goods associated with the burials placed the kiva in a Pueblo III
context. What event might have occurred in association with the deaths
of these individuals is not known, but the fact that the majority of them
seem to be maternally related presents an interesting question.

In looking to see if the interplay of age and sex might also reflect a
pattern that would aid in understanding the distribution of this haplotype, there was little information on these haplogroup A individuals.
One was a female, who died between 35 and 49 years of age, and another
was a male who died between 20 and 34 years of age. The rest of the
individuals were of unknown sex, with three between the ages of 10 and
19, and one between the ages of 5 and 9.

The other individuals found in Kiva B were also younger, with the
haplogroup B individuals between 15 and 19 and 0 and 4 years of age,
and the haplogroup C individual between 10 and 14 years of age. Among
the untyped individuals, a single male and female (ages 35 to 49) were
also found. Overall, there are too many unknowns to get a clear sense of
what might have been going on; however, hopefully, this can be further
analyzed by genetic sex-determination testing.

Despite missing or unavailable data, what these data do say about
the use of kivas in the Southwest is of interest. The fact that women
and children are present in the kiva is particularly puzzling. There is
no solid answer to what might have occurred here, but it calls for more
attention.

At the Tommy site, on the other hand, the majority (n=53) of the
burials come from the midden. There are five burials from within kivas
(Kiva B, Kiva D, and Kiva E); for three of these, data are available. The
remainder of the burials came from backfill, regions around kivas, or
other parts of the site. With the data currently available, it is not possible to analyze any further patterns of how the different haplogroups

and haplotypes might be distributed, other than to say that it stands in contrast to what we see in Kiva B on the Mine Canyon site.

As it stands, the Mine Canyon and Tommy sites appear distinct in terms of their genetic matrilines. While further analysis may not bear this out, it is interesting to question what may be occurring at these sites to create such a difference, especially as they are so close in geographical space and contiguous in time.

As mentioned before, the most parsimonious explanation for what we are seeing here is the effects of sampling. The only areas of the Mine Canyon site that have been sampled are portions of the midden and Kiva B and C. The majority of the individuals that are contributing to the high frequency of haplogroup A are found within the context of Kiva B, which underwent some kind of event that led to the deaths of 14 individuals. This unusual event, accompanied by the limited sample size, seems to be skewing the results. The remainder of the site may contain individuals that bear more typically Southwestern haplogroup frequencies, as well as provide evidence of shared haplotypes between the two sites.

Of course, other factors may be at play here: the Mine Canyon site may indeed have a higher frequency of haplogroup A than we see in the rest of the Southwest. This may be due to several reasons, such as a Founder's Effect, wherein the original occupants of the site carried with them an atypical number of females with haplogroup A. Additionally, genetic drift may have altered the haplogroup frequencies over time. It is important also to note that other aDNA samples from the Southwest have been small and often not from a single site. It is possible that what we are witnessing at these two sites is quite common in this area, and we do not have any comparisons by which to understand that.

The question of where this unique haplotype A comes from is a related question. Migration has long been a topic of interest in the Southwest, and it could possibly account for the differences seen between the sites. Individuals moving into the region during Pueblo III times from either the Mesa Verde region or the Chaco Valley may both account for the shift. Of course, neither region has seen extensive genetic sampling, so further analysis is required to better understand this possibility.

The Mine Canyon and Tommy sites provide a unique perspective on the Chacoan great house communities, especially on the genetic make-up of the Ancestral Puebloan population. If the Tommy site is part of a great house community, it suggests that it was primarily local people who were similar to others in the eastern portion of the northern Southwest. The difference perceived at the Mine Canyon site is softened with the addition of several more haplogroup B samples. The differences between the two sites are therefore possibly based more on sampling bias than anything else. However, where these distinct haplogroup A samples originate from remains to be seen. It is quite possible they represent the effects of population shifts after the end of the Chaco phenomenon. Perhaps further sampling in other regions of the Southwest, or even into Mesoamerica and California, may reveal more information.

To return to the other relevant aDNA study that was mentioned above, Carlyle (2003) provides mtDNA haplogroup (but no haplotype) data for several Chaco sites. He found one haplogroup B for Pueblo Bonito and one haplogroup C for Kin Bineola. In addition, he also found one haplogroup A, two B, and one C for White House Overhang in Canyon de Chelley, which is Pueblo III and may or may not relate to the White House great house. Similarly, he typed five individuals from Aztec as haplogroup B and one as haplogroup C, all of whom are presumably Pueblo III, and not Chacoan in time. These are typical frequencies of these haplogroups in the Southwest and tell us little more than "nothing unexpected was found." Of interest, as discussed below, is the one haplogroup A from Canyon de Chelley.

Skeletal Information and Chaco Great House Communities

There are skeletal samples from great houses themselves and from the communities in which they are imbedded. Unfortunately, the samples from Salmon Ruins and Aztec Ruin are almost all post-Chaco, and those for other great house communities have gone unstudied for hard-to-explain reasons. For craniometrics, the only comparable sample seems to be from the previously mentioned Village of the Great Kivas.

We do have the study of Schillaci et al. (2001). This study compares a number of later sites with the two Pueblo Bonito burial clusters and the Village of the Great Kivas. There are a few difficulties with the data set they used. Sample sizes are very small: Te'ewi (n = 6), Pecos (n=6), and Tsankawi (n=7). Village of the Great Kivas (n=6), Awatovi (n=4), and Arroyo Hondo (n=4) have particularly small sample sizes. Only 5 out of 18 site samples have 15 or more individuals. The Mesa Verde sample is a composite; not all samples are from Mesa Verde National Park nor are all the individuals from the same time period. Some of the sites span multiple centuries. When one looks at the resulting similarity plots, certain incongruities are present. For example, Hawikuh is much more similar to Arroyo Hondo than it is to Heshotauthla. The Salado sample is more similar to Te'ewi than to Aztec, and there are other less dramatic but still potentially problematic relationships. It would appear that the one relevant thing is that the study did not show Pueblo Bonito and Aztec Ruins to be particularly similar.

However, the Durand et al. (2010) dental trait study did include some great house community samples, and it reaches the opposite conclusion (see Figure 7.1). They compared Pueblo Bonito's north burial cluster (but not all of those individuals that are from the cluster) with

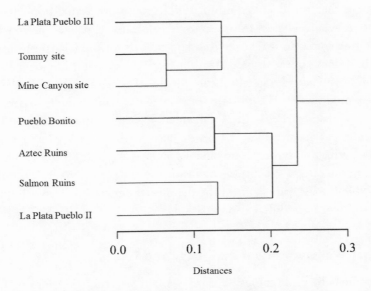

Figure 7.1. A cluster dendrogram showing the distance between prehistoric Southwestern samples based on 21 discrete dental traits. (From Durand et al. 2010)

Aztec Ruin, Salmon Ruin, and the two Bolack Ranch sites of Mine Canyon and the Tommy site, along with combined Pueblo II and Pueblo III samples from the La Plata River. Thus, in this study, only Tommy, Pueblo II La Plata, and Bonito are Chacoan in time. The authors did not have a good set of outgroup samples to ground the comparisons, so these results are somewhat hard to interpret. They found that Salmon looked similar to other Middle San Juan (Totah) Pueblo II samples, while Aztec looked extremely similar to Pueblo Bonito. They also found that the Bolack and La Plata III sites looked similar. Thus, similarities seem to be based on a combination of geographic and temporal similarities, except for the Pueblo Bonito–Aztec similarity. However, this was based on only a portion of the north cluster sample. That is, this analysis is very intriguing, but not at this point convincing.

Summary of Biological Distance Studies

None of these studies are very convincing on their own. They have small sample sizes, they have few good comparison populations, and they assume that the Pueblo Bonito burial groups are actual populations that are relatively close in time. Nevertheless, in aggregate, the conclusion one comes to is that the standard models for the Chaco phenomenon do not appear to be correct. Pueblo Bonito is not homogeneous; Salmon Ruins and Aztec Ruins in Pueblo III times are not as similar as one would predict. Or to state this somewhat more broadly, based on current analyses, sites in the Totah are biologically not internally similar in either Chacoan times or later in Pueblo III (Mesa Verdian) times. Also, at this point, there is no obvious biological link from any Chacoan site, in the canyon or out, to any historic group. And, finally, it is quite possible the individuals from the two burial clusters in Pueblo Bonito were drawn from different populations.

What We Know about Language and Genes

There may be some things we can say about larger relationships within the Southwest that might be helpful in our thinking about Chaco. This is not necessarily the forum for this discussion except that we do have some relevant mtDNA data, and we do have great house communities that span a wide geographical region. What might we expect about their genetic and linguistic affiliations?

While we must fully recognize that language and genes should not be expected to correlate completely, or necessarily even closely, language (and culture) should provide some barrier to gene flow, and so there may well be some correlation between genes and language under certain circumstances. We would not expect language and genes to correlate where there are many languages that are stable over long times, providing ample time for gene flow. Conversely, if a language is spread by biological replacement, and competition exists on the borders between language groups, then we might well expect language and genes to correlate.

For the Southwest, if one accepts the Bellwood, Hill, and Matson model of the spread of Uto-Aztecan (U-A) (see LeBlanc 2008 for a summary of the farmer migration argument), the biological replacement scenario would appear to be met, and we might well expect U-A to be reflected in some genetic markers. On the basis of the farmer migration model, one would make an argument that the present-day Arizona (and southeastern Utah) portion of the Southwest was occupied by peoples who spoke some form of U-A, while most of New Mexico and SW Colorado spoke non-U-A languages. Using the state line is, of course, a bit arbitrary, but it would appear to be not far off from what would appear to be a reasonable boundary line. The exception is that Mimbres and Casas Grandes are likely to have been in U-A territory, but this is not really relevant to the present discussion.

If this model is correct, then we would expect Chaco and most of the great house communities to be outside of the U-A sphere. This would come as little surprise to anyone, but it does raise the question of what would have been the language affiliation of those great house communities that are in Arizona or Utah, the locality of the posited U-A speakers. These communities could be good candidates for emulation sites, or for intrusive sites, or just examples of a multi-language basis for the Chacoan interaction sphere.

One thought is that we might be led to expect more cultural emulation than might have existed in prehistory because of the high levels of

emulation we find between historic Hopi, Zuni, and Acoma.* Here we
have lots of cultural emulation, but three different language families.
The problem with this analogy is that each of these three areas had few
people to interact with except ones with different languages. However,
a few centuries earlier, with many more choices of whom to interact
with, we see lots of movement of people north and south in Arizona
and much less between Arizona and New Mexico. Furthermore, some
archaeologists have proposed considerable movement of people from
the Mesa Verde area in southwestern Colorado to the east and south
(New Mexico), but little movement to the west (Arizona and Utah).
(These proposed movements are well summarized by Kohler et al.
[2010] and Ortman [2012].) Was this because everyone in Arizona was
speaking some form of U-A, making it easier to move between groups?
And could Mesa Verde people move to the Rio Grande relatively easily
because both were within the Tanoan-language sphere? Maybe when
there were many linguistic groups to interact with, language did matter,
but where there were not many choices, language was a weaker barrier.
In such a scenario, biological expansion might be more likely than emulation across a linguistic barrier. Contrary to this expectation, as soon as
one looks at great house communities that were possibly in U-A territory, such as Edge of Cedars and Et Al site in Utah, or White House in
Arizona, they do not look especially Chacoan-like and seem to be good
candidates for emulators.

The above discussion has been to suggest that the broader linguistic
question is of some interest. Now what is actually known at this point?
This discussion would be almost pointless except for the existence of
a small amount of mtDNA data. A series of studies, some already discussed, by Carlyle (2003), Kemp et al. (2010), LeBlanc et al. (2007), and

---

* By emulation, we mean shared cultural traits that are not environmentally driven.
People have contrasted the Western Pueblos with the Rio Grande Pueblos in terms
of similarities in social organization. Zuni and Hopi share not only the katsina cult
but also actual katsinas. They also share the shift in pottery design styles in late prehistoric times. The Western Pueblos share kiva forms in contrast to the Rio Grande
Pueblos, etc. That is, one can argue that from 1300 onward, the Western Pueblos
tend to converge in various ways, including material culture and social relations. It
is not how similar they wind up, but the direction of change considered here. That
is, the direction is one of convergence or emulation.

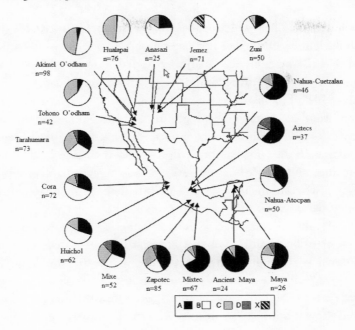

Figure 7.2. The map depicts the locations of populations and their respective frequencies of Native American mitochondrial DNA (mtDNA) haplogroups A, B, C, D, and X. (After Kemp et al. 2010)

Snow et al. (2010) provide some information on the distribution of the four main haplogroups (A, B, C, and D) in the Southwest and Mexico. In short, haplogroup A is very common (often at the 50 percent level) in Mesoamerica, including in those who speak U-A. More northern U-A speakers such as the Cora/Huichol and Tarahumara have substantial (around 25 percent) haplogroup A. Piman speakers in Arizona have somewhat less, while Tewa has none. Zuni has some haplogroup A (Kemp 2006; Kemp et al. 2010) (see Figure 7.2). These data can and have been variously interpreted. One interpretation that LeBlanc favors is that haplogroup A seems to correlate with U-A speakers; the evidence for this conclusion is not overwhelming.

All the prehistoric haplogroup A that has been found comes from Arizona or Utah, except for the haplogroup A found in the Farmington sites. For Carlyle (2003), only 3 out of 28 recovered haplogroup determinations had haplogroup A: 2 from Grand Gulch, Utah, and 1 from Canyon de Chelley, Arizona. Similarly, the prehistoric quids that yielded ancient mtDNA that had haplogroup A were all Western Basketmaker (LeBlanc et al. 2007), and Kemp has found additional haplogroup A in coprolites from Grand Gulch (unpublished data).

This model of haplogroup A corresponding to U-A speaking makes the significant incidence of haplogroup A at the Mine Canyon and Tommy Sites near Farmington of interest. If we assume the cluster of individuals with the same haplotype in Kiva B at the Mine Canyon Site is anomalous and adjust for it, we still have 15 percent haplogroup A. And even if we combine the two sites, despite their distinct haplogroup frequency patterns, we still have an overall 8 percent haplogroup A, which is significant compared with sites farther east. The Farmington sites appear to be small houses that are near the purported Point site (also known as Shannon Bluffs) great house. While this site does have a great kiva, evidence for a classic great house is less clear, but just upstream are the Sterling and Jacques sites, both of which are widely accepted as great house communities. And the Tommy site does appear to be Chacoan in age, or at least overlap with it. Thus, the Tommy site appears to be part of a great house community in some way. So, this is the farthest east any haplogroup A has been found in a Chacoan-related context.

The La Plata River is considered by some to be a cultural dividing line, but whether this is a U-A/non-U-A boundary is another thing. (The question of where and what this boundary would be like and what might have been spoken to the east is complex and not addressed here.) Based on such a dividing line, Farmington is just a bit farther east than where we would expect to find this much haplogroup A mtDNA, if the model is right. Were people sucked into the Chacoan interaction sphere from the west? It is hard to see how population growth alone could have resulted in such a large Chacoan population in the Totah region. Do we know enough about these sites to see subtle evidence for western cultural traits in them as has been done for Pueblo I sites to the north? This is a topic worth further exploration. Alternatively, if the La Plata River is on, or near, a cultural boundary, populations could be rather mixed along it. In this case, we would not necessarily have U-A speakers at Mine Canyon, but gene flow in the past along the linguistic boundary. Or since most of the haplogroup A came from what appears to be a

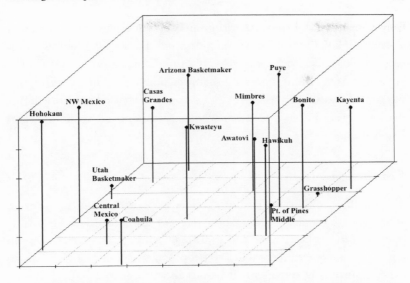

Figure 7.3. A multidimensional scaling plot based on 24 discrete dental traits from Southwestern and Mexican samples. (After Kemp et al. 2010)

family group, maybe they did migrate from the west. There simply are not enough data to take this argument any further.

One dental trait study (LeBlanc et al. 2008) did look at populations that possibly had U-A relationships (see Figure 7.3). There does seem to be evidence, although not very strong, that various Southwestern populations do seem to fit closer to presumed U-A speakers in Mexico than one could explain by geographical distance alone. Pueblo Bonito is not part of this group.

Chaco Was Not Uto-Aztecan Speaking

Based on the above argument about the distribution of haplogroup A (and dental traits), we can weakly suggest that the people of Chaco did not speak a U-A language. This assertion would come as no surprise to anyone, but nevertheless it does seem to be somewhat confirmed based on DNA data and even the dental trait data. Whether we can tie one burial cluster in Bonito to the Tanoan Rio Grande has been suggested but not strongly confirmed nor would it clearly mean that they spoke some form of Tanoan. So far, there is nothing that would link the canyon populations to Zuni; in fact, the craniometrics tend to show that they were not Zuni speakers, although as noted above, there is a Mine Canyon link with modern-day Zuni through a shared haplogroup. One sees no biological evidence that would link Chaco to either Tewa or to Keres speakers. There is nothing that precludes either, just nothing that particularly supports either. It is hard to argue that all the great house communities were in a territory whose inhabitants all spoke the same language.

Conclusion

The obvious conclusion is that there is a lot that could be done to address the biological relationships relevant to Chaco. It is surprising that so little has been done and so little is being done. Overall, we can say that it is very unlikely that the people in Chaco spoke U-A, which is not a surprising statement. It would also appear that biological relationships between Pueblo Bonito and other communities, and within Pueblo Bonito, are not what most people think and do not fit with most standard models of Chacoan development or relationships.

References Cited

Akins, Nancy J. 1986. *A Biocultural Approach to Human Burials from Chaco Canyon, New Mexico*. Reports of the Chaco Center No. 9. Division of Cultural Research, National Park Service, Albuquerque.

Carlyle, Shawn. W. 2003. Geographical and Temporal Lineage Stability among the Anasazi. Ph.D. dissertation, Department of Anthropology, University of Utah.

Durand, Kathy, Meradeth Snow, David G. Smith, and Stephen R. Durand. 2010. Discrete Dental Trait Evidence of Migration Patterns in the Northern Southwest. In *Human Variation in the Americas: The Integration of Archaeology and Biological Anthropology*, edited by B. M. Auerbach. Occasional Paper No. 38:113–134. Center for Archaeological Investigations, Carbondale, IL.

Greene, Michelle. 2007. Exploring the Patterns of Craniometric Trait Variation between Small-House and Great-House Communities. Paper presented at the 72nd Annual Meeting of the Society for American Archaeology, Austin, Texas.

Kemp, Brian M. 2006. Mesoamerica and Southwest Prehistory, and the Entrance of Humans into the Americas: Mitochondrial DNA Evidence. Ph.D. dissertation, Department of Anthropology, University of California, Davis.

Kemp, Brian M., Angélica González-Oliver, Ripan S. Malhi, Cara Monroe, Kari B. Schroeder, John McDonough, Gillian Rhett, Andres Resendéz, Rosenda I. Peñaloza-Espinosa, Leonor Buentello-Malo, Clara Gorodesky, and David G. Smith. 2010. Evaluating the Farming/Language Dispersal Hypothesis with Genetic Variation Exhibited by Populations in the Southwest and Mesoamerica. *Proceedings of the National Academy of Sciences* 107(15):6759–6764.

Kohler, Timothy A., Mark D. Varien, and Aaron M. Wright. 2010. *Leaving Mesa Verde: Peril and Change in the Thirteenth-Century Southwest.* University of Arizona Press, Tucson.

Kohler, Timothy A., and Kathryn K. Turner. 2006. Raiding for Women in the Prehispanic Northern Pueblo Southwest. *Current Anthropology* 47:1035–1045.

LeBlanc, Steven A. 2008. The Case for an Early Farmer Migration into the American Southwest. In *Archaeology without Borders: Contact, Commerce, and Change in the U.S. Southwest and Northwestern Mexico*, edited by Maxine E. McBrinn and Laurie D. Webster, pp. 107–142. University Press of Colorado, Boulder.

LeBlanc, Steven A., Lori S. C. Kreisman, Brian M. Kemp, Francis E. Smiley, Shawn W. Carlyle, Anna N. Dhody, and Thomas Benjamin. 2007. Quids and Aprons: Ancient DNA from Artifacts from the American Southwest. *Journal of Field Archaeology* 32(2):161–175.

LeBlanc, Steven A., and Christy G. Turner II. 2010. The Pecos Dentition: Discrete Morphological Traits. In *Pecos Pueblo Osteology Revisited*, edited by Michèle E. Morgan, pp. 57–70. Peabody Museum Press, Cambridge, Massachusetts.

LeBlanc, S. A., C. G. Turner II, and M. E. Morgan. 2008. Genetic Relationships Based on Discrete Dental Traits: Basketmaker II and Mimbres. *International Journal of Osteoarchaeology* 18:109–130.

Mackey, James C. 1980. Appendix G: Arroyo Hondo Population Affinities. In *The Arroyo Hondo Skeletal and Mortuary Remains*, edited by Anne M. Palkovich, pp. 171–181. School of American Research, Santa Fe.

Monroe, Cara, Brian M. Kemp, and David G. Smith. 2013. Exploring prehistory in the North American Southwest with mitochondrial DNA diversity exhibited by Yumans and Athapaskans. *American Journal of Physical Anthropology* 150(4): 618–631.

Ortman, Scott G. 2012. *Winds from the North: Tewa Origins and Historical Anthropology.* University of Utah Press, Salt Lake City.

Parr, Ryan L., Shawn W. Carlyle, and Dennis H. O'Rourke. 1996. Ancient DNA Analysis of Fremont Amerindians of the Great Salt Lake Wetlands. *American Journal of Physical Anthropology* 99:507–518.

Read, Dwight W., and Steven A. LeBlanc. 2003. Population Growth, Carrying Capacity, and Conflict. *Current Anthropology* 44(1):59–86.

Schillaci, Michael A., Erik G. Ozolins, and Thomas C. Windes. 2001. Multivariate Assessment of Biological Relationships among Southwest Amerindian Populations. In *Following Through: Papers in Honor of Phyllis S. Davis*, edited by Regge N. Wiseman, Thomas C. O'Laughlin, and Cordelia T. Snow, pp. 133–149. Papers of the Archaeological Society of New Mexico Vol. 27. The Archaeological Society of New Mexico, Albuquerque.

Schillaci, Michael A., and Christopher M. Stojanowski. 2003. Postmarital Residence and Biological Variation at Pueblo Bonito. *American Journal of Physical Anthropology* 120:1–15.

———. 2005. Craniometric Variation and Population History of the Prehistoric Tewa. *American Journal of Physical Anthropology* 126(4):404–412.

Snow, Meradeth H., Kathy Durand, and David G. Smith. 2007. Genetic Analysis of the Tommy and Mine Canyon Sites in Context of Southwest Populations. Paper presented at the 72nd Annual Meeting of the Society for American Archaeology, Austin, Texas.

———. 2010. Ancestral Puebloan mtDNA in Context of the Greater Southwest. *Journal of Archaeological Science* 37(7):1635–1645.

Turner, Christy G., II. 1993. Southwest Indian Teeth. *National Geographic Research and Exploration* 9(1):32–53.

8

The House of Our Ancestors

New Research on the Prehistory of Chaco Canyon, New Mexico, A.D. 800–1200

Carrie C. Heitman

In a paper honoring the career of archaeologist Gwinn Vivian presented at the Society for American Archaeology 70th annual meeting, Toll and others (2005) discussed the still often-overlooked role of small house sites in Chacoan prehistory. They pointed out that many of the attributes we reserve for the category of "great house" are in fact present at some small house sites and that both the diversity and overlapping characteristics across this dichotomy require greater attention if we are to understand "how Chaco worked." In this chapter, I present contextual data from 12 house assemblages through a comparative theoretical and ethnographic reading of Lévi-Strauss's house society model (1979, 1982, 1983, 1987, 1991; for cultural approaches see Carsten 1991, 1995; Errington 1987; Fox 1993; Fox, ed. 1993; Hugh-Jones 1995; McKinnon 1983, 1991, 1995, 2000, 2002; Reuter 2002; Waterson 1990, 1993, 1995, 2000; for archaeological applications see Beck 2007; Gillespie 2000, 2007; Joyce and Gillespie 2000; Kirch 2000; Monaghan 1996). The goal of this analysis, in part, is to help resituate small sites within our understanding of Chacoan social organization and to highlight commonalities as well as differences between great houses and small houses. This analysis offers new and ethnographically informed variables and processes with which to think more broadly about Chacoan structures and the importance of looking at lived spaces with a holistic, anthropological lens. Sebastian (2006:421) has encouraged scholars to "redouble our efforts to coax every bit of possible data out of the limited records and large collections from the early years of Chacoan archaeology" and to "strengthen our interpretive frameworks by adopting a broader cross-cultural view and examining the patterned material remains of a wider variety of non-state societies." Coalescing a large body of published and legacy data (http://www.chacoarchive.org), this chapter attempts to embrace both of these directives.

Our enduring reference to great and small houses is shorthand for the obvious hierarchy we see among the structures visible within the boundaries of the Chaco Culture National Historical Park. But social hierarchy emerges from somewhere and, anthropologically speaking, consists in complex ideas of what constitutes power and authority. Using archaeological and ethnographic data, my work examines the connection between symbolic investment in house construction and the construction of social hierarchies during the Chacoan florescence (A.D. 800–1200). In what follows, I first provide a brief summary of my analytical methods and approach to these issues, followed by a discussion of five synthetic data sets summarizing the distribution of ceremonial objects, offering contexts, post features, stratigraphic deposits, and wall resurfacing practices. I conclude with a series of interpretations framed around processes documented in house societies cross-culturally and identified among descendent Puebloan communities of the American Southwest. The difference between great house and small house inhabitants during the prehistoric heyday of Chaco Canyon are often glossed as the social equivalent of the "haves" and the "have nots." This chapter aims to resuscitate a more nuanced approach to small houses in our broader understandings of this particular expression of social complexity by contextualizing the monumental (great houses such as Pueblo Bonito) with what have been described as "vernacular," "everyday," or "domestic" expressions of people's lives. My goal here and in my broader analyses (Heitman 2011) is to advance our understanding of the monumental, not as something *other* but as an emergent phenomenon that magnified social inequalities over time and is best understood in relation to a broader social context.

Data for this study were generated as part of a larger examination of Chacoan ritual and social hierarchy, which included additional axes of variation and comparative ethnographic analyses (Heitman 2011). The aims of the larger study were to assess the utility of house society models for Chaco Canyon and to determine if the insights enabled by such models help us identify if and how social hierarchies were expressed or constructed through the idiom of the house. In an attempt to study the house as a holistic unit of analysis, my research proceeded in four stages of investigation. The first involved an examination of the intellectual history of kinship theory in the American Southwest—as this intellectual history directly pertains to the normative process by which archaeologists map concepts of family and lineage onto built spaces (see also Whiteley, this volume). Using a broadly comparative approach, I then outlined a series of ethnographic patterns and practices based on both proximate and cross-cultural analogs. The goals of this second stage of research were to broaden our understanding of the potential sources of social inequality as evidenced through houses and to analyze the cultural practices inscribed therein. By triangulating between Puebloan ethnography and known archaeological patterns for Chaco, in the third stage I identified object forms and materials as well as dimensions of house construction, maintenance, and features for comparative analysis. Through the examination of 12 house structures and their associated artifact assemblages, this study provides a new body of data yielding insights both on what was shared among canyon inhabitants and what was truly, and hierarchically, different about the great house site of Pueblo Bonito.

The 12 sites selected for analysis include 2 great houses (Pueblo Bonito and Pueblo Alto) and 10 small houses. Seven of the study sites were excavated historically, and the data were made available via the Chaco Research Archive (hereafter referred to as CRA). These sites included Pueblo Bonito, Bc 50, Bc 51, Bc 53, Bc 57, Bc 58, and Bc 59. All of the Bc sites are located on the south side of the canyon, opposite of Pueblo Bonito in the Casa Rinconada cluster. The other 5 sites were excavated in the late 1970s and early 1980s by the Chaco Project and included Pueblo Alto, 29SJ627, 29SJ629, 29SJ633, and 29SJ1360. Sites 627, 629, and 633 are located in an area known as "Marcia's Rincon" opposite the modern-day visitor center. Site 1360 is located at the base of Fajada Butte. In aggregate, occupations of these sites span from the A.D. mid-700s to the A.D. mid-1200s (Pueblo I to mid-Pueblo III).

Sample Size

When analyzing artifact assemblages for sites that were excavated with different methods during different eras, it is difficult to gauge their comparability. There are at least three potential sources of variation impacting this study: excavation methods, sampling, and extramural excavations. First, structures at some sites were excavated nearly in their entirety (e.g., Pueblo Bonito, Bc 50, Bc 51, Bc 53, Bc 57, Bc 58, 29SJ627, and 29SJ629), and some were not (e.g., Pueblo Alto, 29SJ633, and 29SJ1360). Second, extramural areas were sampled at some sites (e.g., Bc 50, Pueblo Bonito, 29SJ629, 29SJ633, 29SJ1360, and Pueblo Alto) but not at others. Third, excavation and screening methods varied from site to site. Not all deposits were screened, and at some sites screening procedures changed from field season to field season.*

Given that houses are the focus of this study, ideally this analysis would only consider intramural excavations across the sample universe. The limited sample sizes available from within architectural units for CRA sites preclude such a limitation, though I retain focus on intramural contexts throughout the discussion. To give the reader a clearer sense of the respective assemblages, Table 8.1 lists the total artifact sample size (n) for each site included in this study as well as the extent of excavation and fill screening conducted at each site. In all but three of these cases (Bc 57, Bc 58, and Bc 59), the site artifact frequencies include material recovered from some extramural excavation.

Pueblo Bonito

If measured by number of rooms, Pueblo Bonito is considered the largest great house in Chaco Canyon, with over 350 ground-story rooms and approximately 650 total rooms. It was one of the three earliest great houses built in the canyon, and its tree-ring dates span a 270-year construction history. The structure evolved over that time period, expanding during numerous construction phases. Each construction stage was "planned" and executed as a unit—a characteristic that often differentiates great houses from small houses.

Pueblo Bonito is unique in a variety of respects, not least of which is the presence of two burial clusters (Figure 8.1). The northern cluster is comprised of four rooms and is located in the oldest section of the building (Lekson's stage I, A.D. 920–935 [1984:Figure 4.20, 127–132]; Windes stage IE, A.D. 900s [2003:20]). Human remains were discovered in all

---

* Excavators at 29SJ627 did not screen the fill during the first field season (1975).

Table 8.1. Summary Table of Extent of Excavation, Extent of Screening, and Total Artifact Sample Size (n) for All Sites Included in Study.

Site	Extent of Excavation	Screening	n
Pueblo Alto	17 rooms, 2 kivas (trenched), midden and trenches	All through 1/4" mesh, floor features through 1/8" or 1/6" mesh	137,204
29SJ627	18 rooms, 7 pit structures, trenches	1974 – no 1975 – yes	100,205
Pueblo Bonito	351 excavation units, 32 kivas	Room 33 only	88,543
29SJ629	9 rooms, 3 pit structures, and trenches	"Most" through 1/4" mesh, floor features through 1/8" or 1/6" mesh	53,795
29SJ1360	13 rooms, 2 pit structures, trenches	None	18,920
29SJ633	1.5 rooms, 1 kiva (partial), trenches, surface sample	All through 1/4" mesh, floor contact material through 1/8" mesh	9,040
Bc 51	45 rooms, 7 kivas, midden and trenches	None	2,878
Bc 59	13 rooms, 3 kivas	None	2,428
Bc 50	26 rooms, 4 kivas, midden and trenches	None	1,698
Bc 53	21 rooms, 4 kivas, and trenches	None	1,224
Bc 57	9 rooms, 3 kivas	None	304
Bc 58	14 rooms, 3 kivas	None	153

four of these rooms, along with cached ceremonial items such as the staffs found in Room 32, ritual assemblages in adjacent rooms, and most notably, the cache of cylinder vessels found in Room 28. Room 33 contained two articulated adult males buried below a hewn plank floor. Pepper (1909) notes the presence of a circular hole cut into one of the wooden planks of the floor in Room 33, and he conjectured that this hole might have functioned similar to a kiva *sipapu* (hole symbolizing

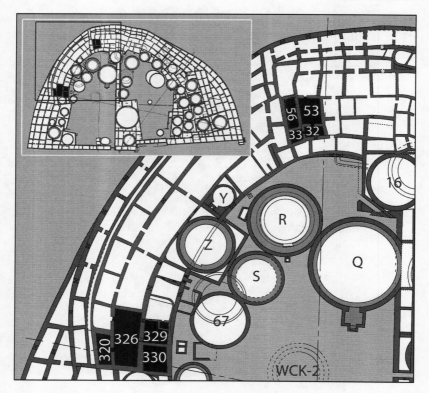

Figure 8.1. Plan view of Pueblo Bonito, highlighting the locations of the two major burial crypts. (Created by Edward Triplett)

the point of emergence/communication with the underworld). Some of the turquoise deposited below the floor may have been introduced through this hole or deposited over time. These individuals were interred with the most elaborate assemblage of grave goods ever encountered in the American Southwest. The disarticulated or semi-articulated remains of at least 12 other individuals were discovered above the floor in this room (CRA, Pueblo Bonito, Room 33 Human Burial Sets 2011).

Some have argued that the disarticulation of the above-floor individuals was due to alluvial disturbance (Pepper 1909, 1920) or to vandals (Judd 1954). In light of some previously unknown archival documentation, Plog and I have argued (Heitman 2007; Heitman and Plog 2005; Plog and Heitman 2010) that the disarticulation of these individuals may instead be attributed to more complex burial practices and the creation of a mortuary repository for ancestors (cf. Marden, this volume, for additional discussion).

The two subfloor males were described by Pepper as skeletons 13 and 14. Skeleton 13 was positioned above skeleton 14, and skeleton 14 showed signs of a violent death, with two holes and a gash in the frontal lobe. More than 30,000 objects were recorded and cataloged from this room, over 95 percent of which were beads, pendants, or other items made from minerals such as turquoise, jet, or shell. Other remarkable items included cylinder jars, ceremonial sticks, a shell trumpet, cylindrical baskets, and flutes. This room is very small—approximately 2 m x 2 m—and yet, enigmatically, it had five vertical support posts. The northwest post was the largest. Offerings were found around the posts both above and below the plank floor. The room had only one entrance—through the doorway in the east wall.

The two subfloor burials and their associated grave good assemblages—laden with over 25,000 pieces of turquoise—have long been interpreted as dating between A.D. 1020 and 1100 (Lekson 2006; Van Dyke 2007; Windes 2003). This interpretation seemed to fit a general evolutionary sense that such prominent individuals could only have come to power and commanded such resources later in the sequence of Chacoan development. Recent AMS radiocarbon dates by Coltrain et al. (2007) (samples numbers AA57715 and AA57713) and others by Plog and myself (2010) demonstrate that these individuals died earlier than researchers previously thought. Using OxCal's R_ combine measure to average paired samples for Burials 13 and 14, we found the following: the median for Burial 13 is A.D. 781, with a 2-σ range of 691–877; the median for Burial 14 is A.D. 774, with a 2-σ range of 690–873. Additional radiocarbon dates on skeletal elements from above the floor exhibit a temporal span of 300–400 years. Plog and I have used these radiocarbon dates, along with other contextual data, to argue that this room was used recurrently as a burial repository (Plog and Heitman 2010).

The western burial cluster is also composed of four rooms. These rooms are again located in the oldest section of the building (Lekson's stage I, A.D. 920–935 [1984:Figure 4.20, 127–132]; Windes stage IA, pre-860 [2003:20]). Room 330 had the highest number of individuals interred (approximately 25). As with the northern cluster, all four of these rooms contained human remains, many of which were disarticulated or semi-articulated. The grave goods encountered in this set of rooms were much less elaborate than that of the northern cluster.

Ceremonial Offerings

One of my units of analysis involved the distribution of ceremonial items. The selection of these specific artifact categories stems both from knowledge of Chacoan archaeological data and from comparative Puebloan ethnographic research (Heitman 2011:84–138). The following categories are generally accepted as having either a clear association with ritual practice or general ceremonial significance.

> *Bifurcate Forms*: Bifurcated baskets and bifurcated ceramic vessel effigies.
>
> *Ceremonial Wood*: All wooden objects of the following form: ceremonial staffs, game sticks, prayer sticks/*pahos*, headdress pieces, and any painted wooden objects.
>
> *Cylinder Vessels*: Ceramic cylinder jars have a strong ritual association with great houses (Crown and Hurst 2009; Crown and Wills 2003; Toll 2001) and thus are considered here.
>
> *Effigies/Figurines*: Effigies and figurines in the overall sample take many forms. They include large, carved, stone effigies as well as ceramic effigy vessels. They also include anthropomorphic forms (like the human figurines found in OP6 in Room 110 at Pueblo Alto). In short, all human and animal forms irrespective of material type are included in this category.
>
> *Parrots*: Any occurrence of this imported Mesoamerican bird species (includes *Ara macao*, *Ara militaris*, *Rhynchopsitta pachyrhyncha*, and *Ara* sp.).
>
> *Musical Instruments*: Includes flutes, whistles, rattles, trumpets, rasps, and bells.
>
> *Paint/Pigment*: The raw materials used for paint and classified as such by the original excavator or analyst. Includes, for example, nodules of yellow ocher, hematite, "pellets" of paint, etc.

Miscellaneous Painted Objects: This category captures all remaining painted objects not included under other headings (excluding ceramic vessels).

Palettes: Objects specifically defined as such by the excavator. Also includes any object defined as a "paint slab."

Pipes: Includes objects classified as pipes or cloud blowers.

Some of the forms analyzed here are relatively unique to Chaco Canyon (e.g., parrots [McKusick 2001] and cylinder vessels used for imbibing cacao [Crown and Hurst 2009]). Others, such as musical instruments (Brown 2005), bifurcated baskets (Jolie 2014; Judd 1954:306–320; Morris and Burgh 1941:54–59; Jolie and Webster, this volume), and pipes are broadly considered to have had a role in ritual practice in Southwestern prehistory and thus are also considered here. The remaining four object categories—effigies/figurines, ceremonial wood, paint/pigments, and palettes—were selected based on Puebloan ethnographic research (Heitman 2011:84–138). For each of the 12 sites, I calculated the frequency of items in these respective categories using published and unpublished (CRA) data sources.

I hasten to note that my analyses ignored other important artifact types that had ritual uses. While numerous other forms of ceramics, lithics, bone, and perishable items can have religious significance, other factors and functions are also likely to affect their frequencies.

In sum, the data presented in Table 8.2 show different spatial distributions: some broad, some more restricted, and others exclusive to the human burial contexts at Pueblo Bonito previously described. Additional context-specific descriptions are available elsewhere (Heitman 2011). Effigies and figurines, paint and pigments, palettes, and pipes were present across the sample universe. Wood paraphernalia, musical instruments, parrots, and cylinder jars were more restricted in their distribution. None of the categories of ceremonial objects were exclusive to great house sites, but some specific object forms were exclusively recovered from great houses. Bifurcate forms, flutes, shell trumpets, rasps, a cache of ceremonial staffs, and a cache of cylinder jars were only recovered from Pueblo Bonito. With the exception of rasps, all of the items exclusive to Pueblo Bonito were found in association with or adjacent to (Room 28) the two human mortuary contexts at that site.

Table 8.2. Frequencies of Selected Ceremonial Items from All 12 Sites in the Sample Universe.

Site	Bifurcate Form	Ceremonial Wood	Cylinder Vessel	Effigy/Figurine	Parrot	Musical Instrument	Paint/Pigment	Misc. Painted Object	Palette	Pipe	Total
Pueblo Alto			1[1]	13[2]		3[3]	2406[4]		31[5]	1	2,455
Pueblo Bonito	11	919	192[6]	175	31[7]	49	334	29	12	84	1,836
29SJ627				47[8]		2	957		22	1	1,029
29SJ629		1[9]		4[10]			554[11]		6[12]	2	567
29SJ1360			1[13]	17[14]	4		177[15]		4		203
29SJ633			1[16]	4[17]		1	138		3		147
Bc 51				10			7	2	8		27
Bc 50		1[18]		6		1	1	6	10	1	26
Bc 53				3			1	2	11	2	19
Bc 58									7	1	8
Bc 57				2			1	1	1	2	7
Bc 59		3		1				1	1	1	7

Note: Table sorted by total number of ceremonial items.

1. Data from Toll and McKenna (1987:213–216, Table 1.1.7).
2. Two human effigy vessels (ceramic), two duck pots (ceramic), and nine effigy/zoomorphs (ornaments).
3. Two copper bells (Mathien 1987:402); one whistle (Mathien 1987:418).
4. Data from Mathien (1987:418).
5. Data from Windes: one metate with pigment classified as a paint palette, five undifferentiated palettes, and 24 incidental palettes (1987b:367); one paint mortar (1987b:369).
6. Total from Toll and McKenna (1987:Table 1.53).
7. Number from Hargrave (1970).
8. Twenty-seven ceramic effigies and 14 duck pots (Toll and McKenna 1992); six zoomorphic ornaments (Toll and McKenna 1992:Table 4.3).
9. Wooden cylinder inset with turquoise flecks (Mathien 1993:230); according to Mathien's later analysis, the wooden cylinder had green paint on both ends, not turquoise (Mathien 1993:307).
10. Ceramics—one duck pot (unpolished mineral on white) and two effigies (Red Mesa). Two zoomorphic ornaments (Mathien 1993:Table 5.3).
11. Number from Mathien (1993:Table 5.8).
12. Five palettes and one mano with traces of red paint (Windes 1993).
13. One cylinder jar recovered; see Table 3.15 (McKenna 1984:176).
14. Five duck pots and eight effigy pots (McKenna 1984:Table 3.17). Table 5.3 lists four fetishes/anthropomorphs.
15. Paint/pigment total created from Mathien's raw data; using mineral types noted in other site monographs as soft minerals probably used for pigments.
16. One possible cylinder jar fragment (McKenna and Toll 1991:171, 175).
17. Four effigy/duck pots (McKenna and Toll 1991:156).
18. The published text describes a "tablita" recovered from Room 1, painted turquoise blue.

Ceremonial Caches and Offering Contexts

In an effort to reveal the formal variability of such contexts, Table 8.3 summarizes the presence/absence of data for the 13 identified forms of caches and offerings evident in the study sample. These typically included offerings (most often shell, turquoise, and jet) left on kiva benches, placed in ceilings/roofs, sealed in firepits, scattered across floor surfaces, put in formal caches or repositories placed in floors, sealed within niches, identified as paho or prayer stick features, placed in kiva radial beam pilasters, placed around posts, placed inside postholes, placed in kiva ventilators, and immured within walls.

Two important observations can be drawn from this inter-site comparison. First, diverse ritual contexts are present across both great

Table 8.3. Ceremonial Cache and Offering Contexts for Sites in the Study Sample.

	Bench	Ceiling/Roof	Firepit	Floor	Floor Cache Repository	Niches	Paho Feature	Plaza Cache/ Repository	Pilasters	Post	Postholes	Ventilator	Walls
Pueblo Bonito	X	X	X	X	X	X	X		X	X	X	?	X
Bc 50					X	X							
Bc 51					X	X							
Bc 53													
Bc 57					X							X?	
Bc 58													
Bc 59									?				
Pueblo Alto		X		X			X	X	X?		X	X	
29SJ627			X	X							X	X	
29SJ629						X?		X			X		
29SJ633													
29SJ1360	?												

house and small house site types, but the two great houses stand out with greater diversity of contexts represented (11 [possibly 12] at Pueblo Bonito and 7 at Pueblo Alto). Second, this table demonstrates just how different Pueblo Bonito is from the other sites in the study sample. We know more about Pueblo Bonito than we might ever know about any other great house given the extent of excavations at that site (over 95 percent). That said, the redundancy and elaboration of ritual contexts, the discrete clusters of human remains, and the extensive offerings specifically made in and around those burial contexts differentiate this house relative to the other 11 sites investigated.

While a few offering assemblages were recovered from small house kivas—such as the wall cache found in the kiva known as "Feature 5" at Bc 50 (a cache containing nine assorted smooth stones [Museum Catalog #:Bc 50 20/433a–i] and a chipped white stone pipe), the ceremonial deposits at Pueblo Bonito entail a far broader array of contexts, including pilaster offerings (Kivas 2B, 16, 162, B, C, D, F, G, H, I J, K, L, M, N, P, R, S, and T), subfloor repositories (Kivas 162, D, and N), offerings strewn across floors (e.g., floor of Kiva Q, CRA Descriptive Strata Level PBKQL01.04), offerings placed on benches (Kivas 16 and C), and offerings placed in ceilings (Kivas L and R).

Table 8.4 presents grouped frequency distributions for Pueblo Bonito kivas with ceremonial offering frequencies greater than 500. All 13 of the kivas shown here have radial log pilaster offerings. Notably, the kivas with the highest frequency of ceremonially deposited items are *not* the largest kivas. Kivas A and Q, for instance, are the two largest kivas at Pueblo Bonito (with the possible exception of the West Sub-Court kiva that was buried prehistorically). A variety of formation processes (such as looting, the prehistoric removal of ceremonial contents, etc.) play an important role in the differential preservation of such contexts in the archaeological record. That said, a few exceptional characteristics of Kiva R demand further scrutiny (see Figure 8.1 for kiva location).

Like the rooms in both of the human burial clusters at Pueblo Bonito, Kiva R was initially constructed around A.D. 860 (Windes 2003:20 [Stage 1A]), and it is the oldest, continuously utilized kiva at Pueblo Bonito. Its features include a bench, six radial log pilasters with intact offerings, a south bench recess, a north bench niche, a "floor repository"

Table 8.4. Pueblo Bonito Kivas with Ceremonial-Offering
Frequencies >500 Listed in Descending Order of Frequency.

Frequency = 1,000–6,000	Frequency = 500–1,000	Frequency = 100–500
Kiva R / 32.72 m^2	Kiva T / 36.96 m^2	Kiva P / 49.27 m^2
Kiva L / 23.67 m^2	Kiva M / 21.73 m^2	Kiva Q / 116.71 m^2
Kiva B / 33.49 m^2		Kiva I / 18.32 m^2
		Kiva G / 33.49 m^2
		Kiva N / 23.24 m^2
		Kiva 16 / 30.68 m^2
		Kiva 2B / 38.05 m^2
		Kiva C / 39.48 m^2

Note: Floor areas are included for each.

below the north niche, an above-floor ventilator, and a fireplace. Beads
and the beak of a Redhead duck found among the decayed ceiling poles
were interpreted as a possible ceiling offering. The initial Kiva R structure was partially razed by the prehistoric occupants of Pueblo Bonito,
and subsequent reconstructions were built upon the foundations of the
first. This process of reconstruction happened three times—resulting in
four total iterations of Kiva R in the same location. The initial floor of
Kiva R was laid upon 36 cm of intentionally deposited carbonaceous
shale (Judd 1921–1927:106). Kiva R also has the highest frequency of
ceremonial items for all the kivas at Pueblo Bonito and included 2,691
pieces of turquoise and 2,256 pieces of shell.

Posts

Though the Chacoan great house site of Chetro Ketl was not in the
study, it is important to mention it here because it represents one
extreme end of the Chacoan post-feature-investment spectrum. Vivian
and Reiter (1960:Figure 16) describe how below the two northern vertical support posts in the Great Kiva at Chetro Ketl, four, 180- to 455-kg
shaped sandstone disks were found. Below the disks under the northeast post were four alternating layers of lignite and adobe. Below the
lowest layer of adobe, within sand fill, excavators found a sueded bag
containing an ounce of turquoise dust. An archival document (Woods
1931) scanned by the Chaco Research Archive team shows a similar

Figure 8.2. Original image caption, "Coal layer under wall. Coal often used under floor or for packing, probably absorbed moisture." (Courtesy of the Maxwell Museum of Anthropology, University of New Mexico, 88_43_161)

alternation of lignite layers between the fourth and fifth floors of the Chetro Ketl Great Kiva, as documented by Janet Woods.

Both historic and modern excavators have noted lignite packing as a common component of prehistoric Chacoan building practices. Take for instance the original caption for a photograph of an unidentified Chacoan small house site excavation (Figure 8.2): "Coal layer under wall. Coal often used under floor or for packing, probably absorbed moisture."

At small house site 29SJ633, lignite packing was noted by Mathien as a feature common to postholes in excavated rooms (1991:47). In the Pueblo Alto report, Windes similarly notes: "Crushed lignite often partially filled the largest pits at Pueblo Alto. Almost all postholes in excavated canyon-bottom sites contained lignite" (1987a:276). In his publication on the *Architecture of Pueblo Bonito*, Neil Judd (Judd 1964:202) emphatically noted the ubiquity of these kinds of deposits in a range of contexts:

Shale, occurring with low-grade subbituminous coal that sometimes approaches lignite in quality, is a product of the Menefee formation which underlies Chaco Canyon's Cliff House sandstone. It was lavishly employed at Pueblo Bonito both as a wall packing about pilasters and elsewhere and as an under-floor spread but was never, to my knowledge, used as a fuel.

The post interment in the Great Kiva at Chetro Ketl is unique in its degree and complexity of elaboration (cf. Aztec Ruins Great Kiva, Lowry Pueblo, and the Village of the Great Kivas). My comparative research (Tables 8.5 and 8.6) shows, however, that it also shares aspects of practices described at Chacoan sites more broadly.

Packing lignite or low-grade coal around posts occurs in both great house and small house contexts and in rooms as well as kivas and pit structures. Sites in the study sample with recorded occurrences include small house sites Bc 50, 29SJ1360, 29SJ627, and 29SJ629 and both great house sites (Pueblo Bonito and Pueblo Alto).

Based on the elaborated post feature at Chetro Ketl, is it fair to assume that the practice of lignite packing was ritually or cosmologically significant? Perhaps this was a dimension of Chacoan geomancy?

Table 8.5. Room Provenience and Frequency of Postholes with Lignite "Packing" or Lignite Shims.

Site	Room	Frequency
Bc 50	North Plaza	1
Bc 50	Substructure 6	1
Bc 50	East of Substructure 7	1
Bc 50	Feature 5	1
Pueblo Bonito	Kiva Q	4
Pueblo Bonito	Kiva A	2
Pueblo Bonito	(Pilasters) East Court Kiva	2
Pueblo Bonito	Room 108	1
Pueblo Bonito	Room 323*	6
Pueblo Bonito	Room 325*	5
Pueblo Bonito	Room 326*	6
Pueblo Bonito	Room 329*	4

Note: Data for CRA sites in the study sample.

* = These rooms also had shale packed around the ceiling beams.

Table 8.6. Room Provenience and Frequency of Postholes with Lignite "Packing" or Lignite Shims.

Site	Room	Frequency
29SJ1360	House 1, Room 11	2
29SJ1360	Ramada	33
29SJ1360	Pithouse B	3
29SJ1360	Plaza—Area 1	2
29SJ1360	Room 4	1
29SJ1360	Plaza Surface 1	2
29SJ627	Room 10	2
29SJ627	Room 11, Ramada Area D1-B	1
29SJ627	Room 14	2
29SJ627	Room 23, Plaza-Facing Ramada Area	2
29SJ627	Room 3	3
29SJ627	Room 3, Ramada	2
29SJ627	Room 5, Ramada Area	6
29SJ627	Room 6, Ramada Area D-2 (overlying D-1)	1
29SJ627	Room 8	7
29SJ627	Pit Structure F	3
29SJ627	Pithouse C	3
29SJ629	Kiva (Pithouse 1)	2
29SJ629	Pithouse 2	4
29SJ629	Room 3	3
29SJ629	Room 4	2
29SJ629	Room 9	3
Pueblo Alto	Plaza 1, Grid 8	1
Pueblo Alto	Room 139	8

Note: Data for Chaco Project sites in the study sample.

Minimally, lignite packing served a functional purpose in securing posts. Its functional attributes do not, however, preclude additional symbolic or cosmological meanings entailed in these and other contexts. The Puebloan ethnographic data describing the importance of the color black, its association with the nadir, and the demonstrated importance of jet/lignite/carbonaceous shale objects help us better contextualize and interpret these prehistoric practices (Heitman 2011:Table 5.5).

Additional observations for the occurrence of lignite deposits only strengthen its spatial association with ritually significant contexts. The lining of a prayer stick or paho feature in Kiva N at Pueblo Bonito (CRA Floor Feature, Kiva N) further supports an association of lignite (chips, packing) with important house contexts, as does its occurrence packed around the radial log pilaster beams anchored in kiva walls as noted by Judd for one of the East Court kivas* at Pueblo Bonito (Judd 1964:67). Judd also notes that the posts of the Kiva Q deflector screen at Pueblo Bonito were packed in shale (1964:209). Given the extreme lengths canyon builders went to in order to procure beams from high elevations (English et al. 2001:11892; Windes and Ford 1996:303) and what we know ethnographically about the religious importance of trees and wood among Pueblo groups (Heitman 2011:Table 5.4), it is per-haps not surprising that these posts were interred with varying degrees of veneration. But this broadly shared practice of investment in post interments extends beyond large-diameter, labor-intensive, high-eleva-tion tree species to include smaller-diameter, locally available species in public spaces such as ramadas (e.g., 29SJ1360 [McKenna 1984:87] and 29SJ627 [Truell 1992:Table 5.3]).

The data from both of these tables (8.5 and 8.6) demonstrate how the practice of packing lignite around posts is broadly distributed across sites, but the formality and degree of elaboration differs markedly. One of the postholes in western burial cluster Room 326 at Pueblo Bonito had an adobe collar as well as lignite packing. The formality of that feature is rather different from that shown in a posthole in Pithouse B at 29SJ1360 (McKenna 1984:Figure 2.58).

In aggregate, the data on posthole features from sites in the study sample exhibit a shared set of ideas about how to build. These prac-tices included the broad use of lignite as a packing material executed in more (Pueblo Bonito, Room 326 [Judd 1954:Plate 93]) or less (29SJ1360,

---

*Also at the Great Kiva of Chetro Ketl. The only recorded cases I know of are at great house kivas—which is perhaps not surprising given the rare occurrence of radial log pilasters at small house sites. Such deposits have also been noted by national park stabilizations crews (Dabney Ford, personal communication, Janu-ary 9, 2008).

Pithouse B [McKenna 1984:Figure 2.58]) formal ways, as well as elaborated lignite deposits layered beneath posts in more significant contexts—such as the Great Kiva at Chetro Ketl. The use of lignite as the material source for ritual elaboration is in keeping with the ethnographic data on the importance of black (perhaps referencing the nadir, as in the Zuni case [Tedlock 1979:499; see also Bunzel 1932:645n6; Parsons 1939:626, 630, 687]) and color-directional symbolism among the pueblos more broadly (Heitman 2011:84–138), as well as the artifactual data on the distribution of jet/lignite items as shown by Neitzel (2003b).

Lignite Layering

Given the associations of lignite documented above, we might conclude that special materials (wood posts/beams/prayer sticks) as well as special contexts require ritualized acts of dedication—such as lignite or offerings. Additional cultural deposits from the study sample support this interpretation. According to stratigraphic drawings done by Pepper for Room 32 in the northern burial complex (Pepper 1896), the Chacoans made a series of "closure" deposits above the floor prior to interring the remains of at least one individual. These stratigraphic layers bear some resemblance to those used in the Chetro Ketl Great Kiva seating pit. The layers alternated between sand and charcoal (Layer B) or "black soil" (Layer D). These deposits occur adjacent to Room 33 in the northern mortuary complex at Pueblo Bonito.

Cases of lignite layering within rooms (either below, between, or above floors) were recorded at five sites in the study sample (Table 8.7): Pueblo Bonito, 29SJ629, Bc 50, Bc 51, and Bc 59. Intentional stratigraphic deposits are predominantly associated with Pueblo Bonito, small house sites in the Casa Rinconada cluster, and an older pit structure from 29SJ629 (Pithouse 2, a ninth-century construction [McKenna 1986]). Minimally, we can conclude that this practice was not restricted to great house sites and that it appears to occur more commonly in kivas at the great house of Pueblo Bonito. Certainly not all rooms and kivas received this treatment, but its recorded presence at 4 of the 10 small house sites in the study sample further complicates our understanding of ritual investment in Chacoan houses. These observations also disrupt characterizations that define the monumental in opposition to the vernacular (see also Bustard 1997).

Table 8.7. Proveniences where Lignite Was Used as an Intentional Between-Floor Fill or Sub-floor Fill.

Site	Room
Pueblo Bonito	Kiva T
Pueblo Bonito	Kiva L
Pueblo Bonito	Kiva V
Pueblo Bonito	Kiva N
Pueblo Bonito	Kiva R
Pueblo Bonito	East Court Kiva
Pueblo Bonito	Room 336
Pueblo Bonito	Room 317
Pueblo Bonito	Room 32 (above floor)
29SJ629	Pithouse 2
Bc 50	Substructure 5
Bc 51	Room 3
Bc 59	Room 1
Bc 59	Room 12
Bc 59	Kivas 2 and 2A

Similar to the posthole deposits, the practice of layering lignite in structures spans both great house and small house contexts—indicating a shared set of ideas about how to build that includes a cosmological dimension. The layering of this substance in particular spaces suggests, at times, a process of ritual closure (as in the case Room 32, Pueblo Bonito), in others an iterative process of sanctification (e.g., between construction episodes at Kiva R, Pueblo Bonito), and further still, a mimetic recapitulation of a layered worldview. Pueblo Bonito stands out in this regard with more documented episodes of lignite layering for sites in the study sample.

Kiva Wall Surfacing

The last characteristic of Chacoan houses addressed here involves wall surfacing events. As with many of the characteristics of interest to my research, these data were not uniformly available and thus present some analytical challenges. While data on wall surfacing events are available for many kivas and square rooms in the study sample, for present purposes I focus only on kivas because the data are more consistently available for those contexts.

Although we cannot know the precise meaning these practices held prehistorically, it is worth considering replastering events in light of empirical data from descendant communities. Based on my reading of the Puebloan ethnographic literature (e.g., Parsons 1939:358; Hopi: Stephen 1969 [1936]:238, Figures 143–146, Plates V–VII), archaeologically we should expect kiva walls of Ancestral Pueblo sites to have numerous layers of wall plaster. Such acts may have been part of rituals of renewal, as argued by Crown and Wills (2003), or acts performed as a prayer for rain.

There are a variety of rooms in the study sample that had evidence of kiva murals, created either with colored layers (Pithouse B, 29SJ1360 [McKenna 1984:57]), painted designs (Kivas 5, 6, and 7 at Bc 51 [Kluckhohn 1939:38–39]), incised designs (Kiva 3, Bc 50 [Brand et al. 1937:78–79, Plate X]), or alternating non-pigment colors (Kiva G, 29SJ627 [Truell 1992:89]). Beyond these notable elaborations, there are a number of kivas in the study sample that contained evidence of numerous wall plastering events (Table 8.8). Pueblo Bonito has at least seven kivas with nine or more plaster layers. All of the Pueblo Bonito contexts, however, are within the range of layer frequencies at other small house sites. Interestingly, four of the six sites in the Casa Rinconada cluster also have kivas with numerous plaster layers. Kiva 6 at Bc 51 had the highest frequency of plaster layers (31). This structure dates to the A.D. late 1000s to A.D. mid-1100s (Truell 1986:162). According to Truell (1986:189), the high number of replastering events in Kiva 6 may be indicative of "more assiduous upkeep" and special use of pit structures evident after the A.D. mid-1000s.

House Society Models

To conclude, the data presented above are interpreted through a modified house society model (Heitman 2011:60–83; see also Mills and Whiteley, this volume; cf. Hays-Gilpin and Ware, this volume). The three sets of concepts and processes I will be emphasizing include Precedence and Continuity, Ancestors and Heirlooms, and Animation and Performance.

Table 8.8. Kivas with Plaster Layers ≥ 5.

Site	Room	Frequency of Plaster Layers
29SJ1360	Pithouse B	8, various colors
29SJ627	Kiva G	6, alternating colors
Bc 50	Kiva 2	14
Bc 50	Kiva 4	7
Bc 51	Kiva 6	31
Bc 51	Kiva 5	13
Bc 51	Kiva 2	5
Bc 53	Kiva B	6
Bc 57	Kiva A	12
Bc 57	Kiva C	6
Pueblo Bonito	Kiva G	21
Pueblo Bonito	East Sub-Court Kiva 3	19
Pueblo Bonito	Kiva D	19
Pueblo Bonito	Kiva R (sub-structure)	14+
Pueblo Bonito	Kiva 2A	10
Pueblo Bonito	Kiva E	10
Pueblo Bonito	Kiva 2E	9

Note: Data for sites in the study sample.

Precedence and Continuity

The great houses of Chaco Canyon were massively engineered and built to last. One need only to visit Chaco today to see how these edifices endure. In this overt sense, these robust physical structures were meant to exude a form of physical permanence on the landscape. As the structural footprint of Pueblo Bonito evolved, Chacoan architects endeavored to preserve that original core of rooms (Neitzel 2003b). Through numerous planned construction stages, these rooms remained at the center of the final building. Instead of razing these early rooms (as was the practice in a variety of other contexts), these spaces were buttressed and enveloped, preserved as the central core of the great house. Room repositories for ritual sacra were also contained in this original arc.

These practices show an orientation toward precedence and continuity by referencing and maintaining that which came before. This orientation toward precedence also helps us contextualize the complex building sequences, long occupation histories, and multicomponent occupations evident at many small house sites. Long occupation sequences are yet another way Chacoan houses are unique relative to contemporaneous sites in the region and exhibit a cultural valuation for the precedence and continuity of house structures and house sites.

Ancestors and Heirlooms

Curated heirlooms and ritual sacra have the capacity to materialize connections to ancestral origins and thereby re-create those origin places. The new radiocarbon dates from the northern human burial cluster discussed earlier (Plog and Heitman 2010) make clear that the burial sequence contained in Room 33 began very early in the occupation of Pueblo Bonito and was seemingly added to over time. The evolution of Pueblo Bonito over its 300-year occupation history shows a concern for preserving the original core of the house (construction stage I), while constantly expanding and rebuilding. This process included the bodies of ancestors and associated heirlooms housed in that oldest section of the pueblo. The periodic addition of human remains after the initial interment of the two subfloor males also suggests a deliberate strategy of maintaining continuity with these proximate ancestors.

In addition to interring the two males (skeletons 13 and 14) below the plank floor of Room 33, a variety of other attributes are similar to those described in association with kivas (discussed below). The first burial placed in this room was interred on a layer of sand covered by a layer of wood ash. Individual 13 was then interred above skeleton 14, followed by the placement of a plank wood floor. A hole carved into the plank floor was interpreted by Pepper (1909) as a *sipapu* similar to those present in kivas. Offerings of shell, turquoise, malachite, and jet were interred with these individuals (maybe even deposited through the hole in the plank floor) and also placed around the vertical posts at various depths, both above and below the plank floor. Despite the small room size, measuring roughly 2 x 2 m square, there were five substantial vertical support posts (SW, NW, SE, and two in the NE). The cosmological significance of these elements far exceeds any pressing functional reason for their placement, even if one existed.

The repeated placement of offerings around the wooden posts adds another layer of meaning and importance to this mortuary context at Pueblo Bonito and to the pueblo as a whole. Here we have the addition of the bodies of venerated ancestors, ensconced within wood, turquoise, shell, and jet, buried in the heart of the oldest portion of Pueblo Bonito, surrounded by heirlooms. Human remains as well as offerings continued to be added in Room 33 over the coming centuries, showing an iterative series of investments—as a place of origin, anchored with the physical remains of ancestors, containing unique forms of curated heirlooms (staffs, flutes, a shell trumpet, cylinder jars, etc.), and heavily laden with cosmologically significant materials (e.g., turquoise and shell). These practices mapped connections between the bodies of proximate ancestors and materializations of cosmological, apical ancestors as sources of power, legitimacy, and authority.

Animation and Performance

The frequent, redundant, iterative, and ritualized investments in Pueblo Bonito yield insights into how this great house attained and maintained primacy relative to other sites in the canyon. The archaeological data presented here demonstrate that both seen and unseen dimensions of houses were broadly shared between great house and small house occupants and that, to some degree, all house occupants were endeavoring to layer their houses with meaning in accordance with a shared set of practices centered upon houses. These structures also show a mutual orientation toward cosmologically significant materials, objects, and attributes. These shared dimensions shed new light on the ritual fabric in which a variety of canyon occupants participated. These data also corroborate earlier observations regarding the continuum of architectural styles and features evident across great house and small house sites made by Chaco Project analysts McKenna (1986), Toll et al. (2005), and Truell (1979, 1986).

Kivas offer the clearest examples of the processes that animated houses and through which ancestral connections were achieved and maintained. Using the origin myth of Acoma as relayed by Parsons

(1939:310–311), there are at least six ways kivas are imagined to connect and replicate the conditions of emergence: First, the kiva itself represents the hole (*shipap*) through which the people emerged. Second, the round structure replicates the sky and thus the conditions into which "the people" emerged. Third, the beams used to create the kiva replicate the trees used to exit the underworld at the time of emergence and thus mediate between the two worlds. Fourth, the floor features of the kiva (e.g., the first altar created by Iyatiku) replicate the conditions of origin as experienced by their apical ancestor. Fifth, ancestors and other sprits are thought to be present in this liminal context and are communicated with via the *sipapu* of the kiva itself. And lastly, a pit representing a door (typically located on the north side of the kiva) is a conduit of connection to cosmologically significant topographic markers associated with the cardinal directions (cf. Ashmore 2007).

In this ethnographic example, a kiva replicates the place/moment of emergence, enacts the process of emergence, and is the product of emergence. By virtue of these features, the kiva also creates a liminal space in which to connect to those apical ancestors who brought "the people" into being.

The architectural and artifactual data presented in my research make clear that similar narratives of emergence were manifested through kivas during the Chacoan era. The classic, defining "Chaco-style" kivas included a formal suite of characteristics consisting of radial log pilasters (6, 8, or 10), pilaster offerings, cribbed roofs, subfloor vaults, a *sipapu*, a firepit, a fire screen, a bench, a shallow southern recess, and a subfloor ventilator. The ceremonial deposits placed in wooden elements are multifold: pilaster offerings at the convergence of the underlying support structure with the overlying cribbed roof elements, the use of lignite to root vertical support posts, and at times, offerings placed within the ceiling timbers. We see in these contexts a repetition of materials, of which turquoise, shell, and lignite are the most dominant. Based on Puebloan ethnographic data, the association of black with the underworld seems likely. The redundancy of these deposits used repetitively in specific kiva contexts strongly suggests that these materials were connected to a narrative of origin. As such, these deposits and practices provided what Helms has called "tangible forms of contact with the conditions of origins for house members" (Helms 1999:57). We can thus proceed with the knowledge that part of what gave these materials, practices, places, and (by extension) *people* value was their connection to narratives of origin.

Pueblo Bonito kivas include a full range of these deposits. Very limited kiva excavations at Pueblo Alto tentatively suggest that similar deposits were made within kivas at that site (e.g., one exposed pilaster offering, Kiva 3). As described earlier, some similar practices were recorded in kivas and pithouses at small houses in the study sample. These include the layering of lignite below floors, lignite packing around posts, wall niche offerings, and offerings below posts. The small house sites analyzed for this study do not, however, have pilaster offerings nor do they have the same consistent suite of features or offering materials as described above or the same degree of masonry craftsmanship as that of great house kivas. Additionally, to the best of my knowledge, there are no known examples of pilaster offerings at any excavated small house sites in the canyon.

The data available demonstrate a continuum of shared practices evident within this synchronic comparison. Enabled by a house society model, this interpretation of kivas as contexts in which one's connections to a point/process of origin are exerted and made manifest allows us to make sense of those practices shared by great house and small house occupants. By contrast, great house occupants and affiliates—especially those of Pueblo Bonito—invested a tremendous amount of labor and resources into building kivas and layering them with such deposits. By my analysis, part of what allowed Pueblo Bonito to achieve prominence was the ability of house occupants/affiliates to mobilize and enact their connections to a point of origin through kivas and other means and to connect proximate ancestors (e.g., the burials in Room 33) to narratives of cosmological origin. The data show how such practices resonated and were enacted—albeit to lesser degrees—across a broader community of canyon residents. A shared religious valuation of particular materials (shell, turquoise, wood, birds, etc.) was clearly an integral part of the system of trade and exchange that tied communities together across the Chacoan sphere of influence.

This process of enactment by which Pueblo Bonito achieved prominence did not only include the aforementioned contexts and materials. Architectural evidence for massive and constant rebuilding efforts directed specifically toward kivas (Crown and Wills 2003) shows that the process of enactment entailed partially (or completely) razing a finished kiva, only to build it again (as with the example of Kiva R discussed above). The cross-cultural ethnographic data on house societies in which houses are animated through precisely these kinds of acts—repeated over the life of a house in order to continually exert and maintain precedence—provide a theoretical context for how these processes contributed to the construction of hierarchical differences between house occupants/affiliates.

Conclusion

Comparative ethnographic data from descendant Pueblo communities in conjunction with house society models help us to create archaeological expectations and recognize how certain processes contributed to the creation of emergent social hierarchies. The artifact assemblages, artifact distributions, and stratigraphic contexts examined here show how a house-based hierarchy was defined by processes of house consecration and sanctification achieved through post offerings, cached heirlooms, and ritualized deposits, as well as human burials. These processes had the greatest longevity and achieved the highest form of elaboration at Pueblo Bonito. As described for kivas, such offerings created cosmological connections to sacred directions and to ancestral origins, and we see in Pueblo Bonito the most complete conception of the cosmic order. The nested series of offerings at Pueblo Bonito, Pueblo Alto, and various small house sites inscribed and located these structures within a cosmologically defined landscape—creating connections between local and supra-local places of power, authority, and spiritual assistance.

The results of this study contribute to a more holistic understanding of houses occupied during the Chacoan era in at least three ways: first, by identifying new materials, forms, contexts, and processes used to add value and meaning to structures during the Chacoan era, thus augmenting the available tools used to understand variability between houses and the emergence of social hierarchy in Chacoan prehistory; second, by demonstrating that many of these processes were shared amongst great houses and small house occupants; and third, by demonstrating how frequent, redundant, iterative, and ritualized investments in

Pueblo Bonito were intended to demonstrate precedence and its status as an origin house.

As argued by Kroeber (1916), Ortiz (1969), Parsons (1939), and Whiteley (1998), "ritual" among many Pueblo groups is not a separate domain of cultural practice: it is the matrix of cultural practice. Thus, in my analysis, I have foregrounded ritual practices and deposits within houses in an effort to resituate such practices at the center of how we approach studies of Chacoan prehistory. Based on my analysis, ritual is not a curtain to be pulled back in order to glimpse what lay behind. Most likely, ritual was the fabric of lived experience into which all other dimensions (economy, subsistence, politics) were woven. The hierarchical differentiation between structures and, by extension, between people was thus defined not just by built spaces, but by spaces built right.

References Cited

Ashmore, Wendy. 2007. Building Social History at Pueblo Bonito: Footnotes to a Biography of Place. In *The Architecture of Chaco Canyon, New Mexico*, edited by Stephen H. Lekson, pp. 179–198. University of Utah Press, Salt Lake City.

Beck, Robin A. (editor). 2007. The Durable House: Architecture, Ancestors and Origins. Paper presented at the 22nd Annual Visiting Scholar Conference, Center for Archaeological Investigations, Southern Illinois University, Carbondale.

Brand, Donald D., Florence M. Hawley, Frank C. Hibben, et al. 1937. *Tseh So, A Small House Ruin, Chaco Canyon, New Mexico (preliminary report)*. University of New Mexico Bulletin No. 308, Anthropological Series 2(2). University of New Mexico, Albuquerque.

Brown, Emily J. 2005. Instruments of Power: Musical Performance in Rituals of the Ancestral Puebloans of the American Southwest. Ph.D. dissertation, Department of Anthropology, Columbia University.

Bunzel, Ruth. 1932. *Zuñi Ritual Poetry*. Forty-Seventh Annual Report of the Bureau of American Ethnology, 1929–1930. U.S. Government Printing Office, Washington, D.C.

Bustard, Wendy. 1997. Space as Place: Small and Spatial Organization in Chaco Canyon, New Mexico, AD 1000–1150. Ph.D. dissertation, Department of Anthropology, University of New Mexico, Albuquerque.

Carsten, Janet. 1991. Children in Between: Fostering and the Process of Kinship on Pulau Langkawi, Malaysia. *Man* 26:425–443.

————. 1995. Houses in Langkawi: Stable Structures or Mobile Homes? In *About the House: Lévi-Strauss and Beyond*, edited by Janet Carsten and Stephen Hugh-Jones, pp. 105–128. Cambridge University Press, Cambridge.

Coltrain, Joan Brenner, Joel C. Janetski, and Shawn W. Carlyle. 2007. The Stable- and Radio-Isotope Chemistry of Western Basketmaker Burials: Implications for Early Puebloan Diets and Origins. *American Antiquity* 72(2):301–321.

Crown, Patricia L., and W. Jeffrey Hurst. 2009. Evidence of Cacao Use in the Prehispanic American Southwest. *Proceedings of the National Academy of Sciences* 106:2110–2113.

Crown, Patricia L., and Wirt H. Wills. 2003. Modifying Pottery and Kivas at Chaco: Pentimento, Restoration, or Renewal? *American Antiquity* 68:511–532.

English, Nathan B., Julio L. Betancourt, Jeffrey S. Dean, and Jay Quade. 2001. Strontium Isotopes Reveal Distant Sources of Architectural Timber in Chaco Canyon, New Mexico. *Proceedings of the National Academy of Science* 98(21):11891–11896.

Errington, Shelly. 1987. Incestuous Twins and the House Societies of Insular Southeast Asia. *Cultural Anthropology* 2(4):403–444.

Fox, James L. 1993. Comparative Perspectives on Austronesian Houses: An Introductory Essay. In *Inside Austronesian Houses: Perspectives on Domestic Designs for Living*, edited by James J. Fox, pp. 1–28. Department of Anthropology in association with the Comparative Austronesian Project, Research School of Pacific Studies, Australian National University, Canberra.

Fox, James J. 1993 (editor). *Inside Austronesian Houses: Perspectives on Domestic Designs for Living*. Department of Anthropology in association with the Comparative Austronesian Project, Research School of Pacific Studies, Australian National University, Canberra.

Gillespie, Susan D. 2000. Beyond Kinship: An Introduction. In *Beyond Kinship: Social and Material Reproduction in House Societies*, edited by Rosemary A. Joyce and Susan D. Gillespie, pp. 1–21. University of Pennsylvania Press, Philadelphia.

————. 2007. When Is a House? In *The Durable House: House Society Models in Archaeology*, edited by Robin A. Beck, pp. 25–52. Southern Illinois University Occasional Paper 35. Southern Illinois University, Carbondale.

Hargrave, Lyndon L. 1970. *Mexican Macaws: Comparative Osteology and Survey of Remains from the Southwest*. Anthropological Papers of the University of Arizona No. 20. University of Arizona Press, Tucson.

Helms, Mary. 1999. Why Maya Lords Sat on Jaguar Thrones. In *Material Symbols: Culture and Economy in Prehistory*, edited by John E. Robb, pp. 56–69. Center for Archaeological Investigations, Southern Illinois University Series, Occasional Paper No. 26. Southern Illinois University, Carbondale.

Heitman, Carrie C. 2007. "Houses Great and Small: Re-evaluating the Construction of Hierarchy in Chaco Canyon, NM, AD 860–1180." In *The Durable*

House: Architecture, Ancestors and Origins, edited by Robin A. Beck, pp. 248–272. 22nd Annual Visiting Scholar Conference, Center for Archaeological Investigations, Southern Illinois University, Carbondale.

————. 2011. Architectures of Inequality: Evaluating Kinship and Cosmology in Chaco Canyon, New Mexico, AD 850–1180. Ph.D. dissertation, Department of Anthropology, University of Virginia, Charlottesville.

Heitman, Carolyn C., and Stephen Plog. 2005. Kinship and the Dynamics of the House: Rediscovering Dualism in the Pueblo Past. In *A Catalyst for Ideas: Anthropological Archaeology and the Legacy of Douglas W. Schwartz*, edited by Vernon Scarborough, pp. 69–100. School of American Research Press, Santa Fe.

Hugh-Jones, Stephen. 1995. Inside-Out and Back-to-Front: The Androgynous House in Northwest Amazonia. In *About the House: Lévi-Strauss and Beyond*, edited by Janet Carsten and Stephen Hugh-Jones, pp. 226–252. Cambridge University Press, Cambridge.

Jolie, Edward A. 2014. Cultural and Social Diversity in the Prehispanic Southwest: Learning, Weaving and Identity in the Chaco Regional System, AD 850–1140. Ph.D. dissertation, Department of Anthropology, University of New Mexico, Albuquerque.

Joyce, Rosemary A., and Susan D. Gillespie (editors). 2000. *Beyond Kinship: Social and Material Reproduction in House Societies*. University of Pennsylvania Press, Philadelphia.

Judd, Neil M. 1921–1927. Note Cards, Pueblo Bonito, Notes on Excavations. Papers of Neil M. Judd, Box 8, National Anthropological Archives, Smithsonian Institution, Washington, D.C. Electronic documents, http://www.chaco archive.org/media/pdf/Pages_1_250_from000174complete.pdf and http:// www.chacoarchive.org/media/pdf/Pages_251_500from000174complete. pdf, accessed September 1, 2010.

————. 1954. *The Material Culture of Pueblo Bonito*. Smithsonian Miscellaneous Collections No. 124. Smithsonian Institution, Washington, D.C.

————. 1964. *The Architecture of Pueblo Bonito*. Smithsonian Miscellaneous Collections No. 147. Smithsonian Institution, Washington, D.C.

Kirch, Patrick V. 2000. Temples as "Holy Houses": The Transformation of Ritual Architecture in Traditional Polynesian Societies. In *Beyond Kinship: Social and Material Reproduction in House Societies*, edited by Rosemary A. Joyce and Susan D. Gillespie, pp. 103–114. University of Pennsylvania Press, Philadelphia.

Kluckhohn, Clyde. 1939. Discussion. In *Preliminary Report on the 1937 Excavations, Bc 50–51, Chaco Canyon, New Mexico*, edited by Clyde Kluckhohn and Paul Reiter, pp. 151–162. University of New Mexico Bulletin No. 345, Anthropological Series 3(2). University of New Mexico, Albuquerque.

Kroeber, A. L. 1916. Thoughts on Zuñi Religion. In *Holmes Anniversary Volume*, edited by F.W. Hodge, pp. 269–277. J. W. Bryan Press, Washington, D.C.

Lekson, Stephen H. 1984. *Great Pueblo Architecture of Chaco Canyon.* Publications in Archeology 18B, Chaco Canyon Series. National Park Service, Santa Fe.

———. 2006. Chaco Matters: An Introduction. In *The Archaeology of Chaco Canyon: An Eleventh-Century Pueblo Regional Center*, edited by Stephen H. Lekson, pp. 3–44. School of American Research Press, Santa Fe.

Lévi-Strauss, Claude. 1979. *La voie des masques.* Plon, Paris.

———. 1982. *The Way of the Masks.* Translated by Sylvia Modelski. University of Washington Press, Seattle.

———. 1983. Histoire et ethnologie. *Annals: Économies, Sociétés, Civilisations* 38:1217–1231.

———. 1987. *Anthropology and Myth: Lectures 1951–1982.* Translated by Roy Willis. Blackwell, Oxford.

———. 1991. Maison. In *Dictionnaire de l'ethnologie et de l'anthropologie*, edited by Michel Izard, pp. 434–436. Presses Universitaires de Frances, Paris.

Mathien, Frances Joan. 1987. Ornaments and Minerals from Pueblo Alto. In Investigations at the Pueblo Alto Complex, Chaco Canyon, New Mexico, 1975–1979, Vol. III, *Artifactual and Biological Analyses*, edited by Frances Joan Mathien and Thomas C. Windes, pp. 381–428. Publications in Archeology 18F, Chaco Canyon Studies. National Park Service, U.S. Department of the Interior, Santa Fe.

———. 1991 (ed.). *Excavations at 29SJ633: The Eleventh Hour Site, Chaco Canyon, New Mexico.* Reports of the Chaco Center No. 10. Division of Cultural Research, National Park Service, Albuquerque.

———. 1993. Ornaments and Minerals from 29SJ629. In *The Spadefoot Toad Site: Investigations at 29SJ629, Chaco Canyon, New Mexico*, Vol. II, *Artifactual and Biological Analyses*, edited by Thomas C. Windes, pp. 269–316. Reports of the Chaco Center No. 12. Division of Cultural Research, National Park Service, Santa Fe.

Mathien, Frances Joan, and Thomas C. Windes (editors). 1987a. *Investigations at the Pueblo Alto Complex, Chaco Canyon, New Mexico: Tests and Excavations, 1975–1979*, Vol. III, *Artifactual and Biological Analyses*. Publications in Archeology 18F, Chaco Canyon Studies. National Park Service, U.S. Department of the Interior, Santa Fe.

———. 1987b. *Investigations at the Pueblo Alto Complex, Chaco Canyon, New Mexico, 1975–1979*, Vol. IV, microfiche. Publications in Archeology 18F, Chaco Canyon Studies. National Park Service, U.S. Department of the Interior, Santa Fe.

McKenna, Peter J. 1984. *The Architecture and Material Culture of 29SJ1360, Chaco Canyon, New Mexico.* Reports of the Chaco Center No. 7. Division of Cultural Research, National Park Service, Albuquerque.

———. 1986. *A Summary of the Chaco Center's Small Site Excavations: 1973–1978.* Part I in *Small Site Architecture of Chaco Canyon, New Mexico*, by Peter J. McKenna and Marcia L. Truell, pp. 5–114. Publications in Archaeology

18D, Chaco Canyon Studies. National Park Service, U.S. Department of the Interior, Santa Fe.

McKenna, Peter J., and H. Wolcott Toll. 1991. Ceramics from 29SJ633, The Eleventh Hour Site. In *Excavations at 29SJ633: The Eleventh Hour Site, Chaco Canyon, New Mexico*, edited by Frances Joan Mathien, pp. 139–205. Reports of the Chaco Center No. 10. Division of Cultural Research, National Park Service, Santa Fe.

McKinnon, Susan. 1983. Hierarchy, Alliance, and Exchange in the Tanimbar Islands. Ph.D. dissertation, Department of Anthropology, University of Chicago.

———. 1991. *From a Shattered Sun: Hierarchy, Gender, and Alliance in the Tanimbar Islands*. University of Wisconsin Press, Madison.

———. 1995. Houses and Hierarchy: The View from a South Moluccan Society. In *About the House: Lévi-Strauss and Beyond*, edited by Janet Carsten and Stephen Hugh-Jones, pp. 170–188. Cambridge University Press, Cambridge.

———. 2000. The Tanimbarese *Tavu*: The Ideology of Growth and the Material Configurations of Houses and Hierarchy in an Indonesian Society. In *Beyond Kinship: Social and Material Reproduction in House Societies*, edited by Rosemary A. Joyce and Susan D. Gillespie, pp. 161–176. University of Pennsylvania Press, Philadelphia.

———. 2002. Kinship Studies in Socio-Cultural Anthropology and Archaeology. Paper presented at the 67th Annual Meeting of the Society for American Archaeology, Denver.

McKusick, Charmion R. 2001. *Southwest Birds of Sacrifice*. Arizona Archaeological Society No. 31. Arizona Archaeological Society, Tucson.

Mills, Barbara J. 2002. Recent Research on Chaco: Changing Views of Economy, Ritual, and Society. *Journal of Archaeological Research* 10:65–117.

———. 2008. Remembering while Forgetting: Depositional Practices and Social Memory at Chaco. In *Memory Work: Archaeologies of Material Practices*, edited by Barbara J. Mills and William H. Walker, pp. 81–108. School for Advanced Research Press, Santa Fe.

Monaghan, John. 1996. Mesoamerican Community as a "Great House." *Ethnology* 35(3):181–194.

Morris, Earl Halstead, and Robert Frederic Burgh. 1941. *Anasazi Basketry, Basket Maker II through Pueblo III: A Study Based on Specimens from the San Juan River Country*. Carnegie Institution of Washington Publication No. 533. Carnegie Institution, Washington, D.C.

Neitzel, Jill E. 2003a. (editor) *Pueblo Bonito: Center of the Chacoan World*. Smithsonian Books, Washington, D.C.

———. 2003b. Artifact Distributions at Pueblo Bonito. In *Pueblo Bonito: Center of the Chacoan World*, edited by Jill E. Neitzel, pp. 107–126. Smithsonian Books, Washington, D.C.

Ortiz, Alfonso. 1969. *The Tewa World: Space, Time, Being, and Becoming in a Pueblo Society.* University of Chicago Press, Chicago.

Parsons, Elsie Clews. 1939. *Pueblo Indian Religion.* 2 vols. University of Chicago Press, Chicago.

Pepper, George H. 1896. Rooms #32 and 33, also measurements of Rooms Pueblo Bonito. American Museum of Natural History, Division of Anthropology. Electronic document, http://www.chacoarchive.org/media/pdf/000157_public.pdf, accessed September 1, 2010.

———. 1909. The Exploration of a Burial-Room in Pueblo Bonito, New Mexico. In *Putnam Anniversary Volume: Anthropological Essays Presented to Frederic Ward Putnam in Honor of His Seventieth Birthday, April 16, 1909, by His Friends and Associates,* edited by Franz Boas, Roland B. Dixon, Alfred L. Kroeber, Frederick W. Hodge, and H. I. Smith, pp. 196–252. G. E. Stechert & Co., New York.

———. 1920. *Pueblo Bonito.* Anthropological Papers of the American Museum of Natural History Vol. 27. Trustees of the American Museum of Natural History, New York.

Plog, Stephen. 2003. Exploring the Ubiquitous through the Unusual: Color Symbolism in Pueblo Black-on-White Pottery. *American Antiquity* 68:665–695.

Plog, Stephen, and Carrie C. Heitman. 2010. Hierarchy and Social Inequality in the American Southwest, AD 800–1200. *Proceedings of the National Academy of Science* 107(46):19619–19626.

Reuter, Thomas. 2002. The House of Our Ancestors: Precedence and Dualism in Highland Balinese Society. KITLV Press, Leiden, Netherlands.

Sebastian, Lynn. 2006. The Chaco Synthesis. In *Archaeology of Chaco Canyon: An Eleventh-Century Pueblo Regional Center,* edited by Stephen H. Lekson, pp. 393–422. School of American Research Press, Santa Fe.

Stephen, Alexander. 1969 [1936]. *Hopi Journal of Alexander M. Stephen,* edited by Elsie Clews Parsons. 2 vols. Columbia University Press, New York.

Tedlock, Dennis. 1979. Zuni Religion and World View. In *Southwest,* edited by Alfonso Ortiz, pp. 499–508. Handbook of North American Indians, Vol. 9, William C. Sturtevant, general editor. Smithsonian Institution, Washington, D.C.

Toll, H. Wolcott. 2001. Making and Breaking Pots in the Chaco World. *American Antiquity* 66:56–78.

Toll, H. Wolcott, and Peter J. McKenna. 1987. The Ceramography of Pueblo Alto. In Investigations at the Pueblo Alto Complex, Chaco Canyon, New Mexico, 1975–1979, Vol. III, *Artifactual and Biological Analyses,* edited by Frances Joan Mathien and Thomas C. Windes, pp. 19–230. Publications in Archeology 18F, Chaco Canyon Studies. National Park Service, U.S. Department of the Interior, Santa Fe.

———. 1992. *The Rhetoric and the Ceramics: Discussion of Types, Function, Distribution, and Sources of the Ceramics of 29SJ627.* In *Excavations at 29SJ627,*

Chaco Canyon, New Mexico, Vol. II, *The Artifact Analyses*, edited by Frances Joan Mathien, pp. 37–248. Reports of the Chaco Center No. 11. Division of Cultural Research, National Park Service, Santa Fe.

Toll, Wolcott, Marcia Newren, and Peter McKenna. 2005. Always There, Often Overlooked: The Roles and Significance of Small Houses in the Chaco World. Paper presented at the 70th Annual Meeting of the Society for American Archaeology, Salt Lake City.

Truell, Marcia. 1979. Preliminary Report 29SJ627. Manuscript on file, Chaco Culture National Historical Park Museum Archive, University of New Mexico, Albuquerque.

———. 1986. A Summary of Small Site Architecture in Chaco Canyon, New Mexico. In *Small Site Architecture of Chaco Canyon*, by Peter McKenna and Marcia Truell, pp. 115–508. Publications in Archaeology 18D, Chaco Canyon Studies. National Park Service, U.S. Department of the Interior, Santa Fe.

———. 1992. *Excavations at 29SJ 627, Chaco Canyon, New Mexico. Volume I. The Architecture and Stratigraphy.* Reports of the Chaco Center No. 11. Division of Cultural Research, National Park Service, Albuquerque.

Van Dyke, Ruth. 2007. Great Kivas in Time, Space, and Society. In *Architecture of Chaco Canyon, New Mexico*, edited by Stephen H. Lekson, 93–126. University of Utah Press, Salt Lake City.

Vivian, R. Gordon, and Paul Reiter. 1960. *The Great Kivas of Chaco Canyon and Their Relationships.* Monograph No. 22. School of American Research, Santa Fe.

Vivian, R. Gwinn. 1990. *The Chacoan Prehistory of the San Juan Basin.* Academic Press, New York.

Waterson, Roxana. 1990. *The Living House: An Anthropology of Architecture in South-East Asia.* Oxford University Press, London.

———. 1993. Houses and the Built Environment in Island South-East Asia: Tracing Some Shared Themes in the Uses of Space. In *Inside Austronesian Houses: Perspectives on Domestic Designs for Living*, edited by James J. Fox, pp. 221–235. Department of Anthropology in association with the Comparative Austronesian Project, Research School of Pacific Studies, Australian National University, Canberra.

———. 1995. Houses and Hierarchies in Island Southeast Asia. In *About the House: Lévi-Strauss and Beyond*, edited by Janet Carsten and Stephen Hugh-Jones, pp. 47–68. Cambridge University Press, Cambridge.

———. 2000. House, Place and Memory in Tana Toraja (Indonesia). In *Beyond Kinship: Social and Material Reproduction in House Societies*, edited by Rosemary Joyce and Susan Gillespie, pp. 177–188. University of Pennsylvania Press, Philadelphia.

Whiteley, Peter M. 1998. *Rethinking Hopi Ethnography.* Smithsonian Institution Press, Washington, D.C.

Windes, Thomas. 1987a. *Investigations at the Pueblo Alto Complex, Chaco Canyon, New Mexico, 1975–1979. Volumes I and II.* Publications in Archeology 18F, Chaco Canyon Studies. National Park Service, U.S. Department of the Interior, Santa Fe.

————. 1987b. *Some Ground Stone Tools and Hammerstones from Pueblo Alto. In Investigations at the Pueblo Alto Complex, Chaco Canyon, New Mexico: Tests and Excavations, 1975–1979,* Vol. III, *Artifactual and Biological Analyses,* edited by Frances Joan Mathien and Thomas C. Windes, pp. 291–358. Publications in Archeology 18F, Chaco Canyon Studies. National Park Service, U.S. Department of the Interior, Santa Fe.

————. 1993. Ground Stone, Chopping, and Percussion Tools from 29SJ 629. In *The Spadefoot Toad Site: Investigations at 29SJ 629, Chaco Canyon, New Mexico,* Vol. II, *Artifactual and Biological Analyses,* edited by Thomas C. Windes, pp. 201–268. Reports of the Chaco Center No. 12. Division of Cultural Research, National Park Service, Albuquerque.

————. 2003. This Old House: Construction and Abandonment at Pueblo Bonito. In *Pueblo Bonito: Center of the Chacoan World,* edited by Jill E. Neitzel, pp. 94–106. Smithsonian Institution Press, Washington, D.C.

Windes, Thomas. 1993 (editor). *The Spadefoot Toad Site: Investigations at 29SJ629, Chaco Canyon, New Mexico.* Reports of the Chaco Center, no. 12. Division of Cultural Research, National Park Service, Albuquerque.

Windes, Thomas C., and Dabney Ford. 1996. The Chaco Wood Project: The Chronometric Reappraisal of Pueblo Bonito. *American Antiquity* 61:295–310.

Woods, Janet. 1931. "Excavation Work, the Great Bowl, Chetro Ketl." Chaco Culture National Historical Park, Museum Archives. Electronic document, http://www.chacoarchive.org/media/pdf/001869_public.pdf, accessed September 1, 2010.

9

Unpacking the House

Ritual Practice and Social Networks at Chaco

Barbara J. Mills

In the past 15 years there have been three important shifts in the way that archaeologists view past agricultural societies in the Southwest. First is the more widespread recognition that there were differences in prestige and hierarchy among prehispanic inhabitants. Second is the acknowledgement that power and authority rest not just in economic advantages but also in the realms of ritual and ideology. And third is the realization that there are many alternative social forms in which status, prestige, and hierarchy are manifested. Each of these shifts in thinking has resulted in an opening up of interpretations about past societies in the Southwest, although there are still major differences in how archaeologists think that these different prestige structures came about, were organized, and were transformed.

There are several significant obstacles that stand in the way of more holistic interpretations of power and prestige among Southwestern societies. One of these is an undertheorized and uncritical use of the term "ritual" by Southwest archaeologists. Another is the widespread distinction between "ritual" and "domestic"—even though this dichotomization has been heavily critiqued by archaeologists working in other areas (e.g., Bradley 2005; Brück 1999; Stahl 2008). And although Southwest archaeologists are now more comfortable with talking about elites and the presence of hierarchy in many areas, especially Chaco, there is also a dichotomization (or trichotomization) of ritual, economic, and political realms of society. For example, Lekson (2006:37) suggests that Chaco was ruled by kings and queens, representing "one of the Pueblo world's few garden-variety chiefdoms or petty kingdoms or cacicazgos." He dichotomizes leadership as either "something political, permanent, and hierarchical or something ritual and ceremonial, spiritual, situational, and evanescent" (2006:28). Lekson views Chaco hierarchies as based exclusively in political power, excluding its intersection with ritual power. His proof is in three "facts" about Chaco: the presence of "retainers" buried with two high-status burials, the presence of great houses, and the regional primacy of Chaco.

In the same volume as Lekson's chapter cited above, Sebastian (2006) points out the logical problems with dichotomizing political and ritual power and discusses several ethnographic cases to show how ritual may be the basis for both a hierarchy and political power. Her observation that the opposite of political organization is not ritual but anarchy (Sebastian 2006:409) draws attention to how simplified many of our ideas about religious organization have been. I agree with Sebastian that we need to look at other models, and her comparison of cases from the volume edited by Susan McIntosh (1999), *Beyond Chiefdoms,* was a welcome discussion and one long overdue. Nonetheless, African models are not the only ones that we can draw upon for our comparisons. What they do point out, however, is that there is a diversity of structures in which religious authority may be expressed and in how religious, economic, and political power may intersect. I use religion rather than ritual here because it is not just the practice but also the overarching ideology in which power is vested.

I think that this state of affairs in Chaco research reflects wider changes and approaches in archaeology as a whole. Religion was seen as epiphenomenal to economy and society and ideology, and belief systems were placed on the upper (more inaccessible) end of Hawkes's (1954) ladder of inference. We are in a very new situation now—one where ritual (the practice) and religion (beliefs) have become primary topics of interest, and we might be in danger of making political and economic organization epiphenomenal. Unfortunately, this derives exactly from the problem mentioned above—that many archaeologists see ritual as something separate and "nondomestic" rather than as something that is inherent in political, economic, and other social actions.

To correct this situation requires thinking about ritual as a practice (Bell 1992), not to be dichotomized with domestic life (or, as Fowles [2013] suggests, they are inseparable). The dichotomization is a legacy of post-Enlightenment philosophy, and in the social sciences, it derives from Durkheimian contrasts between the "sacred" and "profane" (Fogelin 2007:60). A number of archaeologists have begun to explore the process of ritualization, as advocated by Bell, to link different spheres of action. This has been especially important in research that takes a biographical or genealogical approach and that tracks objects, animals, plants, and other materials from middens to shrines (e.g., chapters in Mills and Walker, eds. 2008). Such an approach is particularly germane to Chaco because it allows us to identify ritual practices in many different contexts, from middens to kivas and from small houses to great houses (see Heitman 2007 and Heitman, this volume for an example of the latter). At Chaco there are multiple contexts in which we can look for materials that we know were important to people at Chaco, including turquoise, pigments, fossils, birds, wood, and even black-on-white pottery (Mills 2004; Plog 2003; Jolie and Webster, this volume).

Nonetheless, Pueblo Bonito was unique in the Chaco world, and many aspects of Chaco seem to have been unique for the Pueblo world. In order to argue for the distinctiveness of Chaco, new approaches to the archaeology of ritualization in the Southwest are necessary, including an understanding of how the materiality of ritual life was expressed. We need to reassess how value was assigned in the past—the meaning and materiality of things—and use these reassessments to look at communities of practice (Lave and Wenger 1991). A fundamental part of such a research program is to look at how objects are used in constructing and promoting social memory. These concepts have only begun to be embraced by Southwestern archaeologists (e.g., Mills 2008; Mills and Walker 2008; Van Dyke 2004, 2007a; Walker 2008), but there is much in the Southwestern material record that suggests these approaches offer great potential for understanding past societies in the region. By building from the ground up, we can begin to understand indigenous systems of practice rather than imposing our own—and understand how they intersect with political and economic practices.

This chapter is divided into four parts. First, I argue for taking a biographical or genealogical approach to objects to understand what was valued at Chaco and how these varied pathways can be used as the basis for identifying different communities of practice. Second, I suggest that the house society model provides an apt way to look at Chaco social organization. Third, I look at multiple communities of practice and how these networks of relationships were or were not part of different

Chaco "houses." And finally, I explore the implications of the house society model for understanding regional organization, small and great houses, and great house interaction.

Memory, Materiality, and Communities of Practice

Although archaeologists are quick to identify objects that have been used in ritual practice, they are usually focusing on attributes of the objects themselves, such as their forms. An alternative to this functional approach is to understand the value of objects by their depositional contexts and their associations (Mills and Walker, eds. 2008; Murray and Mills 2013; Walker 1995; Zedeño 2008). The choices made in what to place in caches, caves, shrines, burials, beneath floors, in niches, and in empty and filled rooms of different shapes and sizes are not random decisions. These biographical or genealogical pathways have an underlying social logic, and these logics of depositional practice are one of the most important ways of understanding what was valued in the past. Some things were clearly more powerful or valuable than others, and they had to be treated appropriately. For example, some objects that were communally owned were considered to be inalienable and therefore were discarded differently than more mundane objects (Mills 2004). As another example, we can point to the ways in which objects were used to commemorate individuals, places, and events through their placement with people, their use in structure dedication and termination, and their use in other memory-making processes. Their depositional contexts help archaeologists to understand these differences and to look at indigenous distinctions in value, the ways in which people and objects were engaged, and different communities of ritual practice.

A deposit-oriented approach has several advantages over an object-oriented approach (McAnany and Hodder 2009), though in reality archaeologists must focus on both. The container or archaeological context is just as important as is what is placed within it. There are logics to where things are discarded just as there are to the associations of things (Murray and Mills 2013). These logics are linked to individual and group identities and to the communities of practice in which ceremonial knowledge was shared and transmitted. The locations of these deposits and what they might tell us about the size and structure of the social networks that participated in their production, use, consumption, and ultimate deposition are what we archaeologically have to work with. This approach is centered in understanding the materiality of ritual practice—how people and things interact within sets or fields of social actions.

Included within such an approach to depositional practice are ways in which we can identify the connectivities of people and groups within social networks or communities of practice, such as mortuary ritual and the construction and termination of ceremonial structures. The idea of communities of practice comes out of learning theory (e.g., Lave and Wenger 1991), and it has recently been applied to studies of apprenticeship, social identity, and migration in the Southwest (Crown 2001; Fenn et al. 2006; Stark 2006; see also Jolie and Webster, this volume). Underlying this approach are several important ways of thinking about the transmission of ritual practice. For example, we might begin by differentiating those practices that have low visibility vs. those that have high visibility. In terms of ritual practices, the former can take the form of private or very small-scale activities or object use (socially and spatially), as well as actions that are covered up, such as the placement of dedicatory offerings in architectural spaces such as niches, pilasters, and floor boxes. The acts of concealment and revealing are important ways in which ritualization practices take form and become meaningful—a process that was clearly used at Pueblo Bonito and other great houses (Ashmore 2007:183). Architecturally and artifactually, things with high visibility may be those whose surfaces are not covered, that are used and/or seen by large groups of people, and that have high performative value. If we take a perspective that is based in learning theory, communities of practice, and the transmission of memory, we can begin to not only think about the exclusiveness or inclusiveness of different ritual practices and the scale of participation but also be able to identify specific networks through which the transmission of knowledge took place.

A community of practice approach intersects with considerations of identity, but that is not the main focus. Instead, I focus on identifying similarities and distinctions in practices that help address some of the main themes of this volume, particularly the ways in which relationships were constructed among people who lived in great houses and small houses, changing ritual practices in houses and kivas, and the identification and significance of different organizational units and social networks over time. In particular, I look at the house society model as an alternative way of thinking about Chaco social organization—one that bridges economic, political, and ritual dimensions—and how the community of the "house" overlaps, or not, with other communities of practice.

The Chaco House Society

The house society concept has recently been proposed as an apt model for Chaco social organization by a number of researchers (Heitman 2007; Heitman and Plog 2005; Mills 2008; Wills 2005). Originally proposed by Lévi-Strauss (1982) as an alternative to lineage-based social organization, there are now many archaeological applications (Beck, ed. 2007; Joyce and Gillespie 2000; Lansing et al. 2011). Importantly, the house concept is not to be confused with the household. Instead, it is a principle of kinship that is on par with "family, lineage, and clan" (Beck 2007:4), rather than one that specifies the specific structure of that kinship principle itself. As Beck (2007:5) also points out, there is great flexibility in the concept, given that "houses are dynamic structures with governing principles that are subject to manipulation through time," with membership that may be based on a number of different kinds of kinship ties. In Lévi-Strauss's original formulation, the house society (or *société à maison*) was an intermediate form of social organization, between the more simple or "elementary" structures and those of more complex societies. As Whiteley (2012; see also Whiteley, this volume) discusses, this "semi-complex alliance" is often a feature of Crow-Omaha kinship systems, which are the major forms found in all the Pueblos. One of the advantages is its flexibility in extending marriage relationships out to a diverse group of relatives, which allows social formulations that are based on both descent and affinity.

There are several principles that underlie the concept of the house society (e.g., Beck 2007; Gillespie 2000, 2007; Heitman 2007; Helms 2007). First, it involves the heritability of the house estate, which may include material and immaterial property. Second, it occurs with others of like structure—houses do not exist on their own but rather in societies with other houses. Third, the house should be considered as a "moral person," and the house is often viewed as a living being, embodied by its architecture. And finally, houses may be archaeologically identified on the basis of architectural permanence, ancestors, origins or primacy, and inalienable objects. People are the major constituents of houses, and so the house society model fits comfortably with discussions of labor organization, particularly for large-scale agricultural investments. In fact, Wills's (2005) application of the concept speaks specifically to the Hohokam and Chaco agricultural labor requirements that would have been needed for irrigation and other forms of water control. Indeed, these are two areas of the Southwest where there is evidence for the kinds of inequality, durability, and materiality that we might expect of house societies. Although Wills seems to apply it to only the Classic period Hohokam, Craig (2007) makes a good case for house societies as early as the Preclassic period based on significant changes and differences in residential permanence. Wills (2005:56) mentions how in both the Hohokam and Chaco areas "agricultural systems stand out against regional patterns by virtue of large-scale, expensive, and technically elaborate communal irrigation systems."

The argument for the presence of house societies at Chaco rests on several criteria. The most important is the presence of burials and other human remains that are clustered in the oldest sections of Pueblo Bonito, along with the rich array of ritually significant materials in burial rooms and their immediately adjacent spaces (Heitman 2007; Heitman and Plog 2005). These point to the repeated interring of individuals over several generations, some of who probably represent secondary burials. Shared cosmology and symbolism is another hallmark, especially as Heitman (2007) and Heitman and Plog (2005) have drawn out the house society at Chaco, including directional symbolism, the importance of wood posts, and resurfacings and rituals of renewal (for the latter see also Crown and Wills 2003). None of these on their own is sufficient for the application of the house society concept, but together they offer a more compelling interpretation than previous interpretations of the Pueblo Bonito burial data. To these criteria may be added the storage of items that were clearly used in collective ritual, such as painted wood, especially in the oldest sections of Pueblo Bonito and

Chetro Ketl (Mills 2004, 2008; Vivian et al. 1978; Jolie and Webster, this volume) and the diversity and density of materials found in these specific rooms—in terms of their actual forms and where these materials came from. For example, turquoise in the north cluster came from multiple sources, demonstrating widespread networks of interaction (Hull et al. 2014). These networks may be some of the best evidence we have of the extension of marriage networks and "semi-complex alliances." The archaeological criteria outlined by Beck (2007) cited above are all manifested in the material evidence from Pueblo Bonito, viz., architectural permanence, ancestors, origins or primacy, and inalienable heirlooms.

Every society has a number of alternative prestige structures, and at Chaco, it is increasingly clear that there was at least one particularly powerful distinction that is materially evident in the two clusters of human remains within Pueblo Bonito found within two of the oldest sections of the building (Akins 2003). These two clusters are the best evidence for different "houses" at Chaco. These clusters include both primary and secondary burials, and their distinctive locations in rooms without outside access and in the oldest sections of Pueblo Bonito suggest "family" crypts—or at least the burial of people related to each other in some way. There is greater similarity in genetic traits within each cluster than between (Schillaci 2003; see also Snow and LeBlanc, this volume), but it should be remembered that descent is not the sole basis for membership in a particular house within a house society. In fact, the house society model specifically replaces a solely lineage-based system of social organization by including affiliations based on alliances (especially but not exclusively marriage). It is the evidence for hierarchy and status from the depositional history of these burial areas that bolsters the house society model.

The rooms clustered around burials were where some of the highest densities of material at Pueblo Bonito were placed (Neitzel 2003), with many objects that were likely used in ritualization practices. Objects in the two clusters of rooms appear to have been placed in those rooms at different times in repeated acts of remembrance (Heitman and Plog 2005; Mills 2008). Members of these groups memorialized those who were buried in these crypts by placing objects of memory in and near them and redepositing parts of bodies with those who had been previously interred. Many of these objects are those that would be considered as communally owned and inalienable, such as altar pieces, though others were most likely individually owned, such as staffs of ritual office (Mills 2004).

The actual length of time that elapsed must have been on the order of several generations, but questions of great interest are how many generations and the relationship of different individuals within each burial chamber. The lower paired burials in Room 33 have been referred to as dating to the "Gallup" period based on the presence of Gallup Black-on-white ceramics in the room assemblage (Lekson 2009). However, none of the Gallup vessels are actually associated with these two burials. Akins reports a Red Mesa Black-on-white bowl and a smudged bowl "resting against the north wall" as the only ceramics in this earlier layer (Akins 1986:117). This generally fits with Windes's (2003:Figure 3.4) hypothesized date for the construction of the rooms in the area of Room 33—roughly in the A.D. 900s. But more recently, AMS direct dating of Burials 13 and 14 suggests a date in the early A.D. 800s (Coltrain et al. 2007:Table 1; Plog and Heitman 2010)—slightly earlier than the earliest tree-ring cutting dates from the entire building.* Red Mesa Black-on-white is generally considered to have been produced ca. A.D. 900–1050 (McKenna and Toll 1984), not in the early or even mid-800s, which suggests that there was access to this space for at least a couple of generations after the individuals were placed there.[†] The size of a hole in the planks that covered the burials is reported by Akins (2003:97) to have been 10 cm, which could have been accessed over a longer period of time and through which some of the items of turquoise, shell, and other materials could have been deposited later in time. However, it

---

*Coltrain et al. (2007:Table 1) report a confidence interval midpoint for Burial 13 as A.D. 821 and for Burial 14, A.D. 817. The 95 percent confidence interval is A.D. 690–944 and 690–940, respectively. These are remarkably close in time and suggest that the two individuals died at the same time and presumably were buried contemporaneously. The earliest tree-ring cutting dates are 828r (Room 317), 852rTent and 864r (Room 323), and 859r (Rooms 108/109) in the western room block and 851r (Room 62) in the eastern room block (tree-ring date database from the Chaco Research Archive, http://www.chacoarchive.org, accessed August 14, 2010).

[†] One tree-ring date of 852vv from Room 33 was obtained from the second-story door lintel and one date of 1081v from the second-story roof (Chaco Research Archive, http://www.chacoarchive.org, accessed August 14, 2010).

is not large enough to have allowed the Red Mesa vessel to have been placed in there (unless the planks themselves were removed or are later than the burials). Thus, the evidence suggests that the northern cluster was used for close to 200 years, or at least eight generations.

The western cluster contains rooms that also date to the mid-800s. The 21 individuals (not all of whom were complete) in Room 320 were accompanied by a variety of ceramics. The 2 adult women lying on a mat within the room are associated with a Red Mesa Black-on-white pitcher and half of a Red Mesa Black-on-white bowl (Akins 2003: Table B.1). The Room 320 ceramic assemblage also includes later styles of ceramics, including six Chaco Black-on-white (ca. A.D. 1075–1150) cylinder jars. Like the northern cluster, then, the western cluster appears to have great time depth, and later burials were accompanied by cylinder jars. Based on pottery and architectural context, it is difficult to tell which clusters' first interments were earlier, but as several have noted, they are clearly in the oldest sections of the building and raise interesting parallels with ethnographic discussions of first-comers and late-comers in establishing claims over property, people, and other resources (e.g., Whiteley 1998).

Of particular importance in discussing the burial clusters is that many of the objects placed in these rooms are not directly associated with individuals interred in these spaces. Instead, these objects are found in contexts in the same chambers or in rooms adjacent to or in the same construction units, but are not burial goods. For example, the turquoise heishi necklace that Judd excavated from Room 320 was not directly associated with a burial. It came from a subfloor cache in the floor that had been covered with mud plaster before the individuals were placed within the room. Similarly, the four offerings in the corners of the floor of the burial room of Room 33 that contained Burials 13 and 14, considered to be among the most elaborate in the Southwest, were placed to dedicate the space rather than to adorn the bodies of the two individuals who were placed on the floor. In both cases we do not know whether these dedicatory deposits were immediately before burials were placed in the rooms or not, but they speak to shared communities of practice linking the two houses.

Other shared ritual practices that distinguish the mortuary behavior in the two house clusters from others at Chaco include the combination of paired, extended primary burials with multiple secondary burials in layers above them or in nearby rooms. Outside of these two clusters, including at small sites, most burials are placed in flexed positions, occur alone, and were placed in middens (Akins 1986:Table 5.13). Akins and others have interpreted these distinctions as evidence for ranking within a model of managerial elites, and Lekson refers to the associated individuals as "retainers." Yet, these distinctions alternatively fit with the house society model, in which the important house members' bones were placed in the architectural container of the house. In this way, the room became an archive of the social house, representing the history of that particular social network and reminding those who participated in each act of burial of their place in society.

Gillespie (2007:32) notes that one of the consistent patterns found in ethnographic cases of house societies is that there are usually distinctions between houses and that archaeologists should be more attuned to these differences, such as "greater" or "lesser" houses (Chesson 2007). She points to Craig's (2007) analysis from the Grewe site where higher-ranked houses may have more evidence of craft specialists. Akins's analysis of the two burial clusters lends support to a discussion of "greater" and "lesser" houses. The north cluster contains the largest number of burials and the highest density of objects that we might associate with ritual practices (Neitzel 2003). This fits one of the expectations for a house society in that there should be multiple houses, not just one, and that there should be variation among them. At Pueblo Bonito there appears to be at least two, with the northern cluster having significantly higher densities of valuable goods than the western cluster. But in relation to probable other Chaco houses in other great houses, the two houses at Pueblo Bonito were ranked higher.

It is both the nestedness—what Wills (2005) refers to as the segmentary quality of its organization—and the transformative nature of the house society concept that I would like to discuss in the rest of this chapter. I find the application to Chaco compelling, but what I would like to explore is how they were related to each other, that is, what evidence there is for social networks that were nested within or that might crosscut the houses. I use depositional practice as one of the primary ways in which these social networks may be identified archaeologically. This requires looking at both shared materialities and other social units within great houses. To paraphrase Robert Netting (1990), what we need to do is unpack the Chaco house society portmanteau.

Unpacking the Chaco "House"

One of the surprising outcomes of recent work on caches in kivas is the degree of homogeneity found in pilaster dedicatory deposits (Mills 2008). Whereas great kivas each had very different cache compositions,* there was remarkable homogeneity in non–great kiva "round rooms" at Pueblo Bonito, which suggests a shared ideology and transmission of ritual practice by a circumscribed social unit. In particular, I noted that the assemblages from the horizontal log pilasters excavated by Pepper showed striking similarities in that while they only contained a handful of offerings, the assemblages were redundant in including a few fig-ure-eight beads, olivella shell, discoidal beads, worked and unworked turquoise, and occasionally other materials such as small fragments of animal bone. Judd's (1959:61–62) tabulation of offerings reports a simi-lar range of offerings from kivas that he excavated. I interpreted this great homogeneity as evidence for a shared tradition that involved the proper way to dedicate these structures.

Subsequently, Tom Windes (2014) has more carefully defined a set of Chaco kivas that he calls "court kivas." Although Lekson defined court kivas on the basis of their size and location next to courts, Windes's analysis is more logical in that he defines them on the basis of sets of shared features—a single floor vault and their hidden quality below grade in courts or surrounded by square rooms. He tabulated 70 kivas like this, of which 46 are in Chaco Canyon (26 from Pueblo Bonito) and the rest largely from north of Chaco. Most date to the A.D. 1000s but also extend into the early 1100s.

Distinguishing the court kivas built in Chaco Canyon itself was the use of low horizontal log pilasters (6 to 10 depending on the size of the structure). As Windes noted, this particular kind of pilaster con-struction is absent in small houses. Truell (1992:100) notes one case of

---

*Compare, for example, the long strands of beads in Great Kiva II at Chetro Ketl with the contents of the Great Kiva Q niche at Pueblo Bonito. In retrospect, the latter seems most like the contents of a Plains bundle (e.g., Zedeño 2008).

a "decorative pilaster" in Kiva E at 29SJ627—in possible emulation of the pilasters in the court kivas. And while there are other pilasters at small sites (McKenna and Treull 1986:181–182), they are more like pit-structure pilasters than those in the court kivas. The horizontal log pilasters and the pilaster log offerings—the caches discussed above— were absent outside of Chaco Canyon except for kivas at Aztec West Ruin, linking the builders of Chacoan court kivas directly to those at Aztec because of the replication of technologies that could not be seen once the kivas were completed. Windes (2014) concluded that these kivas were constructed by "skilled builders" who must have had first-hand knowledge of the way these structures were built.

Even less often found in the court kivas was the use of wainscoting, an additional interior wall layer that extends about halfway to the roof. Windes (2014) challenged Cameron's (2008) and Lekson's (2007) inter-pretations of these as part of the roofing structure that formed a bowl because they co-occur with obvious examples of cribbed roofing. I agree with Windes that this was a true wainscoting—part of the lower wall and separate from the roofing system—and that the wainscot would have been covered by the bottom of the cribbed roofing. Wainscoting may have functioned to provide insulation because the space between the wainscot and the outer wall was often filled with organic material, but this technique was very specific. Judd (1964:187) specifically notes "bunch grass" as the major packing material between the hewn plank or pole wainscots and the outer walls of kivas "in every instance" of the kivas he excavated at Pueblo Bonito. The best preserved was identified as rice grass (*Oryzopsis hymenoides*). Breternitz (1967) also identified rice grass as the packing material at Double Wall Ruin in northern Arizona, dating between A.D. 1100 and A.D. 1300. Interestingly, rice grass is used in the construction of some ritual architecture at Hopi and is "used for the matting that covers the opening of the *Kwan* kiva" (Lomaomvaya et al. 2001:45). The use of grasses in wainscoting is another example of depositional practice that was shared, hidden, and therefore must have been transmitted through the builders and not through emulation.

I think that Windes's conclusion is largely correct—that these struc-tures were built by a group of builders who shared the knowledge of how to construct them within a relatively restricted network. This net-work was heavily involved in the construction of ritual architecture in "downtown" Chaco since there are court kivas at Pueblo Bonito, Chetro Ketl, and Pueblo del Arroyo (Judd 1959, 1964; Lekson 1983). One particularly relevant question is the relationship between the network that constructed the court kivas, the burial clusters or "houses," and great kivas. The presence of specifically hidden attributes of the court kivas and their construction at multiple settlements within and outside of the canyon suggests that the builders were part of a network that crosscut different villages and therefore crosscut different houses that made up the Chaco house society. The builders may have been members of different houses, but the important point is that the community of practice that built court kivas was not isomorphic with a Chaco house.

In contrast to the court kivas, with their redundant deposits, are the highly variable dedicatory and termination deposits found in great kivas (Mills 2008). Although the floor features are similar, these are highly visible architectural attributes. Caches in great kivas are similar in the sense that they usually include shell, but this material ranges from the deposition of whole shells, including *Strombus* and *Murex* trumpets (Mills and Ferguson 2008), to finished beads. In some cases, other items, including turquoise, augment the shell. But comparison of the contents of these caches (Mills 2008) underscores the conclusion that there is no single overarching community of practice in what was deemed appropriate to place in these structures at either their dedication or termination.

Along with the more limited number of great kivas in any single settlement, I suggest that the network that built and maintained great kivas was coeval with individual houses within the Chaco house society at Pueblo Bonito. The great kivas at Pueblo Bonito were not built or even used at the same time—the four that have been identified were constructed between A.D. 900 to after A.D. 1100 (Van Dyke 2007b:97). Their sequence and locations on either side of the central wall suggest an alternation and even competition between the groups who built them. It is particularly interesting that their construction is associated with the major construction episodes of the great house itself. Both would have required labor pools that drew upon members of the house. Within the house society model, these need not have been individuals who lived at Pueblo Bonito but instead individuals who were drawn from throughout the basin.

Although the social units that constructed and maintained great kivas, at least at Pueblo Bonito, were isomorphic with Chaco houses, I do not think that a great kiva is necessary for a Chacoan house to have been present. As Van Dyke (2003) points out, 17 of the 56 known great houses in the San Juan Basin are without great kivas (and great houses closer to Chaco Canyon have the lowest percentages). Larger great houses, except those closest to Chaco Canyon, tend to have at least one, but I think that the great house itself is the minimal identifying structure for this social network. Nonetheless, the number of great kivas may be an indication of the minimum number of houses in a particular community.

Conclusion

I referred to Pueblo Bonito as an archive earlier in this chapter. In a very interesting book about contemporary memory practices, Bowker (2005) discusses memory archives, which are different ways of storing information. The invention of the printing press was one such dramatic shift in the way that memory archives were made and transmitted. Women's role in transmitting information was supplanted, and historical reconstructions may have seen a more abrupt shift than there actually was because the source of those reconstructions changed (rather than the actual practices) (Bowker 2005:11). And today, the dramatic changes from tangible books to digital, from hard copy to soft, and within the latter to changes in different storage mediums are all revolutionizing our archival practices.

I would argue that the many different depositional practices at Chaco were in fact building archives. The practice of depositing objects of ritual significance in rooms in Pueblo Bonito was a particular memory regime that has few precedents or antecedents in the Pueblo world. The different acts of deposition were distinctive ways in which the archive was constructed and information was stored. It was how particular social networks memorialized their ancestors and maintained their authority.

One can imagine Pueblo Bonito itself as one grand archive, but in fact the differentiation of burial clusters suggests at least two separate networks. The northern cluster was clearly the dominant one, with the highest concentrations of objects arguably used in ritual practice. The membership of this house likely drew from outside of Pueblo Bonito for the construction of additions to the building, the many court kivas, and the great kivas. On the one hand, the court kivas share many distinctive construction details that tie them together in a single community of practice, perhaps within a guild of builders that crosscut many of the houses. On the other hand are the great kivas, which I think are more closely associated with the social unit of the Chaco house.

What I find particularly intriguing about the origins and the demise of the social networks that define the Chaco house society is that at both ends they have been suggested to correspond with evidence for migration. Judge and Cordell (2006:194) suggest that the earliest great houses of Una Vida, Pueblo Bonito, and Peñasco Blanco were established by newcomers who moved into areas with poorer agricultural land that required more labor (see also Vivian 1990:600; Wilshusen and Van Dyke 2006). At the other end of the time span of the Bonito phase, in the early to mid-1100s, Wills (2009) has recently suggested another migration of people from the San Juan region, accounting for the disjunctures in architectural and ceramic styles, depositional practices, and mortuary ritual, among other patterns.

The negotiation of latecomers with existing populations in an area is one of the hallmarks of social changes within migration scenarios. In a book of case studies addressing leadership in the prehispanic Southwest (Mills 2000), many of the authors cited evidence for pronounced changes in leadership and the ritualization process in their respective areas. A particularly important commonality among the case studies was that they took diachronic perspectives on how leadership changed, grounding their discussions within longer-term events within each area. Although the specifics of the migrations into Chaco can be debated, the significance of these new interpretations helps to explain much about the Bonito phase and the origins and dissolution of the Chaco house society. New identities often emerge in these situations of contact and negotiation. Ritual practice was a way of establishing claims to property and other resources, and especially to labor.

Gillespie (2007:41) points out that house societies "tend to appear when property and political power become salient values in organizing social life but in the absence of contractual or class-based relationships binding people to one another." Her latter point is particularly important because it gets at how houses might lead to social transformation—one of Lévi-Strauss's original interests. As noted earlier, the burial clusters at Pueblo Bonito suggest that the distinctions between groups and the long-term acts of remembering associated with different groups date to the A.D. mid-800s, at the peak of the Pueblo I period. The Pueblo I period is receiving renewed attention not just because it was when great houses were first founded but also because it was when there was a high degree of mobility from valley to valley, evidence for inter-village violence, and construction of some of the largest communal structures ever built in the Southwest (Wilshusen et al. 2012). This tension between cooperation and conflict at the intra-village and inter-village scales was the crucible for the Chaco house society.

Arising out of the mid- to late 800s inequalities and conflicts, Chaco houses were established to perpetuate claims to land and to organize labor through a system that meshed political, economic, and ritual power. By paying closer attention to how these inequalities and conflicts played out at Chaco, we have a much better way of viewing Chaco society, with models that go beyond dichotomization and include multiple sources of power in a more cohesive model.

References Cited

Akins, Nancy J. 1986. *A Biocultural Approach to Human Burials from Chaco Canyon, New Mexico*. Reports of the Chaco Center No. 9. Division of Cultural Research, National Park Service, Albuquerque.

———. 2003. The Burials of Pueblo Bonito. In *Pueblo Bonito: Center of the Chacoan World*, edited by Jill E. Neitzel, pp. 94–106. Smithsonian Institution Press, Washington, D.C.

Ashmore, Wendy. 2007. Building Social History at Pueblo Bonito: Footnotes to a Biography of Place. In *The Architecture of Chaco Canyon*, edited by Stephen H. Lekson, pp. 179–198. University of Utah Press, Salt Lake City.

Beck, Robin A., Jr. 2007. The Durable House: Material, Metaphor, and Structure. In *The Durable House: House Society Models in Archaeology*, edited by Robin A. Beck Jr., pp. 3–24. Center for Archaeological Investigations Occasional Paper No. 35. CAI, Southern Illinois University, Carbondale.

Beck, Robin A., Jr. (editor). 2007. *The Durable House: House Society Models in Archaeology*. Center for Archaeological Investigations Occasional Paper No. 35. CAI, Southern Illinois University, Carbondale.

Bell, Catherine M. 1992. *Ritual Theory, Ritual Practice*. Oxford University Press, Oxford.

Bowker, Geoffrey C. 2005. *Memory Practices in the Sciences*. MIT Press, Cambridge.

Bradley, Richard. 2005. *Ritual and Domestic Life in Prehistoric Europe*. Routledge, London.

Breternitz, David A. 1967. Ceremonial Structures at Double Wall Ruin, Site NA 4207, Navajo County. *Plateau* 40(1):22–28. Flagstaff.

Brück, Joanna. 1999. Ritual and Rationality: Some Problems of Interpretation in European Archaeology. *European Journal of Archaeology* 2(3):313–344.

Cameron, Catherine M. 2008. Comparing Great House Architecture: Perspectives from the Bluff Great House. In *Chaco's Northern Prodigies: Salmon, Aztec, and the Ascendency of the Middle San Juan Region after AD 1100*, edited by Paul F. Reed, pp. 251–269. University of Utah Press, Salt Lake City.

Chesson, Meredith S. 2007. House, Town, Field, and Wadi: Landscapes of the Early Bronze Age Levant. In *The Durable House: House Society Models in Archaeology*, edited by Robin A. Beck Jr., pp. 317–343. Center for Archaeological Investigations Occasional Paper No. 35. CAI, Southern Illinois University, Carbondale.

Coltrain, Joan Brenner, Joel C. Janetski, and Shawn W. Carlyle. 2007. The Stable- and Radio-Isotope Chemistry of Western Basketmaker Burials: Implications for Early Puebloan Diets and Origins. *American Antiquity* 72(2):301–321.

Craig, Douglas B. 2007. Courtyard Groups and the Emergence of House Estates in Early Hokokam Society. In *The Durable House: House Society Models in Archaeology*, edited by Robin A. Beck Jr., pp. 446–463. Center for Archaeological Investigations Occasional Paper No. 35. CAI, Southern Illinois University, Carbondale.

Crown, Patricia L. 2001. Learning to Make Pottery in the Prehispanic Southwest. *Journal of Anthropological Research* 57:451–469.

Crown, Patricia L., and W. H. Wills. 2003. Modifying Pottery and Kivas at Chaco: Pentimento, Restoration, or Renewal? *American Antiquity* 68(3):511–532.

Fenn, Thomas R., Barbara J. Mills, and Maren Hopkins. 2006. The Social Contexts of Glaze Paint Ceramic Production and Consumption in the Silver Creek Area. In *The Social Life of Pots: Glaze Wares and Cultural Dynamics in the Southwest, AD 1250–1680*, edited by Judith A. Habicht-Mauche, Suzanne L. Eckert, and Deborah L. Huntley, pp. 60–85. University of Arizona Press, Tucson.

Fogelin, Lars. 2007. The Archaeology of Religious Ritual. *Annual Review of Anthropology* 36:55–71.

Fowles, Severin M. 2013. *An Archaeology of Doings: Secularism and the Study of Pueblo Religion*. School for Advanced Research Press, Santa Fe.

Gillespie, Susan D. 2000. Beyond Kinship: An Introduction. In *Beyond Kinship: Social and Material Reproduction in House Societies*, edited by Rosemary A.

Joyce and Susan D. Gillespie, pp. 1–21. University of Pennsylvania Press, Philadelphia.

———. 2007. When Is a House? In *The Durable House: House Society Models in Archaeology*, edited by Robin A. Beck Jr., pp. 25–52. Center for Archaeological Investigations Occasional Paper No. 35. CAI, Southern Illinois University, Carbondale.

Hawkes, C. 1954. Archaeological Method and Theory: Some Suggestions from the Old World. *American Anthropologist* 56:155–168.

Heitman, Carolyn C. 2007. Houses Great and Small: Reevaluating the "House" in Chaco Canyon, New Mexico. In *The Durable House: House Society Models in Archaeology*, edited by Robin A. Beck Jr., pp. 248–272. Center for Archaeological Investigations Occasional Paper No. 35. CAI, Southern Illinois University, Carbondale.

Heitman, Carolyn C., and Stephen Plog. 2005. Kinship and the Dynamics of the House: Rediscovering Dualism in the Pueblo Past. In *A Catalyst for Ideas: Anthropological Archaeology and the Legacy of Douglas W. Schwartz*, edited by Vernon L. Scarborough, pp. 69–100. School of American Research Press, Santa Fe.

Helms, Mary W. 2007. House Life. In *The Durable House: House Society Models in Archaeology*, edited by Robin A. Beck Jr., pp. 487–504. Center for Archaeological Investigations Occasional Paper No. 35. CAI, Southern Illinois University, Carbondale.

Hull, Sharon, Mostafa Fayek, F. Joan Mathien, and Heidi Roberts. 2014. Turquoise Trade of the Ancestral Puebloan: Chaco and Beyond. *Journal of Archaeological Science* 45:187–195.

Joyce, Rosemary, and Susan D. Gillespie (editors). 2000. *Beyond Kinship: Social and Material Reproduction in House Societies*. University of Pennsylvania Press, Philadelphia.

Judd, Neil M. 1959. *Pueblo del Arroyo, Chaco Canyon, New Mexico*. Smithsonian Miscellaneous Collections Vol. 138. Smithsonian Institution, Washington, D.C.

———. 1964. *The Architecture of Pueblo Bonito*. Smithsonian Miscellaneous Collections Vol. 147(1). Smithsonian Institution, Washington, D.C.

Judge, W. James, and Linda S. Cordell. 2006. Society and Polity. In *The Archaeology of Chaco Canyon: An Eleventh-Century Pueblo Regional Center*, edited by Stephen H. Lekson, pp. 189–210. School of American Research Press, Santa Fe.

Lansing, J. Stephen, Murray P. Cox, Therese A. de Vet, Sean S. Downey, Brian Hallmark, and Herawati Sudoyo. 2011. An Ongoing Austronesian Expansion in Island Southeast Asia. *Journal of Anthropological Archaeology* 30:262–272.

Lave, Jean, and Etienne Wenger. 1991. *Situated Learning: Legitimate Peripheral Participation*. University of Cambridge Press, Cambridge.

Lekson, Stephen H. 2006. Chaco Matters: An Introduction. In *The Archaeology of Chaco Canyon: An Eleventh-Century Pueblo Regional Center*, edited by Stephen H. Lekson, pp. 3–44. School of American Research Press, Santa Fe.

————. 2007. Great House Form. In *The Architecture of Chaco Canyon, New Mexico*, edited by Stephen H. Lekson, pp. 7–44. University of Utah Press, Salt Lake City.

————. 2009. *A History of the Ancient Southwest*. School for Advanced Research Press, Santa Fe.

Lekson, Stephen H. (editor). 1983. *The Architecture and Dendrochronology of Chetro Ketl, Chaco Canyon, New Mexico*. Reports of the Chaco Center No. 6. Division of Cultural Research, National Park Service, Albuquerque.

Lévi-Strauss, Claude. 1982. *The Way of the Masks*. Translated by Sylvia Modelski. University of Washington Press, Seattle.

Lomaomvaya, Micah, T. J. Ferguson, and Michael Yeatts. 2001. *Öngtuvqava Sakwtala: Hopi Ethnobotany in the Grand Canyon*. Produced by the Hopi Cultural Preservation Office. Work Performed under the Guidance of the Hopi Cultural Resources Advisory Task Team, The Hopi Tribe. Kykotsmovi, Arizona.

McAnany, Patricia, and Ian Hodder. 2009. Thinking about Stratigraphic Sequence in Social Terms. *Archaeological Dialogues* 16:1–22.

McIntosh, Susan (editor). 1999. *Beyond Chiefdoms: Pathways to Complexity in Africa*. Cambridge University Press, Cambridge.

McKenna, Peter J., and H. Wolcott Toll. 1984. Ceramics. In *The Architecture and Material Culture of 29SJ1360, Chaco Canyon, New Mexico*, pp. 103–222. Reports of the Chaco Center No. 7. Division of Cultural Research, National Park Service, Albuquerque.

McKenna, Peter J., and Marcia Truell. 1986. *Small Site Architecture of Chaco Canyon, New Mexico*. Publications in Archeology 18D, Chaco Canyon Studies. National Park Service, U.S. Department of the Interior, Santa Fe.

Mills, Barbara J. 2004. The Establishment and Defeat of Hierarchy: Inalienable Possessions and the History of Collective Prestige Structures in the Puebloan Southwest. *American Anthropologist* 106:238–251.

————. 2008. Remembering while Forgetting: Depositional Practice and Social Memory at Chaco. In *Memory Work: Archaeologies of Material Practices*, edited by Barbara J. Mills and William H. Walker, pp. 81–108. School for Advanced Research Press, Santa Fe.

Mills, Barbara J. (editor). 2000. *Alternative Leadership Strategies in the Prehispanic Southwest*. University of Arizona Press, Tucson.

Mills, Barbara J., and T. J. Ferguson. 2008. Animate Objects: Shell Trumpets and Ritual Networks in the Greater Southwest. *Journal of Archaeological Method and Theory* 15(4):338–361.

Mills, Barbara J., and William H. Walker. 2008. Introduction: Memory, Materiality, and Depositional Practice. In *Memory Work: Archaeologies of Material Practices*, edited by Barbara J. Mills and William H. Walker, pp. 3–23. School for Advanced Research Press, Santa Fe.

Mills, Barbara J., and William H. Walker (editors). 2008. *Memory Work: Archaeologies of Material Practices*. School for Advanced Research Press, Santa Fe.

Murray, Wendi Field, and Barbara J. Mills. 2013. Identity Communities and Memory Practices: Logics of Material Deposition in the U.S. Southwest. In *Relational Archaeologies: Humans, Animals, Things*, edited by Christopher Watts, pp. 135–153. Routledge, London.

Neitzel, Jill E. 2003. Artifact Distributions at Pueblo Bonito. In *Pueblo Bonito: Center of the Chacoan World*, edited by Jill E. Neitzel, pp. 107–126. Smithsonian Institution Press, Washington, D.C.

Netting, Robert McC. 1990. Population, Permanent Agriculture, and Polities: Unpacking the Evolutionary Portmanteau. In *The Evolution of Political Systems: Sociopolitics in Small-Scale Societies*, edited by Steadman Upham, pp. 21–61. School of American Research Press, Santa Fe.

Plog, Stephen. 2003. Exploring the Ubiquitous through the Unusual: Color Symbolism in Pueblo Black-on-White Pottery. *American Antiquity* 68(4):665–695.

Plog, Stephen, and Carrie Heitman. 2010. Hierarchy and Social Inequality in the American Southwest, AD 800–1200. *Proceedings of the National Academy of Sciences* 107(46):19619–19626.

Schillaci, M. A. 2003. The Development of Population Diversity at Chaco Canyon. *Kiva* 68(3):221–245.

Sebastian, Lynne. 2006. The Chaco Synthesis. In *The Archaeology of Chaco Canyon: An Eleventh-Century Pueblo Regional Center*, edited by Stephen H. Lekson, pp. 393–422. School of American Research Press, Santa Fe.

Stahl, Ann B. 2008. Dogs, Pythons, Pots, and Beads: The Dynamics of Shrines and Sacrificial Practices in Banda, Ghana, 1400–1900 CE. In *Memory Work: Archaeologies of Material Practices*, edited by Barbara J. Mills and William H. Walker, pp. 159–186. School for Advanced Research Press, Santa Fe.

Stark, Miriam T. 2006. Glaze Ware Technology, the Social Lives of Pots, and Communities of Practice in the Late Prehistoric Southwest. In *The Social Lives of Pots: Glaze Wares and Cultural Dynamics in the Southwest, AD 1250–1680*, edited by Judith A. Habicht-Mauche, Suzanne L. Eckert, and Deborah L. Huntley, pp. 17–33. University of Arizona Press, Tucson.

Truell, Marcia L. 1992. *Excavations at 29SJ627, Chaco Canyon, New Mexico, Volume 1: The Architecture and Stratigraphy*. Reports of the Chaco Center No. 11. Division of Cultural Research, National Park Service, Santa Fe.

Van Dyke, Ruth M. 2003. The Chacoan Great Kiva in Outlier Communities: Investigating Integrative Spaces across the San Juan Basin. *Kiva* 67(3):231–247.

————. 2004. Memory, Meaning, and Masonry: The Late Bonito Chacoan Landscape. *American Antiquity* 69(3):413–431.

————. 2007a. *The Chaco Experience: Landscape and Ideology at the Center Place.* School for Advanced Research Press, Santa Fe.

————. 2007b. Great Kivas in Time, Space, and Society. In *The Architecture of Chaco Canyon, New Mexico,* edited by Stephen H. Lekson, pp. 93–126. University of Utah Press, Salt Lake City.

Vivian, R. Gwinn. 1990. *The Chacoan Prehistory of the San Juan Basin.* Academic Press, New York.

Vivian, R. Gwinn, Dulce N. Dodgen, and Gayle H. Hartmann. 1978. *Wooden Ritual Artifacts from Chaco Canyon, New Mexico: The Chetro Ketl Collection.* Anthropological Papers of the University of Arizona No. 32. University of Arizona Press, Tucson.

Walker, William H. 1995. Ceremonial Trash? In *Expanding Archaeology,* edited by James M. Skibo, William H. Walker, and Axel E. Nielsen, pp. 67–79. University of Utah Press, Salt Lake City.

————. 2008. Practice and Nonhuman Social Actors: The Afterlife Histories of Witches and Dogs in the American Southwest. In *Memory Work: Archaeologies of Material Practices,* edited by Barbara J. Mills and William H. Walker, pp. 137–158. School for Advanced Research Press, Santa Fe.

Whiteley, Peter M. 1998. *Rethinking Hopi Ethnography.* Smithsonian Institution Press, Washington, D.C.

————. 2012. Crow-Omaha Kinship in North America: A Puebloan Perspective. In *Crow-Omaha: New Light on a Classic Problem of Kinship Analysis,* edited by Thomas R. Trautmann and Peter M. Whiteley, pp. 83–108. University of Arizona Press, Tucson.

Wills, W. H. 2005. Economic Competition and Agricultural Involution in the Precontact North American Southwest. In *A Catalyst for Ideas: Anthropological Archaeology and the Legacy of Douglas W. Schwartz,* edited by Vernon L. Scarborough, pp. 41–67. School of American Research Press, Santa Fe.

————. 2009. Cultural Identity and the Archaeological Construction of Historical Narratives: An Example from Chaco Canyon. *Journal of Archaeological Method and Theory* 16:283–319.

Wilshusen, Richard H., and Ruth M. Van Dyke. 2006. Chaco's Beginnings. In *The Archaeology of Chaco Canyon: An Eleventh-Century Pueblo Regional Center,* edited by Stephen H. Lekson, pp. 211–260. School of American Research Press, Santa Fe.

Wilshusen, Richard H., Gregson Schachner, and James R. Allison (editors). 2012. *Crucible of Pueblos: The Early Pueblo Period in the Northern Southwest.* Monograph 71. Cotsen Institute of Archaeology Press, University of California, Los Angeles.

Windes, Thomas C. 2003. This Old House: Construction and Abandonment at Pueblo Bonito. In *Pueblo Bonito: Center of the Chacoan World*, edited by Jill E. Neitzel, pp. 14–32. Smithsonian Institution Press, Washington, D.C.

————. 2014. The Chacoan Court Kiva. *Kiva*, in press.

Zedeño, Nieves. 2008. Bundled Worlds: The Roles and Interactions of Complex Objects from the North American Plains. *Journal of Archaeological Method and Theory* 15(4):362–378.

10

Chacoan Kinship

Peter Whiteley

Introduction

We have become accustomed to imagining archaeological descriptions of Chaco and its ruined settlements, its pots, its walls, even its astronomical alignments as corresponding to actual historical social forms. Yet the *people* and their social arrangements seem largely absent, offstage producers of the material record, as it were. We know there was extensive exchange among settlements and sites—great houses, small houses, center, and periphery. An underlying organization of "house society" type seems very probable (cf. Heitman, this volume). But how were exchange processes articulated? What were the social relationships within and among particular settlements? And how were fieldwork, housework, and ritual events socially configured? In short, what was the structure of Chacoan social life? Answering these questions is no easy task, but the effort, I believe, is important if we are to reconnect the people to the place. My aim in this chapter is to suggest a framework for Chacoan social forms and patterns of organization.

The core target of social-structural analysis for more than a century has been kinship. Kinship systems provide a code for understanding social structures, particularly in societies of lesser complexity than the state. My main concern here is how kinship might shed new light on these Chacoan settlement sites, their internal components, and their interconnections. In brief, my thesis is that two major kinship systems—"Crow" and "Iroquois"—are suggested by certain architectural features, notably at two exemplar cases: Pueblo Bonito and Wijiji. My approach is two-pronged, addressing (1) kinship theory itself and (2) Pueblo, especially Hopi, social structure—a comparison, I argue, that is not so much ethnographic analogy as ethnological homology. And in this regard, I think the conventional distinction between Eastern and Western Pueblos (both per se and as a model for Chaco) is overdrawn.

Puebloan kinship systems are the subject of debate, but the "Crow" type plays a major role. Fred Eggan's landmark study (1950) inferred Crow-matrilineal kinship at the heart of all Pueblo social organization. Recent studies of Crow-Omaha systems (Trautmann and Whiteley, ed. 2012) contain significant implications for the emergence of sociopolitical complexity in the Southwest.

Houses, Kivas, Plazas (I): Pluralism

Chaco's settlement architecture is various (e.g., Lekson et al. 2006), but two prominent great house forms feature D- and E-shapes (Figure 10.1). Pueblo Bonito (D) and Wijiji (E) are especially noticeable in this contrast. Pueblo Bonito is marked by a plurality of round kivas distributed throughout the central part of the structure. At Wijiji, two kivas are arranged as mirror images on opposite sides of a strikingly binary architectural pattern. The sites contrast in other respects: Pueblo Bonito was occupied, developed, and transformed over several centuries, while Wijiji was built at one juncture, ca. 1100 A.D., and only occupied over a short period. Kivas at Bonito shifted over time, as new ones were added and others demolished, but it may be reasonably inferred that, while they changed in time and space, plural kivas were a long-term feature. Against the background of this plural-dual contrast, two points may be taken as given. First, much Chaco architecture is deliberate and reflects particular alignments, astronomical and otherwise (e.g., Van Dyke 2008). Second, as a general matter, American Indian architecture—archaeologically, historically, and ethnographically—typically incorporates conscious symbolic projections of social structural forms (e.g., Morgan 1881; Nabokov and Easton 1989). On these grounds alone, a hypothesis that Chacoan architecture contains correspondences with social structural features seems worth investigating.

The extent to which Pueblo Bonito (Figure 10.2) was a residential site remains in dispute, as well as its population size (e.g., Bernardini 1999; Mills 2002; Windes 1984). Even if Pueblo Bonito were not primarily residential, but received regular (annual, seasonal, etc.) population influxes attached to differentiable architectural units within the pueblo, the arrangement of spaces should reflect social structural principles. This is certainly the case, for example, with the present situation at

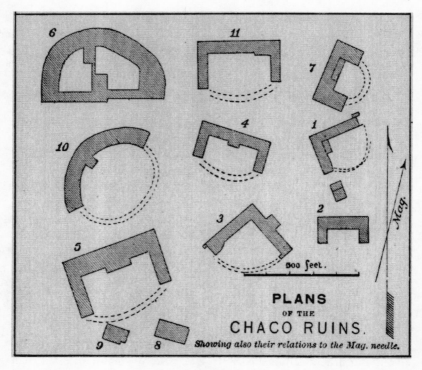

Figure 10.1. Lewis Henry Morgan's (1881) representation of Chacoan plans. While superseded by later mapping, this figure shows that from the earliest formal study, the relationship between settlement patterns and social organization was a key question at Chaco. Morgan, who effectively invented anthropology via the comparative study of kinship (1871), was explicitly interested in correlations between house-forms and kinship systems.

the Hopi village of Walpi on First Mesa: there are very few year-round residents, but many families return to their houses during ceremonial periods. This partly results from modern conditions: people prefer to live at Polacca below First Mesa, where they have running water and electricity. But the pattern of residing away from the main pueblos in field houses at varying distances during the agricultural season, only returning to the main centers for ceremonies, is a well-established one among the Pueblos.

In its overall plan and distribution of kivas, Pueblo Bonito expresses a combination of two obvious social patterns: pluralism and dualism

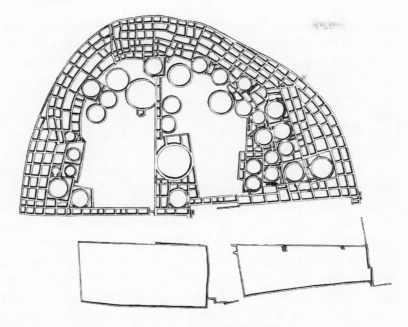

Figure 10.2. Pueblo Bonito plan. (After Morgan 1994)

(east–west). The same set of contrastive architectural components is evident here as at the historic Pueblos: (1) between rectangular and circular rooms—fairly interpreted as an opposition between "houses" and "kivas"—whether or not all rectangular structures were domestic or all round structures were ritual centers; and (2) between built structures and open spaces, the latter of which, as "plazas," probably served as both quotidian and ritual spaces. At Hopi, the same patterns (sans circular buildings) appear in every settlement, each associated with a contrastive term whose stem, *ki-*, refers to built spaces: *kiihu* (house), *kiva*, and *kiisonvi* (plaza)—are all arranged to comprise a *kitsoki* (pueblo or town). All have multiple uses, both everyday and special-purpose; none is intrinsically more or less sacred or profane, but their use-functions reflect a series of binary oppositions. The kiihu is private, domestic, familial, and female centered. The kiva is private, semi-collective, often ritual, and male centered. The kiisonvi is public, collective, both female and male, and alternately secular and ritual. The kiihu is the space of the domestic economy. The kiva is the men's workshop and a space of clan, ritual-sodality, and political action. The kiisonvi is the space of society—where it imagines and, in ritual contexts, performs itself, as a whole entity uniting the various differentiated components. We might summarize this as three intersecting axes of oppositions: (1) kiihu : kiva :: female : male; (2) kiihu : kiisonvi :: familial : collective; and (3) kiva : kiisonvi :: private : public. Within this paradigm, great kivas—not a recent Hopi architectural form, but present in Hopi history, notably on the Mogollon Rim (Herr 2001)—correspond most closely to plazas.

At a Hopi village like Orayvi in 1900 (Figure 10.3), there were approximately 200 *kiikihu* (houses, pl.), comprising single rooms and room-suites on linked stories in clustered room blocks (Whiteley 2008:195–240). Some houses were more important than others: as named clanhouses, they were often the repositories of sacred paraphernalia that indexed the ritual knowledge controlled by the leading segment of the clan associated with the house. Other houses were less important, though all buildings were marked by sacred features, and all houses were associated with people belonging to totemically named social groups (Bear, Sun, Badger, etc.). In a sense, the houses were related to each other as the people who dwelt in and owned them: one house was "in-law" to another or its "niece" or its "sibling" (given Hopi matriliny and female house ownership, the house relationships are most easily thought of as female kin and affines [in-laws]).

Set off from the houses and exterior to the room blocks stood 14 below-ground kivas, not necessarily associated with the individual house blocks and their familial occupants to which they stood adjacent. Ritual specialization and specific matriclan associations differentiated the kivas from each other, and some were more important than others, especially Sakwalenvi (Blue Flute place), Orayvi's *mong.kiva* (chief kiva). Like persons, all kivas were individually named, after totemic imagery of their clan owners. As male clanhouses and/or ritual-sodality chambers, kivas relate to each other in similar fashion as houses, but not so exclusively, since ordinary sodality members include many clans, although each sodality is owned by the leading clan of the same or related name as the clan and kiva (as, for example, with Orayvi's Snake clan, Snake sodality, and Snake kiva). Kivas are the nexus of multiple intersecting kinship relations. However, alliance in ritual is often predicated on marriage alliance (Whiteley 2012). Katsin kiva (Katsina

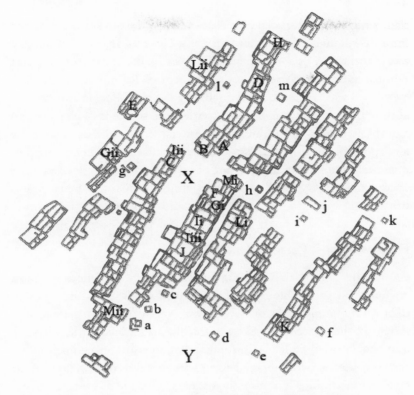

Figure 10.3. Orayvi ca. 1900. X Main kiisonvi; Y "Snake" kiisonvi. Kiva-clanhouse correlations (Whiteley 2008:229–237): *Kiva*: a Hotstitsivi, b Sakwalenvi, c Naasavi, d Marawkiva, e Tsu'kiva, f Kwankiva, g Pongovi/Tawa'ovi, h Tawkiva, I Hawiwvi, j Is.kiva, k Katsinkiva, l Wiklapi, m Hanokiva. *Clanhouse*: A Badger, B Spider, C Bow, D Lizard, E Snake, F Maasaw, Gi Sun/Gii Bear, H Parrot, Ii Sparrowhawki/Iii Squash/Iiii Crane, J Coyote, K Katsina, Li Rabbitbrush/Lii Kookop, Mi Piikyas/Mii Eagle.

kiva) and Hotstitsivi (Zigzag place), for example, were "in-laws," owned respectively by the Parrot-Katsina and Badger clans, who are joint leaders of the Powamuy ceremony (performed by the Katsina and Powamuy sodalities). More than this, though, these two clans also exhibit a pattern of intermarriage.

The principal kiisonvi lay at the heart of the village, surrounded by the most important clanhouses on three enclosed sides. Another kiisonvi stood adjacent to a set of kivas away from the "downtown" room blocks, and it was used for special purposes (notably, the Snake/Antelope and Flute ceremonies). Like other parts of a Hopi village, built structures and spaces are in a sense animate: kiihu as a symbolic concept (referring not just to physical form) appears in many ritual contexts.

Orayvi was far less architecturally regular than Pueblo Bonito, and a clear dual opposition between settlement segments—like Bonito's later-built center-line bifurcation between east and west halves—is less apparent from its built spaces per se, although elements of dual organization are definitely present in several ritual patterns (Whiteley 2008:826–829). Overall, however, discernible similarities are suggested between the organization of space at Bonito and at Orayvi.

Houses, Kivas, Plazas (II): Dualism

Contrasting with Pueblo Bonito, Wijiji (Figure 10.4) is one of the most obviously dualist Pueblo ruins in the Southwest. In its two-kiva pattern built on opposing wings of the E-form, it most suggests the two-kiva system of the Rio Grande Keresan Pueblos, associated with a division into named ritual moieties (Turquoise and Squash). Social dualism has generally been easier to imagine in archaeological reconstructions of the Puebloan past, since it tends to be readily noticeable in the form exhibited at Wijiji (cf. Fowles 2005).

Figure 10.4 Wijiji plan. (After Morgan 1994)

Other Chacoan sites comprising single, dual, triple, or even multiple kivas, which are arranged in apparently paired oppositions across a central architectural axis, may also indicate dualist social forms (Figure 10.5). Let us note in passing Lévi-Strauss's (1963) emphasis that moiety structure is often asymmetrical, occurring "concentrically" (in the social imagination and/or in the symbolic organization of social space) or involving a third element. Lévi-Strauss ascribes "concentric dualism" and triadic structures to emergent "asymmetric" forms of marriage exchange (see below). Kin Ya'a, an outlier great house on Dutton Plateau, expresses an evident dualist or linked triadic pattern: its two circular buildings standing on opposite sides of the ordered rectangular room block seem to mirror each other, with a third in the center, perhaps serving to unite the other two (the fourth round building, a "tower kiva" [surely an oxymoron], should not be confused with actual kivas). In the E-shaped great house Kin Bineola, 12 miles south of downtown Chaco, the multiple kivas within the room blocks also suggest an arrangement into two opposing sets, with one great kiva on the exterior. Hungo Pavi's evident original E-shape and apparently two-kiva system—one interior to the main room block, the other exterior but within the walled plaza—also strongly suggest a dual pattern. Chetro Ketl, somewhat like Bonito in this regard, suggests both dualism and pluralism in its architectural arrangement.

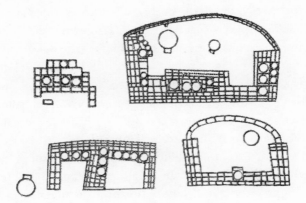

Figure 10.5. Four Chacoan plans: (L to R, top to bottom), Kin Ya'a, Chetro Ketl, Kin Bineola, and Hungo Pavi. (After Morgan 1994)

Efforts to infer dualism in archaeological sites like Wijiji, on the model of Keresan and Tewa moieties and dual- (or single-) kiva systems, have been direct (e.g., Fowles 2005; Lowell 1996; Ware 2014). But like earlier archaeological attempts to identify matrilineal lineages (e.g., Vivian 1970, 1990), or more recently matrilocality (Peregrine 2001), the interest has typically been framed in terms of *groups* (moieties or lineages) rather than *processes* of social reproduction through time. Various forms of dualism (kinship based and otherwise) for organizing social life are globally pervasive (e.g., Maybury-Lewis and Almagor 1989). And as a principle in Native American worldviews, symbolic arrangements of space, ritual practices, and social forms, dualism is thoroughly pervasive (e.g., Lévi-Strauss 1963, 1995). Social-structural *pluralism*, however, seems harder to grasp archaeologically. Does each Pueblo Bonito kiva and adjacent rectangular room-set represent a Prudden-unit component, all of which were somehow inexplicably welded together into a complex? This seems doubtful: the aggregation is too cohesive, the architectural arrangement too regular, at least in the later phases of occupation. Did Pueblo Bonito have named clans, clan-sets, ritual sodalities, or moieties, which are reflected in its architecture? It seems very likely they did.

Pueblo Bonito and Wijiji thus bookend my primary question, which concerns underlying social structural dualism and pluralism at Chaco Canyon specifically, and in the Puebloan Southwest more generally. My use of these examples is suggestive only: I approach the question not as an archaeologist analyzing sites directly but rather as a sociocultural anthropologist noticing general contrasts of architectural form and inferring likely social associations attested in the global ethnographic record (for a more directly investigative approach to kinship and Southwestern archaeology, see Ensor 2013). Obviously, there are implications beyond the San Juan Basin, and imagining these two as a contrastive pair does not exhaust the possibilities. But what we do (or at least did— see below) know from more than a century of ethnological research is that *kinship* provided the "idiom" and the structures for social organization and reproduction in all societies prior to (and in many cases after) the development of full-fledged stratification. Structurally, some key kinship-system types represent markedly dual and plural forms, and the latter especially seem to occupy a cusp of sociopolitical complexity.

Kinship Desuetude

> Kinship is dead. Long live kinship.
> —James D. Faubion (1996)

With a classic case of paradigm fatigue, in the 1980s ethnologists threw out the baby with the bathwater. The immediate catalyst was David Schneider's critique (1984), which, in keeping with other skeptical claims about universalism during that period, targeted anthropological study of kinship as culturally biased, built on European folk theories. The critique opened a useful path for new ways of thinking about relatedness, including emphases on the "house," on the body, and on ideas of shared substance (e.g., Carsten and Hugh-Jones 1995; Franklin and McKinnon 2000; McKinnon and Cannell 2013). But it also precipitated the abandonment of some of the most rigorous methodological and analytical approaches anthropology had developed over more than a century. The abandonment is perhaps most visible in graduate departments, few of which continue to teach this previously core aspect of the discipline. Yet kinship, or under some other name like relatedness, is a protean human concern, simultaneously (ethno-)biological and social, synchronic and diachronic, structural and agentive—the perhaps primary ontological frame of existence and experience in all cultures from birth on. It is for such reasons that kinship never truly died, and it is currently in the midst of a renaissance (e.g., Allen et al. 2008; Barry 2008; Godelier 2012; Héran 2009; Jones and Milicic 2011; Kronenfeld 2009; Trautmann and Whiteley, ed. 2012).

Whether, and if so to what extent, the renaissance will engage archaeologists remains to be seen (for some promising signs, see Ensor 2013 and Ware 2014). However, prior attempts to model kinship structures to Ancestral Pueblo sites were greeted with much skepticism (Sebastian 1992:3). Use of contemporary Pueblo social systems as a source of "ethnographic analogy" was dismissed, from doubt that, after four centuries of colonization, the modern Pueblos truly represented comparable forms to the societies of a thousand years ago. That doubt is justifiable, but the fact remains that there are significant continuities, in material practice, architectural forms, economy, and symbolism: multistory house complexes, kivas, prayer sticks, floodplain and irrigation agriculture, and ceramic and basketry techniques, among other things, show that the modern Pueblos represent *ethnological homologies* with Chaco Canyon, rather than ethnographic analogies (see below).

Even at the height of kinship theory's popularity in archaeology, in the 1960s, archaeological applications mostly derived from Eggan's (1950) influential "descent-theory" analysis of Pueblo social organization. This explicitly structural-functionalist model emphasized corporate matrilineal descent groups, and it was such groups, with their putative joint estates in land and resources, which archaeologists sought to locate in the material record (Longacre 1970; and see Judge and Cordell 2006; Mills 2002; Peregrine 2001; Ware 2014). Structural-functionalism's main shortcoming was its inability to model diachrony, or to identify possible processes of change. On the other hand, "alliance theory" (e.g., Lévi-Strauss 1969 [1949])—representing an opposing view to "descent theory" (Eggan 1950)—was directly concerned with social reproduction and social networks over time, yet largely went unused. Longacre's landmark *Reconstructing Prehistoric Pueblo Societies* (1970), for example, includes not one single reference to Lévi-Strauss's theory, despite its prominence in concurrent social anthropology.

Kinship: Basic Premises

I have already thrown out a few words of kinship jargon, and in view of the recent diminution of awareness, it may be well to summarize a few general points. Kinship systems comprise four intersecting axes: terminology, descent, marriage, and residence.

Terminology. Worldwide only a limited number of basic types are generally recognized, named for the societies where they were originally described: Iroquois, Hawaiian, Eskimo, Sudanese, Crow, and Omaha are the core six. "Eskimo" and "Sudanese" are "descriptive" systems in Morgan's (1871) sense: specific relationships require describing via links among primary kin-types (e.g., "Joe is my cousin because he is my *father's sister's son*"). In contrast, the other systems are "classificatory" (per Morgan), "extending" the same kinship terms, as categorical *classes*, from primary relatives to all members of society (at Hopi, for example, one calls many people "father," "mother," "nephew," "niece," etc., according to one's position within a clan system; if my actual father is Bear clan, all males of the Bear clan, no matter how old, are "father" to me). Figure 10.6 shows the diagnostic differences among kinship systems, for simplicity using a male speaker's classification of female siblings and cousins (the structure is a mirror image if the genders are reversed). In the "Eskimo" system (the standard American and European pattern), Ego distinguishes "sister" from "cousin," all of whom are grouped together with the same term (indeed, without a gender marker). In an "Iroquois" system, by contrast, Ego calls "sister" both his own female siblings and his parallel cousins (cousins via a same-sex link: *father's brother's* daughter [FBD], or *mother's sister's* daughter [MZD]). The Iroquois "cousin" term is reserved only for cross-cousins (i.e., related by a cross-sex link: *father's sister's* daughter [FZD] or *mother's brother's* daughter [MBD]). In the "Sudanese" system, each of Ego-male's female relatives gets a different term. The "Hawaiian," or "generational," system is the opposite: all get the same term.

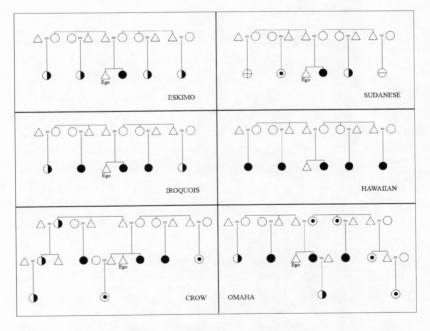

Figure 10.6. Sister-cousin classifications, Ego-male. (After Driver and Massey 1957:diag. 12)

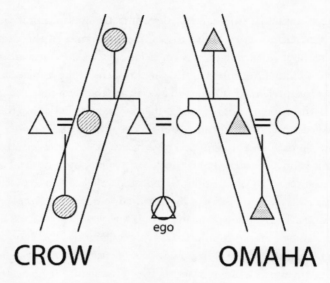

Figure 10.7. Basal sex of Crow and Omaha skewing equations: Crow: female (FZD=FZ=FM); Omaha: male (MBS=MB=MF).

The distinction of parallel from cross relatives—Morgan's (1871) revolutionary discovery—has come to be indexed as "crossness." Crossness marks other systems as well as Iroquois (Crow, Omaha, Dravidian, and Cheyenne—see below). "Crow" and "Omaha" share some basic groupings with Iroquois (Figure 10.6), but add inter-generational "skewing": one cross-cousin (FZD for Crow, MBD for Omaha) is distinguished from the other and grouped with relatives in generations both above and below. Omaha skews down the opposite line. As mirror images, Crow and Omaha are often treated as a pair, dubbed "Crow-Omaha" (Figure 10.7).

To the standard six types, two more have been definitively added: Dravidian and Cheyenne (for others see, for example, Viveiros de Castro 1998). Lounsbury (1964) importantly divided "Dravidian" from "Iroquois" proper,* noting that in addition to distinguishing cross from parallel cousins, Dravidian specifies the former as spouses or in-laws (i.e., the term for cross-cousin simultaneously *means* "spouse"

---

*Note that "Iroquois" in this context refers to the terminology type, not to the Iroquois people themselves.

or "sibling-in-law" in the languages of societies with a Dravidian system). "Cheyenne" looks like the Hawaiian system in Ego's generation, where all cross, parallel, and sibling distinctions are "neutralized." But unlike Hawaiian, Cheyenne retains a distinction between cross and parallel relatives in the generations above and below Ego (F=FB≠MB; M=MZ≠FZ, etc.). This suggests the underlying form of a Cheyenne system is Iroquois; the former probably evolved from the latter over time, losing the cross-parallel distinction in Ego's generation (I here follow Allen's model [e.g., 1989] of progressive loss of "primordial" kinship equations). Of particular interest in the present context are those systems that share the distinctive feature of crossness: Iroquois, Dravidian, Crow-Omaha, and Cheyenne.

Descent. Kinship-based social systems typically designate a primary mechanism for reckoning descent and "affiliating" children accordingly. The principal types are (1) patrilineal, where children of both sexes acquire their primary roles, rights, and duties from their father, who in turn received them from his father; (2) matrilineal, where they acquire their primary roles, rights, and duties from their mother, who in turn received them from her mother; and (3) bilateral, where they acquire primary roles, rights, and duties from both sides of the family, without diagnostic distinctions. Descent does not equate directly with a type of kinship terminology (there are patrilineal Iroquois systems, like the Dakota, and matrilineal ones, like the Seneca and other true Iroquois). However, typically there are close correspondences between Crow-type terminology and matrilineal descent and between Omaha-type terminology and patrilineal descent. Hopi, Zuni, and the Western Keresans—the foundation of Eggan's (1950) conclusions about Pueblo kinship—have Crow terminology and matrilineal descent. Moreover, Fox (1967) suggested the Eastern Keresan system was incipiently Crow.

   In the structural-functionalist model, descent is the organizing principle for corporate social groups, notably "unilineal descent groups"—as for the Nuer and Tallensi (both patrilineal), Trobriands (matrilineal), and other famous cases from the ethnographic record. Such corporate groups were treated as the fundamental frame for political, economic, ritual, and all other social action in the types of society in question: in short, they form the core operational structure in small-scale societies. Valuable as that view proved for identifying some types of synchronic structures, it failed to show how these move through time and space, in short, how a social system reproduces itself from one generation to the next, how it creates networks beyond its immediate setting, and how it may transform.

Marriage. Marriage is the most fundamental form of exchange between human social groups; as such, it is an intrinsically transitive process, the pivot of social and biological reproduction. All or almost all societies have institutionalized marriage practices. Lévi-Strauss (1969 [1949]) showed that in non-state societies, marriages provided the major structural mechanism of alliances produced by intergroup exchange, a key to their operation through time. Marriage, as Viveiros de Castro (1998:368) has put it for Amazonian societies, has a consistently "strategic character." Kin terminologies categorize people into those whom one may and may not marry: with rare exceptions, a person one calls "sibling" is not marriageable; a "cross-cousin" conversely is very often a preferred or prescribed marriage partner, even in societies lacking the direct Dravidian equation. Marriage rules and terminology are thus indissociable; *crossness* is especially marked in this regard (Viveiros de Castro 1998).

Lévi-Strauss (1969 [1949]) postulated two great worldwide structures of "alliance"—referring in the first place to marriage itself, but more broadly to the ties marriages create between social groups and their effect on political and economic structures. "Elementary" structures, he argued, operate by a positive marriage rule, *prescribing* which category of person one must marry (i.e., typically a "cross-cousin"). "Complex" structures (as in Western society) have only a negative rule, *proscribing* close kin, but otherwise indifferent as to marriage partners. Elementary structures showed a dualistic pattern often reflective of a social system organized by moieties (Figure 10.8): Moiety A gives its people as spouses to Moiety B, which reciprocates (A↔B). Such "symmetric-prescriptive" elementary structures dovetail with Dravidian-type terminology and, though less rigidly, also with Iroquois. Inasmuch as, in Ego's generation, all people in society are divided into "siblings" and "cross-cousins," a Dravidian system prescribes marriage with the cross-cousin category, producing a dual pattern of symmetrical exchange that is easily repeated from generation to generation. In one's own generation, those in one's

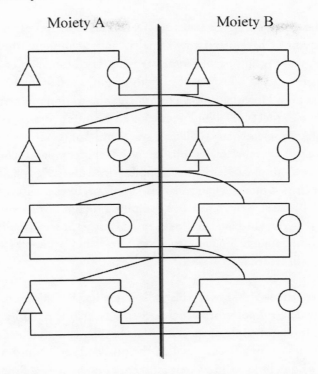

Figure 10.8. Symmetric elementary alliance: sibling-exchange cross-cousin marriage, shown with patrilineal moieties.

moiety are all one's siblings and parallel cousins; those in the opposite moiety are one's cross-cousins, from among whom one must marry.

A permutation of elementary alliance, "asymmetric-prescriptive," involves a minimum of three exchanging groups (e.g., the Kachin of Highland Burma). Unlike symmetric systems, where both sexes are exchanged between two groups (A↔B), asymmetric-prescriptive alliance introduces a "directionality" of gender: men of Group A marry women of Group B, men of Group B marry women of Group C, and men of Group C marry women of Group A (for men: A→B→C→A; for women: C→B→A→C). Reciprocal exchange flows "indirectly": Group C is responsible for "reciprocating" Group A's transaction with Group B. Such systems are thus marked by "indirect" or "generalized" exchange.

Alliance structures, combining both kin terminology and marriage rules, are now again thought of as subject to evolution (e.g., Allen et al.

2008; Godelier 2012). Crossness of Dravidian type appears to underlie Iroquois, Cheyenne, Crow-Omaha, and asymmetric-prescriptive
systems, and evolutionarily to *precede* them (e.g., Godelier et al. 1998;
Trautmann and Whiteley 2012). In this light, Crow-Omaha is twice
removed from Dravidian—via a transformation to Iroquois first (Trautmann and Barnes 1998)—and represents an evolutionary step to another
kind of (non-elementary) alliance structure. For Lévi-Strauss (1966,
1969 [1949]), Crow-Omaha alliance was "semi-complex," combining
aspects of both elementary and complex structures (Héritier 1981; see
below). Crow-Omaha alliance has also been specified as similarly intermediate between elementary and complex structures as "house societies" are between kin-based and class-based systems of social organization
(Carsten and Hugh-Jones 1995:10; see also Whiteley 2008:42–43), to
which I will return later.

Residence. The fourth axis of kinship is residence. Kinship systems usually provide a rule of postmarital residence, which is typically concor-
dant with the principle of descent. Matrilineal systems are usually also
"matrilocal" or "uxorilocal," that is, the husband moves into his wife's
mother's household or into a new adjacent household established by his
wife (likewise patrilineal systems: typically "patrilocal" or "virilocal").

In concert, the four axes show how powerful the kinship system is
overall for the structuring of a social system of small or middle scale,
especially. Kinship systems are often the central articulators of political
and economic institutions, as well as of biological reproduction. Until
kinship's desuetude, it was generally accepted that kinship systems are
the principal mechanism for organizing all human societies (simplisti-
cally termed "bands," "tribes," and "chiefdoms") until the appearance
of the state (organized, conversely, by a market economy, occupational
specialization, class stratification, etc.). Ethnographically, kinship systems have been shown to be relatively stable structures through time
(Jones 2003). Moreover, a century and a half of ethnography has shown
that kinship as an "idiom" or scheme for conceptualizing social relations
is pervasive in the vast majority of human societies.

Whether evolutionary transformations among kinship systems are
reversible has been a major question recently (e.g., Godelier 2012; Godelier et al. 1998). Kinship *terminologies* do not correlate consistently with

sociopolitical forms and economic adaptations: "Eskimo" systems—uniting remotely dispersed Inuit foragers with contemporary Western states—are the prime example. Yet, as Godelier (1998:397) emphasizes, "all the terminologies now known represent different configurations stabilized at various points along different lines of evolution."* If there are systematic relationships among kinship-system types with different "levels of sociocultural integration" (in Steward's [e.g., 1951] terms), this has definite implications for investigating apparently more and apparently less complex archaeological structures.

It seems highly likely that the kinship factors enumerated above were just as important at Chaco Canyon as among societies of small and middle scale anywhere else. Chacoan people surely framed their relationships, their structures of exchange, and both the continuity and transformations of their social orders through time via structures that united and divided them as "kin" and "affines" and provided associated categories and rules for descent, marriage, and residence. Political solidarity among great and small houses was very likely structured and reproduced through marriage-exchange, both within and among the different components comprising the Chacoan sphere, as it evolved through a series of historical phases.

Pluralism and the Middle Range

I have highlighted Chacoan architecture that exhibits marked dual and plural configurations. It is no coincidence, in my view, that Dravidian, Iroquois, and Crow-Omaha exhibit similar structures in the field of social relations. Unlike Dravidian and Iroquois, which align well with dualist types, Crow-Omaha systems are characteristically plural in their social effects, correlating with house societies in important respects. As "semi-complex," Crow-Omaha systems combine elementary (positive) and complex (negative) marriage rules, without the predictable exchange patterns represented by elementary systems. Instead, Crow-Omaha systems create more intricate networks of marriage alliance,

---

* Evolutionary analyses of kinship systems begin with Morgan (1871). Others notably include Allen 1989; Allen et al. 2008; Dole 1972; Fox 1994; Hage 1999; Kryukov 1968, 1998; Lane and Lane 1959; Murdock 1949; Service 1960; and White 1939.

opening out and dispersing ties within a more variegated social field (Lévi-Strauss 1966, 1969 [1949]; McKinley 1971).

Lévi-Strauss's later-developed "house" model (i.e., *sociétés à maison*, "house societies" [especially, Lévi-Strauss 1982]) has proven very effective for the reanalysis of Chacoan social organization (Heitman 2011; Heitman and Plog 2005; Heitman, this volume). The essential difference between "house" and kinship system, in my view, is that between organization and structure, in the sense developed especially by Raymond Firth (e.g., 1961). A system's practical realization in time and space may be distinguished from its underlying structural principles. In his analysis of alliance, as in most of the rest of his work, underlying structures were Lévi-Strauss's abiding interest. In that regard, his house model represents something of a departure. While there is not always a one-to-one correspondence of Crow-Omaha kinship systems with house societies, in the Americas at least there are strong correlations. On the Northwest Coast, the ethnographic origin for Lévi-Strauss's concept of the "house" (Lévi-Strauss 1982), house societies either co-occur with Crow-matrilineal systems (e.g., Haida, Tlingit) or are their close geographic neighbors who participate in shared exchange networks and exhibit many similar cultural features (e.g., Kwakwaka'wakw, Coast Salish). The powerful nineteenth-century Haida and Tlingit great houses combined institutionalized hierarchy, matrilineal descent, matrilocal residence, Crow terminology, and exogamous clans grouped into moieties. Similarly, among Amazonian Gê social systems, another source of useful analogues for the Puebloan Southwest, house societies co-occur with semi-complex alliance, moieties, and Crow-Omaha terminology (Coelho de Souza 2012; Lea 1995).

In Hopi society—an exemplar of semi-complex alliance for Lévi-Strauss (1969 [1949]) and heuristically susceptible to a house model (Whiteley 2008)—marriages are determined by matrilineal clans and their larger groupings into clan-sets (my preferred term for "phratries" in much of the literature). Marriage is formally proscribed within one's own set, one's father's set, and one's mother's father's set. In 1906, Orayvi's ca. 28 Crow-matrilineal clans were grouped into nine exogamous sets (Table 10.1). Thus, if I (male) am Bear clan, my father Greasewood clan, and my mother's father Badger clan, the three sets including these clans are all prohibited to me: my spouse must belong to one of the

Table 10.1. Orayvi Clans and Clan-Sets in 1900.

Set	*ngyam* ("clan")	Trans.	Set	*ngyam* ("clan")	Trans.
I	*Tap-*	Rabbit	VI	*Mas-*	Maasaw
	Katsin-	Katsina		*Kookop-*	"Fire"
	Kyar-	Parrot		*Hoo-*	Cedar
	Angwus-	Crow		*Lee-*	Millet
				Is-	Coyote
II	*Hon-*	Bear		*Paa'is-*	Desert Fox
	Kookyang-	Spider			
			VII	*Honan-*	Badger
III	*Tuwa-*	Sand		*Polii-*	Butterfly
	Tsu'-	Snake			
	Kuukuts-	Lizard	VIII	*Piikyas-*	Young Corn
				Patki-	"Water"
IV	*Tawa-*	Sun		*Siva'p-*	Rabbitbrush
	Kwaa-	Eagle			
			IX	*Kyel-*	Sparrowhawk
V	*Tep-*	Greasewood		*Atok-*	Crane
	Paaqap-	Reed		*Pat-*	Squash
	Awat-	Bow			

other six sets. And unlike an elementary system, Hopi marriage rules are recalibrated with each generation. To continue the example, for my children, the Bear clan remains unmarriageable (as their father's clan), but the ban on marriage with Greasewood and Badger ceases (as their FF's and FMF's clans—two non-prohibited classes). If my wife is Eagle, my children are, too, so the Eagle set becomes off-limits for them, and their mother's father's clan-set (let us say Parrot) is also. My siblings—who share the same prohibitions as me—will produce different arrays of prohibitions for *their* children, depending on whom they marry. The effect of these rules, constantly creating, re-creating, and interweaving ties among the nine clan-sets is a pluralistic pattern of dispersed, "semi-complex" alliances.

Especially given the physical proximity of contemporary great houses in downtown Chaco, it seems unlikely that each one—if indeed it was a residential unit—was endogamous and more likely that its marriage practices embraced a larger social field linking sites to one another in groups. But as a social field comprising plural sites, and as also—in the case of Pueblo Bonito—internally differentiated into plural elements, it seems most probable that marriage exchange followed a plural, semi-complex pattern rather than an elementary one. Further, if this thesis is correct, there may well have been similar exchanges between downtown and peripheral houses (both great and small), as the axis of articulation for a (historically evolving) network based on dispersed alliances.

Crow-Omaha systems in North America have been shown to involve an "opening out" of affinal ties beyond Dravidian and Iroquois systems (Ives 1998; Trautmann and Barnes 1998; Wheeler et al. 2012). These systems (see also Whiteley 2012) consistently correlate with higher population densities, richer resources, and generally more sedentary societal adaptations. Socio-geographically, Crow-Omaha systems are strikingly associated with the areas of most developed political complexity in late prehistoric North America: the Mississippian Southeast (Creek, Choctaw, Chickasaw, Cherokee, Timucua [e.g., Ensor 2002]) and the Midwest (Potawatomi, Illinois, Fox, Osage, etc.). Elsewhere, these systems coincide with high population density, sedentism, hierarchy, or a mixture of all three (Haida and Tlingit). In California, they occur amid the densest populations of aboriginal North America (Ubelaker 2006). In the Plains, with the lone exception of the Crow proper (who had only recently located to the High Plains and adopted bison hunting as their chief adaptation), all Crow-Omaha cases occur in the Prairie-Plains river valleys, areas of sedentary agriculture. Indeed, here, too, homologous ties have been suggested between the Omaha proper and Cahokia, the great Mississippian site at the confluence of the Mississippi and Missouri rivers (e.g., Hall 2004). In aboriginal Australia, the few known cases of Omaha terminology (no Crow) again consistently correlate with relatively higher population densities and richer resources (McConvell 2012; McConvell and Alpher 2002).

There are no known instances of states with Crow or Omaha kinship systems. With the Australian and a few other exceptions, the great majority of cases occur in the middle range of sociocultural complexity. Moreover, the Australian Omaha cases all occur in the context of "downstream" territorial expansion (McConvell 2012; McConvell and Alpher 2002). This may give a clue about Crow types elsewhere. As mirror images, Crow and Omaha cases in North America, Amazonia, and Africa often exist in close geographic proximity, including among closely related peoples of the same language family: for example, among Siouan speakers, the Omaha proper lived close by the Mandan and Hidatsa (Crow systems). This suggests Crow and Omaha systems represent opposite social strategies. If Omaha systems represent an expansionist or outward posture, as their counterpart, Crow systems should be centripetal, attracting people and resources inward.

Among the historically known Pueblos, this orientation seems apposite. Movement in toward a central place was a fact of fourteenth-century Pueblo life and also intermittently at earlier moments. This is clear for the Hopi area ca. A.D. 1300 and is directly echoed in Hopi clan migration narratives and ritual pilgrimages: the narratives always depict final movement *from* the periphery *toward* Tuuwanasavi, the earth-center place, where the present Hopi towns stand. Ortiz (1972) emphasizes that the pattern of centripetalism—gathering symbolic and material resources from the periphery and bringing them into the village center—is the distinctive form in all Pueblo ritual (in contrast, for example, to Navajo). Centripetal territorial concentration, especially in terms of the delivery of outlying products to the downtown center, is also consistently represented in archaeological reconstructions of the relations between the Chaco center and its outliers (e.g., Lekson 2006).

Orayvi, too, was a central place, that for its inhabitants was a capital ("the Jerusalem of the Hopis," as one of my informants put it) to which people residing seasonally in field houses or year-round in colony settlements (e.g., Mùnqapi) return, bringing resources with them. This remains strongly marked in the division of distant territories into clan-owned properties—notably for gathering ritual resources—according to the specific ruins associated with each clan's migrations (like Wupatki, Homol'ovi, Nuvakwewtaqa, Keet Seel, Betatakin, and many others). As an architectural expression of multiple in-migrating clans interwoven at the center by semi-complex alliance, Orayvi's pattern of plural kivas and correlated clanhouses (Figure 10.3) would be hard to improve on. In more compressed and regular form, later Pueblo Bonito may represent a similar pattern. What then of the more dualist cases and their relationship to the Crow type?

Dualism and the Crow-Omaha Transition

In Amazonia, Australia, and North America, Crow-Omaha systems typically occur in geographic proximity to Iroquois systems. In general, evolutionary models identify early human kinship systems as closest in form to a Dravidian type (e.g., Allen et al. 2008). Subsequently, the terminological equation of cross-cousins with affines (Allen 1989) was lost, resulting in a transformation to Iroquois type. Recent comparative analysis of Crow and Omaha systems shows their basis also to lie in the same underlying crossness as Dravidian and Iroquois (Trautmann and Whiteley 2012). Alternate realizations of Crow, Omaha, and Iroquois features among closely related societies thus appear as strategic alternatives. This pattern is especially marked in eastern Amazonia (Coelho de Souza 2012; DaMatta 1982; Turner 1979), the locus classicus of South American Crow-Omaha systems and, not coincidentally, in my view, of large-scale horticulture and "urbanized" chiefdoms in late prehistoric and early historic times (Roosevelt 1993).

Among the Amazonian Gê cases, dualism of Dravidian style is evidenced by moieties based on *descent and/or ritual*, and plural alliance structures may co-exist with patterns of dualism centered in cognatic households (Coelho de Souza 2012). In this context Crow-Omaha and Iroquois are "social technologies" (Godelier 2012), that is, strategically mobilized in agentive processes to procure certain social outcomes (Trautmann and Whiteley 2012). A "full-fledged" Crow or Omaha system only occurs when these social technologies are coordinate with the systematic, strategic production of marriage alliances. Crow and Omaha systems are thus evolved variations on an Iroquois (and ultimately, Dravidian) base.

Both the Amazonian variations and the social technology perspective are extraordinarily resonant with Fox's sense (Fox 1967) of the Keresan Pueblo social system and its relation to the Western Pueblo type (below). The possibility of adaptive oscillation between Dravidian-Iroquois dualism and Crow-Omaha pluralism in alliance structures is a key feature of these arguments. This, it seems to me, is isomorphous with the architectural patterns of dualism and pluralism suggested by Chaco settlement architecture.

Pueblo Homologies

The Amazonian cases provide useful "ethnographic analogies" to the Puebloan Southwest, both prehistorically and more recently. But as noted above, the modern Pueblos themselves are in important respects homologous continuations from Chaco, not analogous metaphors lacking in common derivation. Correlating historic and contemporary Pueblo models with prehistoric Puebloan societies should thus be reconceived for what it is: not ethnographic analogy but *ethnological homology*.

Modern Pueblo systems exhibit various intersecting patterns of duality and plurality, but—and this has been a key problem for analysis of inter-Pueblo similarities—overt dualism is not clearly associated with exogamy. Fox (1967) contested Eggan's (1950) view that Eastern Pueblo social organization had shifted toward an Eskimo-bilateral pattern out of colonial influence and instead suggested the Keresans represented an autonomous, double-descent form (i.e., both Omaha-patrilineal and Crow-matrilineal, associated with moieties, on the one hand, and clans, on the other) that had developed from an Iroquois, and even Dravidian, proto-form. Fox showed that Keresan kin-term usage included both Crow and generational (i.e., Cheyenne) terminology and posited that, instead of declining from a Crow type, Keresan social structure was incipiently Crow-matrilineal; further, the patri-moieties, he claimed, were once exogamous, with prescriptive cross-cousin marriage. Fox suggested that intersecting patrilineal and matrilineal descent lines and a symmetric rule of exchange could be generalized for all Crow systems.

Orayvi's marriage practices show both dispersed alliances—in which all the nine clan-sets are intermarried—together with a simultaneous tendency to prefer classificatory cross-cousin marriage, resulting in repeating alliances between pairs of clan-sets over the generations (Whiteley 2012). Notwithstanding Lévi-Strauss's characterization of semi-complex marriage rules, in actual marriage practices, the Orayvi pattern corresponds exactly with those shown by other detailed studies of Crow-Omaha cases (Héritier 1981). And it directly reflects the tension of opposing forces McKinley (1971) has identified for these systems in general: that they seek, in contradictory fashion, both to expand on and retain their existing alliances at the same time.

The same alliance pattern noted for Orayvi occurs also at Zuni and Laguna—other exemplar cases of Western Pueblo social organization for Eggan—where Parsons (1932:384) identifies a preference for (classificatory) cross-cousin marriage. Of great interest in this regard is her report of the Laguna perspective that cross-cousin and affine terms are conceptualized as equivalent (i.e., Dravidian). Parsons (1932:79) certainly regarded all Pueblo kin terminologies (even at Taos and among the northern Tewa) as marked by elements of crossness (e.g., Parsons 1924).* In short, I agree with Eggan that the Eastern Pueblos lost kinship patterns under colonial pressure, but I think these patterns were likely only full-fledged Crow under certain adaptive conditions and otherwise would have oscillated between a Crow-plural and Iroquois-dual form.† What this means in practice is that Eastern and Western Pueblo social structures are far less divergent than the conventional wisdom has allowed and are more alternate strategic realizations of the same underlying kinship technologies, as among the Amazonian Gê. In that regard, the dual-kiva system of the Rio Grande Keresans and Tewa may be read as approximating a social system with Iroquois crossness, which became neutralized in kin terminology but preserved in ritual and political institutions (Ware 2014). This brings us back to Chaco and the Pueblo Bonito–Wijiji contrast.

Pueblo Dualism ↔ Pluralism

The interrelated Dravidian-Iroquois-Crow possibilities seem to be a deep-structure model hard-wired in Pueblo social thought. It was this model, I suggest, that articulated the production of variant social

---

*My full argument here goes beyond the present scope; I am developing it in another context (e.g., Whiteley 2014).

†Moieties and pseudo-moieties can form by aggregation, of course, an argument preferred by some Southwestern archaeologists (e.g., Fowles 2005; Lowell 1996). But if reproduced from one generation to the next by marriage, and operative within a kinship idiom, they would gravitate to the same Dravidian-Iroquois form as if produced autogenously.

forms with their architectural corollaries at Chaco. As systems developed and diversified their alliance structures, especially in association with hierarchical patterns of sociopolitical complexity, they adopted a full-fledged Crow semi-complex form, often correlative with a house society pattern of practical social organization (again, following Firth's sense of organization vs. structure here). Before that stage was reached, a more Iroquois or even Dravidian model was the likely form, going back into Basketmaker times and, if Allen's tetradic model of original human kinship (e.g., Allen 1989) is correct, much earlier. That underlying Dravidianate-style dualism retained echoes even after a transition to Crow pluralism, and the "house" is suggested by later Pueblo Bonito bifurcation. More than this, however, Wijiji suggests the evolutionary transition was *not* irreversible.

Wijiji is a late Chacoan house and was only occupied for a generation or so. Pueblo Bonito, by contrast, developed over several hundred years. New Hopi villages initially exhibit significant dualism (see e.g., Whiteley 2008:117), either in terms of their foundation by paired clans linked by marriage alliance (Mùnqapi, Supawlavi) and/or ritually organized by single or dual kivas (Paaqavi, Sitsom'ovi, Supawlavi, Kiqötsmovi). Supawlavi, on Second Mesa, is a prime case in this regard, founded as a colony of Songòopavi in the eighteenth century, by the intermarried Bear and Sun Forehead clans. At least since the early twentieth century, Supawlavi has also married with Musangnuvi and with its mother village, Songòopavi, but had it not done so, the two-clan system would have made "reversion" to a moiety-type pattern of cross-cousin marriage a likely outcome. At first, Supawlavi built two kivas—as did Sitsom'ovi after its founding (from its mother village, Walpi) in the eighteenth century and as did Paaqavi in the early years after its founding (from *its* mother village, Orayvi) in 1909 (a third was added later). Sitsom'ovi and Paaqavi were not "two-clan" populations, although there are some clear elements of clan dualism in Orayvi's social structure that were replicated in the constitution of the daughter villages (Whiteley 2008:828–829). Mùnqapi and Kiqötsmovi followed a similar pattern in the construction of dual kivas to Paaqavi, building first one community kiva, followed shortly thereafter by a second, and then quite a bit later, by a third. All three reflect dualist variations of the type described (for alliance structures) by Lévi-Strauss.

If Wijiji was the colony of a larger, plurally organized mother town (like Pueblo Bonito, Pueblo del Arroyo, or Chetro Ketl), the same type of transition, in a different but related architectural modality, may be recognized. Plural Orayvi gave rise to two-kiva Paaqavi and (originally) two-clan Mùnqapi; plural Songòopavi birthed two-clan and two-kiva Supawlavi; plural Walpi gave rise to two-kiva Sitsom'ovi. Had Chaco remained occupied and expanded, we might predict that Wijiji's dual pattern would have expanded by the inclusion of other social units and transformed into a Crow–plural type structure, with more dispersed alliance linking settlements to each other and, as shown at Pueblo Bonito, a multiple kiva system that echoed the multiple origins of alliance partners. But the population would have always retained the structural capacity, in the social technology of the Crow-Iroquois tension, to revert to a simpler alliance structure, based on symmetrical dualism, as historical circumstances dictated.

Conclusion

There is every reason to assume—since they were not states—that Ancestral Pueblo social systems, including the most highly developed versions at Chaco Canyon, were articulated through principles and rules of kinship. Pueblo Bonito, especially in its kiva pluralism, looks like a Crow-Omaha semi-complex system, and the inference—strengthened by the plausible arguments of Vivian (1970, 1990) and Peregrine (2001) for matrilineality and matrilocality—seems more likely that it is Crow. All those goods brought from the periphery to the center would suggest that *people,* too, were a primary subject of alliances (in marriage) in these social transactions. Wijiji by contrast looks like a dual-moiety system, either of the Hopi colony type, or one more directly based in a system of symmetrical exchange reflected in Eastern Keresan and Tewa moiety kivas, or perhaps both.

It seems likely that emergent sociopolitical complexity of the "house" type at Chaco was built on a semi-complex kinship system of Crow form and its capacity, as a social technology, to develop dispersed alliances both within the immediate social environment and throughout the Chacoan system as a whole. The overall system, insofar as it was solidary, was in all probability constituted by marriage alliance, among both great and small houses. For a time at least, formation of new colonies could successfully deploy oscillating dual-plural modalities to maintain and extend social networks. A Dravidianate system, I infer, goes far back into the Puebloan past, from which Iroquois and Crow-Omaha forms crystallized and/or receded under historical forces of an environmental, demographic, or social nature, or all three. I infer that Rio Grande moiety systems evolved from kinship moieties (Ware 2014), particularly since *crossness* seems to underlie even the most bilateral Rio Grande kin terminologies.

Our ability to model Chacoan social structure and organization will always be limited by the nature of the evidence. But Pueblo ethnological homologies and apposite ethnographic analogies can help develop genuinely useful hypotheses coordinate with the global anthropological record. While perhaps not testable in the strict sense, these offer the possibility of more comprehensive explanation than hitherto generated. What we can say with certainty is that kinship and its structural articulation of alliance patterns in non-state societies provide crucial concepts to decode the arrangement of social space among the people who lived, moved, and had their being at Chacoan houses, great and small.

References Cited

Allen, Nicholas J. 1989. The Evolution of Kinship Terminologies. *Lingua* 77:173–185.
Allen, Nicholas J., Hilary Callan, Robin Dunbar, and Wendy James (editors). 2008. *Early Human Kinship: From Sex to Social Reproduction*. Blackwell Publishing, Malden, Massachusetts.
Barry, Laurent S. 2008. *La parenté*. Gallimard, Paris.
Bernardini, Wesley. 1999. Reassessing the Scale of Social Action at Pueblo Bonito, Chaco Canyon, New Mexico. *Kiva* 64:447–470.
Carsten, Janet, and Stephen Hugh-Jones (editors). 1995. *About the House: Lévi-Strauss and Beyond*. Cambridge University Press, New York.
Coelho de Souza, Marcela. 2012. The Making and Unmaking of "Crow/Omaha" Kinship in Central Brazil(ian Ethnology). In *Crow-Omaha: New Light on a Classic Problem of Kinship Analysis*, edited by Thomas R. Trautmann and Peter M. Whiteley, pp. 205–222. University of Arizona Press, Tucson.
DaMatta, Roberto. 1982. *A Divided World*. Translated by A. Campbell. Harvard University Press, Cambridge, Massachusetts.
Dole, Gertrude E. 1972. Developmental Sequences of Kinship Patterns. In *Kinship Studies in the Morgan Centennial Year*, edited by Priscilla Reining, pp. 134–166. Anthropological Society of Washington, Washington, D.C.

Driver, Harold E., and William C. Massey. 1957. Comparative Studies of North American Indians. *Transactions of the American Philosophical Society* 47(2).

Eggan, Fred R. 1950. *Social Organization of the Western Pueblos*. University of Chicago Press, Chicago.

Ensor, Bradley. 2002. Disproportionate Clan Growth in Crow-Omaha Societies: A Kinship-Demographic Model for Explaining Settlement Hierarchies and Fissioning in the Prehistoric U.S. Southeast. *North American Archaeologist* 23(4):309–337.

————. 2013. *The Archaeology of Kinship: Advancing Interpretation and Contributions to Theory*. University of Arizona Press, Tucson.

Faubion, James D. 1996. Kinship Is Dead. Long Live Kinship. *Comparative Studies in Society and History* 38:67–91.

Firth, Raymond. 1961. *Elements of Social Organization*. 3rd ed. Watts and Co., London

Fowles, Severin M. 2005. Historical Contingency and the Prehistoric Foundations of Moiety Organization among the Eastern Pueblos. *Journal of Anthropological Research* 61(1):25–52.

Fox, Robin. 1967. *The Keresan Bridge: A Problem in Pueblo Ethnology*. LSE Monographs on Social Anthropology 35. Athlone, London.

————. 1994. The Evolution of Kinship Systems and the Crow-Omaha Question. In *The Challenge of Anthropology: Old Encounters and New Excursions*, edited by Robin Fox, pp. 215–245. Transaction, New Brunswick, New Jersey.

Franklin, Sarah, and Susan McKinnon (editors). 2000. *Relative Values: Reconfiguring Kinship Studies*. Duke University Press, Durham, North Carolina.

Godelier, Maurice. 1998. Afterword: Transformations and Lines of Evolution. In *Transformations of Kinship*, edited by Maurice Godelier, Thomas Trautmann, and Franklin Tjon Sie Fat, pp. 386–413. Smithsonian Institution, Washington, D.C.

————. 2012. *The Metamorphoses of Kinship*. Verso, New York.

Godelier, Maurice, Thomas R. Trautmann, and Franklin E. Tjon Sie Fat (editors). 1998. *Transformations of Kinship*. Smithsonian Institution Press, Washington, D.C.

Hage, Per. 1999. Marking Universals and the Structure and Evolution of Kinship Terminologies: Evidence from Salish. *Journal of the Royal Anthropological Institute*, n.s., 5:423–441.

Hall, Robert L. 2004. The Cahokia Site and Its People. In *Hero, Hawk, and Open Hand: American Indian Art of the Ancient Midwest and South*, edited by Richard F. Townsend and Robert V. Sharp, pp. 92–103. Art Institute of Chicago, Chicago; Yale University Press, New Haven, Connecticut.

Heitman, Carrie C. 2011. Architectures of Inequality: Evaluating Kinship and Cosmology in Chaco Canyon, N.M., A.D. 800–1200. Ph.D. dissertation, Department of Anthropology, University of Virginia, Charlottesville.

Heitman, Carolyn C., and Stephen Plog. 2005. Kinship and the Dynamics of the House: Rediscovering Dualism in the Pueblo Past. In *A Catalyst for Ideas: Anthropological Archaeology and the Legacy of Douglas W. Schwartz*, edited by Vernon Scarborough, pp. 69–100. School of American Research Press, Santa Fe.

Héran, François. 2009. *Figures de la parenté: Une histoire critique de la raison structurale*. Presses Universitaires de France, Paris.

Héritier, Françoise. 1981. *L'exercice de la parenté*. Gallimard, Le Seuil, Paris.

Herr, Sarah A. 2001. *Beyond Chaco: Great Kiva Communities on the Mogollon Rim Frontier*. Anthropological Papers of the University of Arizona No. 66. University of Arizona Press, Tucson.

Ives, John. 1998. Developmental Processes in the Pre-Contact History of Athapaskan, Algonquian, and Numic Kin Systems. In *Transformations of Kinship*, edited by Maurice Godelier, Thomas Trautmann, and Franklin Tjon Sie Fat, pp. 94–139. Smithsonian Institution Press, Washington, D.C.

Jones, Douglas. 2003. Kinship and Deep History: Exploring Connections between Culture Areas, Genes, and Languages. *American Anthropologist* 105(3):501–514.

Jones, Douglas, and Bojka Mililcic (editors). 2011. *Per Hage and the Renaissance in Kinship Studies*. University of Utah Press, Salt Lake City.

Judge, W. James, and Linda S. Cordell. 2006. Society and Polity. In *The Archaeology of Chaco Canyon: An Eleventh-Century Pueblo Regional Center*, edited by Stephen H. Lekson, pp. 189–210. School of American Research Press, Santa Fe.

Kronenfeld, David B. 2009. *Fanti Kinship and the Analysis of Kinship Terminologies*. University of Illinois Press, Urbana.

Kryukov, Mikhail V. 1968. Historical Interpretation of Kinship Terminology. Institute of Ethnography, USSR Academy of Sciences, Moscow.

———. 1998. The Synchro-Diachronic Method and the Multidirectionality of Kinship Transformations. In *Transformations of Kinship*, edited by Maurice Goedelier, Thomas R. Trautmann, and Franklin E. Tjon Sie Fat, pp. 294–313. Smithsonian Institution Press, Washington, D.C.

Lane, Robert, and Barbara Lane. 1959. On the Development of Dakota-Iroquois and Crow-Omaha Kinship Terminologies. *Southwestern Journal of Anthropology* 15:254–265.

Lea, Vanessa. 1995. The Houses of the Mebêngôkre (Kayapó) of Central Brazil—New Door to Their Social Organization. In *About the House: Lévi-Strauss and Beyond*, edited by Janet Carsten and Stephen Hugh-Jones, pp. 206–225.Cambridge University Press, Cambridge.

Lekson, Stephen H. (editor). 2006. *The Archaeology of Chaco Canyon: An Eleventh-Century Pueblo Regional Center*. School of American Research Press, Santa Fe.

Lekson, Stephen H., Thomas C. Windes, and Peter J. McKenna. 2006. Architecture. In *The Archaeology of Chaco Canyon: An Eleventh-Century Pueblo*

Regional Center, edited by Stephen H. Lekson, pp. 67–116. School of American Research Press, Santa Fe.

Lévi-Strauss, Claude. 1963. Do Dual Organizations Exist? In *Structural Anthropology*, by Claude Lévi-Strauss, pp, 132–166. Basic Books, New York.

———. 1966. *The Future of Kinship Studies. The Huxley Memorial Lecture.* Proceedings of the Royal Anthropological Institute, pp. 13–21. Royal Anthropological Institute, London.

———. 1969 [1949]. *The Elementary Structures of Kinship* (translation of *Les structures élémentaires de la parenté*). Rev. ed. Translated by James Harle Bell and John Richard von Sturmer. Edited by Rodney Needham. Eyre & Spottiswoode, London.

———. 1982. *The Way of the Masks.* Translated by Sylvia Modelski. University of Washington Press, Seattle.

———. 1995. *The Story of Lynx.* University of Chicago Press, Chicago.

Longacre, William A. (editor). 1970. *Reconstructing Prehistoric Pueblo Societies.* University of New Mexico Press, Albuquerque.

Lounsbury, Floyd G. 1964. The Structural Analysis of Kinship Semantics. In *Proceedings of the Ninth International Congress of Linguists*, edited by Horace G. Lunt, pp. 1073–1093. Mouton, The Hague.

Lowell, Julia C. 1996. Moieties in Prehistory: A Case Study from the Pueblo Southwest. *Journal of Field Archaeology* 23:77–90.

Maybury-Lewis, David, and Uri Almagor (editors). 1989. *The Attraction of Opposites: Thought and Society in the Dualistic Mode.* University of Michigan Press, Ann Arbor.

McConvell, Patrick. 2012. Omaha Skewing in Australia: Overlays, Dynamism and Change. In *Crow-Omaha: New Light on a Classic Problem of Kinship Analysis*, edited by Thomas R. Trautmann and Peter M. Whiteley, pp. 243–260. University of Arizona Press, Tucson.

McConvell, Patrick, and Barry Alpher. 2002. The Omaha Trail in Australia: Tracking Skewing from East to West. *Anthropological Forum* 12(2):159–176.

McKinley, Robert. 1971. Why Do Crow and Omaha Kinship Terminologies Exist? A Sociology of Knowledge Interpretation. *Man*, n.s., 6(3):408–426.

McKinnon, Susan, and Fenella Cannell. 2013. *Vital Relations: Modernity and the Persistent Life of Kinship.* School for Advanced Research Press, Santa Fe.

Mills, Barbara J. 2002. Recent Research on Chaco: Changing Views on Economy, Ritual, and Society. *Journal of Archaeological Research* 10:65–117.

Morgan, Lewis Henry. 1871. *Systems of Consanguinity and Affinity of the Human Family.* Smithsonian Institution, Washington, D.C.

———. 1881. *Houses and House-Life of the American Aborigines.* Contributions to North American Ethnology Vol. 4. U.S. Government Printing Office, Washington, D.C.

Morgan, William N. 1994. *Ancient Architecture of the Southwest.* University of Texas Press, Austin.

Murdock, George Peter. 1949. *Social Structure*. Macmillan, New York.

Nabokov, Peter, and Robert Easton. 1989. *Native American Architecture*. Oxford University Press, New York.

Ortiz, Alfonso. 1972. Ritual Drama and the Pueblo World-View. In *New Perspectives on the Pueblos*, edited by Alfonso Ortiz, pp. 135–161.University of New Mexico Press, Albuquerque.

Parsons, Elsie Clews. 1924. Tewa Kin, Clan, and Moiety. *American Anthropologist* 26(3):333–339.

———. 1932. The Kinship Nomenclature of the Pueblo Indians. *American Anthropologist* 34(3):377–389.

Peregrine, Peter N. 2001. Matrilocality, Corporate Strategy, and the Organization of Production in the Chacoan World. *American Antiquity* 66(1):36–46.

Roosevelt, Anna C. 1993. The Rise and Fall of the Amazon Chiefdoms. *L'homme* 126/128:255–283.

Schneider, David M. 1984. *A Critique of the Study of Kinship*. University of Michigan Press, Ann Arbor.

Sebastian, Lynn W. 1992. *The Chaco Anasazi: Sociopolitical Evolution in the Prehistoric Southwest*. Cambridge University Press, New York.

Service, Elman R. 1960. Kinship Terminology and Evolution. *American Anthropologist* 62(5):747–763.

Steward, Julian. 1951. Levels of Sociocultural Integration: An Operational Concept. *Southwestern Journal of Anthropology* 7(4):374–390.

Trautmann, Thomas R., and Robert H. Barnes. 1998. "Dravidian," "Iroquois," and "Crow-Omaha" in North American Perspective. In *Transformations of Kinship*, edited by Maurice Godelier, Thomas Trautmann, and Franklin Tjon Sie Fat, pp. 27–58. Smithsonian Institution, Washington, D.C.

Trautmann, Thomas R., and Peter M. Whiteley. 2012. Afterword: Crow-Omaha, in Thickness and in Thin. In *Crow-Omaha: New Light on a Classic Problem of Kinship Analysis*, edited by Thomas R. Trautmann and Peter M. Whiteley, pp. 281–297. University of Arizona Press, Tucson.

Trautmann, Thomas R., and Peter M. Whiteley (editors). 2012. *Crow-Omaha: New Light on a Classic Problem of Kinship Analysis*. University of Arizona Press, Tucson.

Turner, Terence. 1979. The Gê and Bororo Societies as Dialectical Systems: A General Model. In *Dialectical Societies*, edited by David Maybury-Lewis, pp. 147–178. Harvard University Press, Cambridge, Massachusetts.

Ubelaker, Douglas H. 2006. Population Size, Contact to Nadir. In *Environment, Origins, and Population*, edited by Douglas H. Ubelaker, pp. 694–701. Handbook of North American Indians, Vol. 3, William C. Sturtevant, general editor. Smithsonian Institution, Washington, D.C.

Van Dyke, Ruth M. 2008. *The Chaco Experience: Landscape and Ideology at the Center Place*. School for Advanced Research Press, Santa Fe.

Viveiros de Castro, Eduardo B. 1998. Dravidian and Related Kinship Systems. In *Transformations of Kinship*, edited by Maurice Godelier, Thomas Trautmann, and Franklin Tjon Sie Fat, pp. 332–385. Smithsonian Institution Press, Washington, D.C.

Vivian, R. Gwinn. 1970. An Inquiry into Prehistoric Social Organization in Chaco Canyon, New Mexico. In *Reconstructing Pueblo Societies*, edited by William A. Longacre, pp. 59–83. University of New Mexico Press, Albuquerque.

————. 1990. *The Chacoan Prehistory of the San Juan Basin*. Academic Press, New York.

Ware, John A. 2014. *A Pueblo Social History: Kinship, Sodality, and Community in the Northern Southwest*. School for Advanced Research Press, Santa Fe.

Wheeler, Ward C., Peter M. Whiteley, and Theodore Powers. 2012. Phylogenetic Analysis of Socio-Cultural Data: Identifying Transformation Vectors for Kinship Systems. In *Crow-Omaha: New Light on a Classic Problem of Kinship Analysis*, edited by Thomas R. Trautmann and Peter M. Whiteley, pp. 109–131. University of Arizona Press, Tucson.

White, Leslie A. 1939. A Problem in Kinship Terminology. *American Anthropologist* 41(4):566–573.

Whiteley, Peter M. 2008. *The Orayvi Split: A Hopi Transformation*. Anthropological Papers of the American Museum of Natural History 87. American Museum of Natural History, New York.

————. 2012. Crow-Omaha Kinship in North America: A Puebloan Perspective. In *Crow-Omaha: New Light on a Classic Problem of Kinship Analysis*, edited by Thomas R. Trautmann and Peter M. Whiteley, pp. 83–108. University of Arizona Press, Tucson.

————. 2014. Tewa Crossness and Hopi Skewing: Implications for Pueblo Social Evolution. Paper presented at symposium, "The Present in the Past: Rethinking Ethnographic Analogies in Puebloan Social Formations," annual meeting of the Society for Anthropological Sciences, Albuquerque.

Windes, Thomas C. 1984. A New Look at Population in Chaco Canyon. In *Recent Research on Chaco Prehistory*, edited by W. James Judge and John D. Schelberg, pp. 75–87. Reports of the Chaco Center No. 8. Division of Cultural Research, National Park Service, Albuquerque.

11

Looking North toward Chaco with Awe and Envy . . . Mostly

Paul E. Minnis

I've never met a single person who was not fascinated by Chaco, including students, avocationalists, or even normally too-cool and bored teenagers forced on a family vacation. The widespread interest in Chaco also extends to archaeologists; there is a very substantial cohort of highly competent Chacoan scholars. For example, the recent synthesis volume on Chaco, *The Archaeology of Chaco Canyon: An Eleventh-Century Pueblo Regional Center* (Lekson 2006) cites 125 people as authors of sources directly dealing with Chaco or Chacoan outliers. A second indicator of the robust literature on Chaco is the massive bibliography contained in the Chaco Research Archive (http://www.chacoarchive.org). Chaco is of interest in and of itself, as well as being one of two most commonly discussed examples of the complexity in the U.S. Southwest or northwest Mexico (SW/NW), the other being the Hohokam (e.g., Crown and Judge 1991; Neitzel 1999).

As important, or even more important, our understanding of Chaco is not simply an academic issue. Ancestral Pueblo history, including that of Chaco, is often highlighted as a lesson about humanity that presumably helps us think about the future. The most widely read and important current example is the debate around Diamond's (2005) volume, *Collapse: How Societies Choose to Fail or Succeed*, and its detractors (e.g., McAnany and Yoffee 2009). Whether one agrees with Diamond's Ancestral Pueblo example or not (e.g., Wilcox 2009), it has been widely read beyond the narrow world of professional archaeologists. Unfortunately, the current difficulty in doing original fieldwork at Chaco seems likely to stymie a more precise evaluation of this World Heritage site and its allied archaeological traditions into the foreseeable future.

With some important exceptions, such as Arizona State University's Resilience Solutions Group, the current trend in SW/NW archaeology is not directly focused on the issues that Diamond and others address. Religion and identity are the cultural characteristic de jure for interpretation of prehispanic SW/NW. It is true that these topics had been ignored for many decades and deserve more scholarly attention than they have had in the recent past. However, religion and identity are only two aspects of culture, and they are interactive with others. Few would think that religion and identity, in and of themselves, are sufficient to understand the nature of a society and its history. Was ritual really sufficient to stimulate and organize the resources that needed to be mobilized to create and sustain Chaco? I doubt it. As such, questions about economy, political and social organization, and other cultural characteristics are not out of fashion but remain very salient, both for understanding Chaco and, as importantly, for how archaeological information may help us to deal with modern challenges.

I will focus my comments on farming productivity and its sustainability in what may have been a geographic area requiring more than average creativity in farming. This topic is important for understanding the history of Chaco, especially its end, and it is central to the use of Chaco for historical lessons. It is useful to view the Ancestral Pueblo area as a far-northern extension of maize-focused agriculture that extends from farming originally adapted to the warmer, rain-fed environs of Mesoamerica to the dry and cool/cold regions of the northern SW/NW where water manipulation is normally needed (e.g., Ingram and Hunt 2015). However Chaco was provisioned, it likely required impressive creativity, sufficient labor, and a goodly amount of luck. It is instructive, and more than a little disconcerting, that the innovative and first-rate research leading to the unexpected discovery of cacao use at Chaco (Crown and Hurst 2009) has received far more recent attention that the critical issue of the farming economy that physically sustained the Chaco world.

My comments are partially conditioned by over two decades of research that focuses on Paquimé or Casas Grandes in the "International Four Corners" at the other end of the "Southwest," an area very different from Chaco in several fundamental ways (e.g., Minnis and Whalen 2015a; Whalen and Minnis 2001a, 2009). First, the history of research in the two areas is quite different. Second, Chaco and Paquimé appear to have been quite different settlements. Third, the intellectual history of the two regions has been profoundly divergent.

The history of research has been substantially different because international borders really do make a difference. While Paquimé was one of the first archaeological sites described by European explorers to the SW/NW (Hammond and Rey 1928) and has intrigued scholars and others for the following 400 years, the intensity of archaeological research in Chihuahua is an order of magnitude less than any adjacent state in the U.S. Southwest. A handful of professional archaeologists work in Chihuahua compared to hundreds north of the border. The limited number of archaeologists in other Mexican border states, such as Sonora, is little different. Therefore, the substantial history of Chaco research may be a guide that helps us chart productive research protocols for Casas Grandes and other understudied areas.

The interpretive context is quite different between Chaco and Casas Grandes. Unlike the Ancestral Puebloan area in the northern SW/NW, there is no ethnographic/historical continuity with indigenous groups. We simply have no clear idea which modern indigenous communities, if any, are the descendants of the ancient Casas Grandians. Therefore, the common approach of trying to translate between modern Puebloan communities and Chaco is not very useful for the Casas Grandes area. This is not all bad.

Finally, archaeological research in areas with substantial cohorts of archaeologists, such as the Ancestral Pueblo region and Hohokam core, can focus on the history of the indigenous peoples in those areas: what happened when and why? These are viewed as sufficient questions. In contrast, archaeological research in prehispanic northern Mexico too often has been framed by questions generated by scholars working in its more intensely studied neighbors. Paquimé, for example, has most commonly been discussed in relation to "Mesoamerica/Southwest" relationships, not for its own history. This topic is usually just a one-way question: how did Mesoamerica affect ancient groups in the U.S. Southwest? This has led to a divergence in the intellectual history between areas south and north of the border; in fact, they have been out of sync with each other. While archaeologists north of the border were focused on local regions and ecological settings, Di Peso was emphasizing Casas Grandes's role in long-distance exchange as the "fallen trading center of the Gran Chichimeca." Now that archaeologists north of the border are renewing an interest in long-distance relationships, research south of the border that is filling in our lack of knowledge about the local archaeology may seem anachronistic, but such studies are doing what had been done decades ago north of the border.

While similarities and assumed historical connections between Chaco and Paquimé have received recent attention (Lekson 1999, but see Phillips 2009), there are major differences between the two that limit the value for comparison. First, Paquimé was a community with a large domestic population. There is evidence that Paquimé was the destination for periodic events that drew people from surrounding areas, but I know of no scholar who argues that the residential population was smaller than 2,000 inhabitants. Second, Paquimé seems to have been a single community that was the regional center and was no less than five times larger than any other of its many nearby neighbors. This contrasts with Chaco with its cluster of great houses, not one of which is clearly a magnitude larger or unambiguously more important than the others. Second, I would argue that wealth and exotica—such as a ton and a half of shell artifacts, hundreds of macaw remains, and a notable amount of copper—were more highly concentrated at Paquimé than Chaco. Third, public ritual architecture—such as ball courts, platform mounds, and feasting ovens—are more common and diverse at Casas Grandes than at Chaco. The number of kivas at Chaco is impressive, but so, too, is the amount of "indoor" ritual space at Paquimé. However, the standardization of kiva form at Chaco compared to the diversity of indoor ritual space and outside "monumental" features at Paquimé may be a very salient characteristic. The diversity of ritual architecture at Paquimé, both within rooms and public features, may reflect a greater range of ceremonial, social, and political behaviors compared with Chaco. While there may be "secondary centers" or "administratively important communities" (outliers?) in the Casas Grandes region, they are uncommon—far, far less common—than Chaco outliers (Whalen and Minnis 2001b). I can think of only two obvious ones: El Pueblito (Pitezel 2006, 2011) and Site 242 (Whalen and Minnis 2001a, 2001b).

Of particular significance for my comments, I believe that Paquimé is located in one of the most productive locations in the SW/NW for farming. As discussed below, I suspect that Chaco is not as obviously productive. In short, the Casas Grandes world seems to have been more highly centered on a single community with different connections with outlying populations, and it may well have had a greater diversity of culturally appropriate pathways for political and religious expression. It is not surprising that these differences catch my attention when thinking about Chaco and, for me, thinking about Paquimé.

Provisioning Chaco

Given current issues of feeding an expanding human population under changing conditions, climatic and otherwise, and given the long history of the use of Ancestral Pueblo history to illustrate how ancient human/environmental issues are lessons for modern times, the provisioning of Chaco is certainly worth more consideration. However, SW/NW archaeologists of late have turned away from questions regarding economy, ecology, and agriculture. Religion may have fed the "soul," but the Chacoans were fed mostly by crops. How they did this and how it related to the history of Chaco are important questions. Two chapters in this volume (Geib and Heitman, and Vivian and Watson) directly deal with farming, and both strongly argue for the agricultural productivity of Chaco. Most participants in the Amerind seminar seem to agree that food provisioning was an important issue to consider, especially around A.D. 1130.

During the seminar, I asked the participants to fill out a simple four-topic questionnaire (Tables 11.1 and 11.2). Here I will focus on the responses to questions 3a and 3b: "Were Chacoans able to provision themselves consistently over time?" and "If not, when was this the case?" Most participants believe that Chacoans were able to provision themselves until the A.D. mid-1130s.

How they fed themselves is not completely clear. The apparent documentation of the distant importation of maize (Cordell et al. 2008) and other plant resources (e.g., Windes and McKenna 2001) is interesting. However, to understand how the people of Chaco provisioned themselves, a good place to start is with the issue of local productivity. How bountiful and reliable was farming in the immediate area in and around Chaco Canyon?

Here my Paquimé bias is clear. The primate community of Paquimé is located in an agriculturally robust location. Michael Whalen and I,

Table 11.1. Summary of Questionnaire Responses.[1]

	Questions			
Respondent	1	2	3a	3b
1	400	10,000	yes	—
2	200	20,000	yes	—
3	150–200	30,000	yes	1030–1050, 1090–1100, and 1130–1180
4	400	?	yes	—
5	150	20,000	no	1130–1150
6	500	50,000?	no	around 1130
7	600–800	20,000–40,000	no	"climate change"
8	400–500	less than 10,000	yes	but problem after 1130
9	263	24,750	yes	—
10	100	30,000	yes/no	yes until 1130; no after 1130
11	100	10,000–20,000	no	post-1130
12	100	40,000–50,000	no	—
13	400	200,000	no	mid-1100s

[1] Questions:
One. What was the maximum population of Pueblo Bonito?
Two. What was the maximum population of the Chaco Phenomenon?
Three A. Was food provisioning ever a problem for Chaco?
Three B. If so, when?

among others, have suggested that it was one of the best in the entire SW/NW for farming, with a very large and fertile floodplain that could have been expanded and had ample and dependable water sources amenable to sophisticated irrigation (Doolittle 2000; Minnis and Whalen 2015b; Whalen and Minnis 2001a:59–61). Given the agricultural setting of where I've worked, I find it hard to imagine that the farming potential of downtown Chaco Canyon and its immediate environs was the major draw for prehispanic Chacoans. Its agricultural viability might be better than many have assumed, but was the agricultural potential of the Chaco Wash area really better than the San Juan River valley to

Table 11.2. The Most Critical Characteristic of Chaco.[1]

Respondent	Characteristic
1.	Monumentality, possible a managerial class of architects, engineers
2.	Concentration of ritual-based economic power and authority in the hands of competing corporate groups
3.	Ability of leaders to mobilize a large labor force on a massive scale for construction, craft production, and subsistence
4.	It wasn't a town. Small populations moved there for short duration
5.	Strict conformity to an architectural canon for great houses
6.	Overt social hierarchy as expressed through ritual leadership
7.	Low-level chiefdom of conical clans
8.	Mobilizing and controlling labor
9.	Complex collegial conformity
10.	Ability to extract resources (stuff and labor), with some coercive action
11.	Strong land-holding, kin-based groups
12.	Scale of labor/ritual organization, socially and spatially
13.	Ranked and competitive social groups embedded in houses with overt ritual leadership sanctioned by ritual

1. Answers to the question: "What was the ONE social characteristic that defines Chaco at its 'height' that is different from modern Puebloan communities?"

the north? How productive could Chaco Wash have been? I need to be convinced. It may not take much to convince me, however. Studies of Hopi sand dune farming (Bradfield 1971) and other ancient farming techniques should sensitize us to the ability of indigenous SW/NW farmers to grow crops in what might at first appear to be minimally viable farmland. Other examples abound, including one of my favorites, the Safford grid gardens, massive field systems on terraces above the Gila River, that seem out of place (Doolittle and Neely 2004). Still, there are constraints on agricultural productivity.

Opinions about the productivity Chaco Canyon vary greatly, and they are based on a diversity of data: soil studies, climate reconstructions, various plant remains recovered during excavations, historical observations, and experimental gardens. On one side are Vivian and Watson (this volume), Geib and Heitman (this volume), and Wills and

Dorshow (Dorshow 2012; Wills and Dorshow 2011) who argue that the agricultural potential of Chaco Canyon is quite good. Others, however, suggest that the agricultural productivity of the immediate Chaco Canyon area was significantly limited (e.g., Benson 2011; Benson et al. 2006; Toll et al. 1985).

Despite my Paquimé bias, I am more persuaded by the "pro-farming" arguments that Chaco could be farmed and likely was more productive than I would expect. Like most traditional farmers, Chacoans manipulated microenvironmental differences to use a variety of strategies to grow crops, mostly maize (as well described in chapter 2 by Vivian and Watson). Keeping in mind Chacoans' capacity to mobilize resources, human labor and otherwise, to build the great houses, I suppose that we shouldn't be surprised that Chacoans could have mobilized what was needed to produce crops. The diversity of agricultural strategies that could have been employed could indicate that Chacoans had a reasonable local farming economy well buffered against normal variation of the agricultural-relevant climate fluctuations. Alternatively, this diversity could represent the opposite, that the only way to provision the population with local resources was to construct and maintain complex agricultural features that squeezed barely sufficient yields that might have been augmented on occasion by the importation of bulk foodstuffs. Still, the question about the productivity and reliability of local farming is open. Geib and Heitman's chapter demonstrates how ubiquitous maize pollen is, which they argue is best explained by local production. I am, however, troubled by the fact that Chaco samples have so much more maize pollen compared to other Ancestral Pueblo sites. Again, Chaco surprises us by being different. Could the maize pollen abundance be the result of unusually heavy use of pollen for ceremonial purposes? Still, these two chapters, along other research including the ethnographic evidence, strengthen the case for widespread agriculture in Chaco.

Differing archaeological interpretations are hardly unusual. However, there is a critical problem with the study of the agricultural productivity of Chaco Canyon. While there are a number of general summaries (e.g., Mathien 2008; Vivian 1990; Vivian et al. 2006; Vivian and Watson, this volume), even going back to Fisher's (1934) prescient essay, there is a striking lack of basic published data on ancient farming.

As far as I know, the map of only one field is widely published (Vivian 1990). Like many, I had assumed that this field was the one next to Chetro Ketl when, in fact, it is near Peñasco Blanco (Gwinn Vivian, personal communication 2012).

Other centers of large areas with regional polities in the SW/NW, such as Casas Grandes and Hohokam, are largely situated in locations of exceptional agricultural productivity, the Río Casas Grandes valley and other river valleys in northern Chihuahua on one hand and the Salt/Gila/Santa Cruz river valleys on the other. Can an equally compelling case be made for Chaco? The size, scale, and sophistication of the well-known Hohokam irrigation systems have impressed scholars and others for over a century. There is little question that these massive irrigation systems were central to the history of the Hohokam, including its political dynamics. In addition to irrigation systems and *akchin* farming, substantial rock mulch fields in the Sonoran Desert are recorded (e.g., Fish et al. 1985).

My apologies, but let us return to the Casas Grandes world, another major regional system in the SW/NW. Like the Hohokam, irrigation is only one type of farming used by the Casas Grandians. In addition to its irrigation farming, there is very extensive agricultural terracing in the Casas Grandes areas (Herold 1970; Howard and Griffiths 1966; Luebben et al. 1986; Minnis et al. 2006; Schmidt and Gerald 1988). Enormous numbers of small terrace systems are found not only around Paquimé itself but also in more distant areas in northwestern Chihuahua, both in the lowlands river valleys and in the Sierra Madre Occidental.

Closer to Chaco, Mesa Verde and the northern Rio Grande have widespread agricultural terracing (e.g., Anschuetz 2006; Cordell 1975; Ford 2000). Is there a similar level of agricultural modification in the Chaco area? One would expect so, and summaries, such as Vivian and Watson's chapter, mention their presence, but it is impossible to assess their abundance and distribution until the complete data from the excavations of Chaco water control systems are published.

Agricultural productivity is only one question about the role of farming in the history of Chaco. As shown in Table 11.2, questions about the nature of labor mobilization also were central ones to the Amerind seminar participants. Labor mobilization is usually expressed in relation to the monumental great houses, but this issue should include consideration of the mobilization of agricultural labor. Mobilization of provisioning labor could include transportation of bulk foodstuffs from distant locations as well as local farming. The organization of farming labor at Chaco also could have included some centralized, managed agricultural production. Chief or cacique fields are reported at a number of historic Rio Grandes pueblos (e.g., Parsons 1939), but little description of these is provided. Cacique fields are farm plots controlled by leaders, with labor provided by community members.

We believe that we have documented such fields around Paquimé, the first archaeological examples of cacique fields in the SW/NW (Minnis et al. 2006). These uncommon terraced fields (6 out of 180 terraced fields recorded during archeological survey, a small sample of such fields in northwestern Chihuahua) are distinctive in several ways. First, they are unusually large in size, far larger than most field systems. Second, such fields are located near specialized or administrative sites located away from population concentrations. Given the extremely large size of some earthen ovens in the Casas Grandes region, it is likely that some foods for feasting were produced in the cacique fields. For example, we estimate that the largest oven at Paquimé, one that we believe to have been the largest earthen oven in the SW/NW, could have prepared over 3,000 kg per cooking episode (Minnis and Whalen 2005).

Chaco would be the most logical place in the northern SW/NW to find cacique fields. The size and formality of the Peñasco Blanco field hints to me that there may be some centralized control or at least coordination of farming. What is the variation in the size, distribution, and formality of fields in Chaco, and how do they compare with fields managed and worked differently, such as those at a familial scale of production? Again, we cannot evaluate this topic without more substantial publication of data about Chaco fields.

Provisioning Chaco through Time

Assuming that Chaco had the ability to feed itself during normal times, we need to move on to perhaps an even more important question. If Chaco was a better place for farming than many think, was it always so? There is a profound difference between farming and farming well consistently. Living in Oklahoma for three decades, not surprisingly, makes me think of the Dust Bowl and Great Depression. The Southern Plains witnessed dramatic expansion of farming during economic and climatic boom times, but the amount of farming didn't shield the people of the Southern Plains from the devastating effects of the Dust Bowl and Great Depression; in fact, it contributed to the problem, as did changes in the structure of agrarian economies leading to dispossessed tenant farmers. Addressing the issues of farming success over time will necessitate analysis of multiple data sets as Geib and Heitman (this volume) do in drawing together Chaco's substantial pollen record. Similarly, the viability, resilience, and productivity of the impressive and diverse farming techniques and strategies outlined by Vivian and Watson need to be considered through time. Farming well at one point in time, whether it is by the Ancestral Pueblo, the Navajo in Chaco Canyon, or Oklahomans, doesn't mean, of course, farming well always.

Provisioning adequacy over Chaco's history may have been an important, if not a central, factor contributing to the end of the Classic Chaco era. A small majority of the seminar participants thought that the A.D. post-1130 period was a time of food provisioning problems (Table 11.1). They are not alone, as Chaco is one of many examples used by Diamond (2005) to present his hypothesis about "collapse" of ancient societies. It is true that there is much to critique in Diamond's volume, but it seems to me that the most detailed critique (Wilcox 2009) focuses on the context of his perspective and largely does not evaluate the likelihood that periods of food provisioning problems and anthropogenic environmental changes were critical issues during some of Chaco history.

Despite the importance of understanding the end of Chaco and how it related to provisioning sustainability, there is inadequate modeling about how population, organization, labor, and agricultural dynamics might be related in Chaco. Sebastian's (1992) work was an excellent start, as Vivian and Watson discuss in their chapter. However, such modeling for Chaco is difficult for two basic reasons, certainly more difficult than for some other areas of the Puebloan world, such as the contemporaries of Chaco during the Classic Mimbres period, where I tried to address this question many years ago (Minnis 1985). First, given the documented movement of resources and people within the San

Juan Basin, Chaco's catchment or sustaining area may have been much larger and more complicated than was the case with most such studies in other regions in the SW/NW. Second, estimates of the size and relationships of communities within the Chaco "region" vary widely. For example, estimates of population size of the "Chaco Phenomenon" by seminar participants in response to my short questionnaire vary from 10,000 to 200,000, with the majority within the 20,000–30,000 range (Table 11.1). Clearly, the scale, extent, history, and relationships among communities in the San Juan Basin demand more research, and that research will be complicated.

Without a more detailed understanding of the scale, reliability, productivity, and organization of farming in Chaco Canyon itself and its region, the ability of Chacoan archaeology to offer models or lessons about humanity and its relationships with environments is severely limited. Much data seems to have been collected through field studies but has not yet been published in sufficient detail, especially the substantial work by Vivian (e.g., 1974, 1984, 1991; Vivian et al. 2006). Given the public interest in Chaco and the substantial corpus of research by over 100 scholars, this has been a lost opportunity.

Concluding Comments

We now know far more about Chaco than we did just decades ago. From my northern Mexican perspective, I am in awe and envious of the quantity and quality of work by an impressive cohort of Chaco scholars. Plus, the intellectual potential for Chaco research is also as unlimited as for any other region in the world, and this statement is not hyperbole. Chaco still surprises us. Who would have expected, to mention a recent example, the chemical signature of cacao to be found in Chaco cylinder vessels (Crown and Hurst 2009)? Not me.

My awe and envy is tempered—mostly—by several troubling observations. As I have lamented too often here, publication of basic data on farming systems is essential. However, the greatest potential tragedy of Chaco archaeology is the difficulty now of doing fieldwork, especially original excavation, in Chaco Canyon itself. Contrast the constriction of original field research in Chaco Canyon since the National Park Service's project decades ago with the substantial corpus of recent work in other major regional "systems" in North America, such as Cahokia and the Hohokam heartland. That Chaco is delightfully unusual is recognized by all; however, the exact nature of Chaco is not, by any means. Therefore, more work at the center is clearly needed. Pueblo Bonito was excavated over 100 years ago (Pepper 1920). How can we understand the origins of this very distinctive, if not odd, archaeological phenomenon when the only excavations at one of the three earliest great house communities was conducted a century ago and excavation at the two others, Peñasco Blanco and Una Vida, seems off-limits? What a shame.

Not all is bleak, however. Let us pretend that the questionnaire's results are a fair sampling of Chaco scholars. If so, then one of the most important aspects of Chaco demanding research attention is its regional system. How are "outliers" and other communities related to downtown Chaco and other communities in the northern Southwest? The Newcomb field study hints at the interesting information available at areas outside core Chaco, although the history of this specific and enormous farming system is unclear (Friedman et al. 2003). The chances of gathering new data to study these relationships may be easier than working at the center.

The seeming constraints on some essential Chaco research are more than just lamentable. If Chaco was simply an interesting location where spectacular ruins are juxtaposed against what most would see as a starkly minimalist environment, then the research constraints would be only an annoyance to scholars and others interested in the ancient past of the northern SW/NW. But Chaco is more, so much more; its curious characteristics that defy simple interpretations have extended Chaco fame well beyond the San Juan Basin or the SW/NW. More importantly, Chaco has been and continues to be used as a source of lessons for humanity. Jared Diamond and his critics are only the latest example. Chaco is a WORLD Heritage site for good reason. As such it deserves WORLD-class, ongoing research.

Acknowledgments

Thank you to the session organizers, Stephen Plog and Carrie Heitman, for including a wayward "southwesternist" now professionally in exile south of the border. Thanks to the participants for a very interesting seminar and to John Ware and his staff at the Amerind Foundation for the congenial and collegial setting. Patricia Gilman once again suffered through reading an earlier draft that may have approximated standard English.

References Cited

Anschuetz, Kurt F. 2006. Tewa Fields, Tewa Traditions. In *Canyon Gardens: The Ancient Pueblo Landscapes of the American Southwest*, edited by V. B. Price and Baker H. Morrow, pp. 57–74. University of New Mexico Press, Albuquerque.

Benson, Larry V. 2011. Factors Controlling Pre-Columbian and Early Historic Maize Productivity in the American Southwest, Part 2: The Chaco Halo, Mesa Verde, Pajarito Plateau/Bandelier, and Zuni Archaeological Regions. *Journal of Archaeological Method and Theory* 18:61–109.

Benson, Larry, John Stein, Howard Taylor, Robert Friedman, and Thomas C. Windes. 2006. The Agricultural Productivity of Chaco Canyon and the Source of Pre-Hispanic Maize from the Pueblo Bonito Great House. In *Histories of Maize: Multidisciplinary Approaches to the Prehistory, Linguistics, Biogeography, Domestication, and Evolution of Maize*, edited by John E. Staller, Robert H. Tykot, and Bruce F. Benz, pp. 289–314. Academic Press, San Diego.

Bradfield, Maitland. 1971. *The Changing Pattern of Hopi Agriculture*. Occasional Paper No. 30. Royal Anthropological Institute of Great Britain and Ireland, London.

Cordell, Linda S. 1975. Predicting Site Abandonment at Wetherill Mesa. *Kiva* 40:189–202.

Cordell, Linda S., H. Wolcott Toll, Mollie S. Toll, and Thomas C. Windes. 2008. Archaeological Corn from Pueblo Bonito, Chaco Canyon, New Mexico: Dates, Context, Sources. *American Antiquity* 73:491–511.

Crown, Patricia L., and W. Jeffrey Hurst. 2009. Evidence of Cacao Use in the Prehispanic American Southwest. *Proceedings of the National Academy of Science* 106:2110–2113.

Crown, Patricia L., and W. James Judge. 1991. *Chaco & Hohokam: Prehistoric Regional Systems in the American Southwest*. School of American Research Press, Santa Fe.

Diamond, Jared. 2005. *Collapse: How Societies Choose to Fail or Succeed*. Viking Press, New York.

Doolittle, William E. 2000. *Cultivated Landscapes of Native North America*. Oxford University Press, Oxford.

Doolittle, William E., and James A. Neely. 2004. *The Safford Valley Grids: Prehistoric Cultivation in the Southern Arizona Desert.* Anthropological Papers of the University of Arizona No. 70. University of Arizona Press, Tucson.

Dorshow, Wetherbee Bryan. 2012. Modeling Agricultural Potential in Chaco Canyon during the Bonito Phase: A Predictive Geospatial Approach. *Journal of Archaeological Science* 39:2098–2115.

Fish, Suzanne K., Paul R. Fish, Charles Miksicek, and John Madsen. 1985. Prehistoric Agave Cultivation in Southern Arizona. *Desert Plants* 7:107–113.

Fisher, Reginald G. 1934. *Some Geographic Factors that Influenced the Ancient Population of Chaco Canyon, New Mexico.* University of New Mexico Bulletin 244, Archaeology Series 3(1). University of New Mexico, Albuquerque.

Ford, Richard I. 2000. Human Disturbance and Biodiversity: A Case Study from Northern New Mexico. In *Biodiversity and Native America*, edited by Paul Minnis and Wayne Elisens, pp. 207–222. University of Oklahoma Press, Norman.

Friedman, Richard A., John R. Stein, and Taft Blackhouse Jr. 2003. A Study of a Pre-Columbian Irrigation System at Newcomb, New Mexico. *Journal of GIS Archaeology* 1:1–10.

Hammond, George P., and Agapito Rey. 1928. *Obregón's History of Sixteenth Century Explorations in Western North America Entitled: Chronicle, Commentary, or Relation of the Ancient and Modern Discoveries in New Spain, New Mexico, and Mexico, 1584.* Wetzel, Los Angeles.

Herold, Laurance C. 1970. *Trincheras and Physical Environment along the Rio Gavilan, Chihuahua, Mexico.* Department of Geography, University of Denver Technical Papers No. 65–1. University of Denver, Denver, Colorado.

Howard, William A., and Thomas M. Griffiths. 1966. *Trincheras Distribution in the Sierra Madre Occidental, Mexico.* Department of Geography, University of Denver Technical Paper No. 66–1. University of Denver, Denver, Colorado.

Ingram, Scott E., and Robert C. Hunt (editors). 2015. *Traditional Arid Lands Agriculture: Understanding the Past for the Future.* University of Arizona Press, Tucson.

Lekson, Stephen H. 1999. *The Chaco Meridian: Centers of Political Power in the Ancient Southwest.* Altamira, Walnut Creek, California.

———. 2006. *The Archaeology of Chaco Canyon: An Eleventh-Century Pueblo Regional Center.* School of American Research Press, Santa Fe.

Luebben, Ralph A., Jonathan G. Andelson, and Laurance C. Herold. 1986. Elvino Whetten Pueblo and Its Relationship to Terraces and Nearby Small Structures. *Kiva* 51:165–187.

Mathien, Frances Joan. 2008. *Culture and Ecology of Chaco Canyon and the San Juan Basin*. Publications in Archaeology 18H, Chaco Canyon Series. National Park Service, U.S. Department of the Interior, Santa Fe.

McAnany, Patricia A., and Norman Yoffee. 2009. *Questioning Collapse: Human Resiliency, Ecological Vulnerability, and the Aftermath of Empire*. Cambridge University Press, Cambridge.

Minnis, Paul E. 1985. *Social Adaptation to Food Stress: A Prehistoric Southwestern Example*. University of Chicago Press, Chicago.

Minnis, Paul E., and Michael E. Whalen. 2005. At the Other End of the Puebloan World: Feasting at Casas Grandes, Chihuahua, Mexico. In *Engaged Anthropology: Research Essays on North American Archaeology, Ethnobotany, and Museology*, edited by Michelle Hegmon and B. Sunday Eiselt, pp. 114–128. Museum of Anthropology Anthropological Papers No. 94. University of Michigan, Ann Arbor.

———. 2015a. *Ancient Paquimé and the Casas Grandes World*. University of Arizona Press, Tucson.

———. 2015b. Environment and Food Economy. In *Ancient Paquimé and the Casas Grandes World*, edited by Paul Minnis and Michael Whalen, pp. 41–57. University of Arizona Press, Tucson.

Minnis, Paul E., Michael E. Whalen, and R. Emerson Howell. 2006. Fields of Power: Upland Agriculture in the Prehispanic Casas Grandes Polity, Chihuahua, Mexico. *American Antiquity* 71:707–722.

Neitzel, Jill E. 1999. *Great Towns and Regional Polities in the Prehistoric American Southwest and Southeast*. University of New Mexico Press, Albuquerque.

Parsons, Elsie Crews. 1939. *Pueblo Indian Religion*. 2 vols. University of Chicago Press, Chicago.

Pepper, George H. 1920. *Pueblo Bonito*. Anthropological Papers of the American Museum of Natural History Vol. 27. Trustees of the American Museum of Natural History, New York.

Phillips, David A., Jr. 2009. *A Skeptical View of the Chaco Meridian*. Electronic document, http://wwwunm.edu/~dap/meridian/meridian, accessed June 1, 2009.

Pitezel, Todd A. 2006. Surveying Cerro de Moctezuma, Chihuahua, Mexico. *Kiva* 72(3):353–369.

———. 2011. *From Archaeology to Ideology in Northwest Mexico: Cerro de Moctezuma in the Casas Grandes Ritual Landscape*. Ph.D. dissertation, Department of Anthropology, University of Arizona, Tucson.

Schmidt, Robert H., Jr., and Rex E. Gerald. 1988. The Distribution of Conservation-Type Water-Control Systems in the Northern Sierra Madre Occidental. *Kiva* 53:165–179.

Sebastian, Lynne. 1992. *The Chaco Anasazi: Sociopolitical Evolution in the Prehistoric Southwest*. Cambridge University Press, Cambridge.

Toll, H. Wolcott, Mollie S. Toll, Marcia L. Newren, and William B. Gillespie. 1985. Experimental Corn Plots in Chaco Canyon: The Life and Times of *Zea mays* L. In *Environment and Subsistence of Chaco Canyon, New Mexico*, edited by Frances J. Mathien, pp. 79–132. Publications in Archaeology 18E, Chaco Canyon Studies. National Park Service, U.S. Department of the Interior, Santa Fe.

Vivian, R. Gwinn. 1974. Conservation and Diversion: Water-Control Systems in the Anasazi Southwest. In *Irrigation's Impact on Society*, edited by Theodore Downing and McGuire Gibson, pp. 95–112. Anthropological Papers of the University of Arizona No. 25. University of Arizona, Tucson.

———. 1984. Agricultural and Social Adjustments to Changing Environments in the Chaco Basin. In *Prehistoric Agricultural Strategies in the Southwest*, edited by Suzanne K. Fish and Paul R. Fish, pp. 234–258. Anthropological Research Papers No. 33. Arizona State University, Tempe.

———. 1990. *The Chaco Prehistory of the San Juan Basin*. Academic Press, San Diego.

———. 1991. Chacoan Subsistence. In *Chaco and Hohokam: Prehistoric Regional Systems in the American Southwest*, edited by Patricia L. Crown and W. James Judge, pp. 57–75. School of American Research Press, Santa Fe.

Vivian, R. Gwinn, Carla R. Van West, Jeffrey S. Dean, Nancy J. Akins, Mollie S. Toll, and Thomas C. Windes. 2006. Ecology and Economy. In *The Archaeology of Chaco Canyon: An Eleventh-Century Pueblo Regional Center*, edited by Stephen H. Lekson, pp. 45–66. School of American Research Press, Santa Fe.

Whalen, Michael E., and Paul E. Minnis. 2001a. *Casas Grandes and Its Hinterland: Regional Organization in Northwest Mexico*. University of Arizona Press, Tucson.

———. 2001b. Architecture and Authority in the Casas Grandes Region, Chihuahua, Mexico. *American Antiquity* 66:651–699.

———. 2009. *The Neighbors of Casas Grandes: Excavating Medio Period Communities in Northwestern Chihuahua*. University of Arizona Press, Tucson.

Wilcox, Michael. 2009. Marketing Conquest and the Vanishing Indian: An Indigenous Response to Jared Diamond's Archaeology of the American Southwest. In *Questioning Collapse: Human Resilience Ecological Vulnerability, and the Aftermath of Empire*, edited by Patricia McAnany and Norman Yoffee, pp. 113–141. Cambridge University Press, Cambridge.

Wills, W.H., and Wetherbee Bryan Dorshow. 2011. Agriculture and Community in Chaco Canyon: Revisiting Pueblo Alto. *Journal of Anthropological Archaeology* 31:138–155.

Windes, Thomas C., and Peter J. McKenna. 2001. Going against the Grain: Wood Production in Chacoan Society. *American Antiquity* 66:119–140.

12

Chaco

The View from Downstream

Kelley Hays-Gilpin and John Ware

Each chapter in this volume makes a new contribution to the large and complicated question of what life was like in Chaco Canyon from about A.D. 800 to 1130, but no single chapter gives the reader a sense of the lively discussion that engaged seminar participants for several days at the Amerind Foundation. Hays-Gilpin and Ware were invited to serve as discussants, along with Paul Minnis and Dick Ford, partly because none of us has done more than occasional work in Chaco Canyon, so we bring outsider perspectives to the intense debates that often pervade Chacoan studies. Hays-Gilpin and Ware brought to the table our interests and expertise in collaborative research with descendant communities: contemporary Pueblo people who are stakeholders in the histories archaeologists generate for diverse audiences. Both of us use ethnography together with archaeological methods in our research. We advocate using ethnographies, oral histories, and appropriate ethnographic analogies and homologies in producing more interesting, appropriate, and relevant archaeological narratives. This was our principal contribution to the discussions at Amerind, and it is the main focus of this chapter.

Whatever Chaco was, it was different than the historic pueblos. Nevertheless, Chacoans were among the ancestors of contemporary Pueblo people, and we can productively use the historic pueblos as "end points" in our reconstruction of past trajectories of culture change. Most archaeologists who have used ethnographic data and the direct historical approach rely on Western Pueblo, especially Hopi, data more than all the other pueblos combined (see Whiteley, this volume). Of all the Pueblos, the Hopis were least affected by Spanish colonial programs and are closer to the baseline Pueblo proto-culture hypothesized by Fred

Eggan, the most influential of all Pueblo synthesists. We advise archaeologists to expand their working knowledge of pueblos and working relationships with Pueblo people, especially when considering appropriate analogs and homologs for Chacoan and other eastern Ancestral Puebloan groups. The Keresan- and Tanoan-speaking Pueblos of the Rio Grande and southern San Juan Basin (Acoma and Laguna) have, we suspect, more direct historical links to Chaco and other Ancestral Pueblo groups of the core San Juan region, and their social, political, and ceremonial organizations are very different from the Western Pueblos of Hopi and Zuni. The sodality-based ritual-political organizations of the Eastern Pueblos make more appropriate analogs and homologs for Chaco than the kin-based community organizations of the Western Pueblos. Moreover, Eastern Pueblo oral traditions suggest direct links to sites and shrines in and around Chaco Canyon.

Before we begin, let us emphasize that Chaco was complicated and continually evolving, so that Chaco will be understood in historical context or not at all. Although the following discussion is broken down into topic headings, we emphasize that all things Puebloan tend to be deeply integrated. As Mills explains (this volume), dichotomizing "ritual" and "domestic" realms and trichotomizing "ritual," "economic," and "political" realms are not useful because all these conceptual categories are packed tightly together in Pueblo culture and worldview. Among all historical pueblos, politics, ritual, economics—indeed, all social relations—are cut from the same tightly woven cloth. We also caution our readers that words matter, and we have to be careful about our definitions. Western Pueblo "kivas" house different kinds of activities and organizations than Eastern Pueblo "kivas," and Chacoan "kivas" may well have been different than all historical forms. Chaco has been variously described as a "chiefdom," "kingdom," "ritual center," "segmentary state," and most recently "altepetl" (Toner 2012–2013), but we argue that Chaco may not fit tidily into any of the standard social-political organizational types that anthropologists use, and "name it and nail it" approaches to Chaco complexity inhibit attempts to understand Chacoan social-political relations. This short chapter is no place for long nuanced definitions, but consistency in definition and classification is essential for mutual understanding.

Chaco Roots

From roughly 3,000 to 1,000 years ago, a natural sand dune dam helped stabilize the floodplain of Chaco Canyon, creating a farming oasis in the vast desert of the San Juan Basin (Vivian et al. 2006; but see Hall 2010 and Love et al. 2011 for contrary evidence). As a result, Chaco attracted early Pueblo farmers long before the foundations for the first great houses were laid in the A.D. 800s (two of the largest Basketmaker III communities on the plateau are located on each end of Chaco Canyon). Memory, ancestors, and connections to outlying areas probably were important from the beginning of human settlement in the canyon, as shown in Jolie and Webster's research on fiber perishables (this volume). Twined sandals and burden baskets persist from the Basketmaker period right through to the early 1100s; basket and textile styles and techniques continue from local Basketmaker roots, over time apparently recruited to ritual uses such as altar pieces. These Basketmaker roots were expressed alongside later influences in the 1000s that suggest connections to distant people and places—textile styles that came from points south, in northern Mexico and Mesoamerica, along with such southern items as cylinder jars (some with cacao residues), copper bells, and macaws.

Chaco also has strong local and regional roots in settlement pattern, community plan, architectural design, and rock art. Many of the large great houses in Chaco overlie "proto-great houses" that were constructed as early as the A.D. 850s and did not reach monumental proportions until the eleventh century. Similar proto–great houses have been documented in Pueblo I communities in the central Mesa Verde area, the La Plata River valley, the Chuska front, and along well-watered sections of the central and southern San Juan Basin.

Although it was strongly connected to both local and regional roots, Chaco also differs from other early Pueblo cultures. By the 800s, evidence for ritual intensification is echoed but not exactly replicated elsewhere. For example, the two clusters of "special" burials discussed in this volume by Mills, Heitman, and Marden may be interpreted as placement of ancestors in specially built or retrofit crypts. Some may have served the same roles as Mesoamerican ancestor bundles with whom later generations nurtured ongoing relationships through offerings and prayers, and even by rearranging body parts into new configurations. Chaco Canyon was one of the few places on the plateau that was occupied continuously for over 300 years, so in at least some great houses, ancestors were buried where descendants still lived. Ancestor bundles might have been part of ritual practices and responsibilities that belonged to one segment of a community, but not to others. Variation, too, might have been normal. Ritual practices and responsibilities possibly differentiated early. We think of katsinas as a post–A.D. 1300 ritual practice, but ritual personification might have begun much earlier. Differences in life often correlate with differences in death. We will return to the possibility of evidence for individual identification with mythological personages in kin-group origin stories, founding of sodalities, and personages who create and shape the world we live in, such as the Hero Twins.

Provisioning Chaco

This volume presents evidence that considerable quantities of maize were or could have been grown locally in Chaco and its immediate hinterlands. Vivian and Watson (this volume) document widespread and diverse microenvironments and water control technologies that ancient Chacoans could have exploited. The aforementioned sand dune dam raised the water table and attracted farmers during the 800s, but probably was breached sometime after A.D. 900. Later, around 1050, people apparently filled the breach with masonry and re-created the dam to keep Chaco Wash from down cutting and to maintain a higher water table in canyon sediments. Though Chaco looks dry and desolate compared to the Rio Grande valley to the east or the San Juan to the north, the canyon contains many potential agricultural niches. Chaco is similar to the Hopi Mesas in this regard. At Hopi and other persistent settlement loci on the plateau, people produced substantial quantities of maize and other crops using a variety of risk-averse farming strategies. The key to risk reduction is diversity: diversity of crops, planting and watering strategies, and field locations. Like all farmers on the high, dry Colorado Plateau, Chacoans diverted runoff to fields, built grid gardens, used slope wash, and likely planted crops in sand dunes, perhaps using techniques that would be perfected by historic Hopi farmers. In addition to their crops and fields, Chacoans undoubtedly minimized risk by diversifying their economic, social, and ritual networks as well.

Maize farming in Chaco in any given year likely was a gamble—farmers dealt with differential rainfall from year to year and spotty distribution of storm episodes. Wind can be ferocious in the San Juan Basin, especially in the spring when young plants are most vulnerable. Today, Pueblo and Navajo farmers use tin cans to protect young plants, but early historic photographs show brush windbreaks and stone slabs set on the west side of each plant to deflect blowing sand. High-intensity summer storms can do more harm than good. Crop-damaging insects also appear sporadically; wise farming families eat them and encourage their turkeys to eat them.

How did farmers coordinate such diverse systems? How was land use negotiated within the community? Did individuals own the fields they worked? Was improved farm land passed down within families or were fields communally owned and controlled? Did leaders tell farmers what, when, and where to plant? The historic pueblos practice a variety of land use strategies, mirroring their variety of crops and fields. At Hopi the most productive cornfields typically are owned by elite lineages that grant use rights to other descent groups in the village based on their contribution to community ceremonies. Usufruct rights to more marginal farmland go to any individual or family willing to invest time and effort in field improvement. In the Eastern Pueblos, farmland is communally owned. Use rights to individual fields are granted by the pueblo leadership, who also organize and direct community labor in ditch cleaning and planting and harvesting the fields of religious leaders.

During the seminar, Vivian described the complex field systems, ditches, and head gates in Chaco Canyon, which are so uniform and consistent that they almost certainly required central planning, direction, and use of skilled labor: the same kind of centrally directed cooperative labor that was necessary for great house and road construction. Chaco's smaller-scale gridded fields, which are perfectly laid out and precisely engineered, may have been constructed with labor above the household level as well, but this could have been organized by kin-based or other supra-household corporate groups. As mentioned above, in the historic Eastern Pueblos, gangs of workers plant and harvest the fields of religious leaders. Leaders also assign work groups to community construction and maintenance projects. When the work is finished, the groups disband until the next project is organized.

Ritual may also play a role in structuring and modulating community provisioning. Richard Ford (1972) notes that Eastern Pueblos timed communal feasts to periods in the annual cycle when food shortages were most likely to occur. Ford explained another example of ritual modulation at the Amerind seminar. The major colors of Pueblo corn have persistent ceremonial roles, and community members need access to a variety of colored corn to complete their ceremonial obligations. If a farmer plants different-colored seeds in one field, cross pollination will produce speckled corn, not the pure colors that the ritual system calls for. A religious requirement thus encourages farmers to plant their corn in widely spaced fields, which coincidentally minimizes the risk of major crop loss. Vivian and Watson's description of field systems in Chaco Canyon, based on historic Navajo field locations, fits the risk-averse Pueblo pattern of spreading maize into different ecological niches. Ethnography tells us that this pattern could have been partly driven by a ritual system.

Geib and Heitman (this volume) show that large quantities of corn pollen were deposited in a variety of archaeological contexts in Chaco Canyon. Some of these deposits could result from food-processing activities, as well as long-term storage, but pollen also could have been deposited in the course of ritual activities—and of course ritual and economic activities are difficult to distinguish, not only in the archaeological record but also in historic and contemporary Pueblo practice. In many pueblos today, men grow corn in the fields and women do the husking in the plaza, as a public event in which everyone's effort is monitored and appreciated. Just as important, pollen was almost certainly used as ritual offerings. Geib and Heitman provide many examples from Pueblo ethnographies, and we also cite our own experience in both Eastern and Western Pueblos. Today, corn pollen is often mixed with finely ground white cornmeal, turquoise, and shell, and carried in small bags. This mixture is sprinkled to confer blessings on people and places, to mark pathways and boundaries, and to feed all manner of beings, including houses, shrines, and supernatural personages. For example, Pueblo men sprinkle cornmeal mixture on women grinding

corn to bless them and thank them for their efforts on behalf of their
families and the community. In the seminar, Ford explained that in
Tewa Pueblos, Ash Boy, a helpful domestic god, lives on trash mounds.
Each community usually has a space on the mound where one commu-
nicates in prayer to Ash Boy. At Okay Owingeh, a white quartz stone
placed on the mound marks this important place. The souls of ancestors
buried in trash mounds gather at the quartz shrine to get their cornmeal
and hear the prayers of their descendants. Reciprocity between living
humans and ancestors (and other supernatural personages), enacted in
the form of feeding with corn and bringing rain that helps corn grow, is
at the heart of Pueblo worldview. The high density of corn pollen Geib
and Heitman document in Chaco Canyon might testify to long-term
continuity of Pueblo ritual involving corn pollen and the reciprocal
offerings its use evokes.

In our seminar discussion, Laurie Webster described additional
evidence for how corn was processed and stored in the Chaco world.
Earl Morris's notes describe a room at Aztec with Early Bonito phase
trash that contained 6.5 feet of refuse, and much of the refuse consisted of corn husks. Morris noted (and sometimes collected) a large
number of artifacts made of corn husks. He also found chains of corn
tassels that were probably hung in rooms. Nearby Salmon Ruins had a
trash deposit near its tower kiva that contained large quantities of corn
tassels. Archaeologists should therefore expect to find abundant corn
pollen in pueblo plazas, trash mounds, rooms, and almost every other
archaeological context.

Diversity of field, crop, and planting techniques, at least temporary
coordination of labor, and sequential coordination of ritual activities,
are part and parcel of historical Pueblo farming strategies and probably figured in Chacoan strategies as well. We see artifact assemblages
that include carved and bent wooden sticks that resemble pueblo prayer
sticks (some seem to refer at once to digging sticks and prayer sticks). In
pueblos today, farmers set up prayer sticks in fields when planting (see,
for example, Cushing 1920). They are often made of willow, a riparian
species that is symbolically linked to water, and are often adorned with
waterbird feathers. Prayer sticks with spatulate or curved ends symbol-
ize agriculture and may date back to the Basketmaker era (Jolie and
Webster, this volume). Using such prayer sticks in fields serves to link

water, soil, and human labor and links Ancestral Pueblo with descendant Pueblo communities.

Organization of Labor

Centrally directed skilled labor is obvious in Chacoan provisioning systems, and in other cultural practices as well. In just about everything, Chacoans seem to have invested more labor than would have been practically necessary. Most Chacoan architecture is "overbuilt" and labor intensive: massive buildings; carefully dressed masonry; precise, carefully planned, and symmetrical arrangements of rooms and open spaces. Craft production involved elaborate pottery, textiles, basketry, stone tools, and painted wooden ritual paraphernalia. Distinctive and labor-intensive "Chaco Style" architectural details are found not only in great houses but also in utilitarian constructions, including carefully executed stone boxes in canals and banded masonry in dams. Whatever else Chaco was, it was a style, an aesthetic that could not be precisely replicated without intensive investments of knowledge, skill, and labor.

Facsimiles of the Chaco Style probably spread through emulation throughout the core San Juan Basin region, but the expertise necessary to accomplish the style was more likely transmitted by intensive instruction. At Aztec Ruins, for example, hidden details of construction technique suggest similarities that go well beyond emulation, and such details provide some of the best evidence for the migration of people from downtown Chaco to the San Juan in the early twelfth century.

Barbara Mills (this volume) notes that Chacoans' investment in craftsmanship must mean that both objects and the procedures for creating objects were infused with deep meaning. Construction procedures had to follow a strict form, even when they were not visible after the fact. Heitman's (this volume) revelations of lignite layers in both great house and small house foundational deposits are a case in point. These features were not visible after the houses were erected, but details were not left out for the sake of expediency. Many Chaco small houses show investments of "care" and special materials that probably express shared cosmological principles and relationships, such as directional symbols and colors that evoke human emergence from the underworld. Shared cosmology links, rather than divides, large and small houses in Chaco, and the presence of these links argues strongly against major cultural or ethnic divides in downtown Chaco (cf., Vivian 1990). Although elite-commoner divides are almost certainly present in Chaco, as they are present in all historic pueblos, strong evidence of a shared ideology and a strong sense of shared community are apparent in Chaco as well.

The organization of labor is another instance where Pueblo homology may yield useful insights into Chaco organizations. Among most Western Pueblos, ceremonial authority and status are enmeshed in ranked kinship relations and there is little or no authority at the village level to direct communal labor. At Hopi and Zuni, nearly all labor, from house construction to craft manufacture to agricultural work, is organized by either kin-based groups—usually households or lineage segments—or individuals. Houses are traditionally built and owned by matrifocal households (women dress, stack, and plaster the walls, while men pitch in with the lifting and placement of heavy roof timbers), and rooms are added or modified as needed to accommodate changes in family size and constituency. Individuals willing to invest work in the development of small fields and orchards earn usufruct rights to the land they improve. However, the community's most productive cornfields are owned by a minority of prominent village descent groups, who validate their enhanced status by means of a mythic history and ownership of communal ceremonies.

The organization of labor in the East is very different and is reminiscent of Chacoan-style construction. Labor for field preparation, ditch cleaning, road construction, house and room block construction and repair, and church and kiva maintenance is performed by organized work groups directed by leaders appointed by the religious hierarchy (Hill 1982; Ortiz 1972; White 1942). Centralized planning and direction is evident in the uniformity of eastern house blocks, a result of centrally directed "ladder-style" room block construction, resulting in identical dimensions on at least one room block axis. Cameron (1999:232) describes the standardization that comes from this construction technique, which requires a high degree of centralized planning and direction, as a "muted echo of Chacoan building techniques."

Other forms of standardized manufacture are apparent in the East as well. Elizabeth Brandt has argued that central planning and what amounts to intervillage trade agreements among Eastern Pueblo ritualists has standardized Eastern Pueblo craft industries: "One Rio Grande Pueblo prohibits the manufacture of pottery or woven belts by its members. Ordinary community members do not know the reasons for these prohibitions, but only that whenever they make pottery for sale they will receive a visit warning them that such a practice is prohibited, and if they persist, they will be denied rights in their own community in an increasing scale of sanctions culminating in expulsion from the Pueblo and loss of all rights" (Brandt 1994:16). According to Brandt, "some religious societies functioned essentially as trade guilds, holding resource locations and manufacturing methods secret, and selling or trading to other communities. While we have looked for Pochtecas (Mesoamerican traders), they have been right in the village" (1994:16).

Ritual and Cosmology

Decades ago, Fred Eggan said there are no people on earth who are as invested in ritual as the Southwestern Pueblos. Based on historical pueblo homologs, we think it unlikely that conformity and labor investment in Chaco were enforced by some guy with a whip or a ration bowl. Ritual labor provides sufficient inducements. Measured against classic heredity-based chiefdoms and simple states, Chaco may appear "strange," but much of this strangeness disappears when we consider that the Eastern Pueblos—the most likely Chacoan descendants—have theocratic sodality-based political organizations. Granted, the Eastern Pueblos don't build monumental great houses, earthworks, and roads, and Eastern Pueblo ritualists eschew obvious symbols of rank. However, Chaco is separated from the Eastern Pueblos by a millennium, and the Spanish helped drive Rio Grande ritual underground. No doubt twelfth- and thirteenth-century droughts and other environmental disruptions contributed to changes in overt theocratic expressions as well.

Peter Whiteley asked the seminar participants to think about what rituals do and reminded us that the Pueblos don't discriminate among religion, politics, and economics. When engaged in ritual, Whiteley said, they are trying to change the world's condition. Using ritual "to produce rain" may not accord with Western ideas, but if you believe that it won't rain unless the correct rituals are performed, then ritual activity clearly is instrumental as well as symbolic. Consequently, placing a prayer offering in a field is no different than planting seeds or building a check dam. And if you belong to a group that owns special knowledge that enables you to influence rain, and these ritual resources are inherited in social units, then association between ritual status and social power cannot be reduced to mere superstition. Ritual knowledge is linked to how people understand and act on their physical world. Ritual resources are therefore part of political action and manipulation, every bit as much as economic practices invariably relate to politics.

To resolve environmental uncertainties and to ameliorate fears of drought and hunger, all societies to some extent manipulate cosmological forces through rituals as well as economic intensification. Pueblo cosmology reflects time depth and significant influences from northern Mexico and Mesoamerica. Herbert Spinden (1922) proposed a base Archaic culture for the New World (by which he meant pre-state agricultural communities with roots in Mesoamerica), comprising a set of shared ideas that are selected for or against, that are augmented or transformed as conditions change. Maize agriculture is a fundamental influence on the lives of many indigenous Americans, and ceremonial and cosmological foundations of maize agriculture must have come to the Southwest along with seeds and knowledge of how to plant, maintain, and harvest what became a staple crop and key metaphor. At various points in the diffusion of successive strains of maize from south to north, farmers must have practiced deliberate selection of icons and ritual practices, emulating many practices and images from Mesoamerica.

Like its Mesoamerican counterparts, Pueblo ritual practice keeps the world in order and manages disorder by recruiting powerful natural and human forces to assist one's community. Ritual is organized by partitioning and concentrating power to deal with these forces—weather control, plant and animal fertility, human fertility and childbirth/infant mortality, medicine, conflict, hunting, and ancestors. At this level of abstraction, we can be sure that Chacoans took part in this pan-regional orientation to ritual practice. Whatever the details of their ritual organization, the system they created over many centuries nonetheless could not deal with the drought of the A.D. 1130s. The result was migration and, eventually, reorganization. Chaco people took some rituals along but left others behind. For example, evidence for ritual animation of houses through foundation offerings persists in Pueblos today, but we do not see continuity in the use of sandal imagery, bifurcated burden baskets, and cylinder jars as ritual objects. These apparently dropped out of the Ancestral Puebloan repertoire when Chaco was depopulated.

The Chaco world was unpredictable. Drought, frost, hail, disease, raids from peripheral communities (Gallina neighbors?), and home-grown threats such as witches must have threatened well-being. Religion provides a means of caring for people and defending the community, keeping war leaders and other aggrandizers in check, dealing with witches, allocating scarce resources, and sanctioning antisocial behavior. Ritual keeps uncertainty at bay and resists social disorder. The archaeology of Chaco suggests that cosmological ordering was important very early in Chaco's life cycle. Even before the first great houses reached monumental proportions, houses were symmetrical, centered, and aligned with cardinal directions. Some Chaco ritual expressions seem to refer back to local ancestors. In the words of William Lipe (2006:269), the "builders of Chacoan Great Houses took widely used and long-held San Juan conventions of architecture and layout and made them much more formal and much larger-scale." The same applies to ritual objects. Jolie and Webster (this volume) show that some ritual items, including fancy baskets and textiles, are local productions with deep roots. Other expressions were recruited from other regions. By the A.D. mid-1000s, ritual objects from Mesoamerica show up in increasing frequency in Chacoan deposits: copper bells, macaws, shell ornaments, and other powerful and exotic ritual symbols.

Questions about the role of Mesoamerica and West Mexico in Chaco life cannot fail to spark interesting and often highly polarizing discussions. Were macaws, copper bells, and cacao delivered on the backs of traveling traders from Mexico to feed elite appetites for sumptuary goods? It is much more likely, we think, that exotic goods were integrated into an increasingly complicated (but not necessarily complex) religious system. Just as placing colored corn in dispersed agricultural fields is a wise strategy on the high, dry Colorado Plateau, having a variety of ritual practices from a variety of exotic origins under the control of a variety of ritual associations evidently complemented the risk-averse provisioning strategies of Chaco. Traders and travelers from Chaco probably went out looking for religious objects that would enhance ceremonies at home, as well as new and powerful ceremonies to bring back. Cross-culturally, ritual sodalities are acquisitive by nature. Driver (1969:361) points out that sodality expressions "are normally shared with neighboring tribes, as well as tribes in other culture areas, and must be accounted for by contact of peoples, diffusion, acculturation, and other historical processes." To the extent that we can plot Chaco "exotics" in fine time intervals, we are not seeing a constant flow of such items. Rather, import looks episodic, as we would expect if different kinds of exotic objects and ritual practices were worked into a complicated residential and ritual system in different ways at different times as various corporate groups invent, recruit, compete, cooperate, and emulate outsiders and ancestors.

When many communities in a region have invested in a common ideological system, we can reasonably expect them to exchange ritual practices as well as goods and personnel across a wide area. In the Chaco world, we see plenty of evidence for the movement of goods and ideas over a vast system linked by pathways, shrines, and perhaps even roads. Was Chaco and its system of far-flung outliers multiethnic? Almost certainly. Ethnographic homology suggests several key mechanisms for such system expansion. Daughter villages would have fissioned off from mother villages, in segmentary fashion, to populate unoccupied territory, so the ideological system was always expanding gradually outward. Outlying populations would also be encouraged to join the ideological system, and emulation undoubtedly played an important role in this process (an archaeological example is when the Totah region joined the sphere of Aztec and Salmon Ruins influence). Ritual drama and shock and awe undoubtedly played a crucial role in such regional emulation networks, which is suggestive, again, of homological similarities with the Eastern Pueblos. All of the ritual organizations of the Eastern Pueblos, and many in the West as well, are pan-tribal and intertribal in scale. Most formal training of Pueblo ritualists occurs only in the communities where the ritual association was born. And so, when a Tewa man joins his village Bear Medicine society, he goes to a Keresan village or Jemez to be trained and initiated (Ortiz 1994:298).

Social and Political Organization

Though a great deal of the Amerind seminar discussion focused on ritual and the control of ritual knowledge and techniques (or, Pueblo people would say, having the responsibility for ritual knowledge and techniques), kinship is the basic idiom of social relations in most pre-state societies. Whiteley and Ware championed kinship studies and admonished younger scholars to take kinship seriously. How did kinship relations play out in early Pueblo social history, and can we tease out kinship forms and structures from observed community, settlement, and material culture patterns in Chaco? Whiteley (this volume) and Ware (2014) approach this question from two different but complementary perspectives.

Whiteley's approach follows Lévi-Strauss's theory of elementary and complex kinship systems, with elementary systems (e.g., Dravidian) specifying whom one must marry—typically a cross-cousin in the opposite "moiety" and complex systems specifying categories of kin whom one may not marry—and hence, the decision of whom to marry becomes more complex. Based in part on Pueblo homology, Whiteley sees Pueblo Bonito and other Chacoan great houses with multiple rooms, kivas, and plazas as "semi-complex" Crow organizations that are transitional alliance systems in Lévi-Strauss's model (Crow systems do not prescribe a particular marriage partner, but there are so many negative rules in Crow-Omaha systems that they appear to be hinge-points in the transition from elementary to complex alliance systems). In contrast to Pueblo Bonito, the Wijiji great house has two great kivas enclosed in a perfectly symmetrical room block that Whiteley likens to the two-kiva moiety system of some Eastern Pueblos. Could it be, Whiteley asks, that Wijiji was envisioned as a daughter village (Wijiji was built but perhaps never actually inhabited) established by two intermarrying descent groups from a more complex great house, in a fashion similar to the original establishment of Sitsom'ovi on First Mesa, Supawlavi on Second Mesa, and Paaqavi on Third Mesa at Hopi? Whiteley extends this argument to the classic East-West Pueblo organizational divide that has fascinated anthropologists for over a century and was first formalized in Eggan's (1950) hypothesis of the "Keresan bridge." Whiteley follows Fox (1967) in arguing that Rio Grande moiety systems evolved from kin-based moieties and that Ancestral Pueblo organizations may have oscillated back and forth between semi-complex Crow systems—under certain population densities and adaptive conditions—and "Iroquois-like" elementary dual-alliance systems.

During the seminar, Ware agreed with Whiteley that most of the large great houses and their surrounding communities in Chaco began with some form of semi-complex matrilocal-matrilineal organization (given Pueblo homology, Crow is the most likely model) and that these organizations likely had elementary, Dravidian-like organizational roots extending back into deep prehistory on the Colorado Plateau. Ware traced the emergence of semi-complex organizations to the evolution of the first sedentary farming communities in the core San Juan region in the eighth and ninth centuries A.D. Where Ware departs from Whiteley's model is the role he ascribes to ritual sodalities in the emergence of Chacoan great houses and other monumental features. Ware argued that the earliest Pueblo sodalities germinated from the avunculate but eventually detached from descent groups to create a dialectic that resulted in a basic restructuring of social-political relationships on the eastern plateau—leading eventually to the sodality-based, as opposed to kin-based, community organizations that are ubiquitous among the Rio Grande pueblos (Ware 2014). Social tensions arising from the sodality-kinship dialectic on the eastern plateau likely drove monumental constructions throughout the Chaco interaction sphere in the late eleventh and early twelfth centuries. Although he does not rule out true exogamous moieties in Pueblo prehistory, Ware argues that Eastern Pueblo moieties are actually dual sodalities associated with great kivas that have always functioned mostly outside pueblo kinship systems.

There are, of course, other ways to view social relations than the use of formal kinship theory and analysis. Two of the chapters in the volume (Heitman and Mills) employ Lévi-Strauss's "house society" model to address questions regarding corporate groups larger than the domestic household. Both these chapters contribute important data and insights, but we question the selection of house theory to model Chaco organizations. Nearly every example of material culture and cultural deposit that Heitman and Mills cite as evidence of house societies in Chaco could equally serve as clear evidence of lineages (lineages are socially bounded corporate groups associated with particular practices and rituals performed in some form of bounded architectural space, with shared memories about origins and ancestors, and all Pueblo lineages own inalienable objects that serve to define and sanctify group membership). As the more generalized of the two constructs, house theory allows perhaps more flexibility in populating supra-household corporate groups, so that houses can be constituted on the basis of a variety of kin and non-kin relationships, including fictive kin, surrogate relationships, alternative marriage forms, simple co-residence, and so on. And herein lies house theory's greatest advantage: it can help unpack supra-household corporate groups from larger social matrices when deeper knowledge of kinship and sodality structure is either absent or indeterminate—a likely situation in many if not most archaeological contexts. But is this the case for the Ancestral Pueblos?

There is abundant material evidence for non-kin sodalities in Chaco, but Pueblo homology allows us to posit corporate kin groups with perhaps equal confidence. Roughly two-thirds of all historic pueblos, from every Pueblo language family, have matrilineal descent groups and descent categories that, at minimum, include households, lineages, clans, and in the Hopi case, clusters of related clans, or phratries. And matrilineal ownership of house and land was described by the earliest Spanish explorers to the Southwest in the sixteenth century, so these practices must have evolved at some point in precolonial times. In other words, Pueblo homology allows us to go beyond generalized house theory to explore the implications of the much larger and better developed family of theories around descent and alliance. We are not aware of any aspect of house theory that would allow us to postulate that Ancestral Pueblo communities were likely endogamous because they were predominately matrilocal-matrilineal, or that exogamous moieties are more likely to form in matrilineal as opposed to patrilineal or cognatic ideologies, or that leadership roles in matrilineal communities are more likely to form around a mother's brothers than around a mother's husbands; or that male status is more likely to pass down through the avunculate than through alternative social channels. If something looks like a duck, walks like a duck, and quacks, what is the advantage of calling it a bird instead of a duck?

Matrilineal organizations have a number of political implications as well, since they tend to co-occur with certain leadership styles. Self-aggrandizers and their institutional equivalents tend to be less common when women own the houses and land, so there tends to be a low level of political centralization in matrilocal-matrilineal societies (Murdock 1949:205–206). People, especially males, are invariably political, so we can reasonably expect a certain level of self-promotion in all human societies. In transegalitarian societies (Hayden 1995), however, status seekers often pursue recognition in corporate groups rather than risk the dangers of standing out individually. This fact accords well with the apparent absence of powerful individual leaders in Chaco or anywhere else in the Ancestral Pueblo world. If there were kings and queens in Chaco, they weren't memorialized by stelae or pyramids. The "elite burials" from Pueblo Bonito were buried with ritual objects—wooden staffs and cylinder vessels—rather than the accoutrements one would expect of royalty. If anything was memorialized in Chaco, it was the vernacular house—the modest front-oriented unit pueblo—writ large. The house's living tissue probably was a corporate descent group (Old Bonito is composed of two front-oriented habitation units, which suggests that Bonito was founded by two intermarrying descent groups). Chaco clearly was not egalitarian, which accords well with Pueblo homology. Historical pueblos are deeply ranked societies who have—and Chaco must have had—upper as well as mid-level managers with high levels of expertise who organized ritual activities, architectural construction, farming, water control, defense, trade, and the founding of new communities through alliance and migration.

In pueblos today, we have good evidence for divisions of ritual labor. In Chaco as well, ritual items like bear paws and cylinder jars are not evenly distributed throughout Pueblo Bonito or among great houses. Evidence suggests pluralities, or overlapping networks of ritual responsibilities, with multiple ritual sodalities at work just as we find in the historical pueblos. We can agree that "pluralism" is about segmentation of ritual responsibilities of kin groups, sodalities, or, if one prefers, houses, but architecture and iconography also exhibit dualities that are too pervasive to ignore. Dualism is apparently part of a widely shared "base" cosmology and duality pervades Chaco architecture and iconography. Dualisms are pervasive in historical pueblos as well, and play out in many ways: Male-female symbolism is foundational, but other important dualities include winter-summer, life-death, north-south, sky-underworld, and so on. Old and Young relationships are expressed in the Twin War Gods and the Corn Mothers—in each pair, one is older than the other, and older-younger is sometimes expressed in kinship terminology. Center–periphery is another important duality. People in daughter villages go back to their mother village—their center—for ceremonies. Pluralism crosscut by dualism is a pervasive and long-lived Pueblo pattern. Does small-private contrast with great-public? And if so, is this space gendered, with kivas as masculine spaces, and aboveground rooms as feminine spaces? A gender inversion may also be expressed, with kivas as feminine womb-underworld spaces for masculine activities.

Heitman (this volume) ties historical Pueblo dualisms to her comparison of architectural deposits in small houses with those of Pueblo Bonito. Ceremonial material such as lignite layers under foundations expresses oppositions between vertical and horizontal axes. Directional axes and colors are especially important at Acoma, where the vertical axis opposes the sun and the underworld and reconciles these dimensions. We recognize these archaeologically, in understanding the lignite layers as underworld symbols, and these dynamics are still played out in important ways in contemporary pueblos. As Mills (this volume) points out, pueblo houses are living, moral beings. When a family builds a house, they feed it with foundation deposits, seeds placed in mortar, and prayer feathers in the roof beams. Founding, feeding, and periodic renewal animate the house. A house nurtures its inhabitants, and they in turn feed the house and care for it. Chaco foundational deposits are very uniform and reflect a shared technology of how to make and animate a house. But then we see plurality in other ritual deposits, reflecting different functions and sources. Some of these probably were complementary functions, and others could have been competitive. Leaders of different houses or different sodalities might have "recruited" powerful objects from the past or from great distances.

Ware (2014) has argued that Chaco started as a continuation of kin-based Pueblo I communities in the 800s and something happened sometime after 1000 that allowed sodalities to break away from kinship groups, creating tension and competition that may help to explain Chacoan monumentality: great houses, earthworks, road, etc., all based on ritual intensification. What happened? Pueblo oral traditions may hold part of the answer. Some pueblo traditions describe a dysfunctional era of competition for ritual leadership and ostentatious display (Kuwanwisiwma 2004; Lekson 2009:198–200). Alfonso Ortiz (1969) turned to the Tewa origin story as a charter for life. The story explains initial chaos in the world, and in response, the Corn Mothers formed sodalities to take care of people "in here" in light of chaos "out there." Communities tolerated the ritual societies, then accepted them, and then put them in order. Emerging from Sand Lake, the Tewa found the world not ripe, not ready for habitation, so they had to go back to the underworld. The Corn Mothers created hunt chiefs to learn how to deal with a new power, animals. People got sick, so the Corn Mothers created the Bear Medicine society, which practices an ethic of caring for the people in time of stress.

Peter Whiteley added that Western Pueblo sodalities are characterized less by competition than by simple differentiation of function, which is handled calendrically. Sodalities can alternate their performance years, like the Hopi Flute and Snake societies, when their functions are the same (turning the sun). Different sodalities do not compete directly. Hopi sodalities were introduced by clans, who brought them on their migrations to the Center Place. Individual Hopi villages accepted sodalities if their contribution benefitted the whole community.

Identity

As Mills (this volume) notes, the two clusters of human remains found in the two oldest parts of Pueblo Bonito suggest dual houses in which founding ancestors and subsequent generations were interred in special crypts that became "archives" for history and identity for as long as 200 years. Who were these individuals and were they related by descent or by some other kind of identity, such as sodality leadership? Snow and LeBlanc (this volume) explain that we probably know less than we think we do about their biology and need more data and new critical attention to the data we do have.

Marden (this volume) explained some interesting details about the human remains in Bonito's north burial cluster that she has not included in her chapter. Her comments sparked interesting discussion about how ethnography helps explain behaviors that could result in the archaeological patterns we see here. Marden's data suggest that each individual buried in the Bonito crypts had some kind of pathology, such as evidence of head wounds. Were these individuals related to each other—descendants of a founding ancestor, buried in successive layers? Were they leaders and retainers, as Lekson (2009:293n131) supposes? Or were they individuals with unusual physical challenges who could not function independently in society, who were supported by the community as a whole rather than by their individual family units? At this time, we lack conclusive evidence for such a scenario, but believe it is worth considering among other possibilities. In our discussion, Ford explained that Pueblo individuals who cannot care for themselves and who would be a burden on their natal households traditionally were accorded special ritual roles in their communities. While anthropologists have written a great deal about alternate-gender individuals, such as the Zuni man-woman or *llamana* (Roscoe 1991), little has been said about the honored roles of those afflicted with severe arthritis, growth disorders, blindness, albinism, dementia, and other challenges. Were the "special" Bonito individuals elites or individuals who were "adopted" by sodalities in life and in death buried with ritual paraphernalia to transform their identities into mythical beings they may have personated? At Zuni, in order to protect society secrets, patients are often adopted into the medicine sodality that affects a cure.

We briefly discussed "Pax Chaco," that period of Chaco's peak population and regional integration in which we see little evidence for conflict. This period is bracketed by evidence of structural violence that includes what some researchers call "extreme processing events" involving disarticulated human remains. These include both Pueblo I and Pueblo III period "bone beds" that some osteologists, notably Turner, have interpreted as evidence for cannibalism, and others have suggested are evidence for battles or witch executions. Why don't we see similar evidence of structural violence in the A.D. 900s-1100s? Ware suggested that Chacoan sodalities had a role in keeping the peace. He pointed out that sodalities are associations that bridge kinship and ethnicity. Sodalities everywhere tend to emerge and thrive in multiethnic situations, and one of their primary functions is to mediate conflict. He noted that inhabitants of the Kayenta area, west of the Chuska Mountains, endured the same climate uncertainties and crises as Chaco, and we have little evidence of conflict there (cf. Haas and Creamer 1993). Nor do we have evidence for large heterogeneous communities. The Kayenta culture area apparently was biologically and ethnically homogeneous and was characterized for most its history by small, dispersed settlements (at least until the mid-1200s). So we don't need strong, hierarchical leadership integrating the Chaco region to explain the Pax Chaco. Unlike the Kayenta area, the eastern Colorado Plateau is and probably always was multiethnic, but likely had overarching sodalities mediating and dampening conflict.

Conclusion

Looking to the future of Chaco studies, we would like to encourage opening doors to more Pueblo input, interaction, and participation. We need to encourage young Pueblo archaeologists and historians to join what often seems like a closed society of scholars. Pueblo youth today are the ones who will be doing much of the future excavation, as well as park management and interpretation. Navajo participation will be valuable as well, since their land encompasses much of the Ancestral Pueblo world, and the Navajo Nation Historic Preservation Department has an official policy of claiming cultural affiliation with ancient Chacoans. Navajo connections to Chaco are contested by Pueblos, but clearly Navajos are associated by residence and connection to place and intermarriage. In addition, Navajo ritual practitioners transformed Pueblo sodality rituals to Navajo chantways, and some oral traditions from Pueblo histories have been recruited to Navajo purposes.

Over many decades of collaborative research with Pueblos, Ford has seen an evolutionary progression in Pueblos from a negative attitude about archaeology to a feeling that Pueblo people are now helping to set research agendas. Pueblos are now asking questions about their past and collaborating with archaeologists to find answers. Many archaeologists

are now accomplishing research the Pueblos want done, including excavation, dating, and identifying clay sources. If we are willing to help
provide the answers to their questions, someday they may be willing
to work with us to address the questions that we think are important,
and a true collaborative archaeology will emerge that will benefit both
Native communities and scholars.

One obstacle to collaboration should be easy to overcome. Many
Native people think academics are deliberately excluding them by
writing in boring and inaccessible styles. We therefore would like to
encourage clear and concise writing so descendent communities, site
managers, field archaeologists, and the general public have access to our
knowledge. Writing clearly doesn't mean "dumbing down." We need to
stop hiding behind long lists of citations—many to our own work!—
which bury our main points and interesting ideas and result in a sea of
parenthetical references.

Paul Minnis mentioned that, especially in the Southwest, archaeologists think of stakeholders as being indigenous people, but Chaco has
something to say to a broader audience. Avocational archaeologists have
profound interest in and make valuable contributions to our discipline.
We also have a responsibility to the wide cross section of the general
public for whom archaeology is fascinating. We should feed their need
to know about long-term culture change, human responses to climate
change, and many other lessons from deep history.

In conclusion, many countervailing influences helped to shape Chaco's disorderly world, and the ancient Chacoans attempted to order the
chaos through prescribed rituals, complicated social organizations, subsistence diversity and residential mobility, and trade and exchange. We
can't know everything about their lives, but we are developing the tools
and strategies to understand relationships among demography, climate,
and social organization through ethnographic analogy, homology, and a
host of interdisciplinary sciences. We know that in good times for farmers, population grows and spreads out, and people deploy a variety of
possible strategies. Moving to new niches is a first one, but when people
on the edges are also expanding, communities find themselves compet-
ing. Intensification often follows. But in the twelfth century, Chaco
expansion and intensification stopped. What happened was climate
change. When people couldn't feed themselves with the strategies and

leaders they had, some started fighting again, some moved longer distances away and joined communities with different strategies, and some reorganized into smaller communities—some of which apparently kept some Chacoan legacies and some of which rejected all things Chaco.

References Cited

Brandt, Elizabeth. 1994. Egalitarianism, Hierarchy, and Centralization in the Pueblos. In *The Ancient Southwest Community: Models and Methods for the Study of Prehistoric Social Organization*, edited by W. H. Wills and Robert D. Leonard, pp. 9–23. University of New Mexico Press, Albuquerque.

Cameron, Catherine M. 1999. Room Size, Organization of Construction, and Archaeological Interpretation in the Puebloan Southwest. *Journal of Anthropological Archaeology* 18(2):201–239.

Cushing, Frank Hamilton. 1920. *Zuni Breadstuff*. Museum of the American Indian, Heye Foundation, New York.

Driver, Harold. 1969. *Indians of North America*. 2nd ed. University of Chicago Press, Chicago.

Eggan, Fred. 1950. *Social Organization of the Western Pueblos*. University of Chicago Press, Chicago.

Ford, Richard I. 1972. Barter, Gift, or Violence: An Analysis of Tewa Intertribal Exchange. In *Social Exchange and Interaction*, edited by Edwin N. Wilmsen, pp. 21–45. Anthropological Papers No. 46. Museum of Anthropology, University of Michigan, Ann Arbor.

Fox, Robin. 1967. *The Keresan Bridge: A Problem in Pueblo Ethnology*. LSE Monographs on Social Anthropology 35. Athlone, London.

Haas, Jonathan, and Winifred Creamer. 1993. Stress and Warfare among the Kayenta Anasazi of the Thirteenth Century A.D. Fieldiana: Anthropology 21.

Hall, Stephen A. 2010. *New Interpretations of Alluvial and Paleovegetation Records from Chaco Canyon, New Mexico*. New Mexico Geological Society Guidebook, Four Corners Country, 2010, pp. 231–246. New Mexico Geological Society, Albuquerque, New Mexico.

Hayden, Brian. 1995. Pathways to Power: Principles for Creating Socioeconomic Inequalities. In *Foundation of Social Inequality*, edited by D. Price and G. Feinman, pp. 15–86. Plenum Press, New York.

Hill, W. W. 1982. *An Ethnography of Santa Clara Pueblo, New Mexico*. Edited and annotated by Charles H. Lange. University of New Mexico Press, Albuquerque.

Kuwanwisiwma, Leigh J. 2004. *Yupköyvi*: The Hopi Story of Chaco Canyon. In *In Search of Chaco: New Approaches to an Archaeological Enigma*, edited by David Grant Noble, pp. 41–47. School of American Research Press, Santa Fe.

Lekson, Stephen H. 2009. *A History of the Ancient Southwest.* School of American
    Research Press, Santa Fe.
Lipe, William D. 2006. Notes from the North. In *The Archaeology of Chaco Can-
    yon: An Eleventh-Century Pueblo Regional Center*, edited by Stephen H.
    Lekson, pp. 261–313. School of American Research Press, Santa Fe.
Love, David W., Mary L. Gillam, Larry V. Benson, Richard Friedman, Phil L.
    Miller, and Kirk R. Vincent. 2011. Geomorphology, Hydrology, and Allu-
    vial Stratigraphy in Lower Chaco Canyon Do Not Support the Possible
    Existence of Prehistoric Sand-Dammed Ephemeral Lakes. *New Mexico
    Geology* 33(4):107–123.
Murdock, George Peter. 1949. *Social Structure.* Macmillan, New York.
Ortiz, Alfonso. 1969. *The Tewa World: Space, Time, Being, and Becoming in a Pueblo
    Society.* University of Chicago Press, Chicago.
———. 1972. Ritual Drama and the Pueblo World View. In *New Perspectives on the
    Pueblos*, edited by Alfonso Ortiz, pp. 135–161. University of New Mexico
    Press, Albuquerque.
———. 1994. The Dynamics of Pueblo Cultural Survival. In *North American
    Indian Anthropology: Essays on Society and Culture*, edited by Raymond J.
    DeMallie and Alfonso Ortiz, pp. 296–306. University of Oklahoma Press,
    Norman.
Roscoe, Will. 1991. *The Zuni Man-Woman.* University of New Mexico Press,
    Albuquerque.
Spinden, Herbert Joseph. 1922. *Ancient Civilizations of Mexico and Central Amer-
    ica.* American Museum of Natural History, Handbook Series 3. American
    Museum Press, New York.
Toner, Mike. 2012–2013. Chaco, Through a Different Lens. *American Archaeology*
    16(4):26–32.
Ware, John. 2014. *A Pueblo Social History: Kinship, Sodality, and Community in the
    Northern Southwest.* School of Advanced Research Press, Santa Fe.
White, Leslie. 1942. *The Pueblo of Santa Ana, New Mexico.* Memoirs of the Ameri-
    can Anthropological Association 60. American Anthropological Associa-
    tion, Menasha, Wisconsin.
Vivian, R. Gwinn. 1990. *The Chacoan Prehistory of the San Juan Basin.* Academic
    Press, San Diego.
Vivian, R. Gwinn, Carla R. Van West, Jeffery S. Dean, Nancy J. Akins, Mollie S.
    Toll, and Thomas C. Windes. 2006. Ecology and Economy. In *The Archae-
    ology of Chaco Canyon: An Eleventh-Century Pueblo Regional Center*, edited
    by Stephen H. Lekson, pp. 45–65. School of American Research Press,
    Santa Fe.

EDITORS AND CONTRIBUTORS

Editors

Carrie C. Heitman is an assistant professor of anthropology at the University of Nebraska–Lincoln (UNL) and a Faculty Fellow at the Center for Digital Research in the Humanities. Prior to starting at UNL in 2013, she was an American Council of Learned Societies New Faculty Fellow in the Department of Anthropology at Northwestern University. Since 2004, Heitman has helped oversee the building of the Chaco Research Archive (http://www.chacoarchive.org), and her research continues to explore how digital technologies can help us better understand human complexity. Her research on Chaco Canyon integrates disparate data sets to help answer fundamental questions about how and why social inequalities transform into structural inequalities over time in human societies. Heitman's research has focused on the Pueblo region of the American Southwest, particularly aspects of social organization, mortuary behavior, and ritual and cosmology during the period from A.D. 700 to 1150. She has conducted research in east-central Arizona, southeastern Utah, Chaco Canyon in northwestern New Mexico, and the Mixteca Alta of Oaxaca in Mexico.

Stephen Plog is the David A. Harrison III Chair in Archaeology at the University of Virginia where he has been a member of the faculty since 1978. He has conducted fieldwork in the Chevelon Canyon region of east-central Arizona, northern Black Mesa in northeastern Arizona, the Zuni area of west-central New Mexico, Chaco Canyon in northwestern New Mexico, and the Valley of Oaxaca in Mexico. With the support of the Andrew Mellon Foundation and the Institute for Advanced Technology in the Humanities at the University of Virginia, Plog has directed the creation of the Chaco Research Archive (http://www.chacoarchive.org), an online resource that includes a relational database that integrates a wealth of information on the early excavations in Chaco Canyon during the late nineteenth century and the first half of the twentieth century. The Chaco Research Archive provides those interested in the history of Chaco Canyon with access to original field notes and photographs, as well as correspondence, unpublished manuscripts, and catalog records. Through database queries, scholars can explore detailed contextual information from early excavations. Plog's own research has focused on the Pueblo region of the American Southwest, particularly aspects of sociopolitical and ritual change, demography, exchange, mortuary behavior, and ceramics and style during the period from A.D. 800 to 1150. He is the author of *Stylistic Variation in Prehistoric Ceramics: Design Analysis in the American Southwest* and *Ancient Peoples of the American Southwest*. Plog has co-edited *Spatial Organization and Exchange: Archaeological Survey on Northern Black Mesa* and *Papers on the Archaeology of Black Mesa, Vol. II.*

Contributors

Phil R. Geib has worked as a professional archaeologist for thirty-five years, with most of this time focused on prehistoric remains in southeastern Utah and northeastern Arizona. He is currently adjunct faculty at the University of Nebraska–Lincoln. His major research interests include hunter-gatherers, the transition to agriculture, prehistoric technology, and cooperation and warfare; his regional specialties include the North American Southwest and Great Basin. Geib is the author of *Foragers and Farmers of the Northern Kayenta Area: Excavations along the Navajo Mountain Road.*

Kelley Hays-Gilpin is professor and chair of anthropology at Northern Arizona University and Edward Bridge Danson Chair of Anthropology at the Museum of Northern Arizona. Her current research, undertaken in collaboration with the Hopi Cultural Preservation Office, explores Hopi history and culture from prehistory to present through cross-media comparison of style and iconography (including pottery, textiles, basketry, mural painting, rock art), visual and verbal metaphors, traditional ecological knowledge, and gender arrangements. She is the author of *Ambiguous Images: Gender and Rock Art* and co-editor of *Painting the*

Cosmos: Metaphor and Worldview in Images from the Southwest Pueblos and Mexico.

Edward A. Jolie is a post-doctoral research assistant professor and director of the R. L. Andrews Center for Perishables Analysis at Mercyhurst University in Erie, Pennsylvania. His interests are broad but focus primarily on the archaeology of western North America, perishable technologies worldwide, and anthropological ethics.

Steven A. LeBlanc was director of collections at Harvard's Peabody Museum. His primary focus in the American Southwest has been on the Mimbres culture of southwestern New Mexico. He has authored or co-authored several books, including *The Mimbres People: Ancient Pueblo Painters of the American Southwest* and *Prehistoric Warfare in the American Southwest*. He has an interest in ceramics, prehistoric warfare, and a possible farmer migration into the Southwest from Mesoamerica.

Kerriann Marden is currently an assistant professor of anthropology and director of the Forensic Science Program at Eastern New Mexico University. She has ongoing programs of research in both bioarchaeology and forensic anthropology, including extensive analysis of the Chaco Canyon skeletal assemblages at the National Museum of Natural History, the American Museum of Natural History, The Field Museum of Natural History, the Maxwell Museum of Anthropology at the University of New Mexico, and the Peabody Museum of Archaeology and Ethnology at Harvard University.

Barbara J. Mills is a professor in the School of Anthropology at the University of Arizona. She has conducted archaeological research throughout the U.S. Southwest including the Chaco, Zuni, Silver Creek, Mimbres, and northern Four Corners areas. She is currently directing the Southwest Social Networks Project, which extends her past work on social network analysis of the late prehispanic period to the Chaco world. Mills is co-author of *Living on the Edge of the Rim*, co-editor of multiple books, and is senior editor of the forthcoming volume, *The Oxford Handbook of the Archaeology of the American Southwest*.

Paul E. Minnis is professor emeritus at the University of Oklahoma. He conducts research on the prehispanic ethnobotany and archaeology of the U.S. Southwest and northwest Mexico. Minnis conducted fieldwork in the Mimbres region of southwestern New Mexico in the 1970s and 1980s and co-directed research projects on the Casas Grandes/ Paquimé region in northwest Chihuahua beginning in 1989. He is the author or editor of 12 books and numerous articles. Minnis also is a past president of the Society of Ethnobiology, treasurer and press editor for the Society for American Archaeology, and co-founder of the Southwest Symposium.

Meradeth Snow is a molecular anthropologist, focusing on the ancient DNA of the native inhabitants of the New World, with particular focus on the desert Southwest. She is employed by the anthropology department at the University of Montana, Missoula.

R. Gwinn Vivian is curator emeritus at the Arizona State Museum, Tucson. His Chacoan research interests include strategies for agricultural water use, roads, and the dynamics of small house–great house organizational systems. He is the author of *The Chacoan History of the San Juan Basin* and co-author of *Wooden Ritual Objects from Chaco Canyon, New Mexico: The Chetro Ketl Collection* and *Chaco Handbook: An Encyclopedia Guide.*

John Ware recently retired after 13 years as director of the Amerind Foundation in Dragoon, Arizona. A Southwest archaeologist and anthropologist who has participated in fieldwork in multiple regions, he has a long-term interest in Pueblo social organization, both precolumbian and historic. Ware is the author of *A Pueblo Social History: Kinship, Sodality, and Community in the Northern Southwest.*

Adam S. Watson is a post-doctoral fellow at the American Museum of Natural History whose research explores human interaction with the environment, political economy, religion, and the development of societal complexity in precolumbian North America. Specializing in zooarchaeology and GIS, Watson's ongoing research investigates agricultural strategies and the changing roles of wild and domestic animal species in subsistence, ritual, and craft production among the Ancestral Pueblo communities in and around Chaco Canyon, New Mexico.

Laurie D. Webster is an anthropologist and a specialist in Southwestern perishable material culture. She is a visiting scholar in the Department of Anthropology at the University of Arizona and a research associate at the American Museum of Natural History. Her publications include the edited volume, *Beyond Cloth and Cordage: Archaeological Textile Research in the Americas*, and the catalog, *Collecting the Weaver's Art: The William Claflin Collection of Southwestern Textiles*, as well as numerous articles about prehistoric perishable technologies. She lives in Mancos, Colorado.

Peter Whiteley is Curator of North American Ethnology at the American Museum of Natural History. His ethnographic and ethnohistorical research has focused primarily on Hopi, with long-term fieldwork since 1980. Major publications include *Deliberate Acts: Changing Hopi Culture through the Oraibi Split* (1988), *Rethinking Hopi Ethnography* (1998), and *The Orayvi Split: A Hopi Transformation* (2008). Whiteley's research also has examined several New Mexico Pueblos, including Isleta, Kewa, Laguna, and Tesuque.

INDEX

Page numbers in *italics* represent illustrations.

AMERIND STUDIES IN ANTHROPOLOGY

SERIES EDITOR JOHN WARE

Ancient Paquimé and the Casas Grandes World
Edited by Paul E. Minnis and Michael E. Whalen

Chaco Revisited: New Research on the Prehistory of Chaco Canyon, New Mexico
Edited by Carrie C. Heitman and Stephen Plog